Nieuwe Zijde
Pages 70–85

Oude Zijde
Pages 56–69

Eastern Canal Ring
Page 114–123

Plantage
Pages 138–147

EYEWITNESS *TRAVEL GUIDES*

AMSTERDAM

CANALBUS

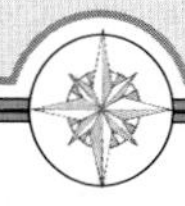

EYEWITNESS *TRAVEL GUIDES*

AMSTERDAM

Main Contributors:
ROBIN PASCOE
CHRISTOPHER CATLING

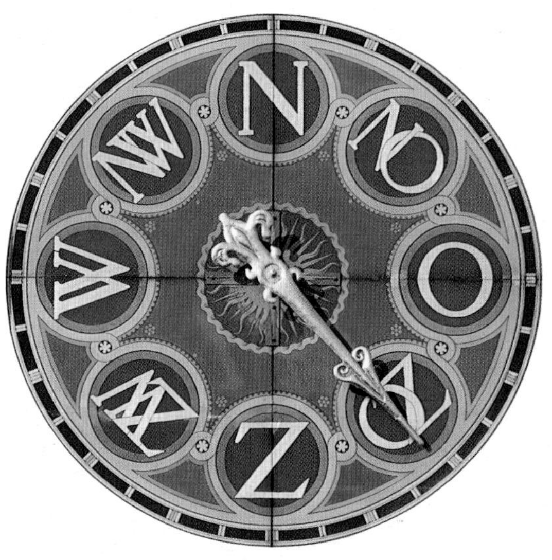

DORLING KINDERSLEY
LONDON • NEW YORK • STUTTGART • MOSCOW

A Dorling Kindersley Book

Project Editor Heather Jones
Art Editor Vanessa Hamilton
Editors Peter Adams, Sasha Heseltine, Fiona Morgan, Alice Peebles, Nichola Tyrrell
US Editor Mary Sutherland
Designers Emma Hutton, Erika Lang Malcolm Parchment
Map Co-ordinators Michael Ellis, David Pugh

Managing Editors Vivien Crump, Helen Partington
Managing Art Editor Steve Knowlden
Senior Editor Peter Casterton
Deputy Editorial Director Douglas Amrine
Deputy Art Director Gaye Allen

Production David Proffit
Picture Research Lorna Ainger
DTP Designer Siri Lowe

Contributors
Paul Andrews, Hedda Archbold, Marlene Edmunds, Adam Hopkins, David Lindsey (Restaurants), Fred Mawer, Alison Melvin, Catherine Stebbings, Richard Widdows

Maps
Jane Hanson, Phil Rose, Jennifer Skelley (Lovell Johns Limited)

Photographers
Max Alexander, Rupert Horrox, Kim Sayer

Illustrators
Nick Gibbard, Maltings Partnership, Derrick Stone, Martin Woodward

•

Film outputting bureau Cooling Brown (London)
Reproduced by Colourscan (Singapore)
Printed and bound by G. Canale & C. (Italy)

First American edition 1995
2 4 6 8 10 9 7 5 3 1
Published in the United States by
Dorling Kindersley Publishing, Inc.,
95 Madison Avenue, New York, NY 10016

Published in Great Britain by Dorling Kindersley Limited.
Distributed by Houghton Mifflin Company, Boston.

Library of Congress Cataloging-in-Publication Data
Amsterdam. -- 1st American ed.
p. cm. -- (Eyewitness travel guides)
Includes index.
ISBN 0-7894-0186-X
1. Amsterdam (Netherlands) -- Guidebooks.
I. Series.
DJ411.A53A6555 1995 95-7625
914.92'3520473 -- dc20 CIP

•

Every effort has been made to ensure that the information in this book is as up-to-date as possible at the time of going to press. However, details such as telephone numbers, opening hours, prices, gallery hanging arrangements and travel information are liable to change. The publishers cannot accept responsibility for any consequences arising from the use of this book.

We would be delighted to receive any corrections and suggestions for incorporation in the next edition. Please write to:
Deputy Editorial Director, Eyewitness Travel Guides
Dorling Kindersley, 9 Henrietta Street, London WC2E 8PS, UK.

Throughout this book, floors are referred to in accordance with European usage, i.e., the "first floor" is one flight up.

Contents

Model boat at Scheepvaart Museum

Introducing Amsterdam

Amsterdam Area by Area

Traditional drawbridge

Children in Dutch costume outside a church in the Zuiderzee Museum

Café terrace in Artis zoo

Travelers' Needs

Survival Guide

Façade of the Rijksmuseum

Wheels of Gouda cheese

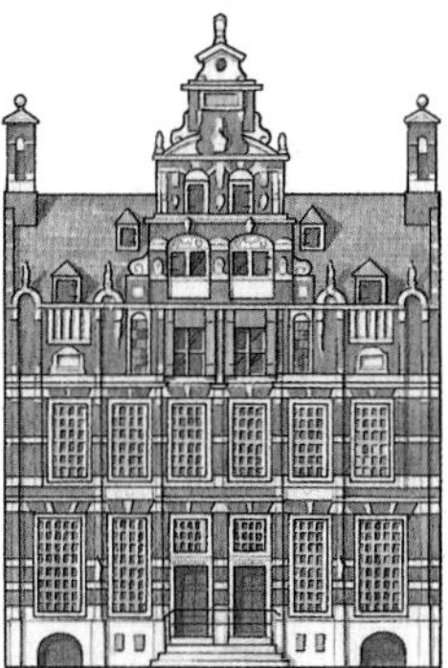

Dutch Renaissance canal house and details of cornices and gables

How to Use this Guide

This guide helps you get the most from your stay in Amsterdam. It provides expert recommendations as well as detailed practical information. *Introducing Amsterdam* maps the city and sets it in its historical and cultural context. *Amsterdam Area by Area* describes the important sights, with maps, pictures and illustrations. *Farther Afield* looks at sights outside the city center and *Beyond Amsterdam* explores other places near Amsterdam. Suggestions on food, drink, where to stay and what to do are made in *Travelers' Needs,* and *Survival Guide* has tips on everything from travel to Dutch telephones.

Amsterdam Area by Area

The center of the city has been divided into seven sightseeing areas. Each area has its own chapter, which opens with a list of the sights described. All the sights are numbered and plotted on an *Area Map*. The detailed information for each sight is presented in numerical order, making it easy to locate within the chapter.

Each area of central Amsterdam has color-coded thumb tabs.

A locator map shows where you are in relation to other areas of the city center.

Sights at a Glance lists the chapter's sights by category: Churches, Museums and Galleries, Historic Buildings, Streets and Canals.

1 Area Map

For easy reference, the sights are numbered and located on a map. The sights are also shown on the Amsterdam Street Finder *on pages 280–87.*

2 Street-by-Street Map

This gives a bird's-eye view of the heart of each sightseeing area.

A suggested route for a walk covers the more interesting streets in the area.

Stars indicate the sights that no visitor should miss.

3 Detailed information on each sight

All the sights in Amsterdam are described individually. Addresses and practical information are provided. The key to the symbols used in the information block is shown on the back flap.

4 Introduction to Beyond Amsterdam

Beyond Amsterdam *has its own introduction, which provides an overview of the history and character of the region around Amsterdam and outlines what the region has to offer the visitor today. The area covered by this section is highlighted on the map of the Netherlands shown on page 165. It covers important cities, such as Den Haag, as well as attractive towns and places of interest in the Dutch countryside.*

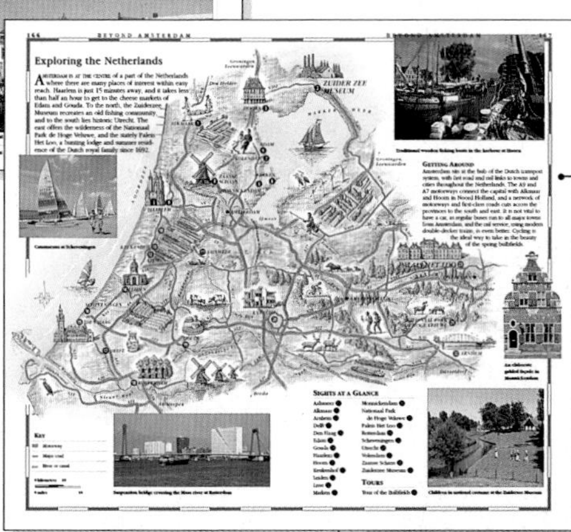

5 Pictorial Map

This gives an illustrated overview of the whole region. All the sights covered in this section are numbered, and the network of major roads is marked. There are also useful tips on getting around the region by bus and train.

6 Detailed information on each sight

All the important cities, towns and other places to visit are described individually. They are listed in order, following the numbering given on the Pictorial Map. *Within each town or city, there is detailed information on important buildings and other sights.*

Stars indicate the best features and works of art.

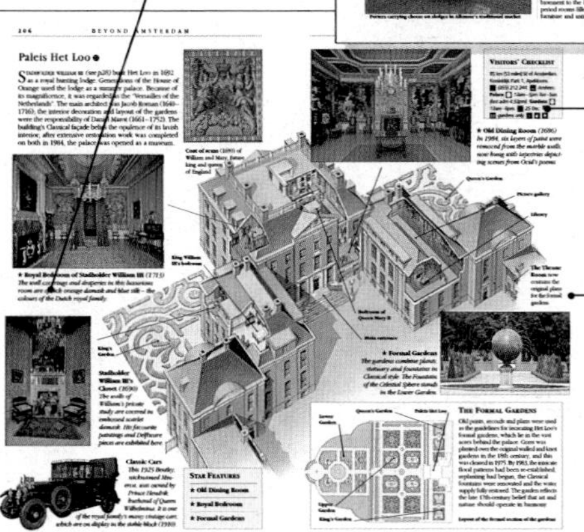

The Visitors' Checklist provides a summary of the practical information you will need to plan your visit.

7 The top sights

These are given two or more full pages. Historic buildings are dissected to reveal their interiors; museums and galleries have color-coded floorplans to help you locate the most interesting exhibits.

Introducing Amsterdam

Putting Amsterdam on the Map

Although the Netherlands' seat of government is at Den Haag, Amsterdam is the nominal capital. It is the country's largest city, with a population in excess of 800,000, and the most visited, receiving over 1.5 million visitors a year. It stands on precariously low-lying ground at the confluence of the Amstel and IJ rivers near the IJsselmeer and, like much of the Netherlands, would flood frequently but for land reclamation and sea defenses. This position places Amsterdam at the heart of the Randstad, a term used to describe the crescent-shaped conurbation covering much of the provinces of Noord Holland, Zuid Holland and Utrecht, and encompassing the cities of Utrecht, Rotterdam, Den Haag, Leiden and Haarlem.

Satellite photograph showing the north-west Netherlands and the IJsselmeer

Western Europe

Amsterdam has a first-class international airport, as well as good road and rail links to all parts of the Netherlands and beyond.

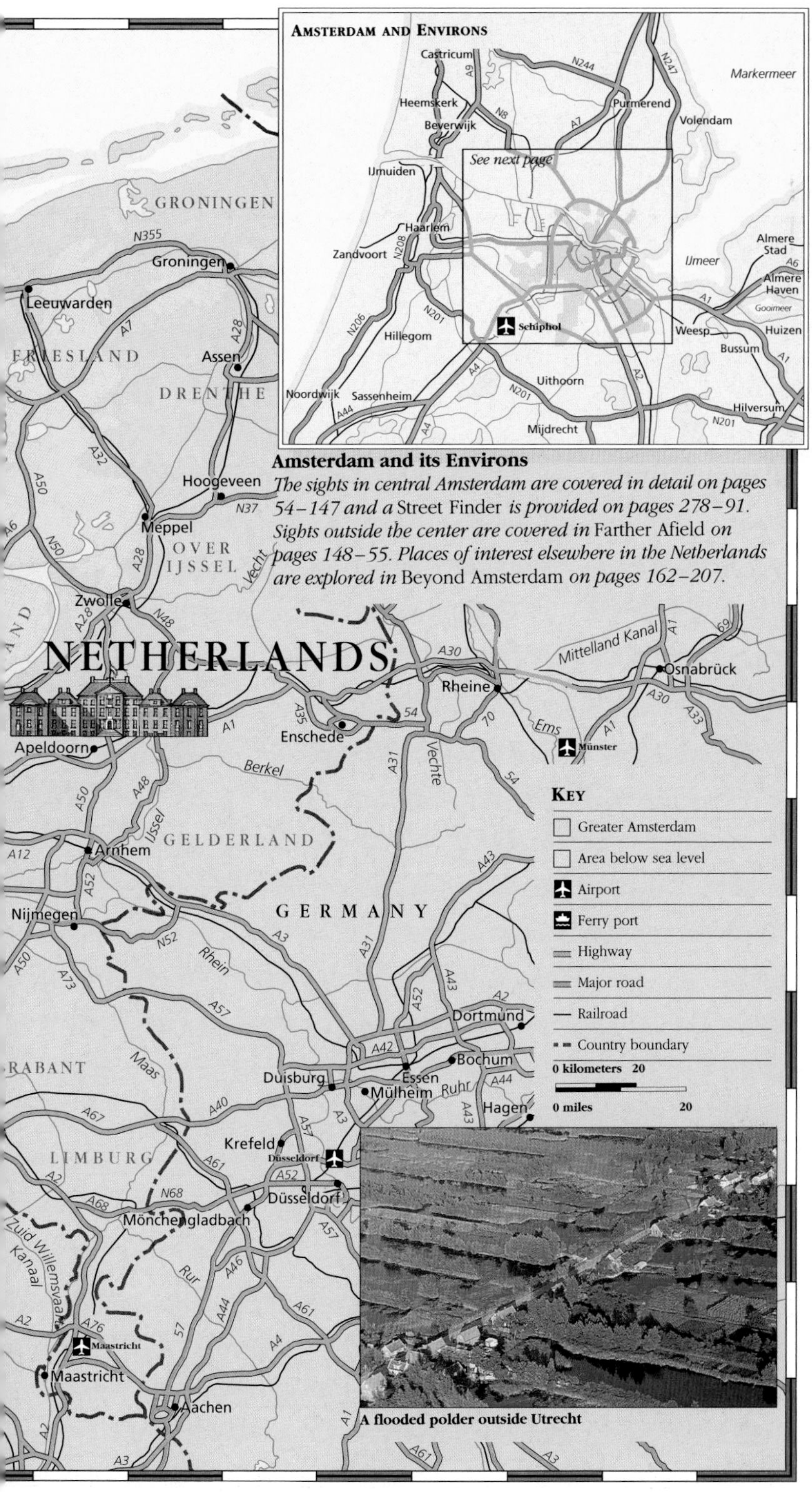

Amsterdam and its Environs

The sights in central Amsterdam are covered in detail on pages 54–147 and a Street Finder *is provided on pages 278–91. Sights outside the center are covered in* Farther Afield *on pages 148–55. Places of interest elsewhere in the Netherlands are explored in* Beyond Amsterdam *on pages 162–207.*

A flooded polder outside Utrecht

Greater Amsterdam

AMSTERDAM RETAINED its characteristic horseshoe shape within the Singelgracht until well into the 19th century. This pattern is still clearly visible in the network of streets and canals in the city center. Since then the city has expanded dramatically in all directions. All of Greater Amsterdam enjoys first-class public transportation *(see Transport Map on inside back cover).*

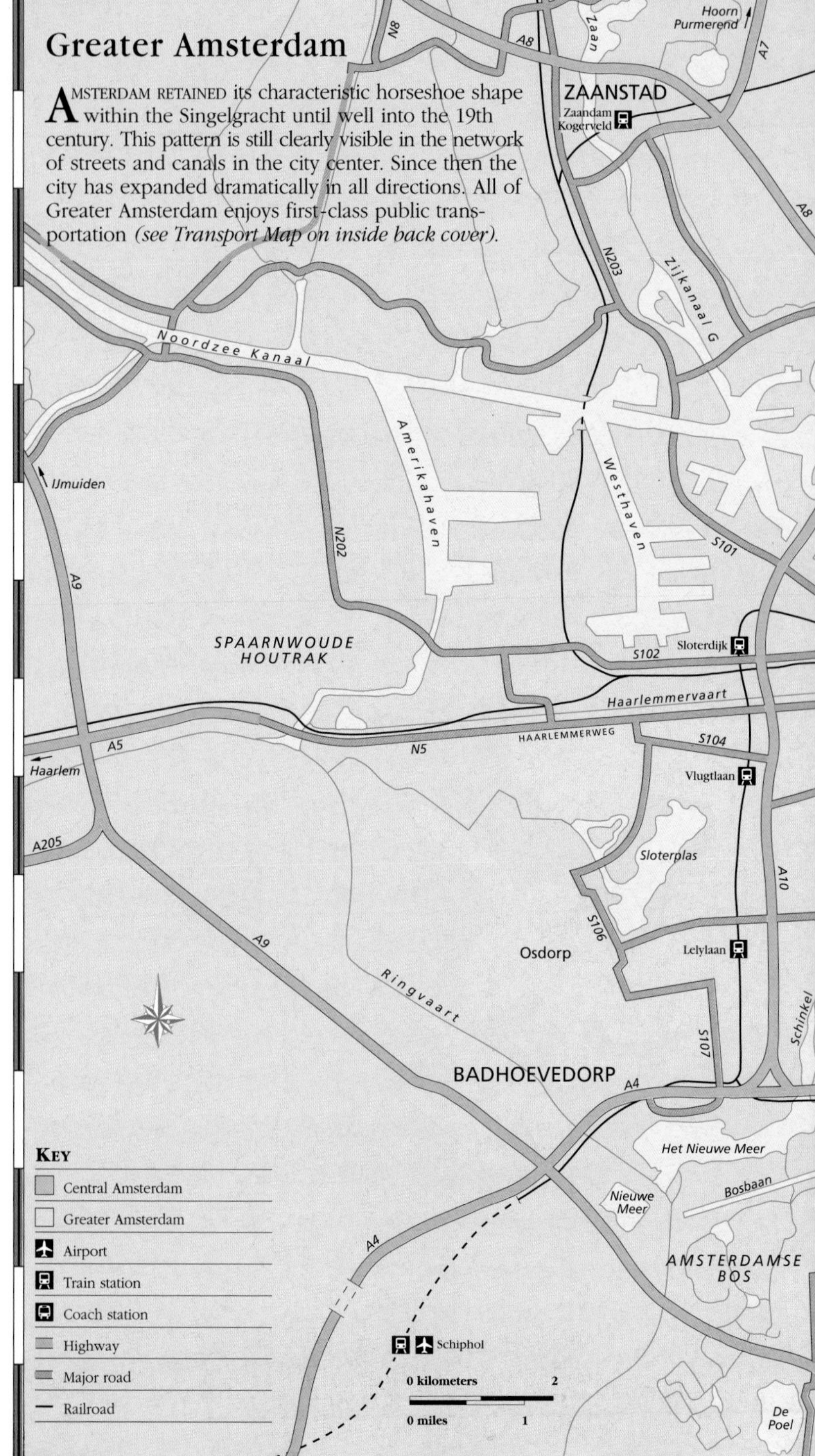

KEY

- Central Amsterdam
- Greater Amsterdam
- Airport
- Train station
- Coach station
- Highway
- Major road
- Railroad

Volendam
Het Twiske
De Leek
Noordhollands Kanaal
N247
A10
WATERLAND
Holysloter Die
Ransdorper Die
S118
S116
Het IJ
S115
Kinselmeer
S101
See next page
Centraal Station
IJ Tunnel
Het IJ
S103
S114
Prinsengracht
Singel
Dam
Buiten IJ
AMSTERDAM
S100
S112
S106
Singelgracht
Muiderpoort
Nieuwe Diep
IJmeer
Rijksmuseum
Amsterdam-Rijnkanaal
S110
Amstel
S108
A1
Diemen
Amstel
BEATRIXPARK
S109
S112
DIEMEN
De Diemen
A10
A1
RAI
Zuid WTC
Hilversum Amersfoort
S211
AMSTERDAM ZUIDOOST
Gaasp
BIJLMERMEER
S112
Amstel
Bijlmer
A2
A9
Gaasperplas
A9
OUDERKERK AAN DE AMSTEL
Gein
Bullewijk
Utrecht

Central Amsterdam

A street musician on Waterlooplein

THIS GUIDE divides central Amsterdam into seven distinct areas, each of which has its own chapter. Most city sights are contained in these areas. The Oude Zijde and Nieuwe Zijde make up the two halves of medieval Amsterdam, while the Museum Quarter was developed in the 19th century and has the three most important national museums. In between lies the Canal Ring, which retains many fine buildings from Amsterdam's Golden Age, while the Plantage *(see pp138–47)*, once an area of green space outside the city, is today best known for the zoological and botanical gardens.

Antiwar Barge on the Singel

The Singel was the first concentric canal to be cut in Amsterdam. It forms the border between the medieval center and the newer Western and Central Canal Rings (see pp86–113).

WESTERN CANAL RING

CENTRAL CANAL RING

MUSEUM QUARTER

VONDELPARK

Anne Frankhuis

Nieuwe Kerk

Amsterdams Historisch Museum

Rijksmuseum

Van Gogh Museum

Stedelijk Museum

Vondelpark

This attractive park in the Museum Quarter (see pp124–37) *is a good place to relax after a visit to one of Amsterdam's museums.*

0 meters 500

0 yards 500

Spires of Nieuwe Kerk and the Postkantoor
The Nieuwe Zijde's skyline (see pp70–85) *is pierced by the Neo-Gothic spire of the former Postkantoor, the steeples of the Nieuwe Kerk and the statues on the Koninklijk Paleis.*

House on the Oudezijds Voorburgwal
This attractive residential canal, which now runs through the Red Light District, was first cut in front of the ramparts protecting the Oude Zijde (see pp56–69).

Flowers at the Bloemenmarkt
A fragrant, floating flower market, the Bloemenmarkt is located beside the Munttoren on the Singel in the Eastern Canal Ring (see pp114–23).

KEY

- Major sight
- Place of interest
- Other building
- Parking
- Tourist information
- Police station
- Church
- Synagogue
- Mosque

THE HISTORY OF AMSTERDAM

AMSTERDAM, the greatest planned city of northern Europe, is today one in which beauty and serenity co-exist happily with a slightly seamy underside. Both parts of this split personality continue to draw visitors. Most of the racier aspects of Amsterdam spring directly from the city's long and honorable tradition of religious, philosophical and political tolerance. Developing at a time when many countries were torn by conflict, a precedent for freedom of speech was established early in Amsterdam. The notion of individual freedom of conscience was fought for, long and hard, during the struggles against Spanish domination in the 16th century. This belief stands firm today, with the caveat that no one should be harmed by the actions of others – a factor that sparked off the riots involving squatters in the 1970s.

Amsterdam's coat of arms on the Munttoren

The city was founded as a small fishing village in an improbable position on marsh at the mouth of the Amstel river. The waters around the village were controlled by a system of dikes and polders, and the young township expanded prodigiously to become the chief trading city of northern Europe, and ultimately, in the 17th century, the center of a massive empire stretching across the world. The construction of the canals and gabled houses in the 16th and 17th centuries – the hallmark Amsterdam – coincided with a period of fine domestic architecture. The glorious result is a city center of unusually consistent visual beauty. By the 18th century, Amsterdam was a major financial center, but internal unrest and restrictions imposed under Napoleonic rule led to a decline in her fortunes.

The city quietly slipped into a period of obscurity, and industrialization came late. In the 20th century, however, the city entered the European mainstream again. Its international airport, expanded in 1993, provides access for the world, and tourists pour in to see the stunning art museums and sample the delights of a modern, vibrant city.

Plan of Amsterdam (c. 1725) showing the Grachtengordel ***(see pp44–5)*** **and Plantage** ***(see pp138–47)***

◁ ***The Maid of Amsterdam Receiving the Homage of her People*** **(c. 1685) by Gerard de Lairesse**

The Origins of Amsterdam

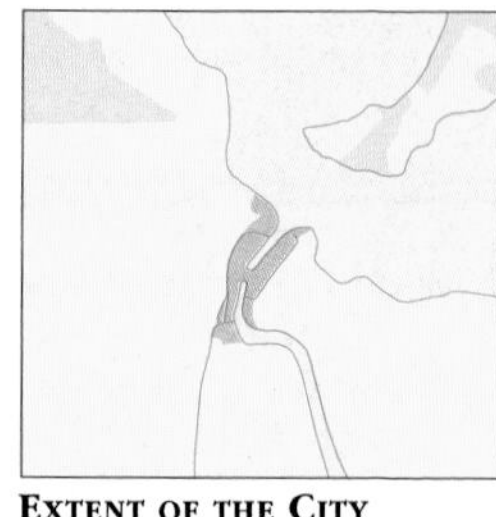

Windmills drained the land

AMSTERDAM emerged from the mists of the Low Countries in about 1200, on a watery site at the mouth of the Amstel river. It was a settlement of fisherfolk before turning to trade. The first permanent dwellings were built on terps, man-made mounds high enough to provide protection from flood water. As the settlement grew, it was molded by dynastic and religious combat, with feudal struggles between the Lords van Amstel and the counts of Holland, who had the backing of the all-powerful bishops of Utrecht *(see p202)*. This rivalry continued into the next century.

Farming on polders outside the village walls

Dam

Cooking Pot

Sturdy earthenware pots were used for cooking communal meals over an open fire in the kitchen area of 13th-century houses.

Wooden defense walls

Lord Gijsbrecht

The 19th-century etching shows Gijsbrecht van Amstel being marched into Utrecht as a prisoner by Guy of Hainaut, brother of the Count of Holland, in 1298.

Livestock grazed on reclaimed land called polder.

THE VILLAGE OF AMSTERDAM IN 1300

This medieval artist's impression shows the first tiny settlement on polders along the Damrak. The village was protected by wooden walls, and it is thought that the castle of the Van Amstels may have been located in the area around today's Dam square *(see pp72–3)*.

TIMELINE

1000 Fishermen float down Rhine in hollow pine logs

Small wooden cog ship used for fishing

1000 | 1050 | 1100

Primitive boat dating from c. 6000 BC

1015 Local feudal leader repels attack by German tribes and declares himself Count of Holland

c. 1125 Fishermen build huts at mouth of the Amstel river

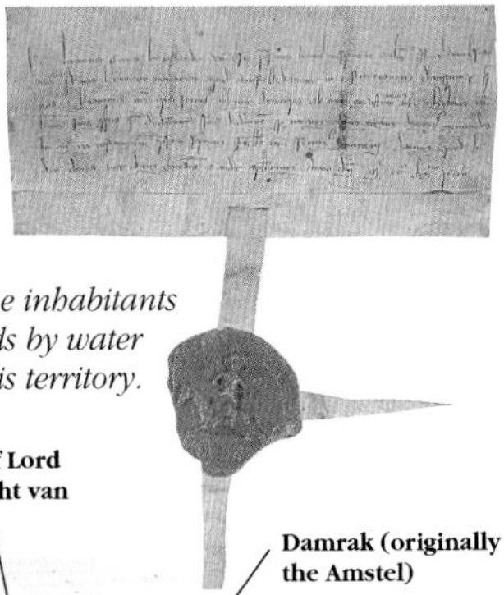

Freedom Charter
The village of Amstelledamme receives its first mention in this document of 1275 – permission from Count Floris V for the inhabitants to move their goods by water toll-free through his territory.

Count Floris V

The powerbase of Floris V, Count of Holland, was in Den Haag, and in 1275 he granted Amsterdammers freedom from tolls when crossing his lands. His political rival, Lord Gijsbrecht van Amstel, feared Floris's growing influence in Amsterdam and assassinated him in 1296. This resulted in the downfall and eventual exile of the van Amstel dynasty.

FLORENT V, XVI Comte de Holl.

19th-century portrait of Floris

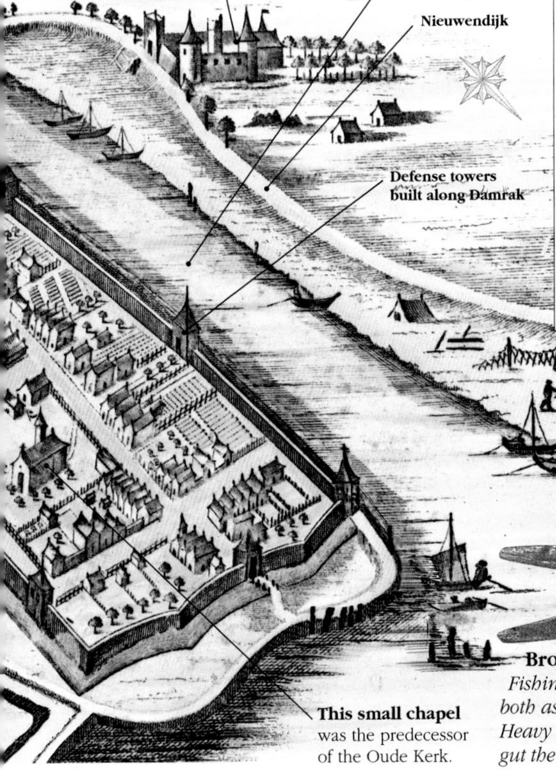

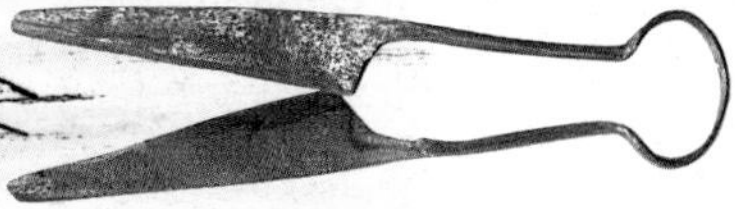

Castle of Lord Gijsbrecht van Amstel

Damrak (originally the Amstel)

Nieuwendijk

Defense towers built along Damrak

Cog ships

Fishermen on Damrak

Bronze Scissors
Fishing was integral to the community, both as a source of food and commerce. Heavy long-bladed scissors were used to gut the catch, which was mainly herring.

This small chapel was the predecessor of the Oude Kerk.

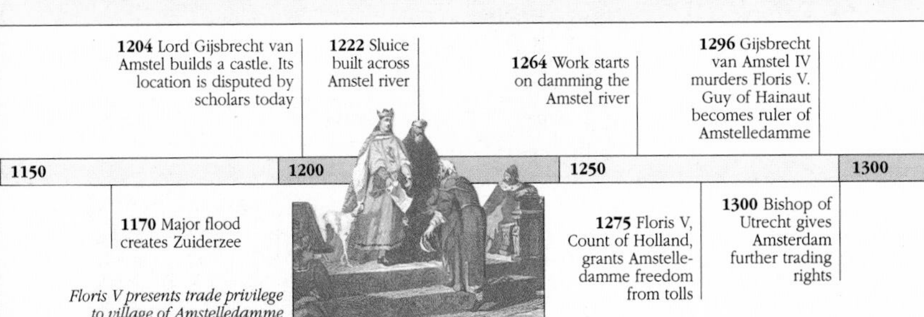

1204 Lord Gijsbrecht van Amstel builds a castle. Its location is disputed by scholars today

1222 Sluice built across Amstel river

1264 Work starts on damming the Amstel river

1296 Gijsbrecht van Amstel IV murders Floris V. Guy of Hainaut becomes ruler of Amstelledamme

1150 | 1200 | 1250 | 1300

1170 Major flood creates Zuiderzee

Floris V presents trade privilege to village of Amstelledamme

1275 Floris V, Count of Holland, grants Amstelledamme freedom from tolls

1300 Bishop of Utrecht gives Amsterdam further trading rights

Medieval Amsterdam

THE LITTLE TOWN at the mouth of the Amstel fortified itself against both its enemies and the surrounding water. Amsterdam grew rich quickly after the discovery of a method of curing herring in 1385, which preserved the fish longer, enabling it to be exported. The town became a port for handling beer from Hamburg. Elaborate waterside houses with warehouses attached were used to service the trade. The Low Countries were under the rule of the Dukes of Burgundy, and control passed by marriage to the Austrian Habsburgs.

Medieval leather boot (c. 1500)

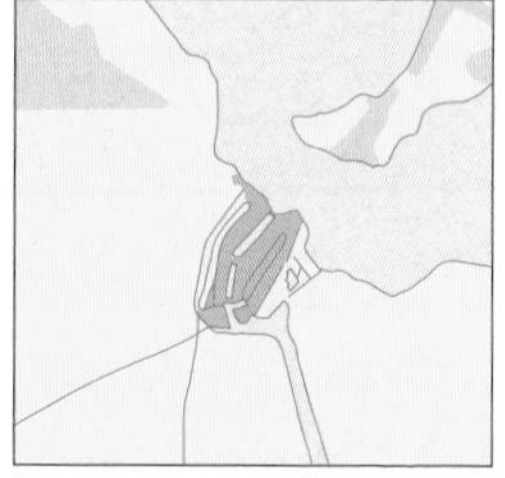

EXTENT OF THE CITY

Miracle of Amsterdam
This tapestry cushion depicts a miraculous event. A dying man was given the Sacrament, which he regurgitated. Thrown on the fire, the Host would not burn.

CANALSIDE HOUSE

Early canal houses were simple structures, built of wood with a thatched roof. From a single-story design with the front and back on different levels, the layouts grew more complex. At the front, side rooms became separated off from the main room, and the back house was similarly divided. The family slept on the first floor and goods were stored under the roof.

The wooden façades had simple spout gables *(see pp96–7).*

Flour, beer and other foodstuffs were stored under the sloping roof.

Timber structure

Philip of Burgundy and Isabella of Portugal
Philip ruled the Low Countries after 1419. His wedding to Isabella in 1430 led to the Habsburg dynasty ruling the Netherlands.

TIMELINE

Misericord in the Oude Kerk

1301 Guy of Hainaut made Bishop of Utrecht

1304 Lord Gijsbrecht van Amstel exiled

Early 1300s Work starts on Oude Kerk *(see pp68–9)*

1323 Count of Holland designates Amsterdam a toll port for beer

1345 Miracle of Amsterdam

1350 Amsterdam becomes a beer and grain entrepôt

1380 Work begins on Nieuwe Kerk *(see pp76–7)*

1385 Willem Beukelszoon discovers method of curing herring

1300 | 1325 | 1350 | 1375 | 1400

Stained-glass window in the Nieuwe Kerk

Making Beer
The brewing industry expanded after 1323, when the Count of Holland permitted Amsterdam to become a toll port for beer. Hops were introduced early in the century.

Thatched roof

The Great Fire of 1452
After Amsterdam's second devastating blaze, which destroyed the Nieuwe Kerk, legislation was passed preventing the use of wood as a building material.

Access to canal at rear

Stone side walls

Wooden support piles were driven into the first stable layer of sand.

Warehouse space

Amsterdam's Seal
The seal shows the diagonal crosses of St. Andrew, the coat of arms of the Habsburgs and the cog ship that brought wealth through trade.

Where to See Medieval Amsterdam

Few buildings remain from this period, since fire destroyed two-thirds of the city. The Oude Kerk *(see pp68–9)* dates from the early 14th century and the Nieuwe Kerk *(pp76–7)* from 1380. The Agnietenkapel *(p61)* was built in 1470 and is one of very few Gothic chapels to survive the Alteration of 1578 *(pp22–3).*

The Waag (p60)
Built in 1488, this was originally a gateway in the city wall.

No. 34 Begijnhof (p75)
The oldest wooden house in the city, it dates from about 1420.

Maximilian marries Maria of Burgundy

1477 Charles' daughter Maria marries Maximilian Habsburg of Austria

1452 Second Great Fire of Amsterdam

1480 Defensive walls built around Amsterdam

1494 Maximilian is Holy Roman Emperor. Power passes to his son, Philip, who marries the daughter of Isabella of Spain

1425 | 1450 | 1475 | 1500

1421 First Great Fire of Amsterdam

1419 Philip the Good of Burgundy begins to unify the Low Countries

1467 Charles the Bold succeeds Philip of Burgundy

Charles the Bold

1482 Maria dies and Maximilian Habsburg rules the Netherlands

1500 Birth of Philip's son, the future Emperor Charles V and king of Spain

The Age of Intolerance

By 1500, Amsterdam had outpaced rivals to become the main power in the province of Holland. Trade in the Baltic provided wealth and the city grew quickly. Spain's Habsburg rulers tried to halt the Protestant Reformation sweeping northern Europe. Dutch resistance to Philip II of Spain resulted in 80 years of civil war and religious strife. Amsterdam sided with Spain but switched loyalties in 1578 – an event known as the Alteration – to become the fiercely Protestant capital of an infant Dutch Republic.

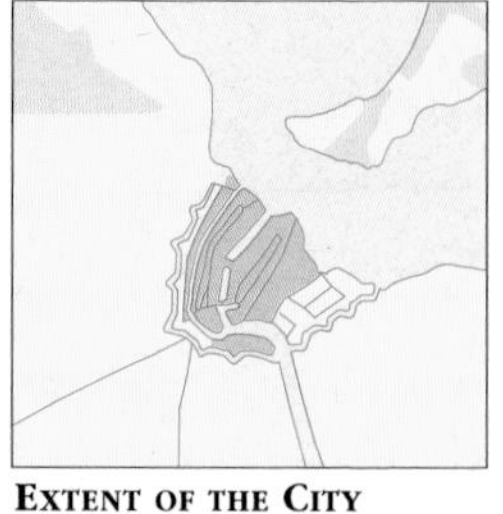

Extent of the City

1500 Today

Anabaptists' Uprising *(1535)*
An extremist Protestant cult of Anabaptists seized the Stadhuis. Many were executed after eviction.

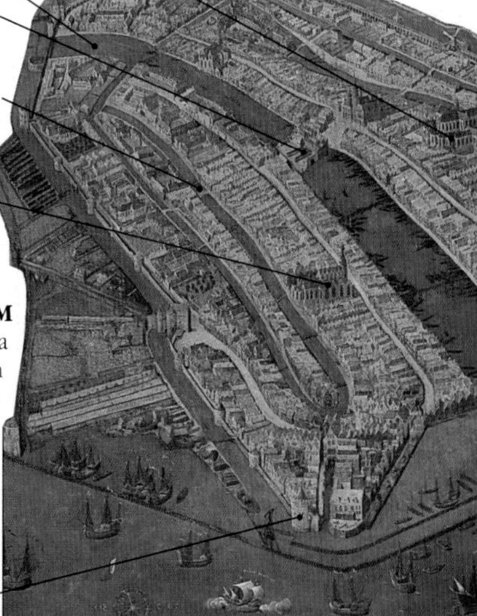

Perspective of Amsterdam
This painted woodcut is a bird's-eye view of Amsterdam by Cornelis Anthonisz (1538). It is a critically important, detailed and precise map, heralding a centuries-long tradition of world-class map making in the city *(see p146)*.

William of Orange
William, portrayed in 1555 by Anthonius Mor, led the Dutch against the Spanish until his assassination in Delft (see p195).

Much of the farmland in the Netherlands is below sea level.

Timeline

1500 | **1510** | **1520** | **1530** | **1540** | **155**

1502 Population of Amsterdam 12,000

1506 Charles rules over the 17 provinces of the Netherlands

1516 Charles becomes king of Spain

1519 Charles becomes Holy Roman Emperor, Charles V

Charles V, Holy Roman Emperor, king of Spain and ruler of the Netherlands

1535 Anabaptists demonstrate on Dam square. Mass executions follow. Start of 40 years of religious strife

1543 Charles V unifies Low Countries

1550 Edict of Blood decrees death for all Protestant heretics

1551 Population of Amsterdam about 30,000

The Guild of St. George *(1533)*
Guilds set up to keep order in the growing city later formed the Civic Guard (see pp82–3). *Map maker Cornelis Anthonisz painted this guild at supper.*

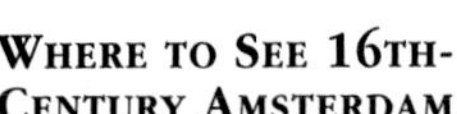

Where to See 16th-Century Amsterdam

Few buildings of early 16th-century provenance remain, but No. 1 Zeedijk *(see p67)* was built mid-century as a hostel for sailors. The Civic Guards' Gallery at the Amsterdams Historisch Museum *(pp80–83)* contains a series of splendid group portraits of 16th-century militia companies and guilds.

Montelbaanstoren
The lower section of the tower was built in 1512 (see p66), *forming part of the city defenses.*

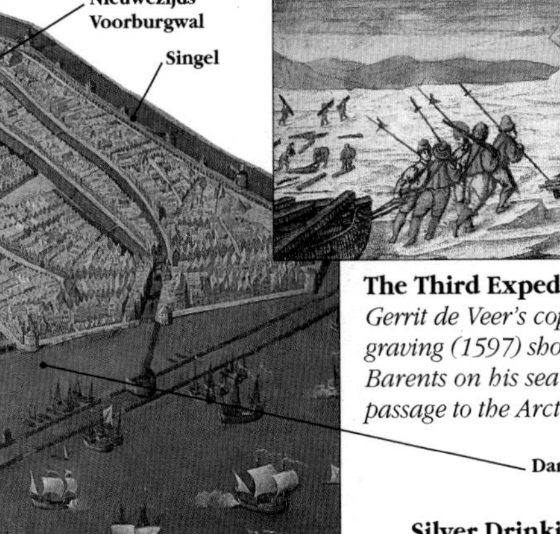

The Third Expedition
Gerrit de Veer's copper engraving (1597) shows Willem Barents on his search for a passage to the Arctic Sea.

Silver Drinking Horn
As the guilds grew richer, ceremony played a larger part in their lives. This ornate drinking horn shows St. George defending the hapless maiden against the dragon.

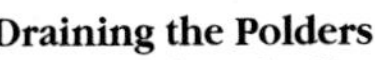

Draining the Polders
"Gangs" of windmills were built to drain the low-lying land. Each mill scooped water up, stage by stage, until it drained away into the sea (see p173).

Duke of Alva

1555 Charles V abdicates. Philip II of Spain succeeds

1566 Calvinist iconoclasts demolish religious art and statuary in *Beeldenstorm*

1567 Duke of Alva introduces heavy taxation in Amsterdam

1572 Beginning of Dutch Revolt under Protestant William of Orange

1576 Amsterdam besieged by William of Orange

1578 Calvinists take civil power and expel Catholics from Amsterdam in the Alteration

1579 Northern provinces sign Union of Utrecht

1580 Spain absorbs Portugal, and Dutch establish new trade routes to the east

1584 William of Orange assassinated in Delft

1596–7 Explorer Willem Barents finds route to Arctic Sea

1598 Philip II dies, unable to subdue Dutch Protestants

1560 | 1570 | 1580 | 1590 | 1600

William was shot on the staircase of his headquarters in Delft in 1584 (see p195)

The Golden Age of Amsterdam

THE 17TH CENTURY was truly a Golden Age for Amsterdam. The population soared, three great canals *(see pp44–5)*, bordered by splendid houses, were built in a triple ring around the city and scores of painters and architects were at work. Fortunes were made and lost, and this early capitalism produced paupers who were cared for by charitable institutions – a radical idea for the time. In 1648, an uneasy peace was formalized with Catholic Spain, causing tension between Amsterdam's Calvinist burgomasters and the less religious House of Orange, dominant elsewhere in the country.

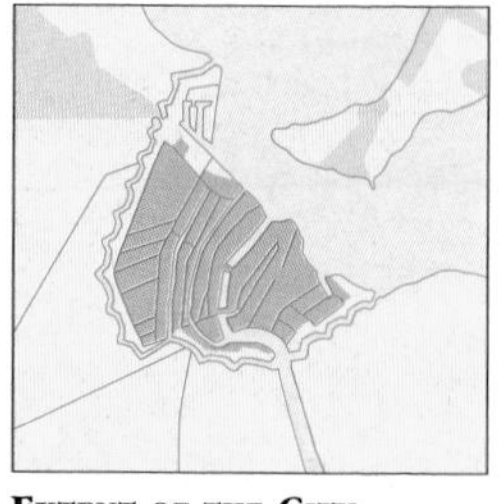

EXTENT OF THE CITY

▭ *1600* ▭ *Today*

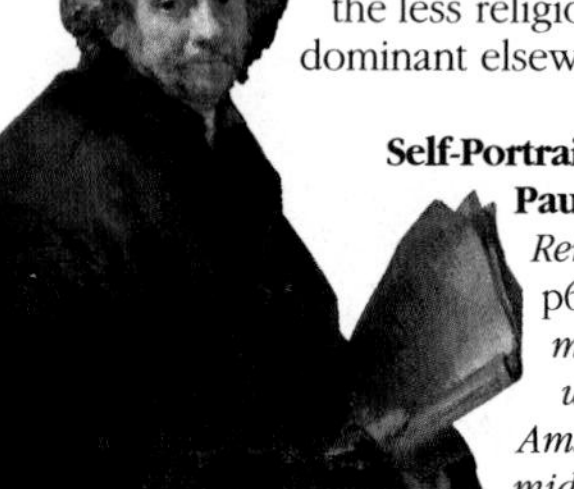

Self-Portrait as the Apostle Paul *(1661)*
Rembrandt (see p62) *was one of many artists working in Amsterdam in the mid-17th century.*

The Love Letter *(1666)*
Genre painting (see p194), *such as this calm domestic interior by Jan Vermeer, became popular as society grew more sophisticated.*

Livestock and grain trading

Nieuwe Kerk (1395)

The new Stadhuis (now the Koninklijk Paleis) was being constructed behind wooden scaffolding.

DAM SQUARE IN 1656

Money poured into Amsterdam at this time of civic expansion. Jan Lingelbach (c. 1624–74) painted Dam square as a busy, thriving and cosmopolitan market, full of traders and wealthy merchants.

Delft Tiles
Delicate flower paintings were popular themes on 17th-century delft tiles (see p195), *used as decoration in wealthy households.*

TIMELINE

1598 Frederick Henry of Orange is stadtholder. Plans to control navy from Den Haag fail

Prince Frederick Henry of Orange

1600

1609 Plan for triple ring of canals around heart of Amsterdam *(see pp44–5)*

1610

1613 Work starts on first phase of canals

1614 Work finishes on Zuiderkerk *(see p62)*

1620 Tulip mania begins

1620

17th-century botanical drawing of a tulip

1628 The philosopher Descartes comes to Amsterdam

1630

1631 Rembrandt comes to live in Amsterdam *(see p62)*

1636 The great tulip crash

1640

1642 Rembrandt paints *The Night Watch (see p131)*

Flora's Bandwagon *(1636)*
Many allegories were painted during "tulip mania." This satirical oil by HG Pot symbolizes the idiocy of investors who paid for rare bulbs with their weight in gold, forcing prices up until the market collapsed.

Giving the Bread
The painting by Willem van Valckert shows the needy receiving charity. A rudimentary welfare system was introduced in the 1640s.

WHERE TO SEE 17TH-CENTURY AMSTERDAM

Many public buildings sprang up as Amsterdam grew more wealthy. The Westerkerk *(see p90)* was designed by Hendrick de Keyser in 1620, the Lutherse Kerk *(p78)* by Adriaan Dortsman in 1671. Elias Bouman built the Portugese Synagoge *(p66)* in 1675 for members of the immigrant Sephardic Jewish community *(p64).*

Apollo *(c. 1648)*
Artus Quellien's statue is in the South Gallery of the Koninklijk Paleis (see p74).

Rembrandthuis *(1606)*
Jacob van Campen added the pediment in 1633 (see p66).

adhuis (Koninklijk Paleis)

1650 Death of adtholder William II

1665 New Stadhuis completed

1672 William III is stadtholder. De Wit brothers killed by mob in Den Haag *(see p186)*

1685 Huguenot refugees reach Amsterdam after Louis XIV's Edict of Nantes

1650	1660	1670	1680	1690

1648 Amsterdam achieves supremacy over Antwerp on the maritime trade routes

1652 Stadhuis burns down

1663 Second phase of canal building

1669 Death of Rembrandt

1677 William III marries Mary Stuart, heiress to the English throne

William and Mary

The Golden Age Overseas

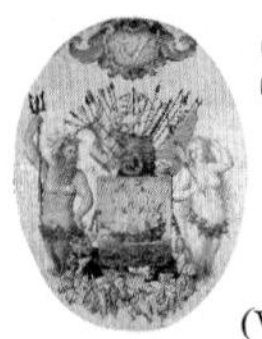

Coat of arms of the VOC

SUPREMACY IN THE NETHERLANDS led to success overseas for Amsterdam. The Dutch colonized the Indonesian Archipelago, establishing a profitable empire based on spice trading in the East. The Dutch East India Company (VOC) thrived, using vast wooden ships called East Indiamen. In the New World, the Dutch ruled large parts of Brazil and bought Manhattan from its native owners, naming it New Amsterdam. However, war with England radically trimmed Dutch sea power by the end of the 17th century.

Purchase of Manhattan
In 1626 explorer Pieter Minuit bought the island of Manhattan from the Native Americans for $24.

Salvaged Silverware
The Batavia *sank off the coast of western Australia in 1629. This bedknob, ewer and plate were salvaged in 1972.*

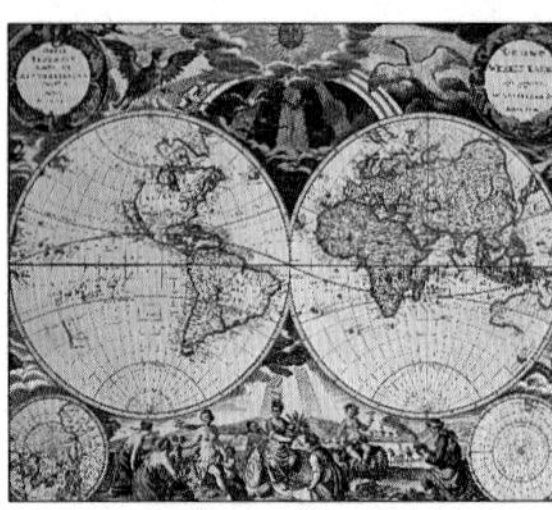

World Map *(1676)*
Jan Blaeu's map charted the known world, with parts of Asia and Australia missing.

THE BATAVIA

Owned by the VOC, the *Batavia* was an East Indiaman, with three main masts. She was 45 m (148 ft) in length and carried a complement of about 350, including crew, soldiers and families.

TIMELINE OF EXPLORATION

1595 First voyage to Indonesia via Cape of Good Hope

1600

1602 Dutch East India Company (VOC) founded

VOC logo

1609 Hugo Grotius advocates freedom of trade at sea

1610

1620 Pilgrim Fathers depart for the New World *(see p185)*

1620

1621 Dutch West India Company founded

1626 Peter Minuit buys Manhattan and founds New Amsterdam

1630

Peter Stuyvesant

1642 Abel Tasman discovers Tasmania

1640

Dutch Battle Ships *(1683)*
Ludolf Backhuysen (1631–1708) painted the Dutch battle fleet routing the rival Portuguese navy off the coast of northern Spain.

The Dutch East India Company

Founded in 1602, the VOC had a monopoly on all profits from trade east of the Cape of Good Hope. It became a public company and many a Dutch merchant's fortune was made. By 1611, it was the leading importer of spices into Europe, with ships ranging as far as China, Japan and Indonesia. For nearly 200 years the VOC ran a commercial empire more powerful than some countries.

The Nederlands Scheepvart Museum (see pp146–7) *has a hall devoted to the VOC. A replica of the East Indiaman, the* Amsterdam, *is moored outside.*

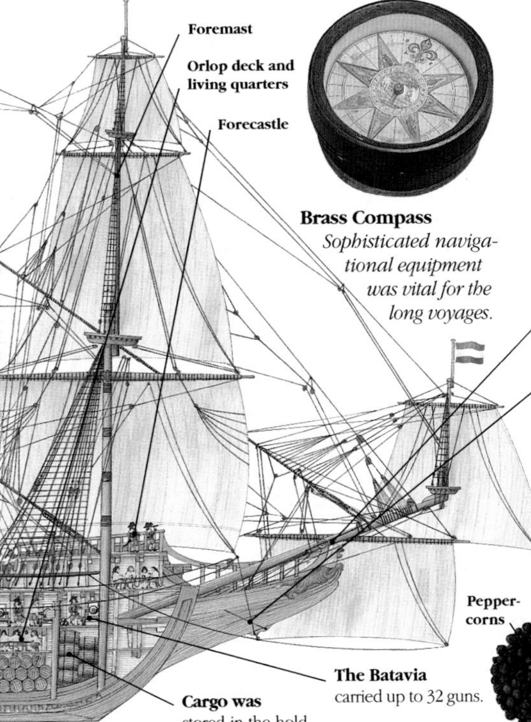

Brass Compass
Sophisticated navigational equipment was vital for the long voyages.

The Batavia
carried up to 32 guns.

Cargo was
stored in the hold.

Transporting Spices
A cargo of eastern spices was of almost inestimable value. Most prized were pepper, cloves, nutmeg, mace and cinnamon.

Nutmeg **Cinnamon** **Cloves** **Ground nutmeg** **Pepper-corns** **Ground mace**

1647 Peter Stuyvesant made governor of New Amsterdam

1648 Treaty of Munster ends war with Spain. Dutch Republic recognized

1664 British take possession of New Amsterdam

1665 Admiral de Ruyter *(see p77)* destroys English fleet

1672 *Rampjaar* (year of disaster). France, under Louis XIV, attacks Holland. War with England breaks out once more

King Louis XIV

1650 | 1660 | 1670 | 1680 | 1690

1652 First maritime war with England

Dutch fleet in river Medway in 1667

1666 Four-day sea battle against English

1667 Dutch sign Breda Peace Treaty with England

1688 William III *(see p25)*, invited to take over English throne, becoming King William III

The Age of Consolidation

THOUGH THE DUTCH EMPIRE declined, the Netherlands remained wealthy. Amsterdam's ships became commercial cargo carriers and by the mid-18th century, the city was the world's financial capital. Tolerance prevailed and the city was flooded with immigrants, including Jews from all across Europe. Dissatisfaction with the ruling House of Orange intensified; although Prussian troops crushed a Patriot uprising in 1787, the Patriots established a short-lived republic, with French backing, only to see Napoleon take over, making his brother Louis king of the Netherlands.

Silver Torah finials *(see p64)*

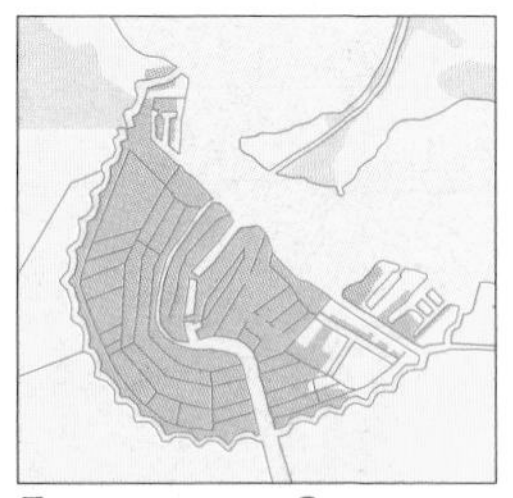

EXTENT OF THE CITY

1700 | Today

Receiving Visitors *(c. 1713)*
Amsterdam was cosmopolitan and decadent; in Cornelis Troost's satire, the ladies of a brothel parade before Prince Eugène of Savoy.

DOLLHOUSE
Costly dollhouses were designed for show rather than play, and are a fitting symbol of the extravagance of the age. This example is a miniature replica of the house of an Amsterdam merchant. Now in the Frans Hals Museum in Haarlem *(see pp178–9)*, it was made around 1750 for Sara Rothé.

Wintertime in Amsterdam *(c. 1763)*
Petrus Schenk's print shows people skating on the frozen canals. The ice-breaking barges in the background are bringing fresh water to the city.

TIMELINE

1695 Tzar Peter the Great of Russia visits Amsterdam to study shipbuilding

Portrait of Tzar Peter the Great (1727) on gold snuff box

1700

1702 Death of William III. Stadtholderless period begins in the Netherlands

1710

1713 Treaty of Utrecht signed. Dutch Republic becomes isolated

1716 Grand Assembly meets in Den Haag *(see p186)*, imposing radical government reforms

French musketeer

1720

1730

1740

1744 France invades Southern Provinces

1747 Stadtholdership becomes hereditary under William IV

1748 Tax collector riots

1751 Death of William IV. Start of 40 years of political strife

17

Prussian Troops Enter Amsterdam *(1787)*
A lithograph by an unknown artist shows Prussian troops entering the city on October 10, 1787, coming to the aid of the House of Orange after pro-French Patriot upheavals.

Where to See 18th-Century Amsterdam

De Gooyer Windmill *(see p144)* produced grain for the city from 1725. A clandestine church was opened in 1735 in today's Museum Amstelkring *(pp84–5)*, in response to the Alteration *(pp22–3)*. Fine canal houses include No. 465 Herengracht *(p112)* and the Felix Meritis Building *(p113)*, designed by Jacob Otten Husly in 1787. Museum van Loon was renovated in 1752 *(p122)*.

Museum Willet-Holthuysen
The elaborate, gilded staircase (see p121) *was built in 1740.*

Pavilioned bed with green canopy

Lying-in room

Library

Florin *(1781)*
By 1750, Amsterdam possessed the most sophisticated and successful banking and brokering system in the world.

Tax Collector Riots *(1748)*
This print by Simonsz Fokke shows an angry mob raiding the house of a tax collector in June 1748.

Porcelain Plate *(c. 1780)*
The wealthy lived in great style, sparing no expense. This hand-painted plate is decorated with mythological figures and ornate gold leaf.

1760 | 1770 | 1780 | 1790 | 1800 | 1810

1763 Freezing winter

1766 William V comes of age

1768 William V marries Wilhelmina of Prussia

1780–84 War with England, whose navy destroys Dutch fleet

1787 Patriots' upheaval ends with Prussian army entering Amsterdam

1791 VOC *(see pp26–7)* goes into liquidation

1795 Provinces unite briefly into republic, ruled jointly by Patriots and French

Louis Napoleon (1778–1846)

1806 Napoleon Bonaparte takes over republic

1808 Louis Napoleon crowned king of the Netherlands

The Age of Industrialization

By the end of Louis Napoleon's rule, Amsterdam had stagnated. The decline continued, with little sign of enterprise and scant investment. Industrialization came late and attempts to revive the city's fortunes by digging a canal to the North Sea were not effective. Politically, the country regrouped around the House of Orange, bringing the family out of exile and declaring a monarchy in 1813. The mid-century saw growth of the liberal constitution; by 1900 the Socialist tradition was well established.

Extent of the City

1800 Today

Cocoa Trading
Cocoa was one of Amsterdam's main exports in the 1890s.

Centraal Station

The station *(see p79)* was completed in 1889. It became a symbol of the emergent industrial age – a sign that Amsterdam was finally moving toward the future rather than looking back to the Golden Age.

Dutch Renaissance-style façade

The gilded "clock" shows the wind direction, acknowledging Amsterdam's earlier reliance on the wind to power her sailing ships.

Main concourse

The Sweatshop by H Wolter
As industrialization increased, sweatshops, with their attendant poverty, became commonplace.

Diamond Cutting
The diamond trade thrived in the late 19th century, when precious stones were imported from South Africa.

Timeline

1813 House of Orange returns from exile

1814 William becomes king of the Netherlands

1824 Noordzeekanaal is dug but proves ineffective

1831 Low Countries split into north and south. Southern provinces become Belgium

1839 Amsterdam-to-Haarlem railroad opens *(see p177)*

1840 William I abdicates. Succeeded by William II

1845 Rioters in Amsterdam call for social reform

1848 New constitution devised by Thorbecke

1850 Population 245,000

1860s Jews begin to arrive in Amsterdam from Antwerp

1820 | 1830 | 1840 | 1850 | 1860

King William I at Waterloo (1815)

Henry Thorbecke

Cycling Poster
Amsterdammers were encouraged to exercise and stay healthy. Cycling was the ideal sport as the city environs were very flat. This poster by Hart Nibbrig, from the 1880s, shows the city skyline.

Steamships unloaded their cargo straight into the railroad terminal.

Tracks ran alongside the Zuiderzee.

Passengers alighted under cover.

The King's Waiting Room

WHERE TO SEE 19TH-CENTURY AMSTERDAM

An outburst of civic pride in the late 19th century led to the construction of some new revivalist-style public buildings. PJH Cuypers's Neo-Gothic Rijksmuseum *(see pp130–33)* opened in 1885, followed ten years later by the Stedelijk Museum *(pp136–7)*, the work of AW Weissman. HP Berlage's Beurs *(p79)* marked the beginning of the radical new style that led to the Amsterdam School *(p97)*.

***Concertgebouw** (1888)*
AL van Gendt's concert hall (see p128) *is Neo-Renaissance in style.*

The Jewish Quarter *(1889)*
The desperate conditions in the ghetto are shown in this painting by EA Hilverdink.

1874 Child Labor Act cuts working hours

1876 Noordzee-kanaal reopened

1878 FD Nieuwenhuis founds the Social Democratic Association

1883 World Exhibition draws a million visitors

1886 26 die in Jordaan riots

1889 Cuypers finishes Centraal Station *(see p79)*

1891 Wilhelmina ascends throne

1894 Foundation of Social Democratic Workers' Party (SDAP)

1902 Socialists win their first seat on city council

1909 Communists split from SDAP and become separate political force

1870 1880 1890 1900 1910

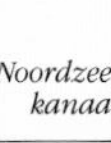

Noordzee-kanaal

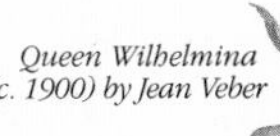

Queen Wilhelmina (c. 1900) by Jean Veber

Amsterdam at War

THE NETHERLANDS remained neutral in World War I. After the war, political unrest was rife and the city council embarked on a program of new housing projects and, in the 1930s, the Amsterdamse Bos was created to counter unemployment. When World War II broke out, the Netherlands again opted for neutrality – only to be invaded by Germany. The early 1940s were bitter years, and many died of starvation in the winter of 1945. During this time, most of the Jewish population was deported; many, like Anne Frank, tried to avoid detection by going into hiding.

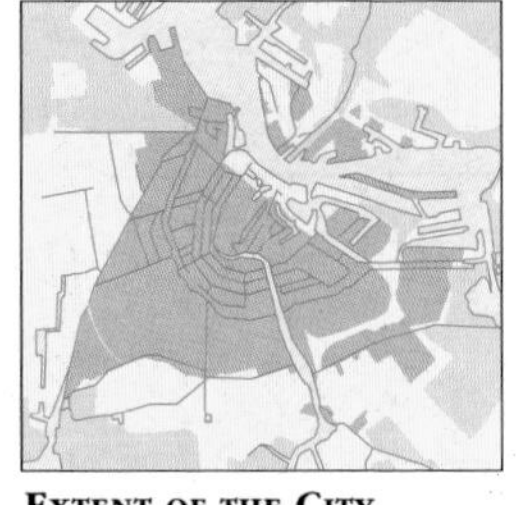

EXTENT OF THE CITY

1945 Today

"Vote Red" Poster *(1918)*
The Social Democratic Party (SDAP) (see p31) *was responsible for the introduction of a welfare state after World War II.*

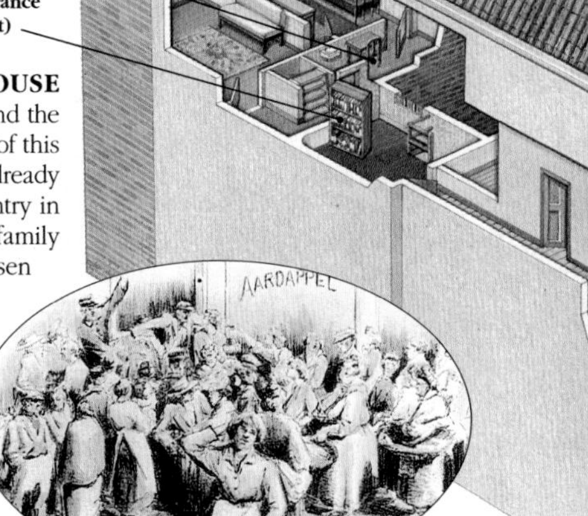

ANNE FRANK'S HOUSE

In July 1942, Anne Frank, her family and the Van Daans went into hiding at the rear of this house *(see p90)*. Anne was 13 and had already begun her diary. She made her last entry in August 1944, three days before her family was arrested. She died in Bergen-Belsen concentration camp in March 1945.

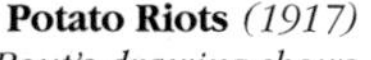

Potato Riots *(1917)*
Daan Bout's drawing shows desperate women fighting for vegetables during World War I. Rioting followed and the army was brought in to quell the uprising.

TIMELINE

1910

1914 World War I begins. Holland remains neutral

1915 SDAP have majority on city council and shape housing policy

1915

Cartoon satirizing the Netherlands' rejection of Germany's offer of friendship in 1915

1917 Potato riots in the Jordaan

1920 Air service from Schiphol to London inaugurated

1920

1920s "Ring" built around southern part of the city. Many canals filled in but work is halted after considerable opposition

Detail on façade of ABN Bank

1925

1926 ABN Bank built on Vijzelstraat

1928 Olympic Game[s] held in Amsterdam

Het Schip by Michel de Klerk
At the end of World War I, Amsterdam School architects (see p97) *designed new housing projects such as "the ship," to replace the slums in the south of the city.*

Where to See Early-20th-Century Amsterdam

Innovative Amsterdam School architecture is found to the south of the city. HP Berlage, PL Kramer and Michel de Klerk collaborated on De Dageraad *(see p151)* and were largely responsible for the Nieuw Zuid *(p154)*. Much of this was built in the run up to the 1928 Olympics; it boasts spectacular housing developments and civic buildings.

Tuschinski Theater *(1921)*
The interior of this exotic complex is awash with color.

Amsterdamse Bos
In 1930, as part of a job-creation plan, 5,000 unemployed Dutch citizens were drafted in to help develop a woodland and leisure area to the southwest of the city.

Offices at the front of the building

Façade of No. 263 Prinsengracht

Dockworker Statue
The statue (see p53) *by Marie Andriessen commemorates the February 1941 protest by dockers and transit workers against the Nazis' treatment of Jews.*

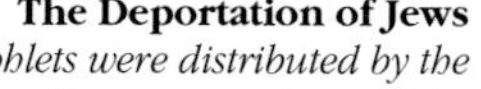

The Deportation of Jews
Pamphlets were distributed by the Resistance vilifying those who stood by and let the Nazis round up the Jews.

1930 Population 750,000. Unemployment worsens. Work on public project of Amsterdamse Bos begins

1932–7 Rise of Dutch Nazi Party under Anton Mussert

1934 Riots in Jordaan over reduction in social security. Seven die

1935 Work parties sent to Germany

1939 Outbreak of World War II. The Netherlands chooses neutrality

1940 Germany bombs Den Haag. The Dutch surrender

1941 450 Jews arrested. Dockworkers strike

1942 Deportation of Jews begins

1944 D-Day Landings

1945 Germany surrenders

1930 | 1935 | 1940 | 1945

Yellow Star of David, which Jews had to wear during Nazi Occupation

Amsterdam Today

Amsterdam trolley

After the end of World War II, Amsterdam suffered a series of social problems – the city's traditional tolerance made it a haven for the hippy culture of the 1960s – and a center of drug use and trafficking. The left-wing Provos challenged social order and by the mid-1980s, families were moving out in droves. A series of riots over squatting and redevelopment of the city led to measures that alleviated the social problems. Amsterdam is once again a tranquil and beautiful city for all to visit.

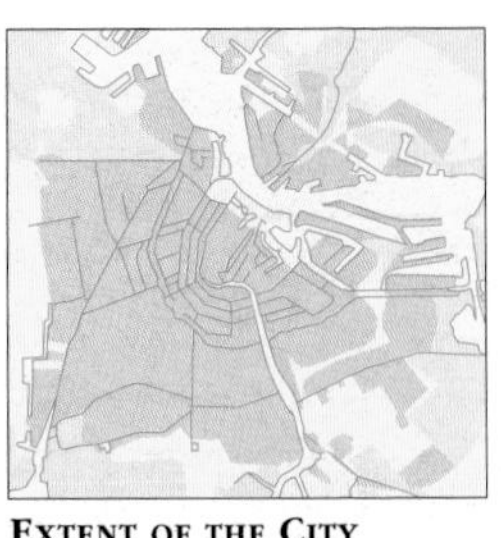

Extent of the City

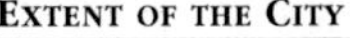

Soccer
The fans were ecstatic when the Dutch national team beat England 3 to 1 in 1988 in the European Championships.

Het Lieferdje
The statue of the Little Urchin *by Carel Kneulman is in Spui. It became a symbol for the Provos in the 1960s.*

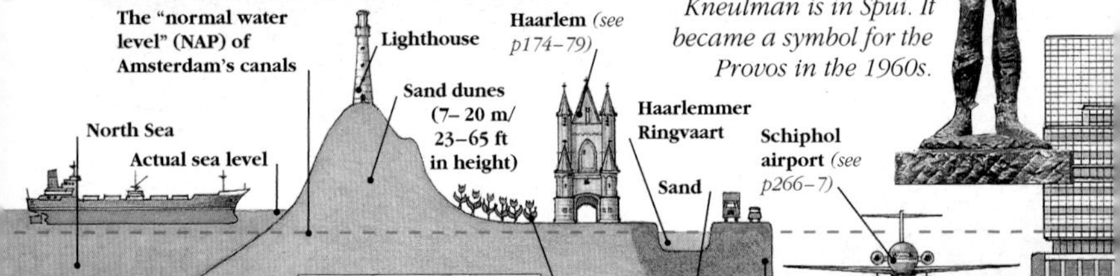

The "normal water level" (NAP) of Amsterdam's canals

Lighthouse

Haarlem *(see p174–79)*

Sand dunes (7– 20 m/ 23–65 ft in height)

Haarlemmer Ringvaart

North Sea

Actual sea level

Schiphol airport *(see p266–7)*

Sand

Bulbfields *(see p266–7)*

Ringdijk

Haarlemmermeer (4.5 m/ 15 ft below sea level)

Locator Map

Normaal Amsterdams Peil
The city's water level (NAP), set in 1684, is displayed near the Stopera (see p63).

Section of Noord Holland

This cross-section shows Holland's polders *(see pp22–3)* lying below sea level. Without the protection of dikes and tide barriers, Amsterdam would be inundated. Its buildings are supported by piles that pass through layers of clay and peat into firm sand.

Timeline

1948 Queen Wilhelmina abdicates after 43 years. Juliana becomes queen

1957 The Netherlands signs Treaty of Rome, joining European Community

1965 Provos win seats on city council for first time

1963 The population peaks at 868,000

1966 Provos demonstrate at wedding of Princess Beatrix to German aristocrat Claus von Amsberg

1950 | 1955 | 1960 | 1965 | 1970

1949 Indonesia officially independent from the Netherlands

Cannabis leaves

1967 Hippies arrive in Amsterdam

1968 First residents move to the vast Bijlmermeer housing project

197 Ajax wi European Cu

Queen Beatrix
Born in 1938, Beatrix was crowned in the Nieuwe Kerk (see pp76–7) *in 1980. She is a popular constitutional monarch, known for her lack of formality.*

House on the Singel
17th-century canal houses often sink since their foundations are shallow. Traditionally they were propped up by wooden support beams, but now technology allows for the replacement of rotten support piles without demolition.

WHERE TO SEE MODERN AMSTERDAM

Amsterdam has many superb new buildings, mostly in a specially built commercial center to the southeast of the city. However, Wilhelm Holzbauer's Stadhuis-Muziektheater *(see p63)*, completed in 1988 amid much controversy, was built in the heart of the old Jewish Quarter.

The ING Bank *(1987) in the southeast of Amsterdam has no right angles to its structure.*

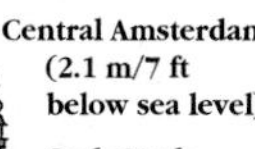

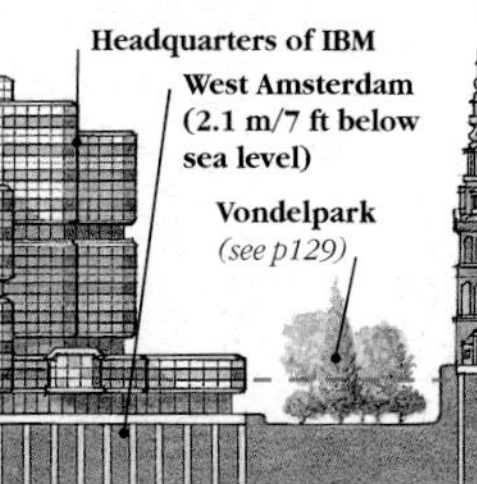

Hippies
In the late 1960s, Amsterdam was known for its tolerance of subcultures. It became a haven for hippies, who gathered in the Vondelpark (see p129).

Abdication speech by Queen Juliana

1980 Start of wave of battles between police and squatters. Queen Juliana abdicates in favor of Beatrix

1989 Center-right comes to power in Dutch Parliament

1992 26 percent of population are now immigrants

1975	1980	1985	1990	1995

1975 Nieuwmarkt riots erupt against destruction of Jewish Quarter. Independence of Surinam. 40,000 migrate to Holland

1981 Amsterdam is recognized as capital of Holland

1984 Population levels off at 670,000

1986 Opera House *(see p63)* opens in Stopera

1993 Schiphol Airport *(see pp226–7)* modernized

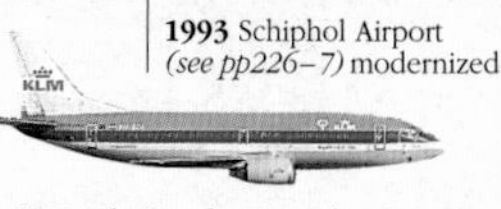

KLM – the Dutch national airline

JACOB BACKER
CORNELIS DE GRAEF
DWOVTER VALCKENIER
CORNELIS BICKER
DALBERT BAS.
NICOLAES CORVER
IAN BICKER
DCORNELIS WITSEN
DNICOLAES TULP
ANDRIES DE GRAEFF 1657
HENDRICK HOOFT 1662
Jan van Waveren
Johannis Hudde 1672
Gerard Bors v. Waveren
Joan de Vries 1686
Jacob Boreel 1691
Cornelis Valckenier
Dirk Bas
JAN GRAAF
Cornelis

AMSTERDAM AT A GLANCE

THERE ARE MORE THAN 100 places described in the *Area by Area* section of this book. The broad spectrum of entries covers recreational as well as cultural sights and ranges from sublime buildings, such as the Oude Kerk, to oddities like the Hash Marihuana Museum *(see p61)*. The Golden Bend *(see p112)* and other impressive canalscapes are also featured, along with suggested walks past some of Amsterdam's finest architecture and notable sights, such as Anne Frankhuis. To help you make the most of your stay, the following 12 pages are a time-saving guide to the best Amsterdam has to offer. Museums, canals and bridges, and cafés and bars all have their own sections. Below is a selection of attractions that no visitor should miss.

AMSTERDAM'S TOP TEN ATTRACTIONS

Nederlands Scheepvaart Museum
See pp146–7

Van Gogh Museum
See pp134–5

Oude Kerk
See pp68–9

Begijnhof
See p75

Koninklijk Paleis
See p74

Rijksmuseum
See pp130–33

Stedelijk Museum
See pp136–7

Museum Amstelkring *See pp84–5*

Magere Brug
See p119

Anne Frankhuis
See pp32–3 & 90–91

◁ **Stained-glass coats of arms in the Lady Chapel of the Oude Kerk**

Amsterdam's Best: Museums

FOR A FAIRLY SMALL CITY, Amsterdam has a surprisingly large number of museums and galleries. The quality and variety of the collections are impressive and many are housed in buildings of historical or architectural interest. The Rijksmuseum, with its Gothic façade, is a city landmark, and Rembrandt's work is exhibited in his original home. For more information on museums see pages 40–41.

Anne Frankhuis
Anne Frank's photo is exhibited in the house where she hid during World War II.

Amsterdams Historisch Museum
A wealth of historical information is on display here. Once an orphanage, it is depicted in Governesses at the Burgher Orphanage *(1683) by Adriaen Backer.*

Rijksmuseum
An extensive collection of paintings by Dutch masters can be seen in the country's largest national museum. Jan van Huysum's Still Life with Flowers and Fruit, *dating from about 1730, is a fine example.*

Stedelijk Museum
Gerrit Rietveld's simple Steltman chair (1963) is one of many exhibits at this ever-changing contemporary art museum.

Rijksmuseum Vincent van Gogh
Van Gogh's Self-portrait with Straw Hat *(1870) hangs in this large, stark museum, built in 1973 to house the bulk of his work.*

Museum Amstelkring
Three 17th-century merchant's houses conceal in their attics Amsterdam's only remaining clandestine church. The buildings have been restored as the Museum Amstelkring.

Nederlands Scheepvaart Museum
This national maritime museum is decorated with reliefs relating to the city's maritime history. Moored alongside is a replica of the East Indiaman, Amsterdam.

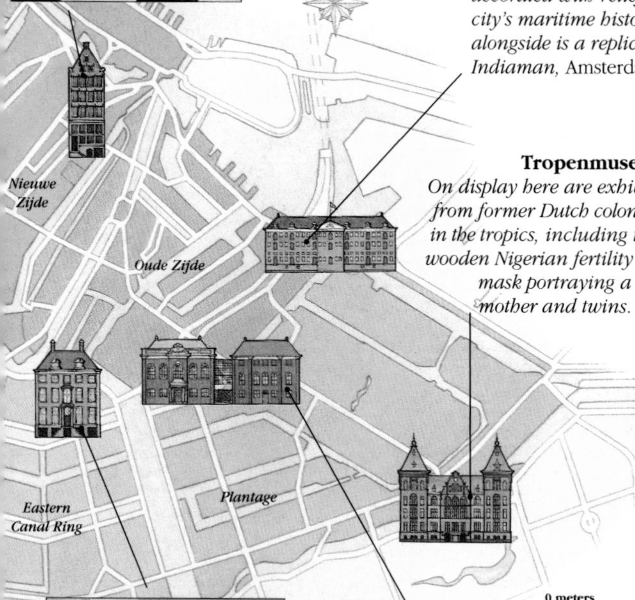

Nieuwe Zijde

Oude Zijde

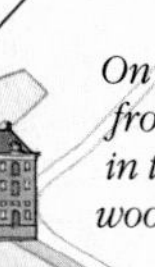

Tropenmuseum
On display here are exhibits from former Dutch colonies in the tropics, including this wooden Nigerian fertility mask portraying a mother and twins.

Eastern Canal Ring

Plantage

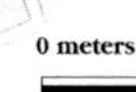

0 meters 500

0 yards 500

Museum Willet-Holthuysen
An impressive collection of furniture, silverware and paintings is housed in this beautifully preserved 17th-century canalside mansion.

Joods Historisch Museum
Four adjoining synagogues are linked to form this museum. The Holy Ark in the Grote Synagoge is the centerpiece of an exhibition on Judaism in the Netherlands.

Exploring Amsterdam's Museums

Wall plaque in St. Luciensteeg

The richness of Amsterdam's history and culture is reflected by its wide range of museums, which cover everything from bibles, beer and African masks to shipbuilding and space travel. Its national art galleries house some of the world's most famous paintings, including Rembrandt's *The Night Watch*. The Nederlands Scheepvaart Museum has the largest collection of model ships in the world, while the Anne Frankhuis is a stark reminder of the horrors of World War II.

Painting and Decorative Arts

The world's most important collection of Dutch art is on display at the **Rijksmuseum**. This vast museum contains approximately 5,000 paintings, including works by Rembrandt, Vermeer, Frans Hals and Albert Cuyp as well as a significant collection of sculptures, prints, artifacts and Asiatic art.

A short stroll across Museumplein will bring you to the **Van Gogh Museum**. Besides a large collection of Van Gogh's paintings and drawings, which traces his entire career, you can see hundreds of his original letters to his brother Theo and the artist's private collection of Japanese prints. Works by other 19th-century Dutch painters are also displayed here.

Modern art in all its forms is the focus of the **Stedelijk Museum**. While the collection features works by artists such as Henri Matisse and Vassily Kandinsky, the emphasis is on paintings, sculptures, drawings, graphics and photographs completed after 1945. Andy Warhol, Edward Kienholz and the Dutch Cobra artist Karel Appel are all represented.

The three-story house where Rembrandt lived for 20 years opened as the **Museum Het Rembrandthuis** in 1911. As well as providing an insight into the artist's life, it contains an important collection of his etchings and drawings, including a fascinating series of self-portraits.

The **Museum van Loon** and the **Six Collection** are based on the outstanding private collections of two wealthy Amsterdam families, each housed in beautiful 17th-century mansions.

Indonesian mask at the Tropenmuseum

Other wonderful collections of art can also be enjoyed by traveling from Amsterdam to the **Frans Hals Museum** in Haarlem, the **Mauritshuis** in Den Haag and the **Museum Boymans-van Beuningen** in Rotterdam.

Rembrandt's *The Jewish Bride* (1663) in the Rijksmuseum

View of a French-style garden from the Museum van Loon

History

Various aspects of Amsterdam's absorbing history is documented in several of the city's museums. The **Amsterdams Historisch Museum** covers the growth of Amsterdam from its origins as a fishing village in the 13th century, by means of maps, paintings and archaeological objects. The city's glorious maritime history is recalled at the **Nederlands Scheepvaart Museum**. Its vast collection of model ships includes a life-size replica of an 18th-century sailing ship. The mechanics of more modern boats is the focus of the **Werf 't Kromhout Museum**, which is housed in one of the few working shipyards left in the city. In the **Museum Willet-Holthuysen**, the richly decorated rooms and collection of Dutch paintings, Venetian glass, silverware and furniture reflects the wealth of Amsterdam in the Golden Age. Catholic ingenuity is revealed at the **Museum Amstelkring**, where a secret church is preserved in the attic of a 17th-century merchant's home. The history of the Dutch trade unions is documented at the **Nationaal Vakbondsmuseum**.

Jewish life in the city is remembered in the fascinating **Joods Historisch Museum**. The famous **Anne Frankhuis** provides a poignant reminder that Amsterdam's Jewish community was almost wiped out in World War II, and its secret annex shows what life was like for those living in hiding. Displays on the activities of the Dutch Resistance at the **Verzetsmuseum Amsterdam** provide more fascinating insights on life in the Netherlands during the Nazi occupation.

Outside the city, the **Zuiderzee Museum** re-creates the life and traditions of the people who once fished these waters.

The open-air reconstruction village at the Zuiderzee Museum

Specialty Museums

Mummies, sarcophagi and bronze effigies of ancient Egyptian gods are just a few of the archaeological displays at the **Allard Pierson Museum**. The **Bijbels Museum**, in adjoining canal houses, also focuses on the archaeology of Egypt and the Middle East, and contains the oldest Bible ever printed in the Netherlands.

The **Theatermuseum** traces the history of Dutch theater through costumes, posters and props, while the **Nederlands Filmmuseum** screens more than 1,000 films a year.

At the **Heineken Brouwerij** you can learn about the history of beermaking on a tour of this former brewery and are rewarded with free samples at the end. More facts can be absorbed at the **Hash Marihuana Museum**, which shows the many applications this product has had through the ages.

The sounds and sights of anything from a North African village to an Indonesian rainforest are re-created at the **Tropenmuseum** by way of an introduction to other cultures.

Model showing the process of precipitation in the Geologisch Museum at Artis

Technology and Natural History

A hands-on approach is encouraged by **Technologie Museum NINT** to explain, for instance, how houses are built, how photography works or how computers process information. The history of aviation and space travel is the focus of the **Nationaal Luchvaartmuseum Aviodome**, which has over 30 historic aircraft on display, including a 1903 Wright Flyer, a Spitfire and a model of Saturn 5. There are also flight simulators on which to try out your flying skills.

Along with hundreds of live animals, the **Artis** complex contains a variety of museums. Rock collectors will be tempted by a huge range of minerals, rocks, fossils and helpful models in the Geologisch Museum. There is also a collection of skulls, skeletons and stuffed animals in the Zoölogisch Museum, which is housed in the zoo's Aquarium.

Finding the Museums

Amsterdam's Best: Canals and Waterways

FROM THE GRACE and elegance of the waterside mansions along the *Grachtengordel* (Canal Ring) to the rows of converted warehouses on Brouwersgracht and the charming houses on Reguliersgracht, the city's canals and waterways embody the very spirit of Amsterdam. They are spanned by many beautiful bridges, including the famous Magere Brug *(see p119)*, a traditionally styled drawbridge. You can relax at one of the canalside cafés or bars and watch an array of boats float by.

Brouwersgracht
The banks of this charming canal are lined with houseboats, cozy cafés and warehouses.

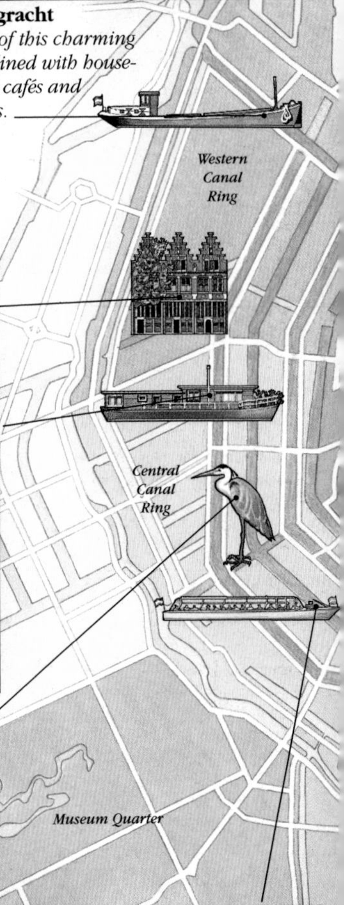

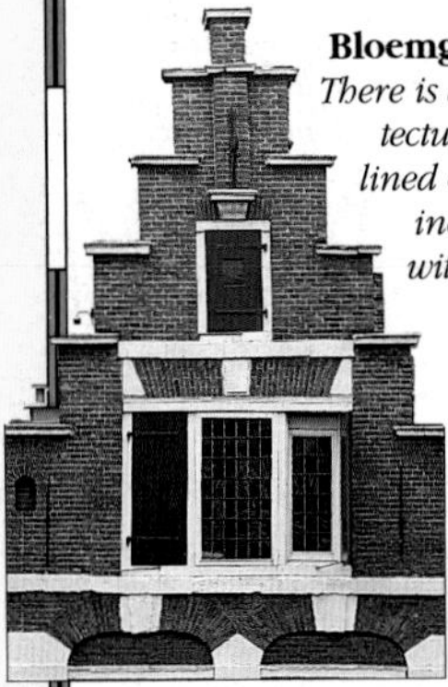

Western Canal Ring

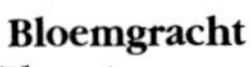

Bloemgracht
There is a great variety of architecture along this lovely, tree-lined canal in the Jordaan, including a row of houses with step gables (see p91).

Prinsengracht
The best way to see all the beautiful buildings along Amsterdam's longest 17th-century canal is by bicycle.

Central Canal Ring

Museum Quarter

Leidsegracht
Relax at a sidewalk café along the exclusive Leidsegracht (see p111).

Keizersgracht
A good view of this elegant canal can be had from any of its 14 bridges, but to get an overview of the Canal Ring go to Metz & Co at No. 455 (see p112).

Singel
The Poezenboot, *a boat for stray cats, is just one of the many sights to be found along the Singel, whose distinctive, curved shape established the horseshoe contours of the Canal Ring.*

Entrepotdok
The warehouses on the Entrepotdok (see p144) *were redeveloped in the 1980s. The quayside is now lined in summer with lively café terraces that overlook an array of houseboats and pleasure craft.*

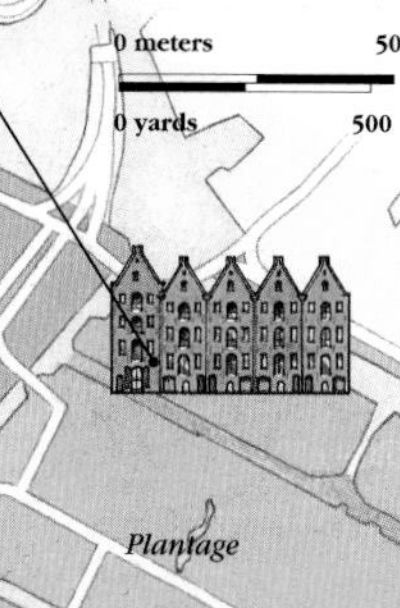

Herengracht
Known as "the twin brothers," these matching neck-gabled houses at Nos. 409–411 are two of the prettiest houses on the city's grandest canal.

Reguliersgracht
Many crooked, brick buildings line this pretty canal, which was cut in 1664. The statue of a stork, located at No. 92, is symbolic of parental responsibility and commemorates a 1571 by-law protecting this bird.

Amstel
This river is still a busy commercial thoroughfare, with barges carrying grain and coal to the city's port.

Exploring Canals and Waterways

Ornate lamps on Blauwbrug

IT IS IMPOSSIBLE to explore Amsterdam's canals and waterways without gaining a sense of the city's rich history. Many are crossed by charming bridges and lined with magnificent buildings, such as the ancient Oude Kerk *(see pp68–9)*, which overlooks the city's oldest canal, the Oudezijds Voorburgwal. First-time visitors are advised to take a cruise *(see pp276–7)* to familiarize themselves with the complex network of waterways. Once you have your bearings, it is fun to explore independently. The Street Finder on pages 280–87 of this guide locates all the waterways highlighted here.

View of the Waag and drawbridge along Kloveniersburgwal

Painting of the Oudezijds Voorburgwal by Cornelis Springer (1817–91)

First Waterways

PEOPLE ARE THOUGHT to have settled near the mouth of the **Amstel** river as early as AD 1200. Around 1264, the river was dammed and the reaches north and south of the dam later became known as **Damrak** and **Rokin**. Although sea dikes, like the **Zeedijk** *(see p67)*, were built in the 13th century, the city's first canals were not cut until the early 14th century. You can still stroll along the **Oudezijds Voorburgwal** and **Grimburgwal**, which were dug on the town's eastern and southern borders.

Early Expansions

AS AMSTERDAM expanded, new canals were added to the city's defense, drainage and transportation network. The first expansion occurred at the end of the 14th century, when the **Oudezijds Achterburgwal** was cut east of the center and **Nieuwezijds Achterburgwal** to the west (now Spuistraat).

This pattern was repeated in the 15th century when the **Kloveniersburgwal** and the **Geldersekade** were dug to the east and the **Singel** was cut to the west and south. In 1481, work began on fortifying the new outer canals with the city's first stone defenses. Remnants include the Waag *(see p60)*, the city's oldest gatehouse, the Munttoren *(see p123)* and the Schreierstoren *(see p67)*.

A major influx of refugees in the 1580s led to the expansion of Amsterdam eastward to the **Oude Schans**. Today, the network of pretty canals in this area is very peaceful.

Amsterdam's Bridges

Amsterdam has nearly 1,300 bridges crisscrossing its canals and waterways. At night, the bridges in the city center are lit by strings of lights, making an evening canal-boat tour a magical experience. One of the prettiest views is found along **Reguliersgracht**, where seven bridges cross the water in quick succession. The most famous bridge is the Magere Brug *(see p119)*, a narrow, wooden drawbridge over the Amstel. Downstream stands Amsterdam's most ornate bridge, the Blauwbrug *(see p118)*. The widest bridge is the Torensluis *(see p78)*, which spans the Singel.

The Torensluis, Amsterdam's widest bridge, overlooked by some of the Singel's finest canal houses

The Grachtengordel

Spurred by a rapidly growing population, an ambitious plan was drawn up by the city planner, Hendrick Staets, at the beginning of the 17th century to quadruple the size of Amsterdam. In 1614, work began on cutting three new residential canals, collectively known as the *Grachtengordel* (Canal Ring), from **Brouwersgracht** in the west, to encircle the existing city. The land along these canals was settled by wealthy citizens and named after the city's ruling factions. The grandest was the **Herengracht** (Gentleman's Canal), named after the commercial patrician class. The **Keizersgracht** (Emperor's Canal) honored the Holy Roman Emperor and the **Prinsengracht** (Prince's Canal) referred to Amsterdam's links with the House of Orange.

Beyond the *Grachtengordel*, workers' houses were put up along the drainage ditches in the Jordaan, and the expanded city was protected by a fortified canal, the **Singelgracht**.

Boats moored in the Waalseilandsgracht

The Industrial Age

In the 19th century, Amsterdam's prosperity was threatened, since the approaches to its harbor were too shallow for a new generation of larger ships. In an attempt to revive maritime trade, the harbor was dredged and the **Noordzeekanaal**, completed in 1876, was cut to provide access to the North Sea. The city's shipbuilding industry was also modernized and docks, such as Werf 't Kromhout *(see p145)*, were adapted from building sailing ships to steamships.

A rapid increase in population in the latter half of the century caused a demand for housing. New streets, such as Jacob van Lennepkade, were built in the western suburbs along canals, to reflect the character of the rest of the city. At the same time, many of the oldest canals in the city center, such as the Nieuwezijds Voorburgwal and much of the Damrak, were filled to improve road access to Centraal Station *(see p79)*.

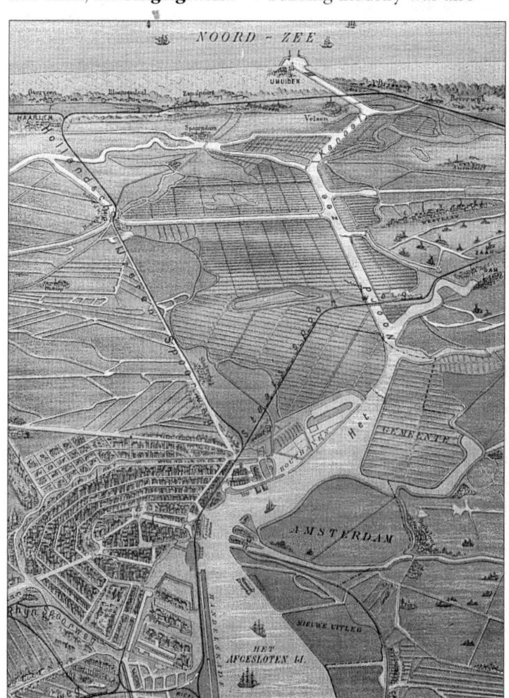

Map (1876) of Amsterdam's network of canals and the Noordzeekanaal

Canals' Modern Usage

After the arrival of road and rail links, the commercial importance of Amsterdam's 75 km (47 miles) of canals declined, although barges still ply the waters of the Amstel river. Canals do, however, play a crucial role in the city's tourist industry, as well as providing Amsterdammers with transportation and a place to live.

In 1994, the city council drew up a series of bylaws aimed at reducing pleasure-boat traffic and imposing stricter rules on houseboats. Despite this, the canals can get very clogged in summer and there are still about 3,000 houseboats officially moored within the city's boundaries. Many of them can be found along the *Grachtengordel* and the Amstel, as well as clustered in the docks near Centraal Station *(see p79)* and the Western Islands *(see p93)*.

Amsterdam's Best: Cafés and Bars

AMSTERDAM IS A CITY of cafés and bars, about 1,500 in all. Each area has something to offer, from friendly and relaxed brown cafés to lively and crowded designer bars. The cafés and bars vary and each has some special attraction: a large range of beers, live music, canalside terraces, art exhibitions, board games and pool tables or simply a brand of *gezelligheid*, the unique Dutch concept of "coziness." More details of Amsterdam's cafés and bars are given on pages 48–9. Addresses are given in the directory on page 237.

De Tuin
This large brown café in the Jordaan is always crowded with regular customers, often local artists.

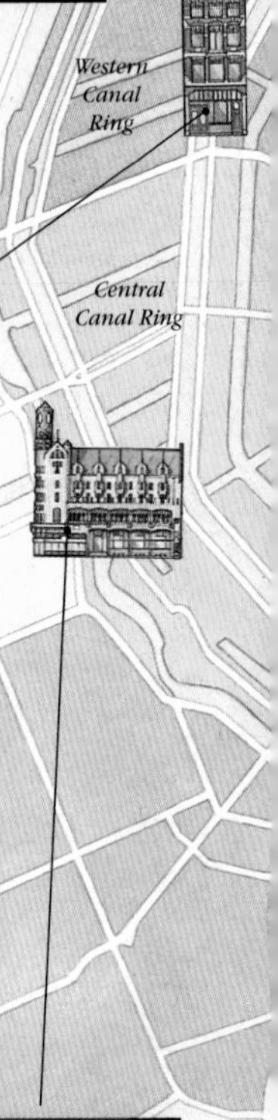

Western Canal Ring

Central Canal Ring

Van Puffelen
A smart and fashionable clientele is attracted to this intimate canalside café, with its impressive 19th-century interior, reading room and restaurant.

Vertigo
The café terrace of the Nederlands Filmmuseum has a splendid view across Vondelpark.

Museum Quarter

Café Américain
The American Hotel's grand café has a beautiful Art Deco interior, and is the place to go to be seen.

Café du Lac
The interior of this quirky grand café, situated on Haarlemmerstraat, mixes Art Deco style with Gothic-kitsch fixtures and fittings.

Nieuwe Zijde

In De Wildeman
There are more than 80 beers from around the world at this modern proeflokaal (see p48).

Oude Zijde

Plantage

De Jaren
Popular with students, this trendy two-story café has a superb view of the Amstel and a wide selection of newspapers.

't Doktertje
This is the ultimate brown café, steeped in cobwebs and atmosphere. It is a dark, friendly and timeless place, tucked away in a tiny side street.

De Kroon
Tastefully restored in recent years, this classic grand café features live classical music and modern art.

0 meters 500
0 yards 500

Exploring Amsterdam's Cafés and Bars

WHEREVER YOU GO in this vibrant city, you are never far from a café or bar. Amsterdammers are at their most friendly over a beer or a Dutch gin, so exploring the city's drinking establishments is an easy way to meet the locals. Table service is standard in most cafés and bars, though not universal. Instead of paying for each drink, bars keep a running total, which you settle as you leave. The exception is outdoor terraces, where you are expected to pay as you order. Most places are open from about 11am until 1am, though some around the Leidseplein stay open until 4 or 5am on the weekends.

Customers sitting outside De Tuin, a traditional brown café

Brown Cafés

THE TRADITIONAL Dutch "local pub," the brown café, is characterized by dark wooden paneling and furniture, low ceilings, dim lighting and a fog of tobacco smoke. It is a warm and friendly place and often a social focus for the neighborhood. Some of the best brown cafés are found in old 17th-century canal houses or tucked away on side streets. The tiny and characterful **'t Doktertje**, just off the Kalverstraat shopping street, is worth a visit, as is the cheap and cheerful **De Pieper**, close to Leidseplein. **De Tuin,** in the heart of the Jordaan, is popular with the local artistic community. Most brown cafés are more than just places to drink and many serve good, reasonably priced food *(see pp236–7)*.

Sampling the wide range of beers in the popular modern tasting bar, Gollem

Proeflokalen and Modern Tasting Bars

LITERALLY MEANING "tasting houses," *proeflokalen* go back to the Dutch Golden Age of the 17th century. In order to increase sales, wine and spirit importers would invite merchants to taste their wares. Today, *proeflokalen* denote bars specializing in either wine, spirits or beer. One of the oldest tasting bars, **De Drie Fleschjes**, dates from 1650, and *jenever* (Dutch gin) is its specialty. **Henri Prouvin** offers a superb range of more than 500 vintage wines and **In De Wildeman** serves beers from around the world, many of them on draft. See the directory on page 237 for other good *proeflokalen*.

What to Drink

The Dutch national drink is beer. A standard *pils* (a lagerlike beer) is served in bars and cafés – the main brands are Heineken and Grolsch. Darker beers like De Koninck have a stronger flavor, and the wheat-brewed *witbiers* like Hoegaarden are white and cloudy. Beers from Amsterdam's 't IJ brewery, such as Columbus, are widely available. The most popular spirit, *jenever*, is the slightly oily Dutch gin. There is either the sharp tasting *jonge* (young), or the smoother *oude* (old) variety. For the complete Dutch experience, drink *jenever* in a single gulp or order a refreshing *pils* with a *jenever* chaser.

Bottle of *jonge jenever*

Traditional *oude jenever*

Hoegaarden, brewed in Belgium

Tarwebok, a strong type of Heineken

Grand Cafés and Designer Bars

GRAND CAFÉS first emerged in the 19th century. Today, these large and opulent venues are the haunts of the upwardly mobile and fashion-conscious. **Café Luxembourg** has a street terrace for people-watching, while **Café Schiller** is more intimate and has a beautiful Art Deco interior. Designer bars cater to a similar clientele, but they are modern, stark and bright in style. Some of the best are the chic **Het Land Van Walem**, **De Balie**, **Vertigo** and the trendy **De Jaren**.

Café Schiller, one of Amsterdam's Art Deco grand cafés

The beautifully restored De Jaren

Smoking Coffeeshops

SMOKING COFFEESHOPS are ones where cannabis is openly sold and smoked. Although technically illegal, the sale of soft drugs is tolerated by the Dutch authorities if it remains discreet *(see p259)*. Many of these cafés are recognizable by their loud music and often psychedelic decor. Smoking coffeeshops appeal to a surprising range of people – old and young alike (under 16 not permitted) from every social and professional background. **Rusland** and **Siberië** are two of the smaller, more relaxed places, while **The Bulldog** is commercial and tourist-filled. Coffee, soft drinks and snacks are generally available. **La Chocolata** specializes in hash confectionery, and **Rookies** is one of the few in the city with an alcohol license. If tempted to smoke, ask for the menu listing what is on sale. The cannabis is strong, especially the local "skunk." Be wary of hash cakes and cookies, since there is no way to gauge their strength. See the directory on page 237 for other good smoking coffeeshops.

Coffeeshops and Salons de Thé

THE MORE CONVENTIONAL type of coffeeshop is where well-to-do ladies go for a chat over coffee and cake. A number of these places use the Dutch spelling, *koffieshop*, or the French *salons de thé* to distinguish themselves from the many smoking coffeeshops, although the differences are obvious. Many, such as **Berkhoff**, **Arnold Cornelis** and **Pompadour**, are attached to confectioners, patisseries or delicatessens, and have a tempting range of cakes and sweets. Several of the city's larger stores and hotels also have tearooms, ideal places to sit down in comfort and relax after a busy day sightseeing or shopping. **Metz & Co** has a comfortable sixth-floor café that offers one of the most impressive canal views in Amsterdam *(see p112)*. The chic **PC** is located on the equally stylish PC Hooftstraat.

Also worth visiting is **Café Françoise**, which houses art exhibitions and lush foliage and features classical music. For something slightly different, **Back Stage** is a wonderfully offbeat café run by eccentric former cabaret artistes, the Christmas Twins.

De Koninck, a dark Belgian beer

Amstel Bockbier, a dark, winter beer

Columbus, brewed in Amsterdam

Where to Find the Best Cafés

All the cafés and bars described on these pages are listed in the directory on page 237. The best, as shown on pages 46–7, are also listed below.

Café Américain
American Hotel, Leidseplein 28–30. **Map** 4 E1.
624 5322.

Café Du Lac
Haarlemmerstraat 118. **Map** 1 C3.
624 4265.

't Doktertje
Rozenboomsteeg 4. **Map** 7 B4.
626 4427.

In de Wildeman
Kolksteeg 3. **Map** 7 C1.
638 2348.

De Jaren
Nieuwe Doelenstraat 20. **Map** 7 C4.
625 5771.

De Kroon
Rembrandtplein 17. **Map** 7 C5.
625 2011.

De Tuin
2e Tuindwarsstraat 13 (near Anjeliersstraat). **Map** 1 B3.
624 4559.

Van Puffelen
Prinsengracht 377. **Map** 4 E1.
624 6270.

Vertigo
Nederlands Filmmuseum, Vondelpark 3. **Map** 4 D2.
612 3021.

Amsterdam Through the Year

Although there is no guarantee of good weather in Amsterdam, the cosmopolitan ambience of this 700-year-old city and the congeniality of the Dutch make it an appealing place to visit whatever time of year you go. Most tourists flock into the city from April to September, when temperatures are mild. Amsterdammers, however, are undaunted by the weather and maintain an active program of festivals and outdoor pursuits throughout the year. Crisp autumn days invite long walks along the city's stately canals, followed by a cosy chat in one of Amsterdam's brown cafés. About twice a decade, the winter temperatures drop so low that the canals freeze over. When this occurs a skating race is held between 11 Dutch cities.

Herons nest on the canals

Spring

Spring begins in late March when daffodils and crocuses blossom overnight all over the city. Flower lovers descend on Amsterdam, using it as a base for day trips to Keukenhof, the Netherlands' 28-hectare (69-acre) showcase for Dutch bulb growers *(see pp180–81)*.

March

Stille Omgang *(second Sun)*, Rokin. Silent nighttime procession celebrating the Miracle of Amsterdam *(see p20)*.

Blues Festival *(mid-March)*, Meervaart. Two days of great blues performances.

April

National Museum Weekend *(mid-Apr)*. Discount or free admission to many state-run museums in the Netherlands.

Koninginnedag *(Apr 30)*. Amsterdam becomes the world's biggest flea market/street party as the Dutch celebrate Queen Beatrix's official birthday. Transportation grinds to a halt as more than 2 million people throng the streets and dance the night away.

Tulip fields in bloom near Alkmaar

Revelers celebrating in the streets to commemorate Koninginnedag

World Press Photo *(mid-Apr–end May)*, Nieuwe Kerk. Exhibition of the very best press photographs from around the world.

May

Herdenkingsdag *(May 4)*. Commemorations throughout the city for the victims of World War II. Largest in Dam square.

Bevrijdingsdag *(May 5)*. Concerts and speeches around the city celebrate the end of the German occupation.

Nationale Molendag *(second Sat)*. Windmills all over the Netherlands are opened to the public and their sails unfurled.

Boeken op de Dam *(late May)* Dam square. The square fills with book stalls and hosts an open-air pop concert.

Drum Rhythm Festival *(end May)*, De Melkweg *(see p110)* and other locations. Jazz, blues and world music extravaganza.

Open Air Theater in Vondelpark *(end May–mid-Aug)*. Program of theater, music and children's shows *(see p128)*.

Sunshine Chart
The summer months are the sunniest, but this is no guarantee of good weather. Amsterdammers will often carry an umbrella even on the hottest July days since bright sunshine in the morning often precedes the arrival of summer rains later.

SUMMER

SUMMER, which starts with the monthlong Holland Festival, is a hectic cultural roller-coaster ride. As well as the events listed below, classic European drama is staged in the Amsterdamse Bos *(p155)*, and open-air concerts are held in the Vondelpark *(pp128–9)*. This is the best time for people-watching in one of Amsterdam's numerous street-side cafés and bars.

A rower training on the Bosbaan in the Amsterdamse Bos

JUNE

Holland Festival *(Jun 1–30)*. In places throughout Amsterdam and in other major cities in the Netherlands, Dutch musicians and composers are joined by top performers from around the world for a monthlong arts festival. A varied program of drama, cabaret, mime and dance is also staged.
Kunst RAI *(first week)*, Amsterdam RAI. Massive exhibition of contemporary art.
Amsterdam Kite Festival *(first week)*, Halfweg. Ten km (6 miles) outside Amsterdam, a festival that allows you to fly your kite alongside experts.
Grachtenloop *(second Sat)*. A choice of 18-, 9- and 5-km runs (11-, 5.5- and 3-mile) around the city's canals. A treasure hunt takes place on the shortest run.
World Roots Festival *(end Jun)*, De Melkweg *(pp110–11)*. A program of music, dance, film and theater performances from Africa and other non-Western countries.

JULY

North Sea Jazz Festival *(mid-Jul)*, the Netherlands Congress Center. Weekend of jazz ranging from Dixieland to jazz rock, a short train ride away in Den Haag.

Orchestral performance at the Prinsengracht Concert

Summer Concerts *(Jul–Aug)*, Concertgebouw *(see p128)*. Annual showcase of classical music.

AUGUST

Prinsengracht Concert *(late Aug)*. Waterborne classical concert performed on barge in front of Pulitzer Hotel *(p221)*.
Uitmarkt *(last week)*. Cultural fair previews new shows and stages music, dance and drama. Location changes annually.

Café-goers relaxing and soaking up the sun at de Jaren Terrace

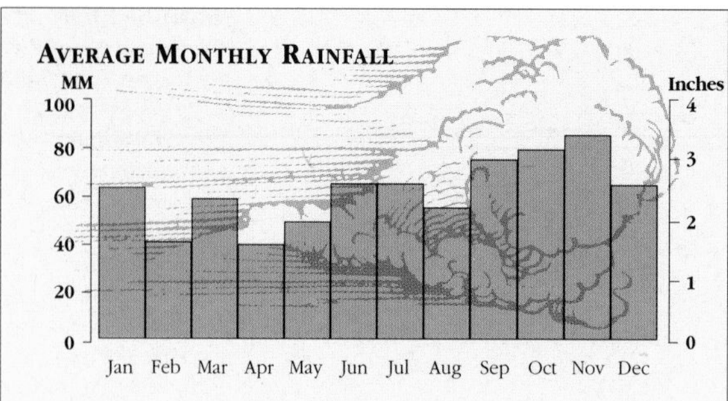

Rainfall Chart

Expect rain all year round in Amsterdam. The pattern, however, is broadly seasonal. Visit the city in spring to enjoy the driest weather of the year. The heaviest rainfall occurs in autumn, reaching a peak in the windy and wet month of November.

AUTUMN

TEMPERATURES DROP quickly at the end of August, but the cultural heat is maintained with the roster of music, dance, opera and drama promoted in the Uitmarkt *(see p51)*. The autumn is also a busy time for more athletic types. There is a range of spectator sports to watch, and it is a good time of year to enjoy brisk walks in one of the city's many parks or along the Amstel. By November, many Amsterdammers retreat indoors on rainy evenings to cafés like Schaakcafé Het Hok in the Lange Leidsedwarsstraat, to cheer on budding chess champions.

SEPTEMBER

Kano Toertocht door de Grachten *(first week)*. Some 500 illuminated canoes and kayaks take part in an evening tour of Amsterdam's canals.
Bloemen Corso *(first Sat)*. Crowds gather to watch a parade of flower-laden floats around Amsterdam. In the evening, there is an illuminated floral procession through the southern suburb of Aalsmeer.
Jordaan Festival *(second and third week)*. Neighborhood festivals are held in this picturesque district, with fairs, street parties, talent contests and music.
Monumentendag *(second Sat)*. A chance to see inside some of the nation's historic, listed buildings, which are normally closed to the public.
European Antiquarian Book and Print Fair *(second week)*, Amsterdam RAI *(see p151)*.

Barges moored along an Amsterdam waterfront in autumn

Amsterdam City Marathon *(last Sun)*. Some 1,500 runners circle the outside of the city and then converge on the center in this 42-km (26-mile) run. Another 10,000 people join in for a 10-km (6-mile) stretch of the marathon.

OCTOBER

Roeisloebengrachten *(third Sat)*, Oosterdok. One of many rowing competitions held in the city throughout the year.
Jumping Amsterdam *(Oct/Nov)*, Amsterdam RAI *(p151)*. International indoor show-jumping competitions.

NOVEMBER

Sinterklaas' Parade *(second or third Sat)*. The Dutch equivalent of Santa Claus arrives by steamboat near St. Nicholaaskerk *(see p79)* with *Zwarte Piet* (Black Peter) and travels through Amsterdam distributing sweets to children.
Caravan and Camping RAI *(late Nov)*, Amsterdam RAI *(p151)*. Annual fair for open-air holiday enthusiasts selling the latest outdoor equipment.

Sinterklaas parading through Amsterdam

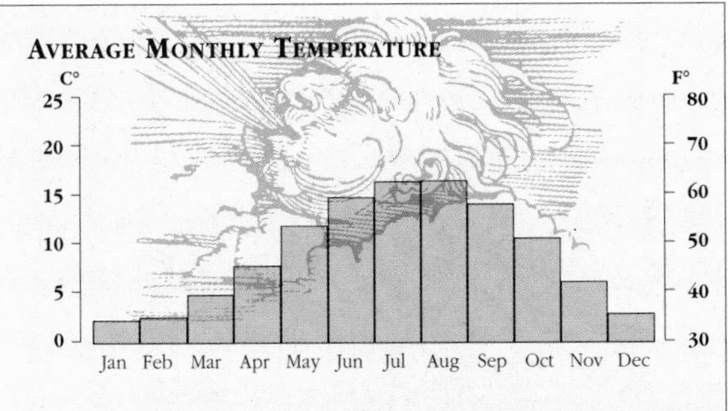

Temperature Chart
The chart shows the average temperature for each month in Amsterdam. Summer is often cooled by the North Sea wind, both spring and autumn can be chilly, and temperatures in winter are frequently freezing.

WINTER

CHRISTMAS is a busy tourist season, with visitors and residents thronging to watch Christmas trees being hawked from barges on the main canals. Barrows appear throughout the city, tantalizing passersby with the smell of freshly fried *oliebollen* and *appelflappen*, two sugary treats not to be missed. After Christmas, the talk of the town is whether or not it will be cold enough for the city authorities to permit skating on the city's canals. If the green light is given – which is rare – whole neighborhoods turn out to skate under the stars.

DECEMBER

Sinterklaasavond *(Dec 5)*. The traditional Dutch gift-giving day when Sinterklaas and his Moorish helpers visit Dutch children to leave a sack of presents. Friends give poems caricaturing each other.

The Dokwerker Monument in JD Meijerplein

Amsterdammers ice-skating on the Keizersgracht

Christmas Day *(Dec 25)*. Increasingly accepted as the main gift-giving day.
New Year's Eve *(Dec 31)*. Firework celebrations throughout the city with an organized display over the Amstel.

JANUARY

Chinese New Year *(Jan or Feb)*, Nieuwmarkt. Traditional lion dance, fireworks, Chinese exhibitions and stage art.

FEBRUARY

Februaristaking *(Feb 25)*, JD Meijerplein. Commemoration of dockworkers' action against deportation of Jewish residents during World War II.

Carnival *(end Feb)*. Parade through Amsterdam designed to shake off the winter blues. Main celebrations held in the southern province of Limburg.

PUBLIC HOLIDAYS

New Year's Day (Jan 1)
Eerste Paasdag (Easter Monday) *
Koninginnedag (April 30)
Bevrijdingsdag (May 5)
Hemelvaartsdag (Ascension Day) *
Pinksteren (Pentecost) *
Eerste Kerstdag (Christmas Day) (Dec 25)
Tweede Kerstdag (Dec 26)
* Dates change in accordance with church calendar.

ARTUSI
ARTUSI

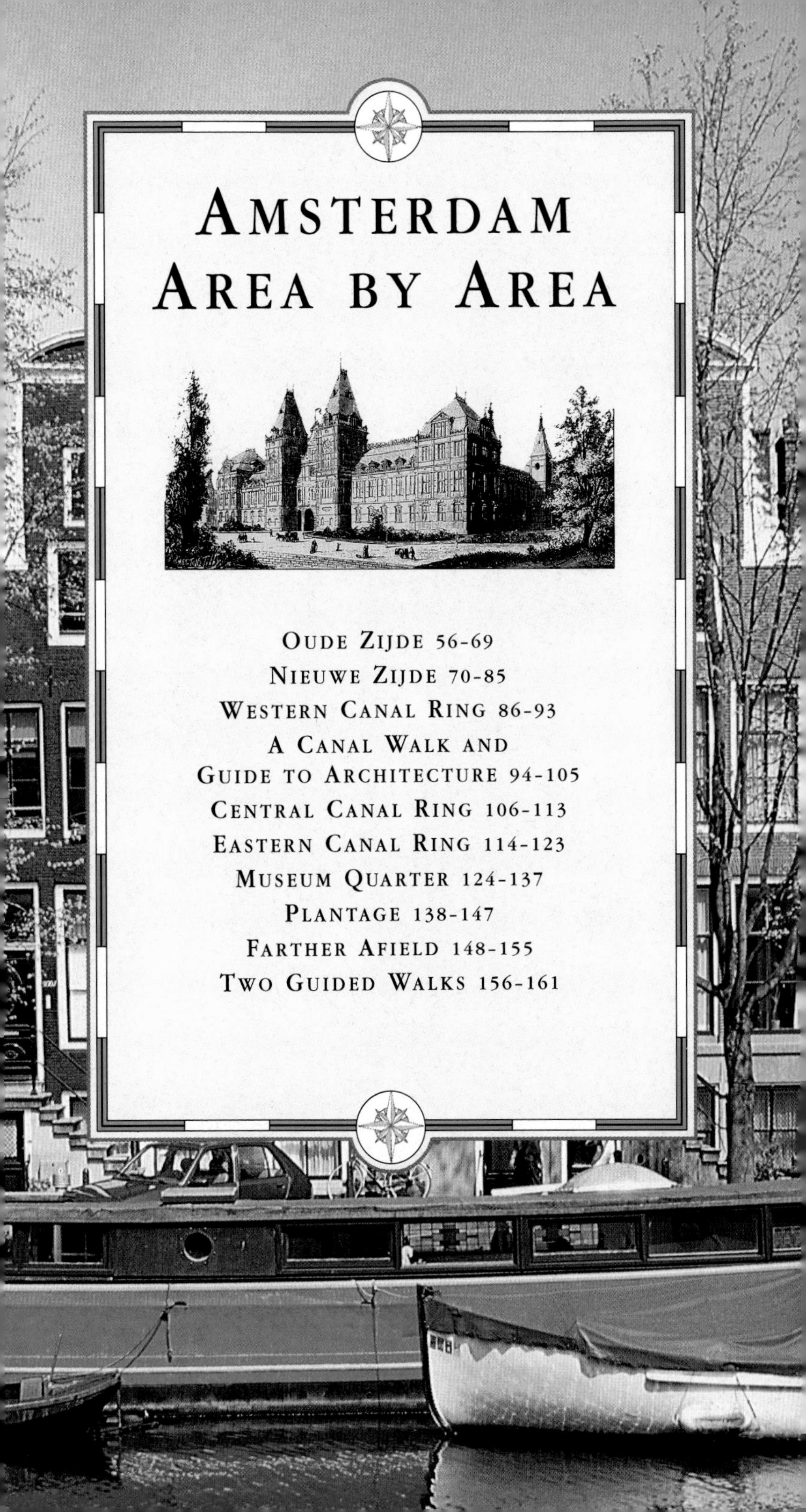

Amsterdam Area by Area

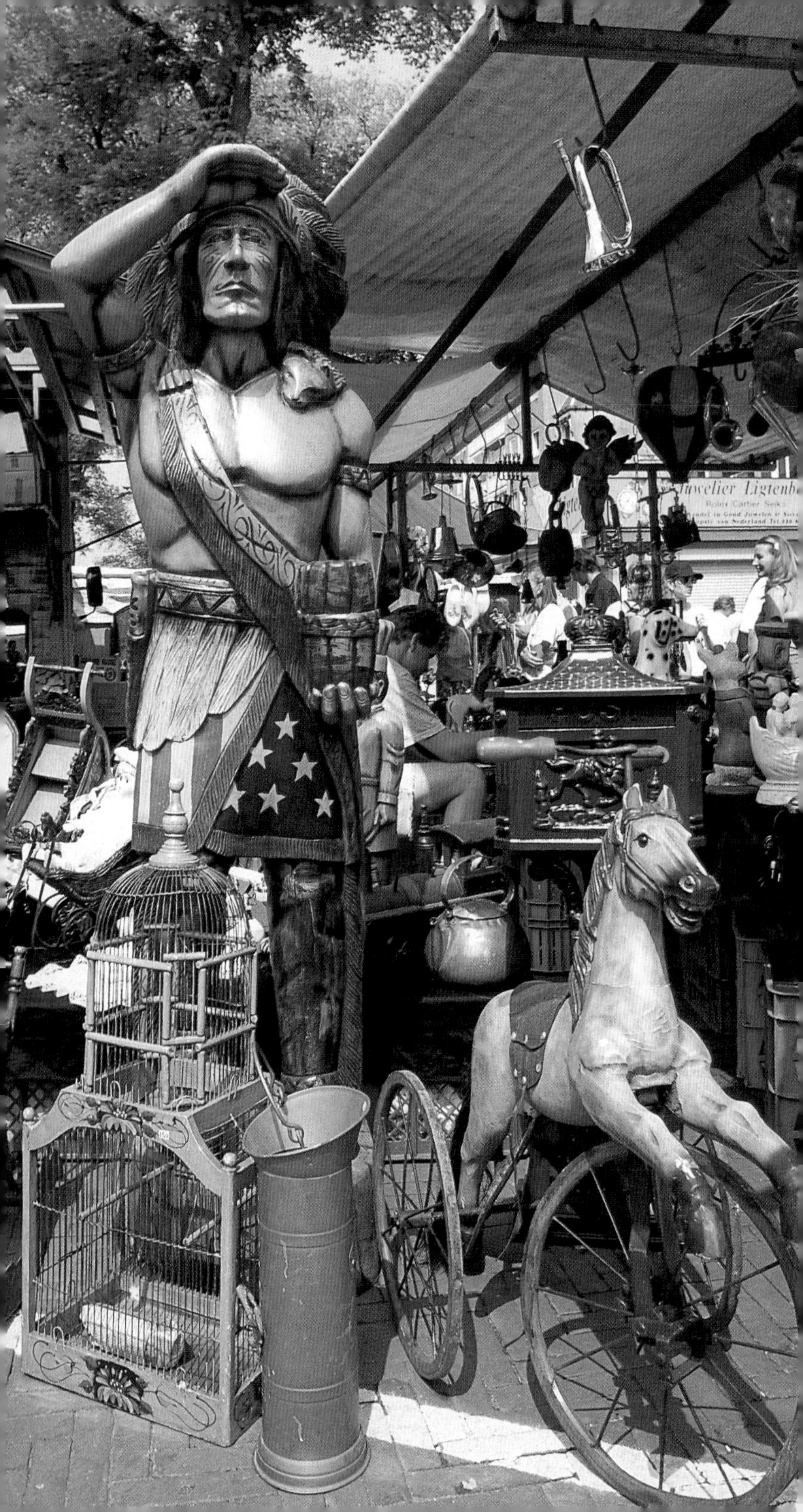
Juwelier
Rolex Cartier Seiko

Oude Zijde

The eastern half of Amsterdam became known as the Oude Zijde (Old Side). Originally it occupied a narrow strip on the east bank of the Amstel river, running between Damrak and the Oudezijds Voorburgwal *(see pp42–5)*. At its heart was built the Oude Kerk, the oldest church in the city. In the early 1400s the Oude Zijde began an eastward expansion which continued into the 17th century. This growth was fueled by an influx of Jewish refugees from Portugal. The oldest of the four synagogues, now containing the Joods Historisch Museum, dates from this period. These were central to Jewish life in the city for centuries. During the Golden Age *(see pp24–7)*, the Oude Zijde was an important commercial center. Boats could sail up the Geldersekade to Nieuwmarkt, where goods were weighed at the Waag before being sold at the market.

Aaron from Mozes en Aäronkerk

Sights at a Glance

Historic Buildings and Monuments
Waag 2
Agnietenkapel 5
Oudemanhuispoort 6
Oostindisch Huis 7
Trippenhuis 8
Pintohuis 16
Montelbaanstoren 17
Scheepvaarthuis 18
Schreierstoren 19

Opera Houses
Stadhuis-Musiektheater 11

Museums
Hash Marihuana Museum 4
Museum Het Rembrandthuis 10
Joods Historisch Museum pp64–5 14

Churches and Synagogues
Zuiderkerk 9
Mozes en Aäronkerk 13
Portugese Synagoge 15
Oude Kerk pp68–9 21

Streets and Markets
Red Light District 1
Nieuwmarkt 3
Waterlooplein 12
Zeedijk 20

Getting There

The best way to reach the Oude Zijde is to get a trolley to the Dam (trolleys 1, 2, 4, 5, 9, 13, 14, 16, 17, 24 and 25), then walk along Damstraat. Or take trolley 9 or 14; the metro goes directly to Waterlooplein or Nieuwmarkt.

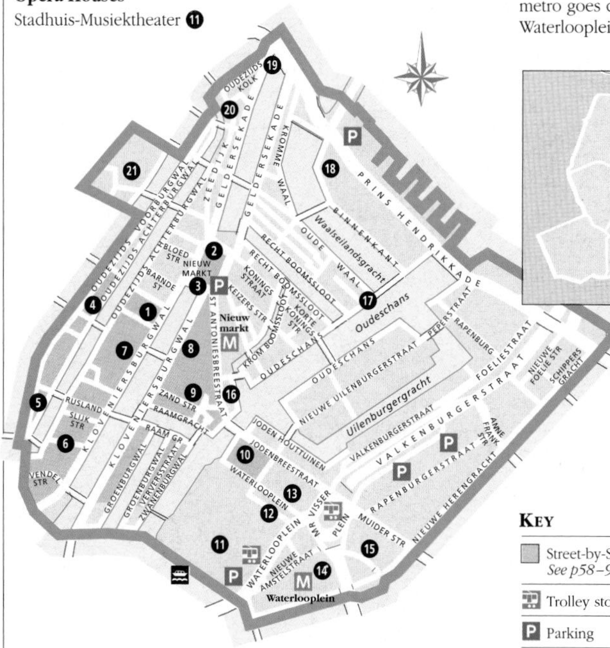

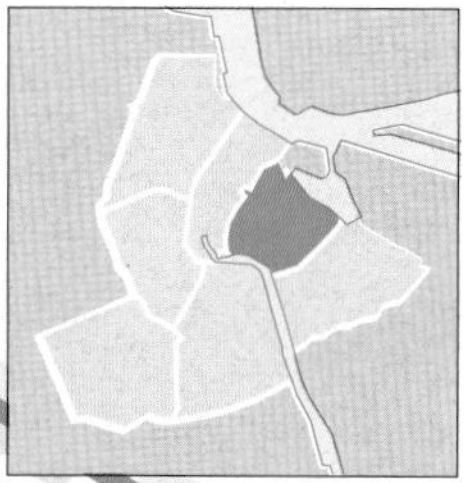

Key

Street-by-Street map *See p58–9*
Trolley stop
Parking
Metro station
Museum boat boarding point

0 meters 250
0 yards 250

Some of the many exotic items to be found at the Waterlooplein flea market

Street-by-Street: University District

THE UNIVERSITY OF AMSTERDAM, founded in 1877, is predominantly located in the peaceful, southwestern part of the Oude Zijde. The university's roots lie in the former Atheneum Illustre, which was founded in 1632 in the Agnietenkapel. Beyond Damstraat, the bustling Red Light District meets the Nieuwmarkt, where the 15th-century Waag evokes a medieval air. South of the Nieuwmarkt, Museum Het Rembrandthuis gives a fascinating insight into the life of the city's most famous artist.

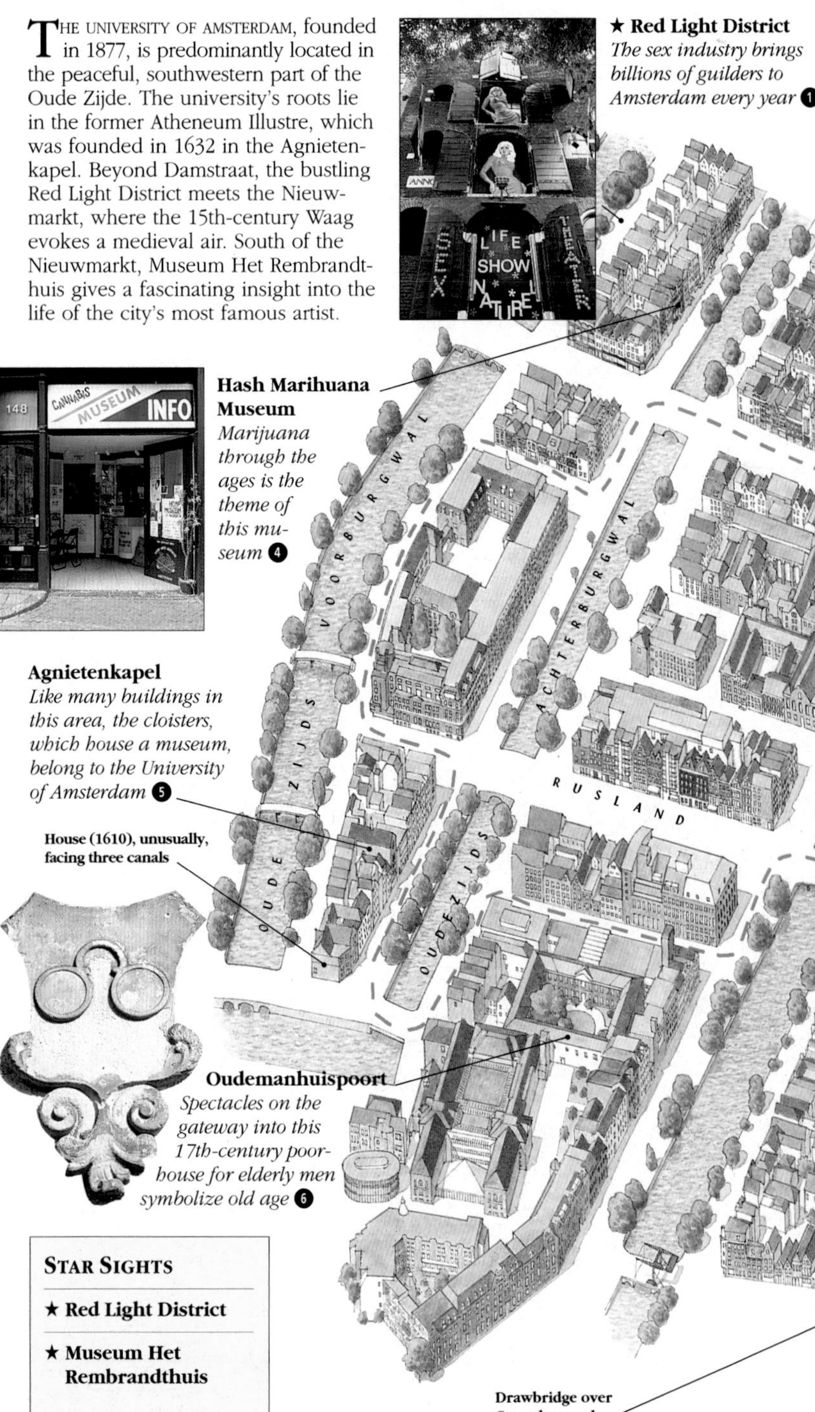

★ Red Light District
The sex industry brings billions of guilders to Amsterdam every year ❶

Hash Marihuana Museum
Marijuana through the ages is the theme of this museum ❹

Agnietenkapel
Like many buildings in this area, the cloisters, which house a museum, belong to the University of Amsterdam ❺

House (1610), unusually, facing three canals

Oudemanhuispoort
Spectacles on the gateway into this 17th-century poorhouse for elderly men symbolize old age ❻

Drawbridge over Groenburgwal

STAR SIGHTS

- ★ Red Light District
- ★ Museum Het Rembrandthuis

Nieuwmarkt
Despite redevelopment southeast of this once-important market square, the Nieuwmarkt itself is still bordered by many fine 17th- and 18th-century gabled houses ❸

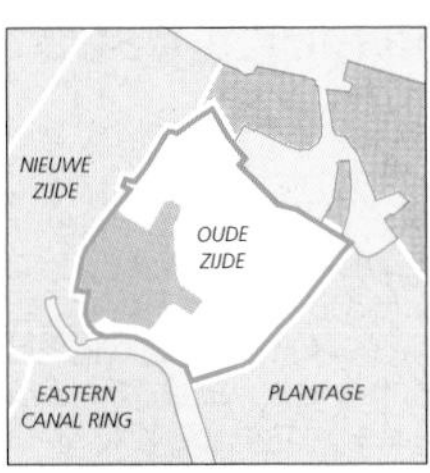

Locator Map
See Street Finder maps 7 and 8

Trippenhuis
Although it appears to be a single 17th-century mansion, this building is in fact two houses, the middle windows being fake to preserve the symmetry ❽

Waag
The octagonal towers of Amsterdam's only remaining medieval gatehouse contain staircases to the upper rooms ❷

Oostindisch Huis
Now part of the University of Amsterdam, this former Dutch East India Company (VOC) building has a fine example of an early 17th-century façade ❼

Zuiderkerk
This prominent city landmark now houses the city's planning information center ❾

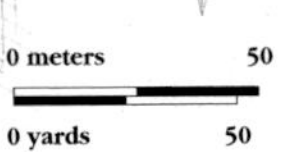

Key

 Suggested route

★ Museum Het Rembrandthuis
Hundreds of Rembrandt's etchings, including many self-portraits, are on display in the artist's former home ❿

Red Light District ❶

Map 8 D2. *4, 9, 16, 24, 25.*

BARELY CLAD prostitutes bathed in a red neon glow and touting for business at their windows is one of the defining images of modern Amsterdam. The city's Red Light District, referred to locally as de Walletjes (the little walls), is concentrated on the Oude Kerk *(see pp68–9)*, although it extends as far as Warmoesstraat to the west, the Zeedijk to the north, the Kloveniersburgwal to the east and then along the line of Damstraat to the south.

Prostitution in Amsterdam dates back to the city's emergence as a port in the 13th century. By 1478, prostitution had become so widespread, with increasing numbers of sea-weary sailors flooding into the city, that attempts were made to contain it. Prostitutes straying outside their designated area were marched back to the sound of pipe and drum.

A century later, following the Alteration *(see pp22–3)*, the Calvinists tried to outlaw prostitution altogether. Their attempts were halfhearted, and by the mid-17th century prostitution was openly tolerated. In 1850, Amsterdam had a population of 200,000, and more than 200 brothels. The most famous of these, like the luxurious Madame Traese's, catered to rich clients.

Entrance to one of the clubs in the Red Light District

Today, the whole area is crisscrossed by a network of narrow lanes, dominated by garish sex shops and seedy clubs, and peppered with junkies, dealers and pickpockets. At night, the little alleys assume a somewhat sinister aspect, and it is not wise to wander around alone. But by day, hordes of visitors crowding in generate a festive buzz, and among the sleaze there are interesting cafés, bars, restaurants and beautiful canalside houses to be discovered.

Waag ❷

Nieuwmarkt 4. **Map** 8 D3. *9, 14.* **M** *Nieuwmarkt.* ● *to the public.*

THE MULTITURRETED Waag is Amsterdam's oldest surviving gatehouse. Built in 1488, it was then, and often still is, called St Antoniespoort. Public executions were held here, and condemned prisoners awaited their fate in the "little gallows room" in one of the towers. In 1617, the building became the public weigh house *(waaggebouw)*. Peasants had their produce weighed here and paid tax accordingly.

Various guilds moved into the upper rooms of each tower. From 1619 the Guild of Surgeons had their meeting room and anatomy theater here. They added the central octagonal tower in 1691. Rembrandt's *Anatomy Lesson of Dr Tulp,* now in the Mauritshuis *(see pp188–9)*, and *The Anatomy Lesson of Dr Deijman,* in the Rijksmuseum *(see pp130–33)*, were commissioned by guild members and hung here.

The weigh house closed in the early 19th century and the guilds moved out. The Waag has since served as a furniture store, fencing academy, fire station and two city museums, but is currently unoccupied.

The 15th-century Waag dominating the Nieuwmarkt, with an antique market on the left

Part of the commemorative photo display in Nieuwmarkt metro

Nieuwmarkt ❸

Map 8 D3. *9, 14.* *Nieuwmarkt.* **Antiques market** *May–Sep: 9am–5pm Sun.*

AN OPEN, PAVED square, the Nieuwmarkt is flanked to the west by the Red Light District. With the top end of the Geldersekade, it forms Amsterdam's Chinatown. The Waag dominates the square, and construction of this gateway led to the site's development in the 15th century as a marketplace. When the city expanded in the 17th century *(see pp24–5)*, the square took on its present dimensions and was called the Nieuwmarkt. It retains an array of 17th- and 18th-century gabled houses. True to tradition, an antiques market is held on Sundays during the summer.

The old Jewish Quarter leads off the square down St. Antoniesbreestraat. In the 1970s, many houses in this area were demolished to make way for the new metro, sparking off clashes between protesters and police. The action of conservationists persuaded the city council to adopt a policy of renovating rather than redeveloping old buildings. In tribute to them, photographs of their protests decorate the metro.

Hash Marihuana Museum ❹

Oudezijds Achterburgwal 148. **Map** 7 C3. *623 5961.* *4, 9, 14, 16, 24, 25.* *Nieuwmarkt.* *11am–10pm.*

THIS MUSEUM is the only one in Europe to chart the history of hemp (marijuana). Exhibits refer back 8,000 years to early Asiatic civilizations, which used the plant for medicines and clothing. It was first used in the Netherlands, according to a herbal manual of 1554, as a cure for earache.

Until the late 19th century, however, hemp was the main source of fiber for rope, and was therefore important in the Dutch shipping industry. Other exhibits relate to the psychoactive properties of this plant. They include an intriguing array of pipes and bongs (smoking devices), along with displays that explain smuggling methods. The museum also has a small cultivation area where marijuana plants are grown under artificial light. Police sometimes raid and take away exhibits, so there may be occasional gaps in displays.

Marijuana bong

Agnietenkapel ❺

Oudezijds Voorburgwal 231. **Map** 7 C4. *525 3339.* *4, 9, 14, 16, 24, 25.* *9am–5pm Tue–Fri.* *public hols.*

NOW HOME to the University Museum, the Agnietenkapel was part of the convent of St Agnes until 1578 when it was closed after the Alteration *(see pp22–3)*. In 1632, the Athenaeum Illustre, the precursor of the University of Amsterdam, took it over and by the mid-17th century it was a center of scientific learning. It also housed the municipal library until the 1830s. While the museum focuses on the history of the University of Amsterdam, the main attraction is the Agnietenkapel itself, dating from 1470. It is one of the few Gothic chapels to have survived the Alteration. During restoration from 1919 to 1921, elements of Amsterdam School architecture were introduced *(see p97)*. Despite these changes and long periods of secular use, the building still has the feel of a Franciscan chapel. The large auditorium on the first floor is the city's oldest, and is used for university lectures. It has a lovely ceiling, painted with Renaissance motifs and a portrait of Minerva, the Roman goddess of wisdom and the arts. The walls are hung with 40 portraits of European humanist scholars, such as Erasmus (1466–1536).

Entrance to Agnietenkapel, home to the University Museum

Oudemanhuispoort ❻

Between Oudezijds Achterburgwal and Kloveniersburgwal. **Map** 7 C4. *4, 9, 14, 16, 24, 25.* **Book market** *10am–4pm Mon–Sat.*

THE OUDEMANHUISPOORT was once the entrance to a complex of old people's almshouses (Oudemannenhuis), built in 1754. The pediment design over the gateway in the Oudezijds Achterburgwal features a pair of eyeglasses, a symbol of old age. A market for secondhand books now operates along the passage.

Trading inside this covered walkway dates from 1757, when 18 small shops opened for the sale of gold, silver and books. The Oudemannenhuis itself was taken over by the University of Amsterdam in 1879. Although the building is closed to the public, visitors can enter its attractive 18th-century courtyard through a door off the arcade.

The spire of the Zuiderkerk, a prominent city landmark

Oostindisch Huis ❼

Oude Hoogstraat 24. **Map** 7 C3.
4, 9, 14, 16, 24, 25.
Nieuwmarkt. *to the public.*

THE OOSTINDISCH HUIS, former headquarters of the Dutch East India Company or VOC *(see pp26–7)*, is now part of the University of Amsterdam. Built in 1605, it is attributed to Hendrick de Keyser *(see p90)*. The premises have been expanded several times, in 1606, 1634 and 1661, to house spices, pepper, porcelain and silk from the East Indies.

The VOC was dissolved in 1800 *(see p29)*, and for a while the Oostindisch Huis was taken over by the customs authorities. Later, the state tax offices also moved in, and the VOC medallion carved in the stone gate was removed and replaced with a lion, which was the traditional heraldic symbol of the Netherlands.

Major restyling in the 1890s destroyed much of the interior decoration, although the façade has remained largely intact. The ornate scrolling on the balustrade that crowns the roof contrasts with the austerity of the rest of the building.

Ornate balustrade of the Oostindisch Huis

Trippenhuis ❽

Kloveniersburgwal 29. **Map** 8 D3.
4, 9, 14, 16, 24, 25. *Nieuwmarkt.* *to the public.*

JUSTUS VINGBOONS designed this richly decorated Classical mansion, completed in 1662. Although it appears to be one house, it is in fact two. The façade, outlined by eight Corinthian columns, features false middle windows. The house was originally designed for the wealthy arms merchants Lodewijk and Hendrick Trip, and hence the chimneys were designed to look like cannons. The city's art collection was housed here from 1817 to 1885, when it transferred to the Rijksmuseum *(see pp130–33)*. The Trippenhuis now houses the Dutch Academy. Opposite at No. 26 is the Kleine Trippenhuis, built in 1698. It is only 2.5 m (7 ft) wide and has very detailed cornicing, which includes two carved sphinxes.

Zuiderkerk ❾

Zuiderkerkhof 72. **Map** 8 D4.
622 2962. *9, 14.*
noon–5pm Mon–Wed & Fri, noon–8pm Thu.

DESIGNED BY Hendrick de Keyser in 1603, the Renaissance-style Zuiderkerk was the first Calvinist church to open in Amsterdam after the Alteration *(see pp22–3)*. The impressive spire, with its free-standing columns, decorative clocks and onion dome, is a prominent city landmark.

The Zuiderkerk ceased to function as a church in 1929. It was, however, restored in 1988, and is now used by the city planning department. The church is surrounded by community housing, including Theo Bosch's modern apartment building, the "Pentagon," completed in the mid-1980s.

Museum Het Rembrandthuis ❿

Jodenbreestraat 4–6. **Map** 8 D4.
624 9486. *4, 9, 14.*
Waterlooplein. *10am–5pm Mon–Sat, 1–5pm Sun and public hols.* *Jan 1.*

REMBRANDT worked and taught in this house from 1639 until 1658. He lived in the ground-floor rooms with his wife, Saskia, who died here in 1642, leaving the artist with a baby son, Titus *(see p200)*.

Many of Rembrandt's most famous paintings were created in the first-floor studio, but it is thought that *The Night Watch (p131)* was painted in a courtyard gallery. Lessons were conducted in the attic. The house was extensively restored

Façade of Museum Het Rembrandthuis

between 1907 and 1911. A fine collection of Rembrandt's etchings and drawings includes various self-portraits showing the artist in different moods and guises. There are also landscapes, nude studies, religious and crowd scenes and sketches of the artist with his wife.

A step-by-step introduction to the traditional etching process is provided in one of the rooms on the ground floor.

Stadhuis-Muziektheater ⓫

Waterlooplein 22. **Map** 8 D4. *9, 14.* *Waterlooplein.* **Stadhuis** *552 9111.* *8:30am–4pm Mon–Fri, 8:30am–7pm Thu.* **Muziektheater** *625 5455. See* ***Entertainment*** *pp246–51.*

FEW BUILDINGS in Amsterdam caused as much controversy as the new Stadhuis (city hall) and Muziektheater (opera house). Nicknamed the "Stopera" by protesters, the plan required the destruction of dozens of medieval houses, which were virtually all that remained of the original Jewish quarter. This led to running battles between squatters and police *(see pp34–5)*.

The building was completed in 1988, a massive confection of red brick, marble and glass that dominates this part of the Amstel. A mural illustrating the Normaal Amsterdams Peil *(see pp34–5)* is shown on the arcade linking the two parts of the complex. The Stopera has the largest auditorium in the country, with a seating capacity for 1,689 people, and it is now home to the Netherlands' national opera and ballet companies. Visitors can join guided backstage tours of the Muziektheater.

Waterlooplein ⓬

Map 8 D5. *9, 14.* *Waterlooplein.* **Market** *10am–5pm Mon–Sat.*

THE WATERLOOPLEIN dates from 1882, when two canals were filled in to create a large market square in the heart of the Jewish quarter. The site was originally known as Vlooyenburg, an artificial island built in the 17th century to house the incoming Jewish settlers *(see p64)*.

Despite encroachment by the Stadhuis-Muziektheater, the northern end of the Waterlooplein still operates a lively market. Stalls sell anything from bric-a-brac to African bedspreads, Indonesian jewelry, Balinese wood carvings and army-surplus clothing.

Mozes en Ääronkerk ⓭

Waterlooplein 205. **Map** 8 E4. *622 1305.* *9, 14.* *Waterlooplein.* *to the public except for exhibitions.*

DESIGNED BY the Flemish architect T Suys the Elder in 1841, Mozes en Ääronkerk was built on the site of a clandestine Catholic church. The later church took its name from the Old Testament figures of Moses and Aaron depicted on the gable stones found on the original building. These are now set into the rear wall.

The church was restored in 1990, when its twin wooden towers were painted to look like sandstone. It is now used for exhibitions, public meetings and the occasional mass.

Clothes for sale at the Waterlooplein market

Joods Historisch Museum ⓮

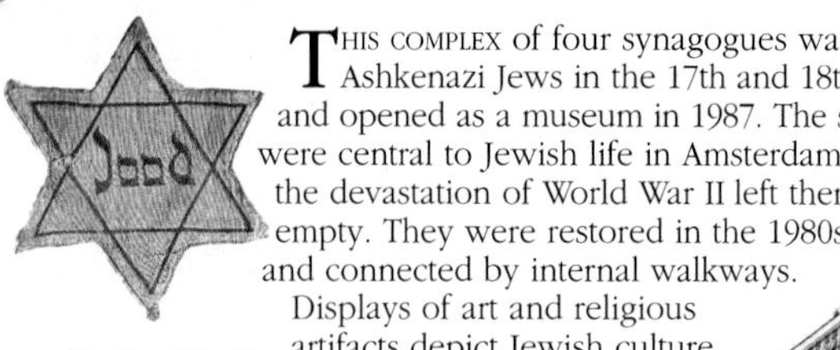

The Star of David, worn by all Jews in the Nazi occupation

THIS COMPLEX of four synagogues was built by Ashkenazi Jews in the 17th and 18th centuries and opened as a museum in 1987. The synagogues were central to Jewish life in Amsterdam, until the devastation of World War II left them empty. They were restored in the 1980s and connected by internal walkways. Displays of art and religious artifacts depict Jewish culture and the history of Judaism in the Netherlands.

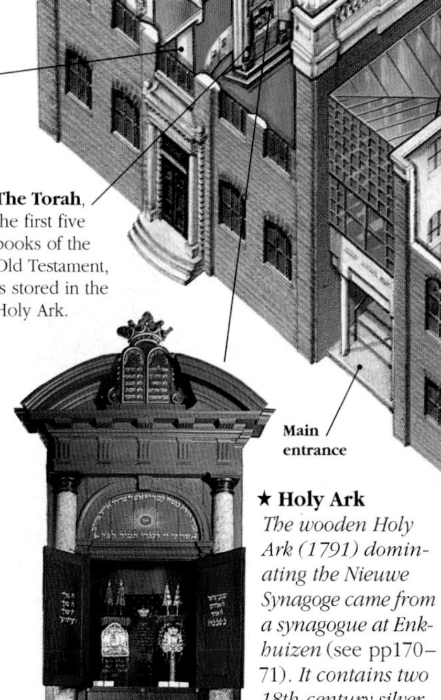

The Nieuwe Synagoge was built in 1752.

The Torah, the first five books of the Old Testament, is stored in the Holy Ark.

Main entrance

★ Haggadah Manuscript
Produced by the scribe Joseph of Leipnik in 1734, this beautifully illuminated manuscript contains the order of service for the Passover celebrations.

★ Holy Ark
The wooden Holy Ark (1791) dominating the Nieuwe Synagoge came from a synagogue at Enkhuizen (see pp170–71). *It contains two 18th-century silver Torah shields and three velvet mantles.*

JEWS IN AMSTERDAM

The first Jew to gain Dutch citizenship was a member of the Portuguese Sephardic community in 1597. The Ashkenazi Jews from eastern Europe came to Amsterdam later, in the 1630s. They were restricted to working in certain trades, but were granted full civil equality in 1796. With the rise of Zionism in the 19th century, Jewish identity re-emerged, but the Nazi occupation decimated the community *(see pp32–3)*.

18th-century Torah scroll finial in shape of the Westerkerk tower

MUSEUM GUIDE

The history of Judaism in the Netherlands is presented thematically. The Nieuwe Synagoge examines the Jewish identity; the Grote Synagoge looks at the philosophies of Judaism, Jewish life in Amsterdam and the growth of the Jewish Quarter. The café and bookstore are found on the ground floor in the Obbene Shul.

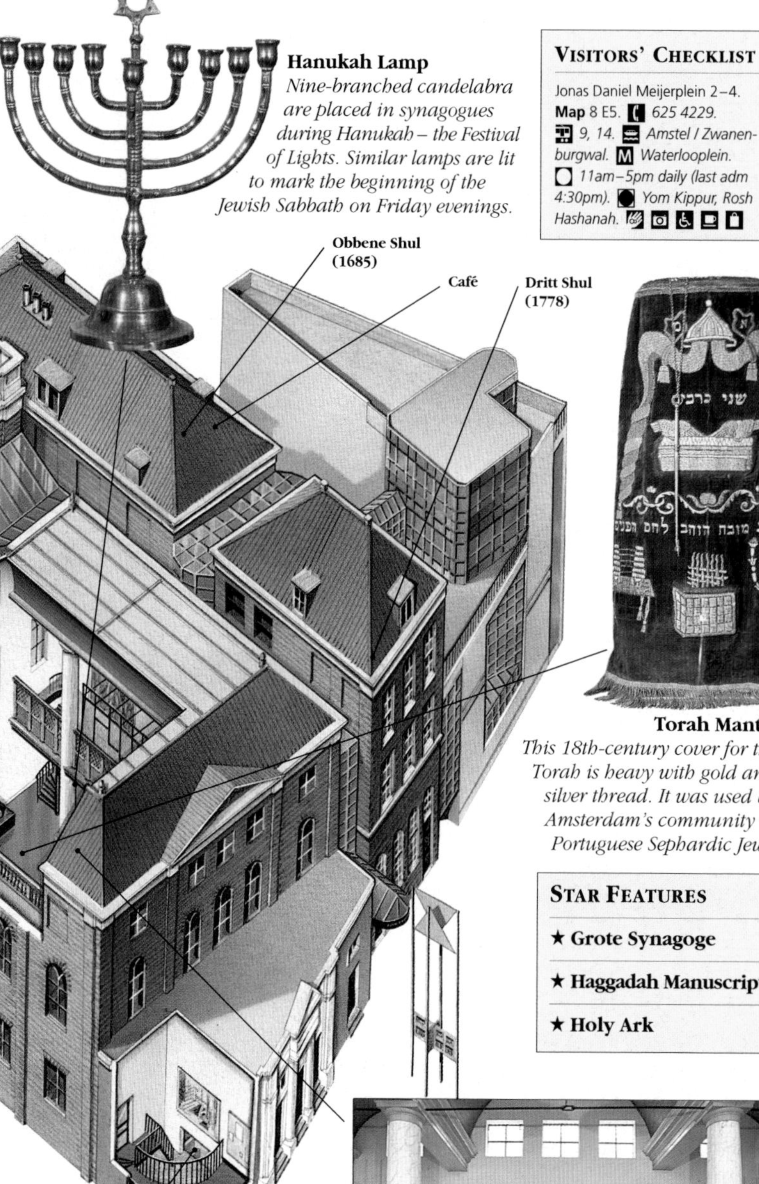

Hanukah Lamp
Nine-branched candelabra are placed in synagogues during Hanukah – the Festival of Lights. Similar lamps are lit to mark the beginning of the Jewish Sabbath on Friday evenings.

Visitors' Checklist

Jonas Daniel Meijerplein 2–4. **Map** 8 E5. 625 4229. 9, 14. Amstel / Zwanenburgwal. Waterlooplein. 11am–5pm daily (last adm 4:30pm). Yom Kippur, Rosh Hashanah.

Torah Mantle
This 18th-century cover for the Torah is heavy with gold and silver thread. It was used by Amsterdam's community of Portuguese Sephardic Jews.

Star Features

- ★ **Grote Synagoge**
- ★ **Haggadah Manuscript**
- ★ **Holy Ark**

The *mikveh*, or bath for ritual purification

★ Grote Synagoge
Designed by Elias Bouman (see p66)*, the hall is lined with galleries. Grilles screen the women's gallery from the male congregation. The Ark was given to the synagogue by Rabbi Abraham Auerbach when it opened in 1671.*

Portugese Synagoge ⓯

Mr Visserplein 3. **Map** 8 E5. *624 5351.* *9, 14.* *Waterlooplein.* *10am–4pm Sun–Fri (Apr–Oct) 10am–4pm Mon–Thu, 10am–3pm Fri, 10am–noon Sun (Nov–Mar)* *Jewish hols.*

ELIAS BOUMAN'S design for the Classically styled Portuguese Synagogue was inspired by the architecture of the Temple of Solomon in Jerusalem. It was commissioned by the Portuguese Sephardic community of Amsterdam *(see p64)*. Inaugurated in 1675, the huge building has a rectangular ground plan with the Holy Ark bearing the covenant in the southeast corner facing Jerusalem, and the *tebah* (the podium from which the service is led) at the opposite end.

The wooden, barrel-vaulted ceiling is supported by four Ionic columns and spans the aisle. More than 1,000 candles and light from 72 windows illuminate the splendid interior, which has retained its original character following careful restoration work.

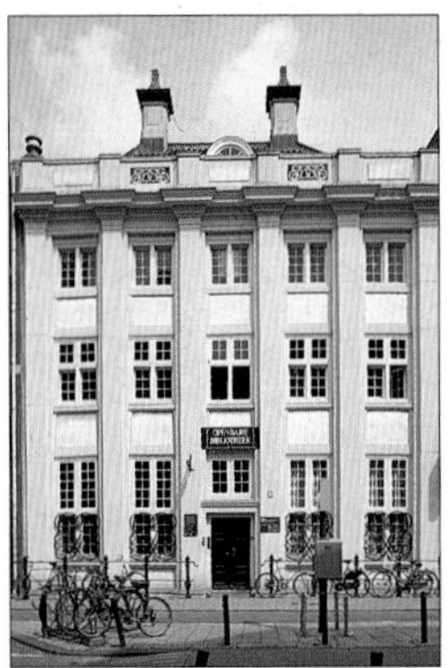

Italianate façade of the 17th-century Pintohuis

Pintohuis ⓰

Sint Antoniesbreestraat 69. **Map** 8 D4. *624 3184.* *9, 14.* **Library** *2–8pm Mon & Wed, 2–5pm Fri, 11am–2pm Sat (except school hols).* *public hols.*

ISAAC DE PINTO, a wealthy Portuguese merchant, bought the Pintohuis in 1651 for the then enormous sum of 30,000 guilders. He had it remodeled over the next decades to a design by Elias Bouman, and it is one of the few private residences in Amsterdam to follow an Italianate style. The exterior design was reworked from 1675 to 1680. Six imposing pilasters break up the severe, cream façade into five recessed sections, and the cornice is topped by a blind balustrade concealing the roof.

In the 1970s, the house was scheduled for demolition because it stood in the way of a newly planned main road. Concerted protest saved the building, which now houses a public library. Visitors can still admire the original painted ceiling, which is decorated with birds and cherubs.

Montelbaanstoren ⓱

Oude Waal/Oudeschans 2. **Map** 8 E3. *9, 14.* *to the public.*

THE LOWER PORTION of the Montelbaanstoren was built in 1512 and formed part of Amsterdam's medieval fortifications. It lay just beyond the city wall, protecting the city's wharves on the newly built St. Antoniesdijk (now known as the Oudeschans) against invasion from the neighboring Gelderlanders.

The octagonal structure and open work timber steeple were both added by Hendrick de Keyser *(see p90)* in 1606. His decorative addition bears a close resemblance to the spire of the Oude Kerk, designed by Joost Bilhamer, which was built 40 years earlier *(see pp68–9)*. In 1611, the tower began to tilt; Amsterdammers attached ropes to the top and pulled it upright again.

Sailors from the VOC *(see pp26–7)* would gather at the Montelbaanstoren before being ferried in small boats down the IJ to the massive East Indies-bound sailing ships, anchored farther out in deep water to the north.

The building appears in a number of etchings by Rembrandt, and is still a popular subject for artists. It now houses the offices of the Amsterdam water authority.

One of many stone carving on the Scheepvaarthuis façade

Scheepvaarthuis ⓲

Prins Hendrikkade 108. **Map** 8 E2. *1, 2, 4, 5, 9, 11, 13, 16, 17, 24, 25.* *Centraal Station.* *to the public.*

BUILT AS AN OFFICE complex in 1916, the Scheepvaarthuis (Shipping House) is regarded as the first true example of Amsterdam School architecture *(see p97)*. It was designed by Piet Kramer (1881–1961), Johan van der May (1878–1949) and Michel de Klerk (1884–1923) for a group of shipping companies that no longer wanted to do business on the quay.

The imposing triangular building has a prowlike front and is crowned by a statue of Neptune, his wife and four female figures representing the four points of the compass.

The medieval Montelbaanstoren, with its decorative timber steeple

No expense was spared on the construction and internal decoration of the building, and local dock workers came to regard the building as a symbol of capitalism. The doors, stairs, window frames and interior walls are festooned with nautical images, such as sea horses, dolphins and anchors. Beautiful stained-glass skylights are also decorated with images of sailing ships, maps and compasses.

The Scheepvaarthuis is now home to the municipal transport department. Although closed to the public, Archivisie *(see p270)* will arrange architectural tours of the building.

Schreierstoren ⓳

Prins Hendrikkade 94–95. **Map** 8 E1. *1, 2, 4, 5, 9, 11, 13, 16, 17, 24, 25.* M *Centraal Station.* *to the public.*

THE SCHREIERSTOREN (Weepers' Tower) was a defensive structure forming part of the medieval city walls, and dates from 1480. It was one of the few fortifications not to be demolished as the city expanded beyond its medieval boundaries in the 17th century. The building now houses a nautical equipment shop.

Popular legend states that the tower derived its name from the weeping (*schreien* in the original Dutch) of women who came here to wave their men off to sea. It is more likely, however, that the title has a less romantic origin and comes from the tower's position on a sharp (*screye* or *scherpe*), 90-degree bend in the old town walls. The earliest of four wall plaques, dated 1569, adds considerably to the confusion by depicting a weeping woman alongside the inscription *scrayer hovck*, which means sharp corner.

In 1609, Henry Hudson set sail from here in an attempt to discover a new and faster trading route to the East Indies. Instead, he unintentionally "discovered" the river in North America that still bears his name. A bronze plaque, placed in 1927, commemorates his voyage.

The Schreierstoren, part of the original city fortifications

Zeedijk ⓴

Map 8 D2. *1, 2, 4, 5, 9, 11, 13, 16, 17, 24, 25.* M *Centraal Station.*

ALONG WITH the Nieuwendijk and the Haarlemmerdijk, the Zeedijk (sea dike) formed part of Amsterdam's original fortifications. Built in the early 1300s, some 30 years after Amsterdam had been granted its city charter, these defenses took the form of a canal moat with piled-earth ramparts reinforced by wooden palisades. As the city grew in prosperity and the boundaries expanded, the canals were filled in and the dikes became obsolete. The paths that ran alongside them became the streets and alleys that bear their names today.

One of the two remaining wooden-fronted houses in Amsterdam can be found at No. 1. It was built in the mid-16th century as a hostel for sailors, and is much restored. Opposite is St. Olofskapel, built in 1445 and named after the first Christian king of Norway and Denmark.

By the 1600s, the Zeedijk had become a slum, and one part was known as "the rats' nest." The area is on the edge of the city's Red Light District, and in the 1960s and 1970s became notorious as a center for drug-dealing and street crime. Despite a clean-up campaign in the 1980s, the Zeedijk still retains its unsalubrious reputation.

Plaques on the gables of some of the street's cafés reveal their former use – the red boot at No. 17 indicates that it was once a cobbler's.

Plaque on the Café 't Mandje (Little Basket), a gay bar at No. 63 Zeedijk

Oude Kerk 21

Carving on 15th-century choir misericord

THE ORIGINS of the Oude Kerk date from the early 13th century, when a wooden church was built in a burial ground on a sand bank *(see pp18–19)*. The present Gothic structure is 14th-century and it has grown from a single-aisled church into a basilica. As it expanded, the building became a gathering place for traders and a refuge for the poor. Its paintings and statuary were destroyed after the Alteration *(see pp22–3)* in 1578, but the gilded ceiling and stained-glass windows were undamaged. The Great Organ was added in 1724, and the stark interior has changed little since.

The Oude Kerk Today
The old church, surrounded by shops, cafés and houses, remains a calm and peaceful haven at the heart of the frenetic Red Light District.

The spire of the bell tower was built by Joost Bilhamer in 1566. François Hemony added the 47-bell carillon in 1658.

Tomb of Saskia, first wife of Rembrandt *(see pp62–3)*

Tomb of Admiral Abraham van der Hulst (1619–66)

Christening Chapel

★ Great Organ *(1724)*
Jan Westerman's oak-encased organ has eight bellows and 54 gilded pipes. Marbled-wood statues of biblical figures surround it.

TIMELINE

1300 Small stone church built

1330 Church consecrated to St. Nicholas

1340 Church enlarged

1412 North transept completed

1462 First side chapel demolished to build south transept

1500 Side chapels added

1552 Lady Chapel added

1566 Spire added to 13th-century tower

1578 Calvinists triumph in the Alteration

1658 Carillon installed

1724 Great Organ installed

1912–14 Partial restoration of northwest corner

1951 Church closes

1955 Restoration of church begins

1979 Church reopens to public

1300 | 1400 | 1500 | 1600 | 1700 | 1800 | 1900

Stained-glass coats of arms in Lady Chapel

★ Gilded Ceiling
The delicate 15th-century vault paintings have a gilded background. They were hidden with layers of blue paint in 1755 and not revealed until 1955.

Visitors' Checklist

Oudekerksplein 23. **Map** 7 C2. 624 9183. 4, 9, 16, 24, 25. **Church** Mar–Oct: 11am–5pm Mon–Sat, 1–5pm Sun; Nov–Feb: 1–5pm Fri–Sun; **Tower** Apr–Sep: 2–4pm. Jun–Sep: Wed–Sat. Jan 1, Apr 30. 11am Sun.

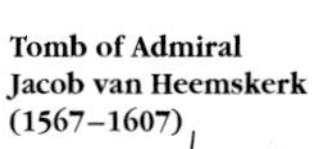

Tomb of Admiral Jacob van Heemskerk (1567–1607)

★ Lady Chapel *(1552)*
The Death of the Virgin Mary *by Dirk Crabeth is one of three restored stained-glass windows in the Lady Chapel.*

Brocaded Pillars
Decorative pillars originally formed niches holding a series of statues of the Apostles, all destroyed by the iconoclasts in 1578.

17th- and 18th-century houses

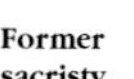

Former sacristy

The Red Door
The inscription on the lintel above the door into the former sacristy warns those about to enter: "Marry in haste, repent at leisure."

Star Features

- ★ Great Organ
- ★ Gilded Ceiling
- ★ Lady Chapel

Nieuwe Zijde

The western side of medieval Amsterdam was known as the Nieuwe Zijde (New Side). Together with the Oude Zijde it formed the heart of the early maritime settlement. Nieuwendijk, now a busy shopping street, was originally one of the earliest sea defenses. As Amsterdam grew, it expanded eastward, leaving large sections of the Nieuwe Zijde, to the west, neglected and in decline. With its many wooden houses, the city was prone to fires and in 1452 much of the area was burned down. During rebuilding, a broad moat, the Singel, was cut, along which warehouses, rich merchants' homes and fine quays sprang up. The Amsterdams Historisch Museum, which is now housed in a splendid, converted orphanage, has scores of maps and paintings charting the growth of the city from these early times to today. One room is devoted to the Miracle of Amsterdam *(see p20)*, which made the city a place of pilgrimage, and brought commerce to the Nieuwe Zijde. Nearby lies Kalverstraat, Amsterdam's main shopping street, and also the secluded Begijnhof. This pretty courtyard is mostly fringed by narrow 17th-century houses, but it also contains the city's oldest surviving wooden house.

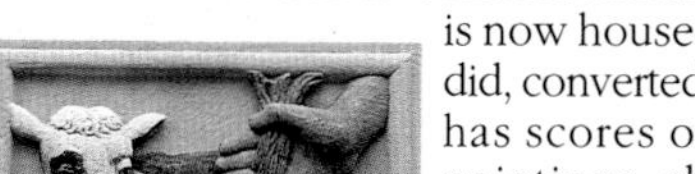

"The calf" emblem on a house in the Begijnhof

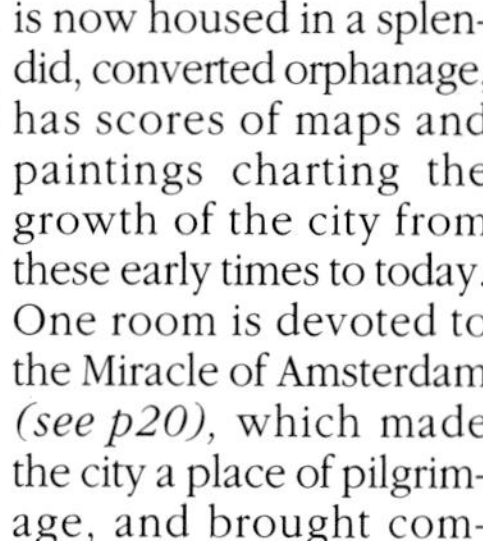

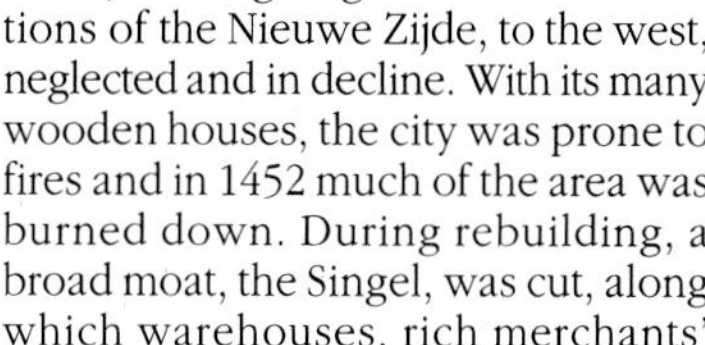

Sights at a Glance

Historic Buildings, Monuments and Bridges
Koninklijk Paleis 2
Nationaal Monument 4
Torensluis 9
Postkantoor 10
Centraal Station 12
Beurs van Berlage 15

Streets and Squares
Nes 5
Begijnhof 7

Churches
Nieuwe Kerk pp76–7 1
Lutherse Kerk 11
St. Nicolaaskerk 13

Museums
Madame Tussauds Scenerama 3
Amsterdams Historisch Museum pp80–3 6
Allard Pierson Museum 8
Museum Amstelkring pp84–5 14

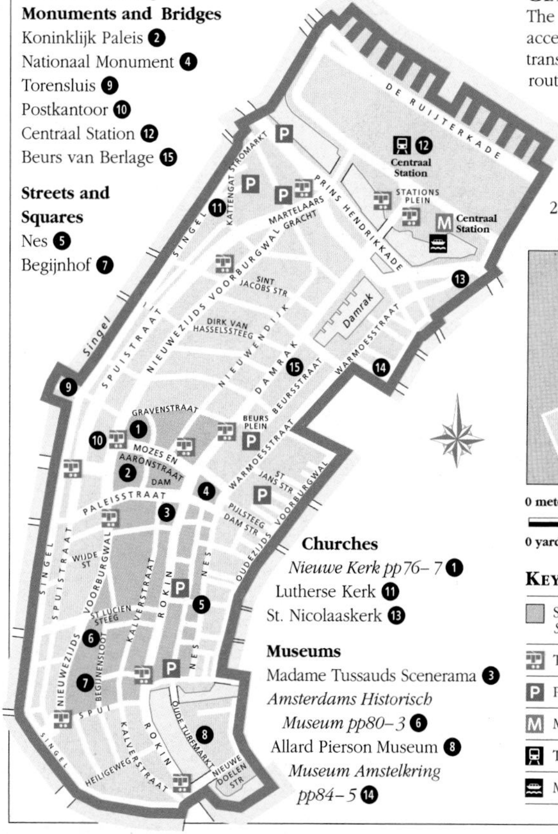

Getting There

The Nieuwe Zijde is easily accessible by public transportation. Most trolley routes terminate at Centraal Station (1, 2, 4, 5, 9, 13, 16, 17, 24 and 25), as does the metro. You can take a trolley (1, 2, 4, 5, 9, 13, 14, 17, 24 and 25) to the Dam.

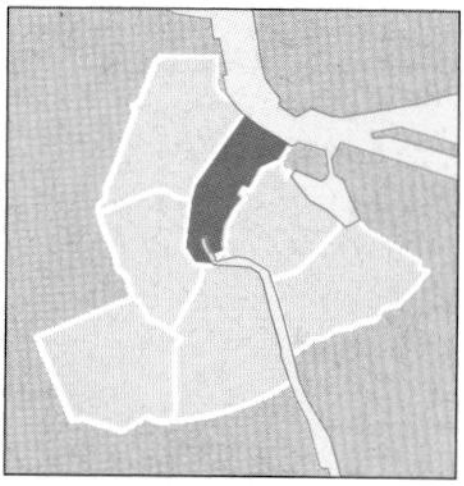

0 meters 250
0 yards 250

Key

Street-by-Street map *See p72–3*
Trolley stop
Parking
Metro station
Train station
Museum boat boarding point

◁ ***The Fatal Fall of Icarus*, one of the many Classical sculptures in the Koninklijk Paleis**

Street-by-Street: Nieuwe Zijde

ALTHOUGH MUCH of the medieval Nieuwe Zijde has disappeared, the area is still rich in buildings that relate to the city's past. The Dam, dominated by the Koninklijk Paleis and Nieuwe Kerk, provides examples of architecture from the 15th to the 20th century. Around Kalverstraat, the narrow streets and alleys follow the course of some of the earliest dikes and footpaths. Here, most of the traditional gabled houses have been turned into bustling stores and cafés. Streets such as Rokin and Nes are now home to financial institutions, attracted by the nearby stock and options exchanges. Nes is also known for its venues that feature alternative theater.

Kalverstraat, now a busy tourist shopping area, took its name from the livestock market that was regularly held here during the 15th century.

★ Amsterdams Historisch Museum
Wall plaques and maps showing the walled medieval city are on display in this converted orphanage that dates from the 16th century ❻

A pillar marks the site of the Miracle of Amsterdam *(see p20)*.

★ Begijnhof
Two churches and one of the few remaining wooden houses in the city nestle in this secluded, tree-filled courtyard ❼

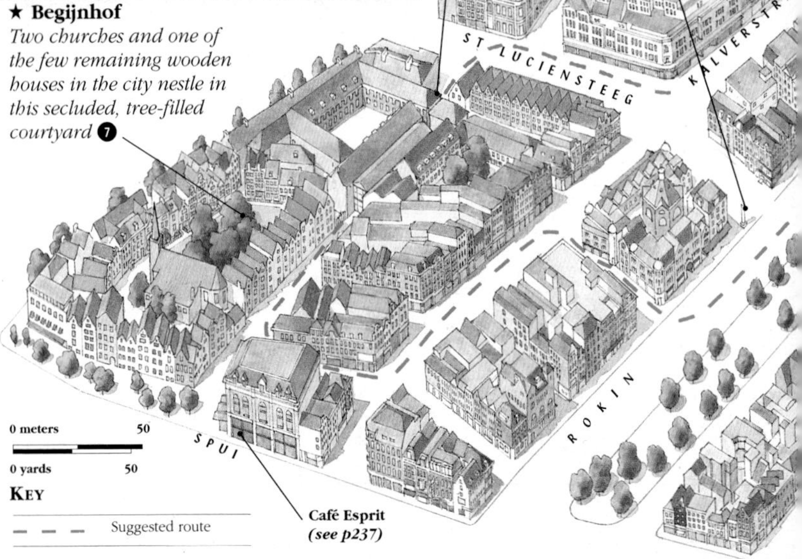

ST LUCIENSTEEG

KALVERSTRA

ROKIN

SPUI

0 meters 50

0 yards 50

KEY

Suggested route

Café Esprit
(see p237)

★ Nieuwe Kerk
The carved and gilded ceiling above the choir was one of the few sections to survive the great fire of 1645 ❶

LOCATOR MAP
See Street Finder, *maps 7, 1 & 2*

De Drie Fleschjes bar ***(see p48)***

St. Nicolaas wall statue, depicting Amsterdam's patron saint, is thought to date from the 15th century.

Nationaal Monument
Two heraldic stone lions represent the Netherlands on this imposing memorial to the Dutch who lost their lives in World War II ❹

Madame Tussauds Scenerama
As well as waxworks and animated scenes, there is a fine view of the city from here ❸

STAR SIGHTS

- **★ Nieuwe Kerk**
- **★ Amsterdams Historisch Museum**
- **★ Begijnhof**

Nes
This street is one of Amsterdam's oldest and has been a center for theater for 150 years ❺

Koninklijk Paleis
Built as the town hall, the building's Classical façade and fine sculptures were intended to glorify the city and its government ❷

The vast marble-floored Burgerzaal in the Koninklijk Paleis

Nieuwe Kerk ❶

See pp76–7.

Koninklijk Paleis ❷

Dam. **Map** 7 B2. 624 8698. 1, 2, 4, 5, 9, 11, 13, 14, 16, 17, 24, 25. Jun–Sep: 12:30–5pm daily; Oct–May: 1–4pm Tue–Thu by appt only. public hols and when queen in residence.

THE KONINKLIJK PALEIS, still used occasionally by the Dutch royal family for official functions, was built as the Stadhuis (town hall). Work began on this vast sandstone building in 1648, after the end of the 80 Years War with Spain *(see pp26–7)*. It dominated its surroundings and more than 13,600 piles were driven into the ground for the foundations. The Classically inspired design by Jacob van Campen (1595–1657) reflects Amsterdam's mood of confidence after the Dutch victory. Civic pride is also shown in the allegorical sculptures by Artus Quellien (1609–68), which decorate the pediments, and in François Hemony's statues and carillon.

The full magnificence of the architecture is best appreciated in the vast Burgerzaal (citizen's hall). Based on the assembly halls of ancient Rome, this 30-m (95-ft) high room runs the length of the building. It boasts a marble floor inlaid with maps of the eastern and western hemispheres, as well as epic sculptures by Quellien.

Most of the furniture on display, including the chandeliers, chairs and clocks, dates from 1808, when Louis Napoleon adopted the building as his royal palace *(see pp28–9)*.

Madame Tussauds Scenerama ❸

Peek & Cloppenburg Building, Dam 20. **Map** 7 B3. 622 9239. 4, 9, 14, 16, 24, 25. Sep–Jun: 10am–5:30pm daily; Jul–Aug: 9:30am–7:30pm daily. Apr 30.

LOCATED ABOVE the Peek & Cloppenburg department store, Madame Tussauds offers an audiovisual interpretation of Amsterdam's history, along with projected 21st-century developments. Some of the symbolic displays, such as the 5-m (16-ft) animated figure of "Amsterdam Man," are somewhat bizarre, but the wax models of 17th-century people give an insight into life in the Golden Age *(see pp24–5)*.

Nationaal Monument ❹

Dam. **Map** 7 B3. 4, 9, 14, 16, 24, 25.

SCULPTED BY John Raedecker and designed by architect JJP Oud, the 22-m (70-ft) obelisk in the Dam commemorates Dutch World War II casualties. It was unveiled in 1956, and is fronted by two lions, heraldic symbols of the Netherlands. Embedded in the wall behind are urns containing earth from all the Dutch provinces and the former colonies of Indonesia, the Antilles and Surinam.

Nes ❺

Map 7 B3. 4, 9, 14, 16, 24, 25.

DATING FROM medieval times, this quiet, narrow street is now home to several theaters. In 1614, Amsterdam's first bank was opened in a pawnshop at No. 57 to lend money to the poor. A wall plaque marks the site, and pawned goods still clutter the shop window.

De Engelenbak, one of several theaters located along Nes

Amsterdams Historisch Museum ❻

See pp80–83.

Begijnhof ❼

Spui. **Map** 7 B4. 🚋 *1, 2, 4, 5, 9, 11, 14, 16, 24, 25.*

The Begijnhof was originally built in 1346 as a sanctuary for the Begijntjes, a lay Catholic sisterhood who lived like nuns, although they took no monastic vows. In return for lodgings within the complex, these worthy women undertook to educate the poor and look after the sick. Nothing survives of the earliest dwellings, but the Begijnhof, which is cut off from traffic noise, still retains a sanctified atmosphere. The rows of beautiful houses that overlook its well-kept green include Amsterdam's oldest surviving house at No. 34. On the adjoining wall, there is a fascinating collection of wall plaques taken from the houses. In keeping with the Begijntjes' religious outlook, the plaques have a biblical theme.

The southern edge of the square is dominated by the Engelse Kerk (English Church), which dates from the 15th century. Despite extensive subsequent remodeling, this attractive building still has its original medieval tower. Directly west stands the Begijnhof Chapel, a well-preserved clandestine church in which the Begijntjes and other Catholics worshiped in secret until religious tolerance was restored in 1795. It once housed relics of the Miracle of Amsterdam *(see pp20–21)*. Four stained-glass windows and paintings depicting scenes of the Miracle remain here.

Plaque on the Engelse Kerk

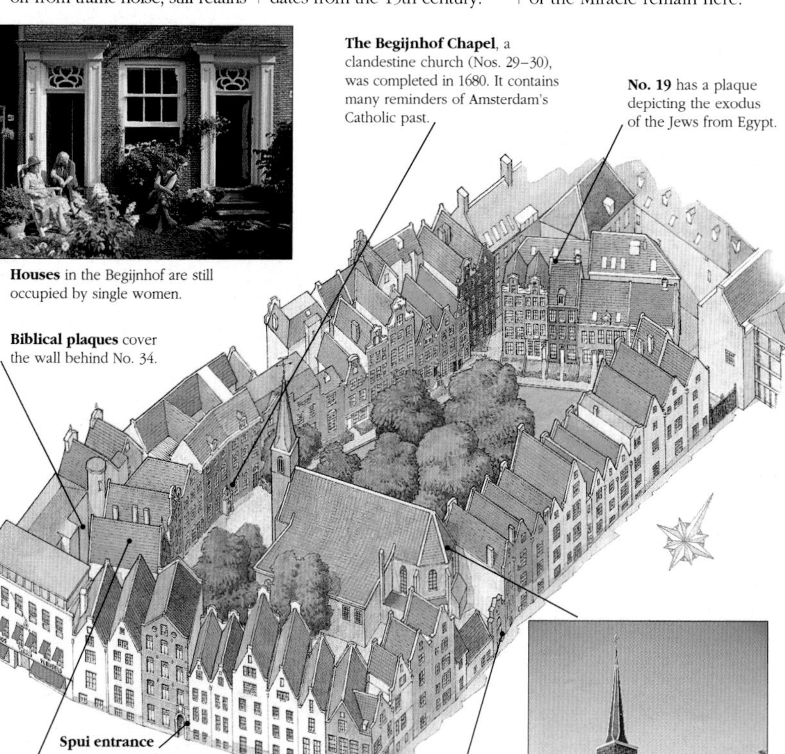

Houses in the Begijnhof are still occupied by single women.

The Begijnhof Chapel, a clandestine church (Nos. 29–30), was completed in 1680. It contains many reminders of Amsterdam's Catholic past.

No. 19 has a plaque depicting the exodus of the Jews from Egypt.

Biblical plaques cover the wall behind No. 34.

Spui entrance

Arched entrance from Gedempte Begijnensloot

Het Houten Huis at No. 34 is Amsterdam's oldest house, dating from around 1420. It is one of only two wooden-fronted houses in the city, as timber houses were banned in 1521 after a series of catastrophic fires. Most of the houses in the Begijnhof were not built until after the 16th century.

Engelse Kerk was built around 1419 for the Begijntjes. The church was confiscated after the Alteration *(see pp22–3)* and rented to a group of English and Scottish Presbyterians in 1607. The Pilgrim Fathers *(see p185)* may have worshiped here.

Nieuwe Kerk ❶

DATING FROM the late 14th century, Amsterdam's second parish church was built as the population outgrew the Oude Kerk *(see pp68–9)*. During its turbulent history, the church has been destroyed several times by fire, rebuilt and then stripped of its finery after the Alteration *(see pp22–3)*. It eventually reached its present size in the 1650s. The pulpit, not the altar, is the focal point of the interior, reflecting the Protestant belief that the sermon is central to worship.

Gilded Cherubs
Grimacing gilded cherubs struggle to support the corners of the wooden barrel vault above the transept crossing.

The New Stadhuis, Dam Square
The Nieuwe Kerk is in the background, at the corner of Dam square, in this painting by Jan van de Heyden (1637–1712). It shows the newly completed Stadhuis, which is now the Koninklijk Paleis (see p74).

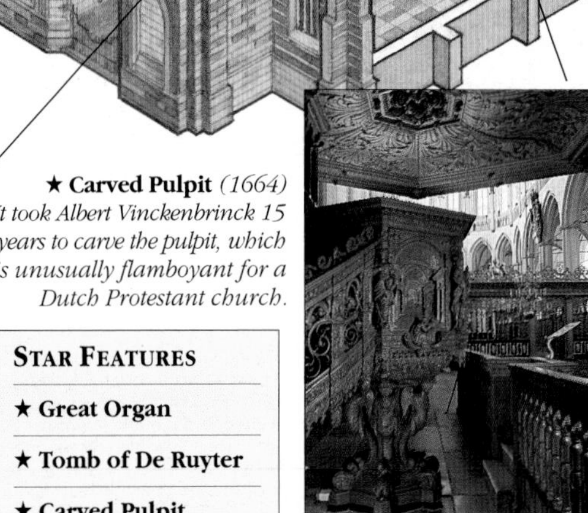

★ Great Organ *(1645)*
Marbled-wood cherubs and angels adorn the elaborate gilded casing of the Great Organ, which was designed by Jacob van Campen.

★ Carved Pulpit *(1664)*
It took Albert Vinckenbrinck 15 years to carve the pulpit, which is unusually flamboyant for a Dutch Protestant church.

STAR FEATURES

- **★ Great Organ**
- **★ Tomb of De Ruyter**
- **★ Carved Pulpit**

Stained-Glass Windows
The lower-right section of the colorful arched window in the south transept was designed by Otto Mengelberg in 1898. It depicts Queen Wilhelmina (see p31) *surrounded by courtiers at her coronation.*

VISITORS' CHECKLIST

Dam. **Map** 7 B2. *638 6909.* *1, 2, 4, 5, 9, 11, 13, 14, 16, 17, 24, 25.* *10am–5pm.*

Brass Candelabra
Magnificent three-tiered brass candelabra were hung from the ceilings of the nave and transepts during restoration work following the fire of 1645.

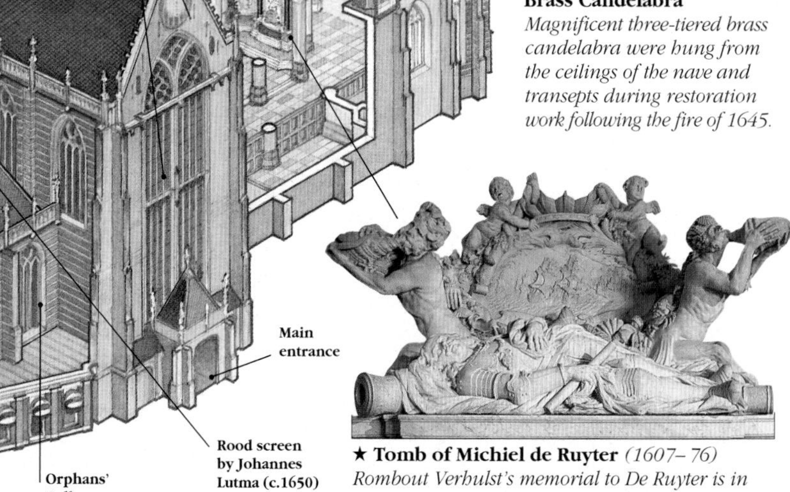

★ Tomb of Michiel de Ruyter *(1607–76)*
Rombout Verhulst's memorial to De Ruyter is in the apse. The admiral, greatly revered by the Dutch, died at sea in battle against the French at Messina.

TIMELINE

Goblet commemorating beginning of renovation of the church (1647)

1380 Estimated date of earliest church on site

1421 Fire destroys much of original building

1452 Damaged in the Great Fire

1540 North transept razed

1578 Church plundered following the Alteration *(see pp22–3)*

1645 Fire destroys all but façade and walls

1646 Work begins on construction of Jacob van Campen's tower

1653 Work on tower halted, reason unclear

1783 Part of tower torn down

1841 First royal investiture in Nieuwe Kerk

1847 Gothic structure built to replace tower

1907 Large-scale restoration

1959 Restoration begins and lasts 20 years

1350 | 1450 | 1550 | 1650 | 1750 | 1850 | 1950

Allard Pierson Museum ❽

Oude Turfmarkt 127. **Map** 7 B4. *525 2556. 4, 9, 14, 16, 24, 25. 10am–5pm Tue–Fri, 1–5pm Sat & Sun. Jan 1, Apr 30, Dec 25.*

AMSTERDAM'S only archaeological collection, now owned by the University, is named after Allard Pierson (1831–96), a humanist and scholar. The collection was moved into this handsome Neo-Classical building in 1976.

The museum contains Cypriot, Greek, Egyptian, Roman, Etruscan and Coptic artifacts. Look for a case of rather gruesome Egyptian mummy remains, scale models of the pyramids, a computer that lets you to write your name in hieroglyphics, a jointed Greek doll from 300 BC and some fine Roman jewelry.

Allard Pierson Museum's Neo-Classical façade made of Bremer and Bentheimer stone

Torensluis ❾

Singel between Torensteeg and Oude Leliestraat. **Map** 7 B2. *1, 2, 5, 11, 13, 17.*

THE TORENSLUIS is one of the widest bridges in Amsterdam. It was built on the site of a 17th-century sluice gate and took its name from two towers that stood here on each side of the Singel until they were demolished in 1829. A lock-up jail was built in its foundations.

In summer, visitors can sit out at café tables on the bridge and enjoy pleasant views down the Singel. The statue dominating the bridge is of Multatuli, the 19th-century Dutch writer who wrote the well-known book *Max Havelaar.*

Postkantoor ❿

Nieuwezijds Voorburgwal 182. **Map** 7 B2. *626 9199. 1, 2, 5, 11, 13, 14, 17.* **Magna Plaza** *11am–5pm Sun, 11am–6pm Mon, 10am–6pm Tue–Wed & Fri–Sat, 10am–9pm Thu. public hols.*

A POST OFFICE building has been here since 1748. A wall panel on the current building's façade depicts the original office, which was taken out of service in 1854. The present building was completed in 1899. CP Peters, the architect, was ridiculed for the extravagance of its Neo-Gothic design. Critics dubbed the Postkantoor's elaborately decorated style and spindly towers "post office Gothic". It has since been redeveloped, and in 1990 opened as the city's first shopping mall. The dimensions and magnificent arched galleries of Peters' original design have been well preserved.

Lutherse Kerk ⓫

Kattengat 2. **Map** 7 C1. *621 2223. 1, 2, 5, 11, 13, 17. appt only. with assistance.*

THE LUTHERSE KERK was designed by Adriaan Dortsman (1625–82) and opened in 1671. It is sometimes known as the Ronde Lutherse Kerk, being the first Dutch Reformed church with a circular ground plan and two upper galleries, giving the whole congregation a clear view of the pulpit.

In 1882 a fire started by careless plumbers destroyed everything except the exterior walls. When the interior and entrance were rebuilt in 1883, they were made squarer and more ornate, in keeping with

An outdoor café on the Torensluis bridge overlooking the Singel canal

the church architectural style of that time. A huge vaulted copper dome replaced the earlier ribbed version.

Falling attendances led to the closure and deconsecration of the church in 1935. The building is now used by the Amsterdam Renaissance Hotel *(see p219)* as a conference and banquet room, and is open to the public for free concerts on Sunday mornings.

Centraal Station ⓬

Stationsplein. **Map** 8 D1. *06 9292 (travel information).* *1, 2, 4, 5, 9, 11, 13, 16, 17, 24, 25.* M *Centraal Station.* **Information office** *7am–midnight Mon–Fri, 8am–midnight Sat, Sun & public hols.*

Weather vane on Centraal Station

When the Centraal Station opened in 1889, it replaced the old harbor as the symbolic focal point of the city *(see pp30–31)* and effectively curtained Amsterdam off from the sea. The Neo-Renaissance red-brick railway terminus was designed by PJH Cuypers, who was also responsible for the Rijksmuseum *(see pp130–31)* and AL van Gendt, who designed the Concertgebouw *(see p128)*.

Three artificial islands were created, using 8,600 wooden piles to support the structure. In the design of the station's twin towers and imposing central section there are architectural echoes of a triumphal arch, and it certainly makes a grand entry point for visitors to the city. The imposing façade is adorned with elaborate gold and colored decoration showing allegories of maritime trade – a tribute to the city's past. Today it is a major meeting point as well as the transit hub of the capital, with 1,400 trains operating daily *(see p268)*, and buses and trolleys terminating here.

Decorative brickwork on the façade of the Beurs van Berlage

Sint Nicolaaskerk ⓭

Prins Hendrikkade 73. **Map** 8 D1. *624 8749.* *1, 2, 4, 5, 9, 11, 13, 16, 17, 24, 25.* M *Centraal Station.* *Good Fri–mid-Oct: 11am–4pm Mon–Sat.*

Sint Nicolaas was the patron saint of seafarers, and as such was an important icon in Amsterdam. Many Dutch churches are named after him, and the Netherlands' principal day for the giving of presents, December 5, is known as Sinterklaasavond *(see p53)*.

The Sint Nicolaaskerk was designed by AC Bleys (1842–1912), and completed in 1887. It replaced some of the clandestine Catholic churches that had been set up around the city when Amsterdam was officially Protestant *(see p84)*.

The exterior is rather grim and forbidding, its twin towers dominating the skyline around the old harbor. Inside, the church takes on a monumental character, with squared pillars and coffered ceiling arches.

Museum Amstelkring ⓮

See pp84–5.

Beurs van Berlage ⓯

Damrak 243. **Map** 7 C2. *626 5257.* *4, 9, 16, 24, 25.* *daily subject to exhibitions and concerts.* *Jan 1.*

Hendrik Berlage's stock exchange was completed in 1903. The building's clean lines and functional appearance mark a radical departure from the revivalist styles of late 19th-century architecture. Many of its design features were adopted by the Amsterdam School *(see p97)*. Inside, there is an impressive frieze showing the evolution of man from Adam to stockbroker. Sadly, the exchange was not popular with traders. It is now used for concerts and shows.

Neo-Renaissance façade of the Sint Nicolaaskerk

Amsterdams Historisch Museum ❻

THE CONVENT OF ST. LUCIEN was turned into a civic orphanage after the Alteration of 1578 *(see pp22–3)*. The original red-brick convent has been enlarged over the years, with new wings added in the 17th century by Hendrick de Keyser *(see p90)* and Jacob van Campen *(see p76)*. The present building, with cobblestone courtyards and Classical façades, is much as it was in the 18th century. The complex houses the city's historical museum, telling the story of Amsterdam's development.

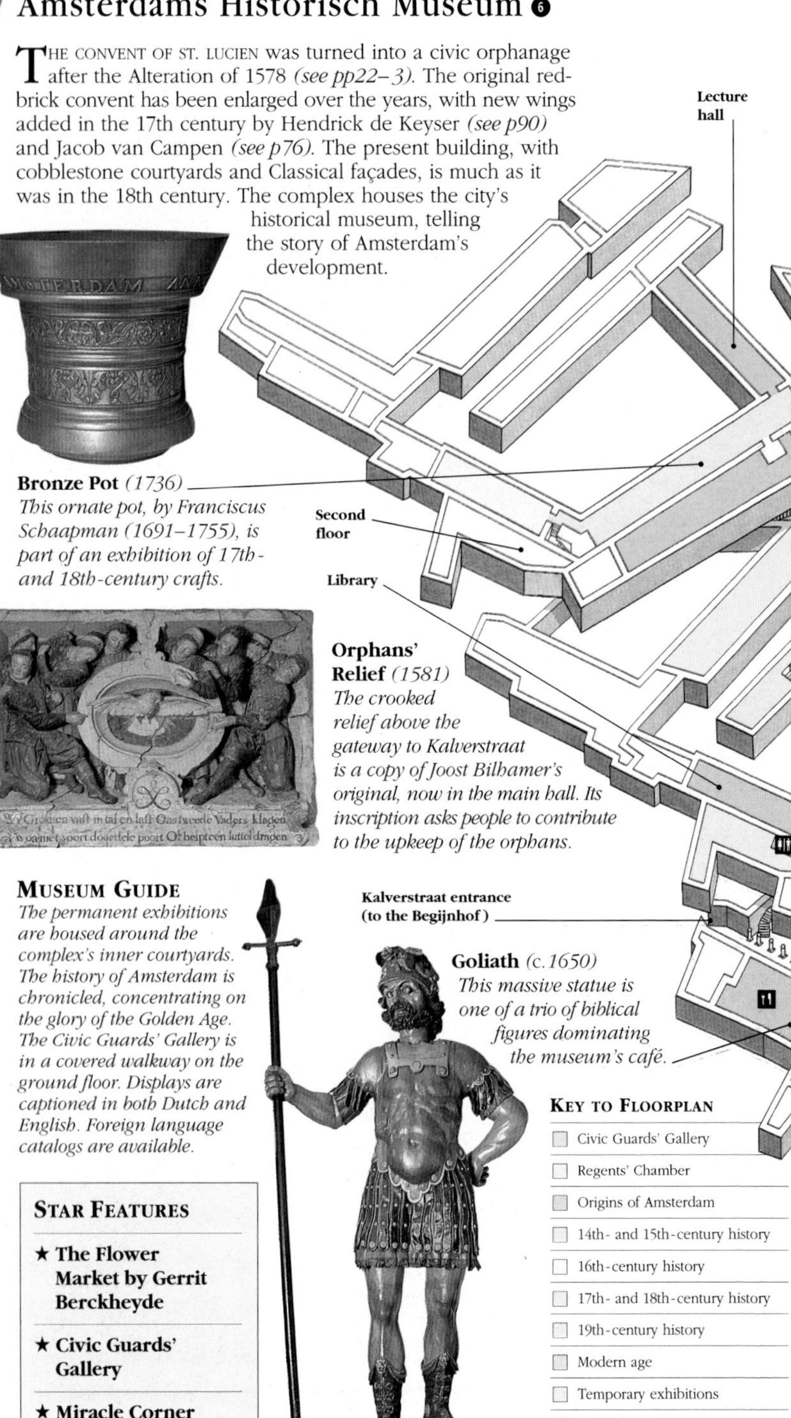

Bronze Pot *(1736)*
This ornate pot, by Franciscus Schaapman (1691–1755), is part of an exhibition of 17th- and 18th-century crafts.

Orphans' Relief *(1581)*
The crooked relief above the gateway to Kalverstraat is a copy of Joost Bilhamer's original, now in the main hall. Its inscription asks people to contribute to the upkeep of the orphans.

Goliath *(c.1650)*
This massive statue is one of a trio of biblical figures dominating the museum's café.

MUSEUM GUIDE

The permanent exhibitions are housed around the complex's inner courtyards. The history of Amsterdam is chronicled, concentrating on the glory of the Golden Age. The Civic Guards' Gallery is in a covered walkway on the ground floor. Displays are captioned in both Dutch and English. Foreign language catalogs are available.

STAR FEATURES

- ★ **The Flower Market by Gerrit Berckheyde**
- ★ **Civic Guards' Gallery**
- ★ **Miracle Corner**

KEY TO FLOORPLAN

- Civic Guards' Gallery
- Regents' Chamber
- Origins of Amsterdam
- 14th- and 15th-century history
- 16th-century history
- 17th- and 18th-century history
- 19th-century history
- Modern age
- Temporary exhibitions
- Nonexhibition space

Visitors' Checklist

Kalverstraat 92, Nieuwezijds Voorburgwal 357, St Luciensteeg 27. **Map** 1 C5. *523 1822.* *1, 2, 4, 5, 9, 11, 14, 16, 24, 25.* *10am–5pm Mon–Fri, 11am–5pm Sat & Sun.* *Jan 1, Apr 30, Dec 25.*

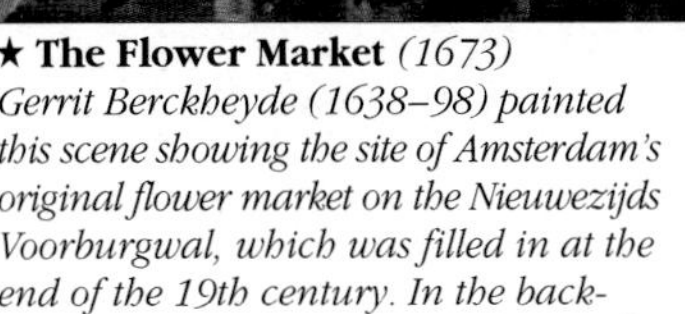

★ The Flower Market *(1673)*
Gerrit Berckheyde (1638–98) painted this scene showing the site of Amsterdam's original flower market on the Nieuwezijds Voorburgwal, which was filled in at the end of the 19th century. In the background is the Koninklijk Paleis (see p74).

Indian Elephant *(c.1700)*
On the long sea voyages of the Golden Age, sailors carved mementos of their journeys, like this wooden elephant.

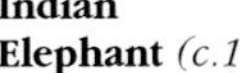

First floor

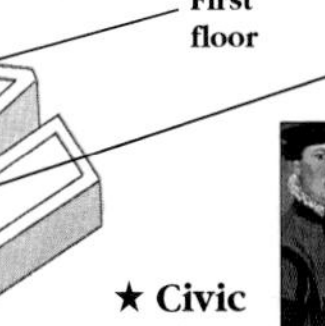

★ Civic Guards' Gallery
This portrait of 17 guardsmen of Company F was painted by an unknown artist in 1552.

Ground floor

17th-century red brick façade

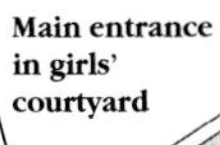

Main entrance in girls' courtyard

Entrance on Nieuwezijds Voorburgwal

St. Luciensteeg entrance

★ Miracle Corner
Four beautifully embroidered altar cushions from the late 15th century are the oldest known representations of the Miracle of Amsterdam in 1345 (see p20). *Tapestry banners once used in the annual procession celebrating the Miracle are also on show.*

The terra-cotta figure of the Maid of Amsterdam

Exploring the Amsterdams Historisch Museum

THE MUSEUM charts the development of Amsterdam from its humble origins as a fishing village on the Amstel in the Middle Ages to the cosmopolitan city of today. The greater section focuses on trade, commerce and culture in the Golden Age *(see pp24–5)*. A series of Civic Guard group portraits are a highlight of the collection, which becomes somewhat disjointed in its display of recent historical artifacts.

Civic Guards' Gallery

THIS COVERED walkway is accessible to all during museum hours. Queen Juliana opened the gallery in 1975 to house the group portraits which were popular during the 16th century. The Civic Guard comprised three guilds of marksmen, which merged in 1580. This is a rare collection as few portraits were commissioned after 1650. Best-known are Rembrandt's works; highlights are by Dirck Barendsz *(see p81)* and Cornelis Anthonisz, such as *The Meal of the 17 Guardsmen of Company H* (1533).

Regents' Chamber

BUILT IN 1634, this room was the meeting place of the orphanage's directors (regents). Its fine ceiling, added in 1656, shows the orphans receiving charity. Portraits of the regents hang on the walls alongside Abraham de Verwer's two paintings of *The Battle on the Slaak* (1634). The long table and cabinets are 17th-century.

17th-century coats of arms on wooden panel

Early History to the 14th Century

THE FIRST ROOMS of the museum contain a series of displays explaining the growth of early Amsterdam around the Amstel river. A map of the city illuminates each area in turn to show when it was developed. The model interior of a medieval wooden house, precise down to the tiny box beds, shows how 14th-century domestic life centered on the hearth, then the only constant source of heat for cooking and warmth.

14th and 15th Centuries

AMSTERDAM'S RISE to prominence in trade and commerce began at this time *(see pp20–21)*. Exhibits include a cauldron used to soften tar for shipbuilding, and many household items such as shoes and tools. A fervent religious revival took place during this period, spurred on by the Miracle of Amsterdam in 1345 *(see p20)*, which caused thousands of pilgrims to flock into the city. The display of relics associated with the miracle is found in Room 3, and includes tapestry cushions and wood carvings from the church built on the site of the alleged phenomenon. Many churches were built in the 14th century and paintings on show include *St. Agnes's Convent* (c. 1490) by Jacob Cornelisz van Oostanen.

16th Century

BETWEEN 1500 and 1560 the city's population tripled. The Civic Guard became defenders of law and order in the overcrowded city. A display of its armor and weaponry in Room 4 stands before a window overlooking the Boys' courtyard. The huge wall relief shows Warmoesstraat, the oldest street in Amsterdam. It details the people who lived there: craftsmen to one side and merchants on the canalside for easy access to their ships. Cornelis Anthonisz's bird's-eye *View of Amsterdam (see pp22–3)* is the oldest city plan to survive, dated 1538. A number of churches and convents are clearly marked. In one corner of Room 4 is Hendrick Cornelisz Vroom's oil painting (1615) of the fortified Haarlemmerpoort, showing how the city defended itself against any outside attack from its political rivals.

Bronze dagger (c. 1500)

17th and 18th Centuries

ROOMS 5 TO 15 form the bulk of the museum's collection, focusing on the Golden Age *(see pp24–7)* and the importance of overseas trade and colonial expansion. In Room 5 is the 17th-century wall map of Asia by the famous cartographer Willem Blaeu *(see p146)*, complete with drawings of the busy principal harbors. Room 6 is full of portraits and busts of dignitaries, as well as official silverware and a 1648 model of the town hall, now the Koninklijk Paleis *(see p74)*. A late 18th-century model of an East Indiaman in Room 8 is resting on a primitive floating

The First Steamship on the IJ **(1816) by Nicolaas Bauo**

dock known as a "camel." This enabled heavily laden ships to travel through the very shallow waters of the Zuiderzee.

Room 11 concentrates on the discrepancy between the rich and poorer inhabitants of the city. Its walls are all hung with huge, gloomy canvases that depict the wealthy governors of Amsterdam's poorhouses.

Art flourished in the Golden Age and artists flooded into the city. Contemporary paintings, often allegorical, portray rich families and their lives. Jacob de Wit's *Maid of Amsterdam* (1741) is in Room 12, and Room 15 is devoted to maps – one shows Watergraafsmeer, where successful merchants built their country houses.

The Old Orphanage

Girls from the Civic Orphanage **(c. 1880) by Nicolaas van der Waay**

The orphanage moved to St. Lucien's convent in 1580. It was open only to the children of burghers, excluding the poorest children. As the city grew, so did the number of orphans. In the 17th century, two wings were built to accommodate more children, and a separate entrance for girls was added on St. Luciensteeg. The building was used as an orphanage until 1960, but the formal uniform was abandoned in 1919.

19th Century

Decline in trade resulted in poverty in the 19th century and charitable institutions developed to deal with the problem. Art reflected social problems: Eduard Alexander Hilverdink's painting, *The Jewish Quarter* (1889) *(see p31)*, depicts the squalor and slum conditions. Melancholic late Hague School works by George Breitner *(see p133)* and somber black-and-white photographs reflect the city's demise. A series of unrealized plans for expansion highlights this stagnation.

The Modern Age

Recent history is not as well documented as earlier times. The museum exhibits a series of evocative photographs taken during the Depression of the early 1930s and the war years *(see pp32–3)*, when the city was under Nazi occupation. Temporary exhibitions cover aspects of 20th-century life in Amsterdam from homosexuality to diamondcutting. There are also displays of archaeological discoveries made during recent excavations.

Museum Amstelkring ⓮

Tucked away on the edge of the Red Light District is a restored 17th-century canal house with two smaller houses to the rear. The combined upper stories conceal a secret Catholic church, known as Ons' Lieve Heer op Solder (Our Dear Lord in the Attic), originally built in 1663. After the Alteration *(see pp22–3)*, when Amsterdam officially became Protestant, many such clandestine churches were built throughout the city. The lower floors of the building became a museum in 1888, and today contain elegantly refurbished and decorated rooms, as well as a fine collection of church silver, religious artifacts and paintings.

Christ and the Dove of Peace in silver

Amstelkring Façade
The house on the canal has a simple spout gable. Along with the two smaller houses behind, it was built by bourgeois merchant Jan Hartman in 1663.

Wooden viewing gallery of church

A priest's tiny box bedroom is hidden off a bend in the stairs. There was a resident priest in the church from 1663.

Main entrance

House on the canal

Reception room in Louis XV style

★ Drawing Room
Restored to its former opulence, the drawing room is an unusually fine example of a living room decorated and furnished in the Dutch Classical style of the 17th century.

Star Features

- **★ Ons' Lieve Heer op Solder**
- **★ Altar Painting by Jacob de Wit**
- **★ Drawing Room**

Visitors' Checklist

Oudezijds Voorburgwal 40.
Map 8 D2. *624 6604.*
4, 9, 16, 24, 25. *10am–5pm Mon–Sat, 1–5pm Sun.*
Jan 1, Apr 30.

Confessional
The landing where the tiny wooden confessional stands was formerly the living room of the rear house.

★ Altar Painting
The Baptism of Christ *(1716) hanging above the mock marble altar is by Jacob de Wit (1695–1754). It is one of three altar paintings that were designed to be interchangeable.*

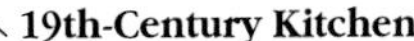

19th-Century Kitchen
The kitchen was originally part of the sacristan's secret living quarters. The delft tiles, fireplace and black-and-white floor are all original.

★ Ons' Lieve Heer op Solder
The original clandestine church was extended in 1735 to create more seating space. It served the Catholic community until St. Nicolaaskerk (see p79) *was finished in 1887.*

GRIETJE

Western Canal Ring

At the start of the 17th century, construction of the *Grachtengordel* began here, just west of the Singel *(see p45)*. At the same time, the city planner, Hendrick Staets, laid out the marshy area beyond these fashionable canals as an area for workers whose industries were banned from the town center. Its network of narrow streets and oblique canals followed the course of old paths and drainage ditches. Immigrants fleeing religious persecution also settled here. It is thought that Huguenot refugees called the district *jardin* (garden), later corrupted to "Jordaan." Historically a poor area, it is famous for its poorhouses *(hofjes)*, and the Claes Claeszhofje is a fine early example. Recently, the Jordaan has taken on a more bohemian air. Farther north are the characterful Western Islands, created in the mid-17th century to meet the demand for warehouses.

"Writing hand" emblem on Claes Claeszhofje

Sights at a Glance

Historic Buildings and Monuments
Huis met de Hoofden 4
Haarlemmerpoort 12

Museums
Theatermuseum 1
Anne Frankhuis 3

Canals and Islands
Egelantiersgracht 5
Bloemgracht 6
Brouwersgracht 11
Western Islands 13

Churches
Westerkerk 2
Noorderkerk 9

Markets
Noordermarkt 10

Hofjes
Claes Claeszhofje 7
De Star and Zon's Hofje 8

Getting There

It is a five-minute walk from the Dam and Centraal Station to reach the Jordaan. Trolleys 13, 14 and 17 go to Rozengracht. No. 3 follows Marnixstraat to Haarlemmerpoort.

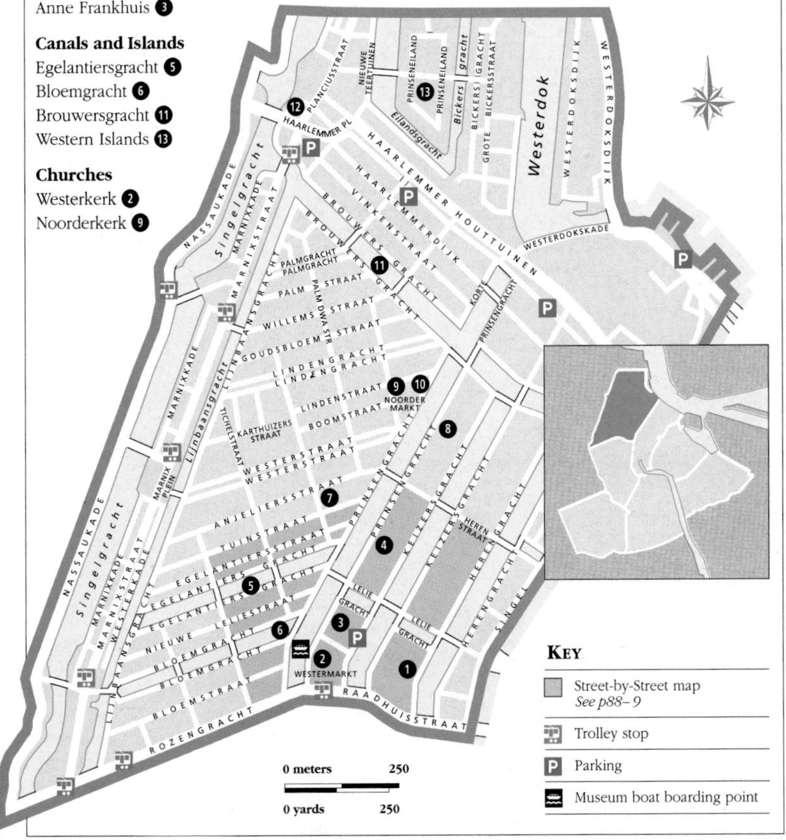

0 meters 250
0 yards 250

Key

Street-by-Street map *See p88–9*
Trolley stop
Parking
Museum boat boarding point

◁ **View of Prinsengracht with its densely packed houseboats and the Westerkerk in the distance**

Street-by-Street: Around the Jordaan

West of the *Grachtengordel* *(see p45)*, the Jordaan still retains a network of narrow, characterful streets and delightful canals. Among the 17th-century workers' houses are dozens of quirky stores, which are well worth a browse, selling anything from designer clothes to old sinks, and lively brown cafés and bars, which spill onto the sidewalks in summer. A stroll along the *Grachtengordel* provides a glimpse into some of the city's grandest canal houses, including the Bartolotti House.

★ Anne Frankhuis
For two years, the Frank family and four others lived in a small upstairs apartment that was hidden behind a revolving bookcase ❸

Bloemgracht
This quiet, pretty canal was once a center for makers of paint and dye ❻

★ Westerkerk
Hendrick de Keyser's church is the site of Rembrandt's unmarked grave, and was the setting for the wedding of Queen Beatrix and Prince Claus in 1966 ❷

Egelantiersgracht
This charming tree-lined Jordaan canal is overlooked by an interesting mixture of old and new architecture. Pretty views are provided from its numerous bridges ❺

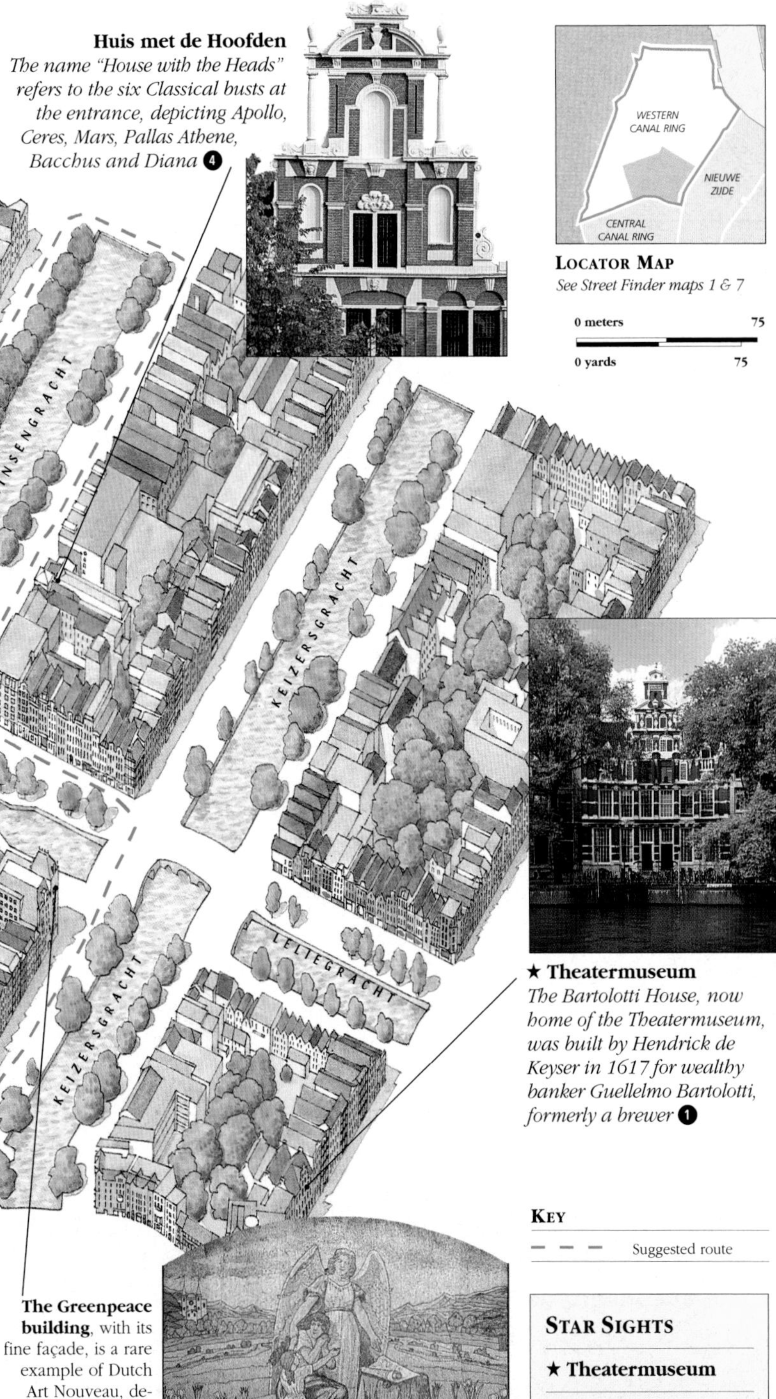

Huis met de Hoofden
The name "House with the Heads" refers to the six Classical busts at the entrance, depicting Apollo, Ceres, Mars, Pallas Athene, Bacchus and Diana ❹

Locator Map
See Street Finder maps 1 & 7

0 meters 75
0 yards 75

★ Theatermuseum
The Bartolotti House, now home of the Theatermuseum, was built by Hendrick de Keyser in 1617 for wealthy banker Guellelmo Bartolotti, formerly a brewer ❶

The Greenpeace building, with its fine façade, is a rare example of Dutch Art Nouveau, designed by Gerrit van Arkel in 1905. It is now home to the environmental group.

Key

– – – Suggested route

Star Sights

- ★ **Theatermuseum**
- ★ **Westerkerk**
- ★ **Anne Frankhuis**

Theatermuseum interior, with 18th-century staircase and stuccowork

Theatermuseum ❶

Herengracht 168. **Map** 7 A2. *623 5104. 13, 14, 17. Prinsengracht. 11am–5pm Tue–Fri, 1–5pm Sat. Jan 1, Apr 30, Dec 25.*

TWO FINE BUILDINGS house the theater museum, which contains costumes, sets and memorabilia. You can even play with antique sound effects and create your own storm. The museum entrance is in the White House, No. 168, a Neo-Classical house designed by Philips Vingboons *(see p99)* in 1638. The interior was restyled in about 1730, and has a magnificent spiral staircase, stuccowork by Van Logteren and rich ceiling paintings by Jacob de Wit *(see p122)*.

The museum extends next door into the exotic Bartolotti House (Nos. 170–172). Built by Hendrick de Keyser (1565–1621) in 1617, its elaborate Renaissance façade contrasts sharply with the austerity of the White House. Its interior decoration was by Jacob de Wit and Isaac de Moucheron.

Westerkerk ❷

Prinsengracht 281. **Map** 1 B4. *624 7766. 13, 14, 17. Apr–Sep: 10am–4pm Mon–Sat.* **Tower**

BUILT AS PART of the development of the Canal Ring *(see pp44–5)*, the West Church has the tallest tower in Amsterdam at 85 m (272 ft), and the largest nave of any Dutch Protestant church. It was designed in Renaissance style by Hendrick de Keyser, who died in 1621, a year after work began.

Rembrandt was buried here but his grave has never been found. The shutters of the huge organ (1686) were painted, by Gerard de Lairesse, with lively scenes showing King David, the Queen of Sheba and the Evangelists. The spire, built in tapering sections, is topped by the gaudy Imperial Crown of Maximilian *(see pp20–21)*. The panoramic views from its top justify the grueling climb.

Anne Frankhuis ❸

Prinsengracht 263. **Map** 1 B4. *556 7100. 13, 14, 17. Prinsengracht. Jun–Aug: 9am–7pm Mon–Sat, 10am–7pm Sun & public hols; Sep–May: 9am–5pm Mon–Sat; 10am–5pm Sun & public hols. Jan 1, Yom Kippur, Dec 25.*

Anne's picture display in her room in the Anne Frankhuis

FOR TWO YEARS during World War II, the Frank and Van Daan families, both Jewish, hid here until their betrayal to the Nazis. In 1957, the Anne Frank Stichting (foundation) took over the house, to carry out "the ideals set down in

The Westerkerk in the 18th century, a view by Jan Ekels

the Diary of Anne Frank." The 13-year-old Anne began her now-famous diary in July 1942. It gives a unique account of growing up under persecution, and of life in confinement *(see pp32–3)*. It was first published in 1947 as *Het Achterhuis (The Annex)* and since translated into dozens of languages, and made into plays and films.

Visitors to the Anne Frankhuis climb to the second floor where an introductory video is shown. They then enter the annex via the revolving bookcase that hid its entrance. Its rooms are now empty, except for the film star pin-ups in Anne's room, and Otto Frank's model of the annex as it was during the occupation. The front of the house has exhibitions on World War II and anti-Semitism. Get here early – with 500,000 visitors a year, the museum gets very crowded.

Huis met de Hoofden ❹

Keizersgracht 123. **Map** 7 A1. *626 3947.* *13, 14, 17.* *9am–5pm Mon–Fri.* *public hols.*

Built in 1622, the Huis met de Hoofden (house with the heads) is one of the largest double houses of the period. It has a fine step gable and takes its name from the six heads placed on pilasters along the façade. Legend has it that they commemorate a housemaid who, when left alone in the house, surprised six burglars and cut off their heads. The sculptures are in fact portrayals of six Classical deities (from left to right): Apollo, Ceres, Mars, Minerva, Bacchus and Diana.

The design of the building is sometimes attributed to Pieter de Keyser (1595–1676), the son of Hendrick. It is now home to the Monumentenzorg, an organization that since 1953 has supervised care of Amsterdam's officially recognized public monuments.

Head of Apollo on the Huis met de Hoofden

Bikes and boats along the tranquil Bloemgracht

Egelantiersgracht ❺

Map 1 B4. *10, 13, 14, 17.*

Many canals in the Jordaan were named after trees or flowers, and this includes the Egelantiersgracht (sweetbrier or eglantine). The canal was cut in the 17th century along a drainage ditch. The houses in this area, built for artisans, are on a more intimate scale than the grand mansions along Herengracht, Keizersgracht and Prinsengracht. As a result, demand for canalside residences in the Jordaan has boomed. Despite some development, the Egelantiersgracht retains much of its original character and one of the most charming spots along the canal is the St. Andrieshofje at Nos. 107–114. This *hofje* was built in 1617, and the passage through to its courtyard is decorated with splendid blue-and-white tiles.

Bloemgracht ❻

Map 1 B4. *10, 13, 14, 17.*

The Bloemgracht (flower canal) was a center for dye and paint manufacturing in the 17th century. Today, only one paint maker remains; This quiet canal is now called the Herengracht (gentlemen's canal) of the Jordaan, because of the fine gable houses along its banks.

The most beautiful are the three houses at Nos. 87 to 91. Built in 1642 in the traditional "burgher" style of the period, they feature stepped gables and a strong use of glass. Their gable stones, which served as house names until numbering was introduced in the 19th century, depict a farmer, a townsman and a seaman.

Stone plaque on the *hofje* founded in 1616 by the merchant Anslo

Claes Claeszhofje ❼

1e Egelantiersdwarsstraat. **Map** 1 B3. *3, 10, 13, 14, 17.* *sporadically.*

THIS IS A GROUP of *hofjes*, the earliest of which was founded in 1616 by a textile merchant, Claes Claesz Anslo. They were renovated by the Stichting Diogenes, a foundation that now rents out the houses to art students.

One of the oldest and most distinctive is the "Huis met de Schrijvende Hand" (house with the writing hand), Egelantiersstraat 52. Once the home of a teacher, it dates from the 1630s.

De Star Hofje and Zon's Hofje ❽

De Star Hofje: Prinsengracht 89–133; Zon's Hofje: Prinsengracht 159–171. **Map** 1 C3. *3, 10, 13, 14, 17.* *sporadically.*

THESE TWO CHARMING *hofjes* are within a short walk of each other. De Star *hofje* was built on the site of the Star Brewery in 1804, and it is officially known as Van Brienen *hofje*. Legend has it that a merchant, Jan van Brienen, founded this poorhouse in gratitude for his release from a vault in which he had been accidentally imprisoned. The peaceful courtyard has a lovely flower garden with a fine laburnum tree.

Zon's *hofje* was built on the site of a clandestine church, known as Noah's Ark, now indicated by a stone plaque of Noah's Ark in the courtyard. The church's original name of Kleine Zon (Little Sun) gave the *hofje* its name. Its rooms are rented to women students.

Noorderkerk ❾

Noordermarkt 44–48. **Map** 1 C3. *626 6436.* *3, 10, 13, 14, 17.* *Mar–Nov: 11am–1pm Sat, or by appointment.* *10am & 7pm Sun.*

BUILT AS A PLACE of worship for poor settlers in the Jordaan, the North Church was the first in Amsterdam to be constructed in the shape of a Greek cross. Its layout around a central pulpit allowed everyone in the encircling pews to see and hear well.

The church was designed by Hendrick de Keyser *(see p90)*, who died in 1621, a year after building began. It was completed in 1623, in time to hold its inaugural service at Easter. The church is still well attended by a widespread Calvinist congregation, and bears many reminders of the working-class origins of the Jordaan. By the entrance is a sculpture of three bound figures, inscribed: "Unity is Strength." It commemorates the Jordaanoproer (Jordaan Riot) of 1934 *(see pp32–3)*.

On the south façade is a plaque recalling the strike of February 1941, a protest at the Nazis' deportation of Jews. And each year on May 4 *(see p50)*, people gather in the church to honor the Jews who died in the war. Major restoration work now in progress is expected to continue until the year 2000.

Visitors to the Saturday morning fair in Noordermarkt

Noordermarkt ❿

Map 1 C3. *3, 10, 13, 14, 17.* **General Market** *9am–noon Mon;* **Boerenmarkt** (fruit and vegetables) *10am–3pm Sat.*

SINCE 1627, the square that surrounds the Noorderkerk has been a market site. At that time, it sold pots and pans and *vodden* (old clothes), a tradition that continues today with a flea market – part of the lively Monday morning market around the church.

Since the 18th century, the area has been a center for bed stores. Bedding, curtains and fabrics are still sold on Monday morning along the Westerstraat, where you can buy anything from net curtain material to buttons.

On Saturday mornings, from about 6am, the weekly *vogeltjes* (small birds) market sells chickens, pigeons, small birds and rabbits. Around 10am, the *boerenmarkt* takes over, selling organic fruit and vegetables, health foods, herbs, essential oils, ethnic crafts and candles.

The square is surrounded by cafés and there is a popular brown café *(see p48)* at No. 34.

The lush garden in the courtyard of De Star *hofje*

A flower-filled houseboat on Brouwersgracht

Brouwersgracht ⓫

Map 1 B2. 🚋 *3.*

BROUWERSGRACHT (brewers' canal) was named after the breweries established here in the 17th and 18th centuries. Leather, spices, coffee and sugar were also processed and stored here. Today, most of the warehouses are fashionable residences that look out on houseboats moored between the canal's picturesque humpback bridges.

Well-maintained examples of these functional buildings, with their simple spout gables *(see pp96–7)* and shutters, can be seen at Nos. 188 to 194. The last distillery in the area, the Ooievaar, is just off Brouwersgracht on Driehoekstraat (Triangle Street). The Dutch gin, *jenever*, has been made here since 1782. The *proeflokaal (see p48)* attached to the distillery is open to the public.

Haarlemmerpoort ⓬

Haarlemmerplein 50. **Map** 1 B1. 🚋 *3.* ● *to the public.*

ORIGINALLY a defended gateway into Amsterdam, the Haarlemmerpoort marked the beginning of the busy route to Haarlem. The present gateway, dating from 1840, was built for King William II's triumphal entry into the city *(see pp30–31)* and officially named Willemspoort. However, as the third gateway to be built on or close to this site, it is still referred to as the Haarlemmerpoort by Amsterdammers.

Designed by Cornelis Alewijn (1788–1839), the Neo-Classical gatehouse was used as tax offices in the 19th century and was made into apartments in 1986. Traffic no longer goes through the gate, since a bridge has been built over the adjoining Westerkanaal. Lying beyond the Haarlemmerpoort is the peaceful Westerpark, one of the city's smaller parks.

Western Islands ⓭

Map 1 C1. 🚋 *3.*

Plaque with shipping motif on a house in Zandhoek, Realeneiland

THIS DISTRICT comprises three islands built on the IJ in the early 17th century to provide space for warehouses and shipyards. Some of these are still in use and many of the period houses have survived.

Bickerseiland was bought in 1631 by the merchant Jan Bicker, who then developed it. Today, the island is residential with a mix of colorful apartment blocks on one side of its walkway and a jumble of houseboats on the other.

Photogenic Realeneiland has one of the city's prettiest spots, the waterside street of Zandhoek. Here, a row of 17th-century houses built by the island's founder, Jacobsz Reaal, overlook the sailboats moored along Westerdok.

Prinseneiland, the smallest island, is dominated by characterful warehouses, many of which are now apartments. The walk on pages 158–9 explores the area in more detail.

DUTCH HOFJES

Before the Alteration *(see pp22–3)*, the Catholic Church usually provided subsidized housing for the poor and elderly, particularly women. During the 17th and 18th centuries, rich merchants and Protestant organizations took on this charitable role and built hundreds of poorhouse complexes, which were built around courtyards and known as *hofjes*. Behind their street façades lie pretty houses and serene gardens. Visitors are admitted to some but are asked to respect the residents' privacy. Many *hofjes* are found in the Jordaan and some still serve their original purpose *(see p75)*.

The "house with the writing hand" (c. 1630) in Claes Claeszhofje

A Canal Walk and Guide to Architecture

With the increase in wealth and civic pride in Amsterdam during the 17th century, an ambitious plan was formed to build a splendid ring of canals around the city *(see pp24–5)*. Conceived in 1609, and added to in 1664 by Daniel Stalpaert, the plan grew to encompass wide canals lined with opulent town houses in a variety of architectural styles *(see pp96–7)*. The houses on the canals of Singel, Keizersgracht, Herengracht, Reguliersgracht and Prinsengracht, illustrated on pp98–105, form a fascinating walk through Golden Age Amsterdam.

Wall plaque, No. 1133 Prinsengracht

Nationaal Monument and Koninklijk Paleis in Dam square

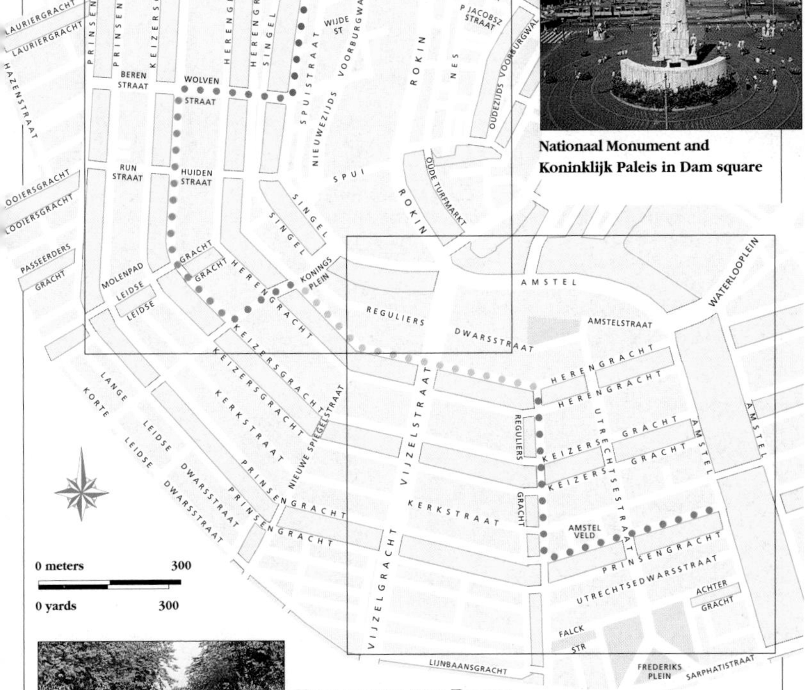

0 meters 300

0 yards 300

A picturesque stone humpback bridge on the Reguliersgracht

Following the Route

The walk begins at Dam square and should be followed from left to right across the next two pages, always walking on the left-hand side of the canal. The colored dots correspond to the stretch of canal illustrated, the gray dots trace interconnecting roads forming part of the route, but are not illustrated.

Key to Walk Route

- ••• Singel
- ••• Keizersgracht
- ••• Herengracht
- ••• Reguliersgracht
- ••• Prinsengracht
- ••• Connecting streets

◁ *Keizersgracht* **(c. 1750) by Hendrick Keun – a scene of beauty and tranquillity**

A Guide to Canal House Architecture

AMSTERDAM HAS BEEN CALLED a city of "well-mannered" architecture because its charms lie in intimate details rather than in grand effects. From the 15th century on, planning laws, plot sizes and the instability of the topsoil dictated that façades were largely uniform in size and built of lightweight brick or sandstone, with large windows to reduce the weight. Canal-house owners stamped their own individuality on the buildings, mainly through the use of decorative gables and cornices, ornate doorways and varying window shapes.

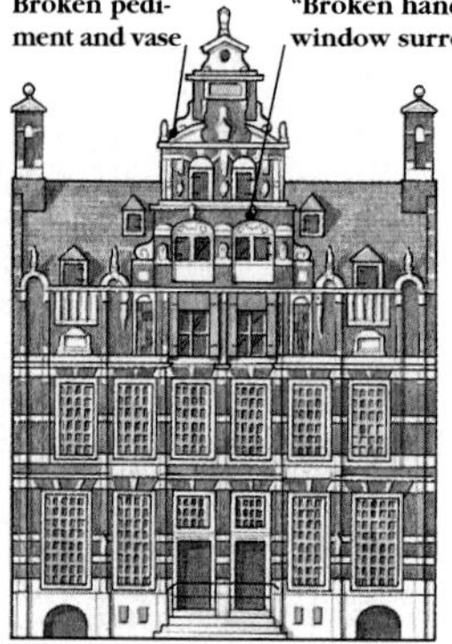

Bartolotti House *(1617)*
The contrasting brick-and-stone, flamboyant step gable, with its marble obelisk and scrolls, is typical of the Dutch Renaissance style of Hendrick de Keyser (see p90).

Felix Meritis Building *(1778)*
The Corinthian columns and triangular pediment are influenced by Classical architecture. This marks the building (see p113) *by Jacob Otten Husly as Dutch Classical in style.*

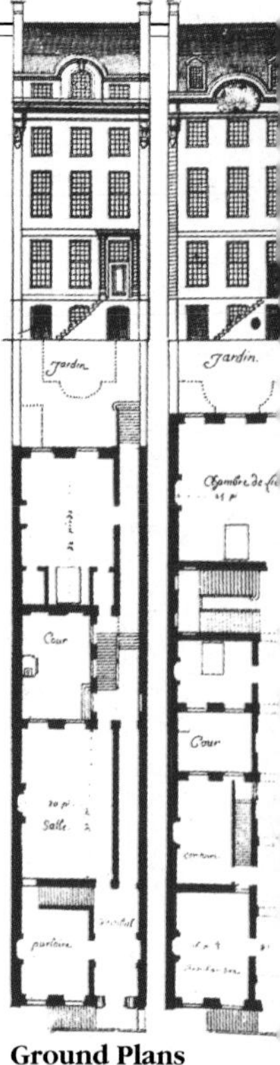

Ground Plans
Taxes were levied accord-ing to width of façade, s- canal houses were often long and narrow, with achterhuis *(back annex) used for offices and stora-*

CORNICES

Decorative top moldings, called cornices, became popular from 1690 onward when the fashion for gables declined. By the 19th century, they had become unadorned.

Louis XV-style with rococo balustrade (1739)

19th-century cornice with mansard roof

19th-century dentil (toothshaped) cornice

GABLES

The term gable refers to the front apex of a roof. It disguised the steepness of the roof under which goods were stored *(see pp20–21)*. In time, gables became decorated with scrolls, crests, and even coats of arms.

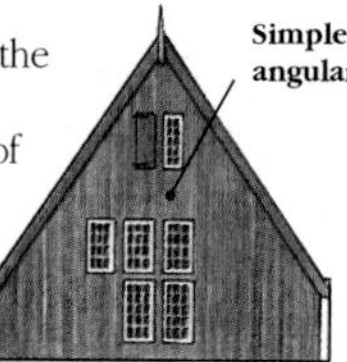

No. 34 Begijnhof (c. 1420) is one of few remaining timber houses *(see pp20–21)*.

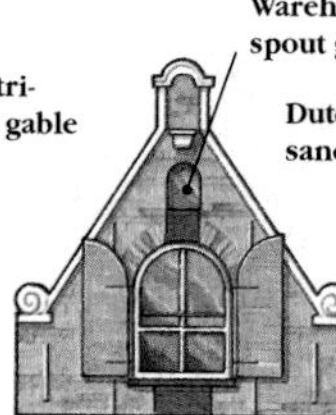

The style of gable on No. 213 Leliegracht (c. 1620) was used for warehouses.

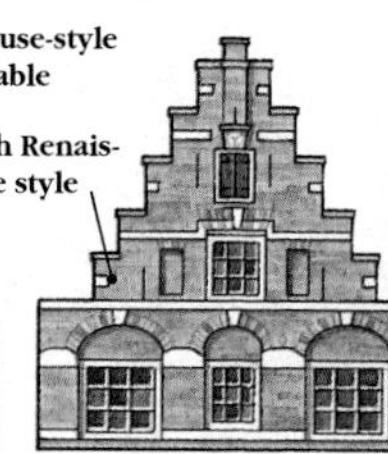

Step gables like the one on No. 2 Brouwersgracht were in vogue between 1600–65.

eaning Façades

anal houses were often built vith a deliberate tilt, allowing oods to be winched to the ttic without crashing against be windows. A law dating from 1565 restricted this lean to 1:25, o limit the risk of buildings ollapsing into the streets.

AMSTERDAM SCHOOL ARCHITECTURE

Michel de Klerk (1884–1923)

Members of the Amsterdam School, a loose grouping of like-minded and idealistic architects, built many distinctive developments between 1911 and 1923 *(see p151)*. They believed in the ability of unusual architecture to enhance residents' lives, many of whom were rescued from appalling slums. Michel de Klerk's development, Het Schip (1921), is on Hembrugstraat in northwest Amsterdam. It is typical of the lively style of the Amsterdam School, with sweeping façades, intricate brickwork and an exotic roofline.

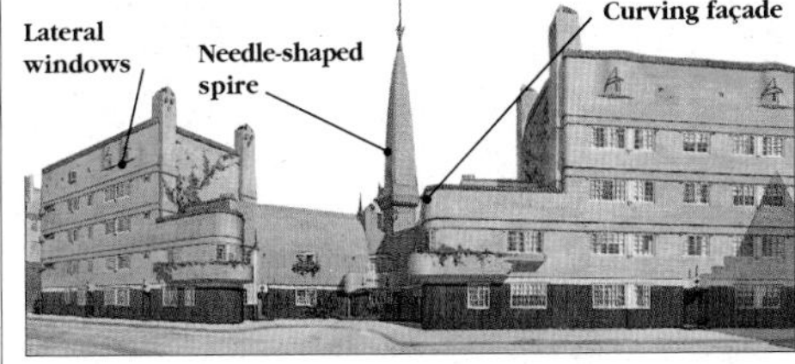

Het Schip (the ship), built to resemble an ocean-going liner

Dutch Hofjes

Poorhouses (hofjes) *were built hroughout the Netherlands by rich benefactors in the 17th and 18th centuries. By providing accommodations for the elderly and infirm* (see p93), *the* hofjes *marked the beginning of the Dutch welfare system.*

Sign of a sailor's hostel

Symbol of a dairyman

Noah's Ark – a refuge for the poor

WALL PLAQUES

Carved and painted stones were used to identify houses before street numbering was introduced in the 16th century. Many reflect the owner's occupation.

No. 419 Singel has a neck gable, a common feature rom 1640 to about 1840.

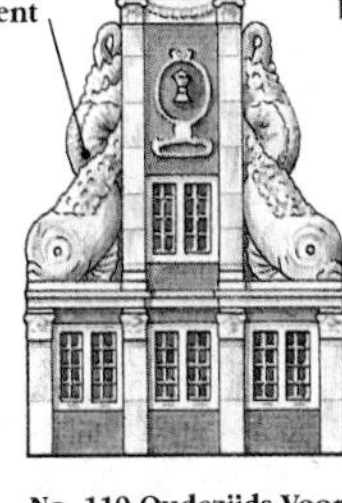

No. 119 Oudezijds Voorburgwal has an ornate 17th-century neck gable.

No. 57 Leliegracht has a plain bell gable, popular from the late 17th century.

No. 298 Oudezijds Voorburgwal has a bell gable dating from the 18th century.

Dam Square to Herengracht 487

THE WALK along Amsterdam's finest canals begins in Dam square *(see pp74)*. Following the gray dots on the map, leave the square past the Koninklijk Paleis *(see p74)*, cross Nieuwezijds Voorburgwal and Spuistraat down Paleisstraat, and turn left along the left bank of Singel, marked by purple dots. Further directions are incorporated into the route below.

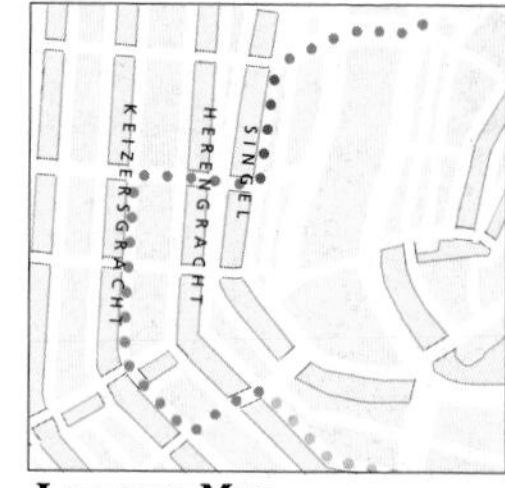

LOCATOR MAP

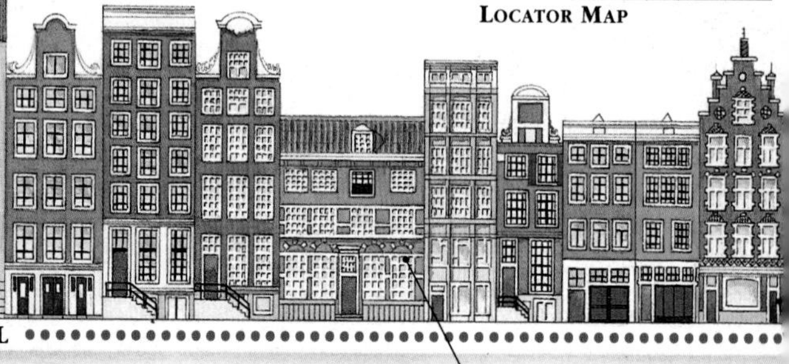

SINGEL

No. 239 Singel
AL Van Gendt (see p128) *designed this massive stone office block for trader Julius Carle Bunge. Known as the Bungehuis, it was completed in 1934.*

The double-fronted 17th-century canal house at No. 265 Singel has been rebuilt several times since it was first constructed.

The step gable at No. 279 Singel dates from the 19th century – most along this canal were built between 1600–65 *(see p96)*.

The three neck gables on Nos. 353–7 Keizersgracht date from the early 18th century *(see pp96–7)*.

Huidenstraat

No. 345a Keizersgracht is a narrow house sharing a cornice with its neighbor.

In 1708, No. 333 Keizersgracht was rebuilt for tax collector Jacob de Wilde. It has recently been converted into apartments.

The Sower at Arles *(1888)*
In March 1878, Vincent van Gogh (see pp134–5) *visited his uncle, who ran a bookstore and art dealership at No. 453 Keizersgracht.*

Keizersgracht

This photograph of the "emperor's canal" is taken at dusk, from the corner of Leidsegracht. The Westerkerk (see p90) *is in the distance.*

Behind the contrasting 18th-century façades at Nos. 317 and 319 Singel are two second-hand bookstores, which are well worth browsing through.

Directions to Keizersgracht

At Raamsteeg, cross the bridge, take the Oude Spiegelstraat, cross Herengracht and walk along Wolvenstraat to the left bank of Keizersgracht.

No. 399 Keizersgracht dates from 1665, but the façade was rebuilt in the 18th century. Its *achterhuis (see p96)* has been perfectly preserved.

No. 409 Keizersgracht

Built in 1671 on a triangular piece of land, this house contains a newly discovered, highly decorated wooden ceiling.

The wall plaque on No. 401 Keizersgracht shows a bird's-eye view of the port of Marseilles.

The plain, spout-gabled building *(see pp96–7)* at No. 403 Keizersgracht was originally a warehouse – a rarity in this predominantly residential area.

No. 469 Herengracht

The modern office block by KL Sijmons replaced the original 18th-century houses in 1971.

Jan Six II
The façade of No. 495 Herengracht was rebuilt and a balcony added by Jean Coulon in 1739 for burgomaster and art expert Jan Six (see p118).

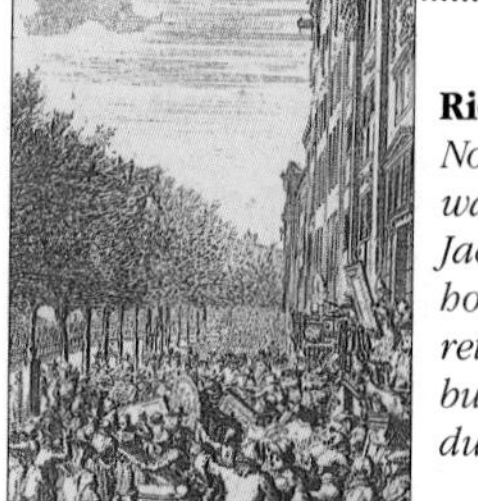

Riots in 1696
No. 507 Herengracht was home of mayor Jacob Boreel. His house was looted in retaliation for the burial tax he introduced to the city.

Three houses boasting typical neck gables, at Nos. 17, 19 and 21 Reguliersgracht, are now much sought after as prestigious addresses.

The Nieuwe Amsterdammer
A weekly magazine aimed at Amsterdam's Bolshevik intelligentsia was published at No. 19 Reguliersgracht from 1914–20.

The spout-gabled *(see pp96–7)* 16th-century warehouses at Nos. 11 and 13 Reguliersgracht are called the Sun and the Moon.

Houseboats on Prinsengracht
All registered houseboats have mailing addresses and are connected to the electricity mains.

Café Marcella, at No. 1047a Prinsengracht, is a typical local bar that has seating outside in summer.

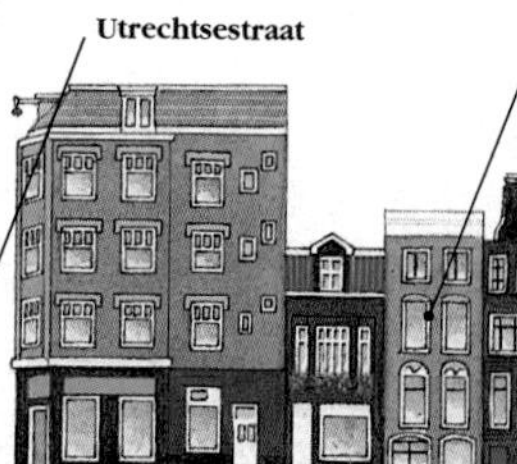

Herengracht 489 to the Amstel

THE SECOND HALF of the walk takes you along Herengracht, winding past grand, wide-fronted mansions. It then follows Reguliersgracht and Prinsengracht down to the Amstel. Many of Amsterdam's prominent citizens lived in this area in the 17th and 18th centuries. Most of these fine houses have recently been converted into banks, offices and exclusive apartment houses.

LOCATOR MAP

HERENGRACHT

The house at No. 491 Herengracht was built in 1671. The façade, rebuilt in the 18th century, is decorated with scrolls, vases and coats of arms.

No. 493 Herengracht
This 17th-century house was given a Louis XV-style façade in 1767 by Anthony van Hemert.

The Kattenkabinet at No. 497 Herengracht was created by financier B Meijer in 1984. It is devoted to exhibits featuring the cat in art.

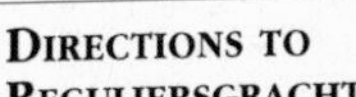

DIRECTIONS TO REGULIERSGRACHT

At Thorbeckeplein, take the bridge to the right, which marks the beginning of Reguliersgracht. Follow the left bank.

REGULIERSGRACHT

Amstelveld in the 17th Century
This etching shows the construction of a wooden church at Amstelveld, with sheep grazing in front of it.

Café Kort
The Amstelkerk (see p119) *has now been converted into a café and offices, while the square itself is a popular play area for local children.*

DIRECTIONS TO PRINSENGRACHT

Turn left by the church, take the left bank of Prinsengracht and walk to the Amstel river.

PRINSENGRACHT

The unusual office block at No. 313 Keizersgracht was built in 1914 by CN van Goor.

No. 319 Keizersgracht was built by the architect Philips Vingboons (1608–78) in 1639. It has a rare, highly decorated façade covered with scrolls, vases and garlands.

Peter the Great *(1716)*
The Russian tsar sailed up Keizersgracht to No. 317, the home of his friend Christoffel Brants. Legend says the tsar got drunk and kept the mayor waiting while at a civic reception.

The Louis XIV-style house at No. 323 Keizersgracht was built in 1728. It has a raised cornice embellished with two hoisting beams, one functional and the other to provide symmetry.

Leidsegracht
This canal marked the end of Daniel Stalpaert's city expansion plan of 1664 (see p24). *It has a mixture of fine 17th- and 18th-century canal houses.*

Art patron Jan Gildemester bought No. 475 Herengracht in 1792. Attributed to Jacob Otten Husly *(see p113)*, it has a stuccoed entrance hall.

Jan Corver
Burgomaster of Amsterdam 19 times, Corver built No. 479 Herengracht in 1665.

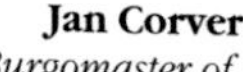

Turn over to continue walk at top of page 102 ▷

Tsar Peter *(see p101)* stayed at No. 527 Herengracht, home of the Russian ambassador, after a night of drunken revelry at No. 317 Keizersgracht in 1716.

Herengracht *(1790)*
A delicate watercolor by J Prins shows the "gentlemen's canal" from Koningsplein.

The asymmetrical building at Nos. 533–7 Herengracht was built in 1910 on the site of four former houses. From 1968–88 it was the Registry of Births, Marriages and Deaths.

The façades of Nos. 37 and 39 Reguliersgracht lean toward the water, showing the danger caused by subsidence when building on marshland.

Reguliersgracht Bridges
Seven arched stone bridges cross the canal, which was originally designed to be a street.

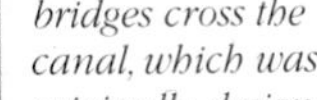

Keizersgracht

Nos. 1059 and 1061 Prinsengracht have tiny basement entrances, rare amid the splendor of the *Grachtengordel* *(see p44)*, where the height of the steps was considered an indication of wealth.

The sober spout-gabled building at No. 1075 Prinsengracht was built as a warehouse in 1690.

My Domestic Companions
Society portraitist Thérèse van Duyl Schwartze painted this picture in 1916. She owned Nos. 1087, 1089 and 1091 Prinsengracht, a handsome row of houses where she lived with her extended family.

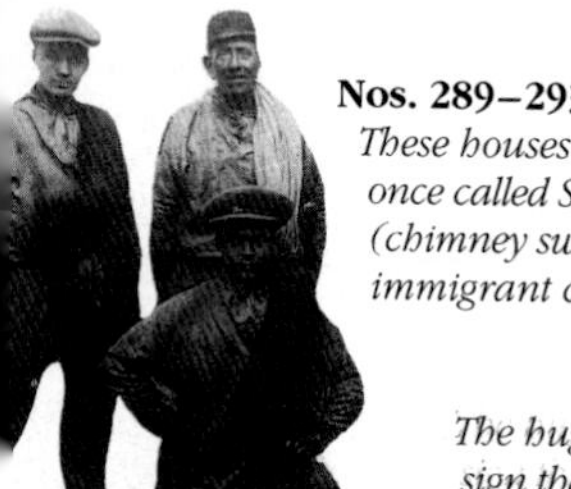

Nos. 289–293 Singel
These houses stand on an alley once called Schoorsteenvegerstag (chimney sweeps' lane), home to immigrant chimney sweeps.

Yab Yum Brothel
The huge lantern is the only sign that this famous brothel operates at No. 295 Singel.

The doorway of No. 365 Keizersgracht was taken from a poorhouse on Oudezijds Voorburgwal in the 19th century.

Jacob de Wit
The artist (see p122) *bought Nos. 383 and 385 Keizersgracht, living in No. 385 until his death in 1754.*

etz & Co is an elegant partment store at No. 455 izersgracht, on the corner Leidsestraat *(see p112).*

Gerrit Rietveld
Rietveld (see p136) *designed the cupola on Metz & Co, and a line of plain, inexpensive furniture for the store.*

De Vergulde Ster (gilded star), at No. 387 Keizersgracht, was built in 1668 by the municipal stonemasons' yard. It has an elongated neck gable *(see p96–7)* and narrow windows.

Directions to Herengracht

Turn left on to Leidsestraat, and walk to Koningsplein, then take the left bank of the Herengracht eastward toward Thorbeckeplein.

HERENGRACHT

Herengracht *(c. 1670)*
GA Berckheyde's etching shows one side of the canal bare of trees. Elms were later planted, binding the topsoil, to strengthen the buildings' foundations.

No. 543 Herengracht was built in 1743 under the supervision of owner Sibout Bollard. It has a double-fronted façade with an ornate balustrade and decorated balcony.

The small houses at the corner of Herengracht and Thorbeckeplein contrast with the grand neighboring buildings.

Isaac Gosschalk
The architect designed Nos. 57, 59 and 63 Reguliersgracht in 1879. They have ornate stone, brick and woodwork façades.

Reguliers Monastery
This engraving by J Wagenaar (1760) shows the monastery that once stood on the canal.

The Amstel
Turn left and follow the broad sweep of the Amstel river, up past the Magere Brug (see p119) *on up Rokin and back to the Dam, where the walk began.*

CENTRAL CANAL RING

THE EXTENSION OF Amsterdam's three major canals continued from the early 17th century *(see pp24–5)*, as the merchant classes sought to escape the overcrowding and industrial squalor in the old city, around the Amstel. They bought plots of land along the new extensions to the Herengracht, Keizersgracht and Prinsengracht, and in the 1660s the wealthiest built opulent houses on a stretch of Herengracht known as the Golden Bend. Designed and decorated by the best architects of the day, such as Philips Vingboons *(see p101)*, the mansions built here were often twice the width of standard canal houses *(see p96)*. Today, many of these grand buildings are owned by institutions. Other architectural landmarks include the Neo-Gothic Krijtberg, with its soaring steeples, the imposing Paleis van Justitie and the Art Nouveau American Hotel overlooking the busy Leidseplein.

Pillar decoration on the Felix Meritis Building

SIGHTS AT A GLANCE

Historic Buildings and Monuments
American Hotel 2
Paleis van Justitie 5
Metz & Co 7

Museums
Bijbels Museum 10

Canals and Squares
Leidseplein 1
Leidsegracht 6
Golden Bend 8

Churches
Krijtberg 9

Markets
Looier Kunst en Antiekcentrum 11

Clubs and Theaters
De Melkweg 3
Stadsschouwburg 4
Felix Meritis Building 12

GETTING THERE

It takes about 15 minutes to walk from the Dam to Leidseplein via the Leidsegracht. Leidseplein can be reached by trolleys Nos. 1, 2, 5 and 11 terminating at Centraal Station. Nos. 6, 7 and 10 also cross the square from the north and west going east toward Plantage.

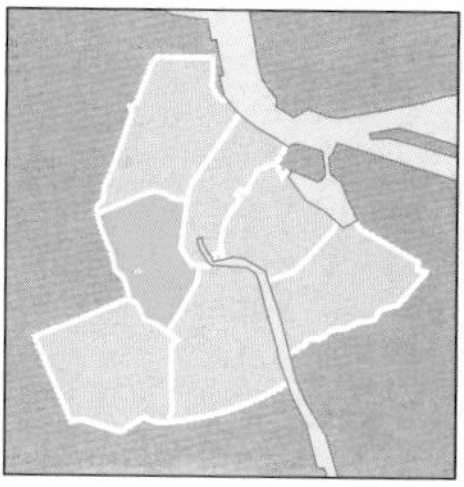

0 meters 250
0 yards 250

KEY

Street-by-Street map *See pp108–9*
Trolley stop
Parking
Museum boat boarding point

◁ **Cyclist crossing one of the many bridges on Leidsegracht**

Street-by-Street: Leidsebuurt

THE AREA around Leidseplein is one of Amsterdam's busiest nightspots. There are various movies to be seen at the many movie theaters, plays at the Stadsschouwburg and lively music programs at De Melkweg. In contrast, there is fine architecture to admire around the Canal Ring, such as the Paleis van Justitie on Prinsengracht, the lavish De Krijtberg on the Singel and many grand houses on the Golden Bend.

Leidseplein street performer

Bijbels Museum
In addition to bibles, there are several archaeological finds from Egypt and the Middle East on display here ❿

Leidsegracht
Cut in 1664, this canal was the main waterway for barges heading for Leiden ❻

Paleis van Justitie
This vast Empire-style building contains Amsterdam's Court of Appeals ❺

Stadsschouwburg
The city's football team, Ajax, uses the theater's balcony to greet fans after winning important games ❹

★ American Hotel
The hotel's recently renovated Café Américain has a fine Art Deco interior and is a popular place to while away an afternoon (see p221) ❷

De Melkweg
This converted milk-processing factory and former hippie hangout survives as one of Amsterdam's key spots for alternative entertainment ❸

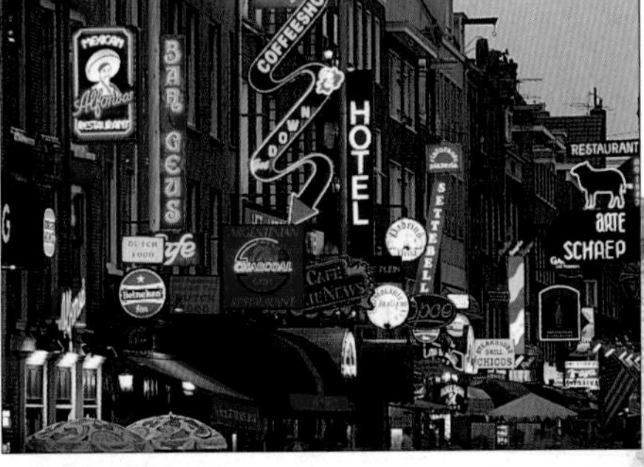

Leidseplein
Young people flock to this square to watch street performances and enjoy the vibrant nightlife ❶

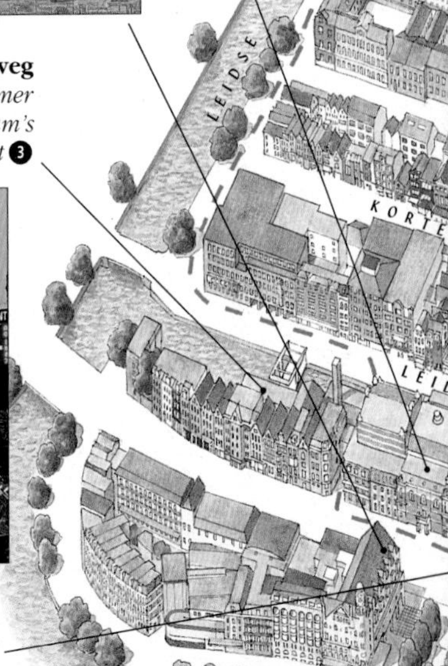

Locator Map
See Street Finder, *maps 4 & 7*

★ De Krijtberg
This Neo-Gothic church houses an ornate wooden carving of the Immaculate Conception ❾

★ Golden Bend
Classical columns and façades on this part of the Herengracht powerfully recall the city's wealth ❽

Metz & Co
The postmodern café at the top of this elegant department store offers one of the best views of Amsterdam ❼

Key

– – – Suggested route

0 meters 100

0 yards 100

Star Sights

- ★ **American Hotel**
- ★ **Golden Bend**
- ★ **De Krijtberg**

Leidseplein ❶

Map 4 E2. [tram] *1, 2, 5, 6, 7, 10, 11.*

THE LEIDSEPLEIN IS Amsterdam's busiest intersection and center of day- and nighttime entertainment.

The square developed in the 17th century as a parking lot on the outskirts of the city – farmers and peasants would leave their carts here before entering the center. It gets its name from the Leidsepoort, the massive city gate demolished in 1862 that marked the beginning of the route southwest to Leiden.

During the day, the square is buzzing with fire-eaters, street musicians and other performers playing to café audiences. At night, it is the focal point for the city's youth, who hang out in the many bars, cafés, restaurants, nightclubs and theaters in and around the square. The revelry often goes on until the early hours.

Street performer in Leidseplein

American Hotel ❷

Leidsekade 97. **Map** 4 E2. [tel] *624 5322.* [tram] *1, 2, 5, 6, 7, 10, 11.* [café] *See **Where to Stay** p221.*

LEIDSEPLEIN WAS quickly becoming a fashionable entertainment area when the American Hotel was built overlooking it in 1882. The hotel got its name because its architect, W Steinigeweg who studied hotel design in the United States, adorned his Neo-Gothic creation with a bronze eagle, wooden figures of Native Americans and murals of American landscapes. Within 20 years it was deemed *passé* and the hotel was demolished. The present building is by Willem Kromhout (1864–1940) and was completed in 1902. His design marked a radical departure, interpreting the Art Nouveau style in an angular Dutch fashion. The building's turreted exterior and elaborate brickwork anticipated the progressive Amsterdam School *(see p97)*. A carved stone plaque on the Leidseplein side of the hotel shows the original building.

The Café Américain *(see p46)*, decorated in Art Deco style, remains one of the most elegant in Amsterdam to enjoy a cup of coffee. It retains its period furnishings, stained-glass windows and lamp shades. The rest of the hotel was redecorated in the 1980s. Samples of the original furnishings are in the Rijksmuseum.

The American Hotel seen from Singelgracht

De Melkweg ❸

Lijnbaansgracht 234a. **Map** 4 E2. [tel] *624 1777.* [tram] *1, 2, 5, 6, 7, 10, 11.* **Box office** [open] *noon–5:30pm, 7:30pm–1am Mon–Sat.* **Performances**: *9:30pm approx.* [wheelchair] [ticket] *See **Entertainment** p249.*

DE MELKWEG (Milky Way) is a multimedia center located in a former dairy behind the Stadsschouwburg. It opened in 1970 and soon gained a dazzling reputation as an alternative cultural meeting place. Nowadays, it offers a wide range of entertainment, including live music, movies, theater, dancing and a photographic gallery. The theater has a stage for new international acts, and De Melkweg's annual World Roots Festival *(see p51)* promotes the latest in world music to a wide audience.

De Melkweg's star-lit façade

Stadsschouwburg ❹

Leidseplein 26. **Map** 4 E2.
624 2311. *1, 2, 5, 6, 7, 10, 11.*
Box office *10am–6pm Mon–Sat. See **Entertainment** p246.*

THIS NEO-RENAISSANCE building is the most recent of three successive municipal theaters in the city, its predecessors having burned down. The theater was designed by Jan Springer, whose other credits include the Frascati building on Oxford Street in London, and AL van Gendt, who was responsible for the Concertgebouw *(see p128)* and for part of the Centraal Station *(see p79)*. The planned decoration of the theater's redbrick exterior was never carried out because of budget cuts. This, combined with a hostile public reaction to his theater, forced a disillusioned Springer into virtual retirement. Public disgust was due, however, to the theater management's policy of restricting use of the front door to patrons who had bought expensive tickets.

Until the Muziektheater was completed in 1986 *(see p63)*, the Stadsschouwburg was home to the Dutch national ballet and opera companies. Today, the theater stages plays by local drama groups such as the resident Toneelgroep, and international companies, including many English-language productions. The theater has become a favorite spot for Amsterdam's premier football (soccer) club, Ajax, and its supporters. Whenever this most popular of teams wins an important competition, the players gather on the theater's balcony to greet their fans, who pack Leidseplein to see their heroes.

Paleis van Justitie ❺

Prinsengracht 434–436. **Map** 4 E1.
541 2111. *1, 2, 5, 11.*
to the public.

CONVERSION of the former city orphanage into the Empire-style Palace of Justice, designed by the city architect Jan de Greef, was completed in 1829. Balustrades run along the roofline and the monotony of the imposing Neo-Classical façade is broken up by Corinthian pilasters. The building houses Amsterdam's Court of Appeal, and the courtrooms inside are set around two open yards.

The orphanage opened in 1666 with space for 800 children. By 1811, the building housed more than 2,000, over half of the city's orphans. To control their rising numbers, a royal decree was passed permitting the relocation of orphans to other towns. When this act was implemented in 1822, there was widespread protest from local people and accusations that the authorities had stolen children. Once all the children were relocated, the orphanage was closed.

Leidsegracht ❻

Map 4 E1. *1, 2, 5, 6, 7, 10, 11.*

No. 39 Leidsegracht, on the right

THE LEIDSEGRACHT was for a few years the main route for barges from Amsterdam to Leiden. It was cut in 1664 to a plan by city architect Daniel Stalpaert, and is now one of the city's best addresses.

Cornelis Lely, who drew up the original plans for draining the Zuiderzee *(see p165)*, was born at No. 39 in 1854. A wall plaque shows Lely poised between the Zuiderzee and the newly created IJsselmeer.

The elongated Neo-Classical façade of the Paleis van Justitie, converted from the city orphanage

Metz & Co ❼

Keizersgracht 455. **Map** 7 A5. *624 8810.* *1, 2, 5, 11.* *11am–6pm Mon, 9:30am–6pm Tue–Wed, Fri–Sat, 9:30am–9pm Thu.* *public hols.* See ***Cafés and Bars*** *p49.*

ON ITS COMPLETION in 1891, this was the tallest commercial building in Amsterdam, measuring 26 m (85 ft). Designed by J van Looy, it was built for the New York Life Insurance Company, whose name still appears above the door. Since 1908, it has housed the luxury store Metz & Co. In 1933, a splendid glass cupola by Gerrit Rietveld *(see p136)* was added. Liberty of London, which bought Metz & Co in 1973, renovated the building and commissioned Cees Dam to design a café on the sixth floor. When the skies are clear, the views across the city from the café and the cupola are superb.

The 1933 cupola of Metz & Co

Golden Bend ❽

Map 7 A5. *1, 2, 4, 5, 11, 13, 14, 16, 17, 24, 25.* **Kattenkabinet** Herengracht 497. *626 5378.* *sporadically for special exhibitions.*

THE STRETCH of the Herengracht between Leidsestraat and Vijzelstraat was first called the Golden Bend in the 17th century, because of the great wealth of the shipbuilders, merchants and politicians who originally lived along here. Most of the opulent mansions have been turned into offices or banks, but their elegance indicates the lifestyle of the first residents. The majority of the buildings are faced with sandstone, which was more expensive than brick and had to be imported. The earliest mansions date from the 1660s. One very fine and largely untouched example is No. 412, designed by Philips Vingboons in 1664 *(see p99)*. Building continued into the 18th century, with the Louis XIV style predominating. No. 475 is typical of this trend. Built in 1730, it is often called the jewel of canal houses. Two sculpted female figures over the front door adorn its monumental sandstone façade. The ornate mansion at No. 452 is a good example of a 19th-century conversion. The Kattenkabinet (cat museum) at No. 497 Herengracht is one of the few houses on the Golden Bend accessible to the public. It is worth visiting for its collection of feline artifacts, views of its formal garden and paintings by Jacob de Wit. The Kattenkabinet is only open to the public, however, during special exhibitions.

Window decoration on No. 475 Herengracht

De Krijtberg ❾

Singel 442–448. **Map** 7 A4. *623 1923.* *1, 2, 5, 11.* *for church services only.* *8:15am, 9:30am, 12:30pm, 5:45pm Mon–Fri; 5:15pm Sat; 8am, 9:30am, 11am, 12:30pm, 5:15pm Sun.*

AN IMPRESSIVE Neo-Gothic church, the Krijtberg (or chalk hill) replaced a clandestine Jesuit chapel *(see p84)* in 1884. It is officially known as Franciscus Xaveriuskerk, after St. Francis Xavier, one of the founding Jesuit monks.

Designed by Alfred Tepe, the church was built on the site of three houses; the presbytery beside the church is on the site of two other houses, one of which had belonged to a chalk merchant – hence the church's nickname. The back of the church is wider than the front, extending into the space once occupied by the original gardens. The narrowness of the façade is redeemed by its two magnificent, soaring, steepled towers.

The ornate interior contains good examples of Neo-Gothic design. The stained-glass windows, walls painted in bright colors and liberal use of gold are in striking contrast to the city's austere Protestant churches. A statue of St. Francis Xavier stands in front and to the left of the high altar; one of St. Ignatius, founder of the Jesuits, stands to the right.

Near the pulpit is an 18th-century wooden statue of the Immaculate Conception, showing Mary trampling the serpent. It used to be housed in the original hidden chapel.

The twin-steepled façade of the Neo-Gothic Krijtberg

Bijbels Museum ❿

Herengracht 366–368. **Map** 7 A4. *624 7949.* *1, 2, 5, 11.* *Herengracht/Leidsegracht.* *10am–5pm Tue–Sat, 1–5pm Sun.* *Jan 1, Apr 30.*

REVEREND Leendert Schouten founded the museum in 1860, when he put his private collection of biblical artifacts on public display. In 1975, the museum moved to its present site, two 17th-century houses in a group of four designed by Philips Vingboons.

The Bible Museum is packed with showcases full of artifacts that attempt to give historical weight to Bible stories. Displays feature models of historical sites, such as King Solomon's Temple, and there are archaeological finds from Egypt and the Middle East. Highlights include a copy of the Book of Isaiah from the Dead Sea Scrolls, and the Delft Bible, dating from 1477, which was the first Bible to be printed in the Netherlands.

Looier Kunst en Antiekcentrum ⓫

Elandsgracht 109. **Map** 4 D1.
624 9038. *7, 10, 17.*
11am–5pm Sat–Wed, 11am–9pm Thu. *public hols.*
Rommelmarkt Looiersgracht 38.
11am–5pm Sat–Thu.

A VAST NETWORK of ground-floor rooms in a block of houses has been turned into the Looier Antiques Center. The market, named after its location near the Looiersgracht (tanners' canal), boasts the largest collection of art and antiques in the Netherlands.

It has around 100 stalls selling everything from glassware to dolls. On Saturdays, anyone can rent a stall here; once a month the facility is rent-free. Lively bridge sessions, open to all, are always going on. On the Looiersgracht, a small street door opens into the Rommelmarkt (rummage market), a long, dimly lit corridor lined with cheaper items: old toys, secondhand records and bric-a-brac. It may even be possible to find a genuine antique hidden among the *rommel* at the far end of the corridor. Upstairs more items are laid out on tables.

The Palladian façade of the 18th-century Felix Meritis Building

Felix Meritis Building ⓬

Keizersgracht 324. **Map** 1 B5.
626 2321. *1, 2, 5, 11, 13, 14, 17.* **Box office & inquiries** *9am–9pm Tue–Sat. See* ***Entertainment*** *p246.*

THIS NEO-CLASSICAL building, with its splendid Palladian façade, is best viewed from the opposite side of the canal *(see p96)*. Designed by Jacob Otten Husly, it opened in 1778 as a science and arts center set up by the Felix Meritis Society. The name means "happiness through merit." An association of wealthy citizens, the society was founded by watchmaker Willem Writs in 1777, at the time of the Dutch Enlightenment *(see pp28–9)*.

Five reliefs on the façade, between the second and third stories, proclaim the society's interest in natural science, drawing, trade, music and letters. Inside, the building contains an observatory, library, laboratories and a small concert hall. Mozart, Edvard Grieg and Johannes Brahms are among the distinguished musicians who have performed here.

In the 19th century, the building became Amsterdam's main cultural center and the elliptical shape of its concert hall inspired the design of the Concertgebouw *(see p128)*. The Felix Meritis Society disbanded in 1889 and the building was taken over by a printing company.

The Dutch Communist Party (CPN) occupied the premises from 1946, but cultural prominence was restored in the 1970s when the Shaffy Theatre Company used the building as a theater and won acclaim for its avant-garde productions.

The building is now used by a reconstituted Felix Meritis Foundation, which specializes in progressive theater productions. From July to September, the Amsterdam Summer University holds courses here in the arts and sciences. Evening events and performances are open to everyone.

Vintage robots on sale at the Looier Kunst en Antiekcentrum

EASTERN CANAL RING

STRETCHING SOUTH from Munttoren, part of a former city gate, this area lies wholly beyond the line of the medieval city wall. From the 1660s, the *Grachtengordel* *(see p43)* was extended farther east toward the Amstel. One of Amsterdam's prettiest canals, Reguliersgracht with its seven bridges, was cut at this time. Today, houses on the major Canal Ring, such as the Van Loon, with its grand façade and fine interior, convey a sense of life in the Golden Age *(see pp24–7)*. Beyond is the 19th-century De Pijp, a working-class district built to relieve the overcrowded Jordaan. De Pijp is now a lively multicultural area, and home to the Albert Cuypmarkt, the city's biggest street market.

Sun motif on a café in Reguliersdwarsstraat

SIGHTS AT A GLANCE

Historic Buildings and Bridges
Blauwbrug 3
Magere Brug 5
Amstelkerk 6
Munttoren 11

Movie Theaters
Tuschinski Theater 10

Squares and Markets
Rembrandtplein 1
Albert Cuypmarkt 7
Bloemenmarkt 12

Museums
Museum Willet-Holthuysen pp120–21 2
Six Collection 4
Heineken Brouwerij 8
Museum van Loon 9

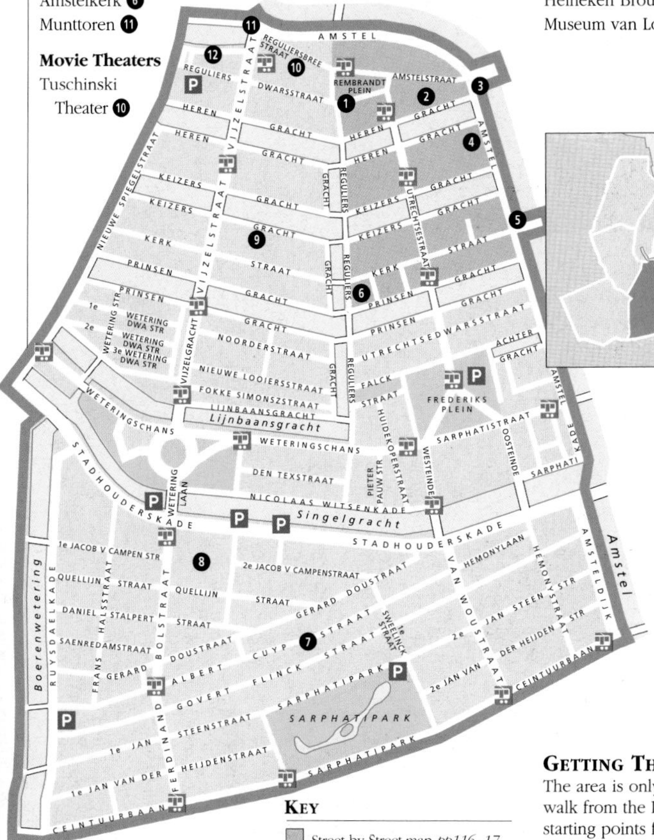

KEY

Street-by-Street map *pp116–17*

Trolley stop

Parking

0 meters 250

0 yards 250

GETTING THERE

The area is only a 10-minute walk from the Dam. Good starting points for exploring this area are the Frederiksplein (trolleys 4, 6, 7 and 10) and the Muntplein (trolleys 4, 9, 14, 16, 24 and 25).

◁ **Colorful display of flowers at the Albert Cuypmarkt, including roses, lilies and sunflowers**

Street-by-Street: Amstelveld

The eastern end of the *Grachtengordel* is quiet and largely residential, especially around the Amstelveld *(see p45)*, with its pretty wooden church and houseboats. A short walk will take you past numerous stores and cafés, particularly on the bustling Rembrandtplein. As you wander down the broad sweep of the Amstel river, Amsterdam suddenly loses its village atmosphere and begins to feel like a city.

★ Rembrandtplein
Looking on to the former Botermarkt (butter market) and the cast-iron statue of Rembrandt, there are dozens of cafés dating from the 19th century, including De Kroon at No. 17 (see p47) ❶

Café Schiller
(see p49)

★ Museum Willet-Holthuysen
This double canal house contains a number of period rooms, including the fine 19th-century-style garden room that looks out on to the restored 18th-century formal garden ❷

Amstelkerk
This wooden church was meant to be a temporary structure while money was raised to build a big new church on Rembrandtplein, but the grand plan fell through. Today, the Amstelkerk houses offices and a café (see p119) ❻

AMSTEL
KEIZERSGRACHT
KERKSTRAAT
PRINSENGRACHT
ENGRACHT

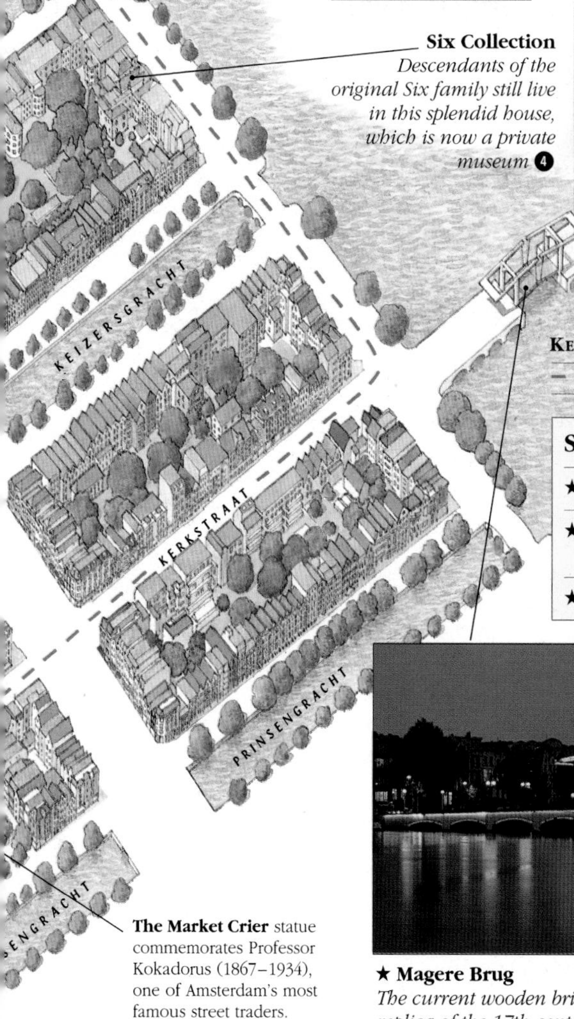

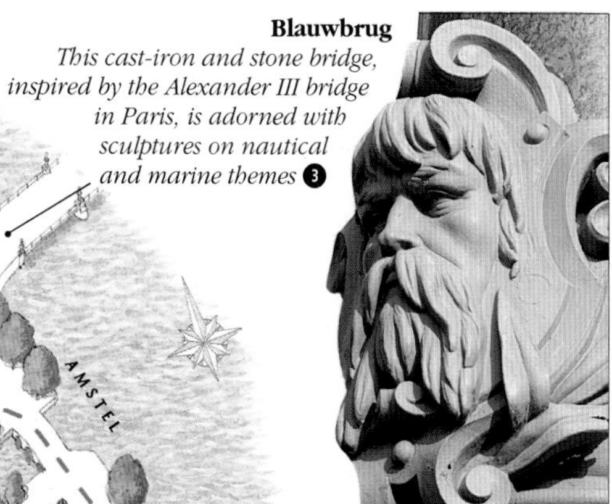

Blauwbrug
This cast-iron and stone bridge, inspired by the Alexander III bridge in Paris, is adorned with sculptures on nautical and marine themes ❸

CENTRAL CANAL RING
EASTERN CANAL RING

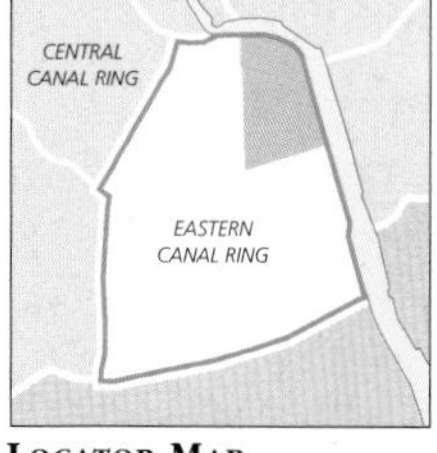

Locator Map
See Street Finder maps 5 & 8

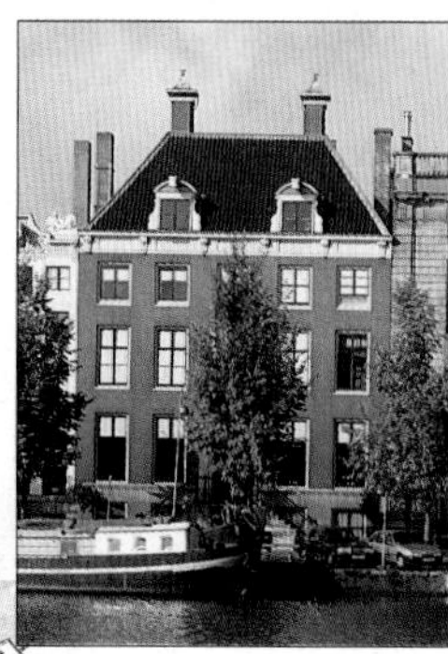

Six Collection
Descendants of the original Six family still live in this splendid house, which is now a private museum ❹

0 meters 100

0 yards 100

Key

– – – Suggested route

Star Sights

- ★ **Rembrandtplein**
- ★ **Museum Willet-Holthuysen**
- ★ **Magere Brug**

The Market Crier statue commemorates Professor Kokadorus (1867–1934), one of Amsterdam's most famous street traders.

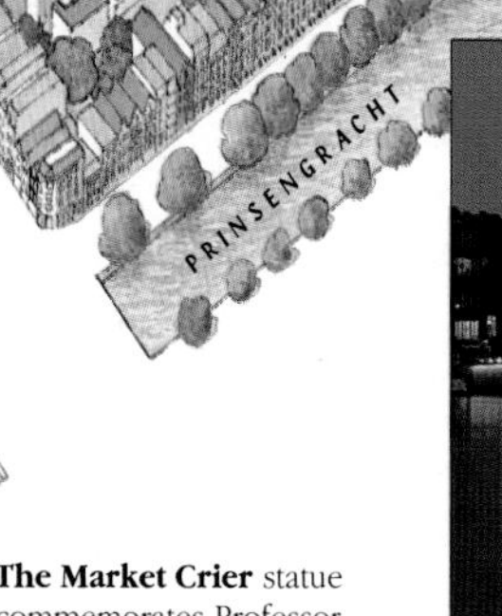

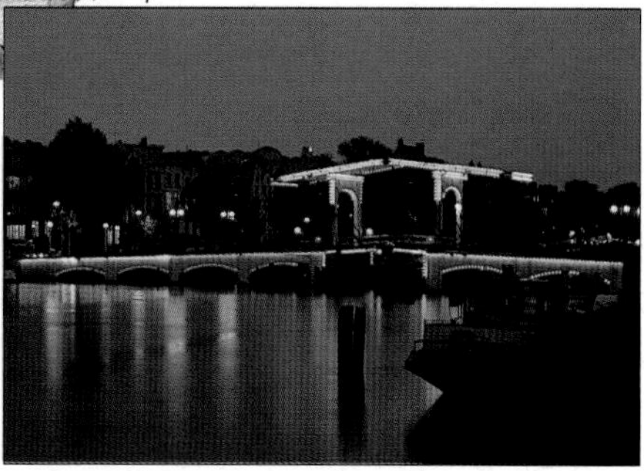

★ Magere Brug
The current wooden bridge is a 20th-century replica of the 17th-century original, but its mechanical drive was only installed in 1994 ❺

Rembrandtplein ❶

Map 7 C5. 🚋 *4, 9, 14.*

FORMERLY CALLED the Botermarkt, after the butter market held here until the mid-19th century, this square acquired its present name when the statue of Rembrandt was erected in 1876.

Soon afterward, Rembrandtplein developed into a center for nightlife with the opening of various hotels and cafés. The Mast (renamed the Mille Colonnes Hotel) dates from 1889, and the Schiller Karena hotel *(see p221)* and the Café Schiller *(see p49)* both opened in 1892. De Kroon *(see p47)*, which epitomizes a typical grand café, dates from 1898. The popularity of Rembrandtplein has persevered, and the café terraces are packed during summer with people enjoying a pleasant drink and watching the world go by.

Two of the many outdoor cafés on Rembrandtplein

Museum Willet-Holthuysen ❷

See pp120–21.

Blauwbrug ❸

Amstel. **Map** 8 D5. 🚋 *9, 14.* Ⓜ *Waterlooplein.*

THE BLAUWBRUG (Blue Bridge) is thought to have gotten its name from the color of the wooden bridge that originally crossed this particular stretch of the Amstel in the 17th century. This bridge is made of stone and was built in preparation for the World Exhibition, which attracted thousands of visitors to Amsterdam in 1883.

The Blauwbrug is decorated with sculptures of medieval boats, fish and the imperial crown of Amsterdam and is surmounted by ornate lamps. The design was inspired by the plans for the elaborate Alexander III bridge in Paris.

Detail of the ornate stone carving on the Blauwbrug

Six Collection ❹

Amstel 218. **Map** 8 D5. ☎ *673 2121.* 🚋 *4, 9, 14.* ◯ *10am & 11am Wed & Fri.* ● *public hols.* *obligatory; apply to the Rijksmuseum information desk for tickets.*

THE SIX COLLECTION comprises an accumulation of fine paintings, furniture, silverware and porcelain objects belonging to the descendants of Jan Six (1618–1700). He was one of the richest men in the city, who, it was said, had "innumerable boxes of money" at his disposal. Before he was appointed burgomaster of Amsterdam in 1691, Jan Six had been a friend and patron of Rembrandt *(see p62)*.

The father-in-law of Jan Six was the subject of Rembrandt's painting *The Anatomy Lesson of Professor Tulp*, now in the Mauritshuis *(see pp188-9)*. Six's extensive art collection includes two portraits by the artist: one of Six himself, and the other of his mother, Anna Wijmer. The painting of Jan Six is considered by many to be Rembrandt's finest portrait. It is also thought that this work was Rembrandt's way of paying back a 1,000-guilder loan he had received from Six.

In addition to the Rembrandt paintings, the Six collection also includes works by other Dutch masters such as Frans Hals *(see pp178–9)*, Thomas de Keyser (1596–1667) and Albert Cuyp *(see p120)*. Descendants of Jan Six still live in part of the building, which was designed by Adriaan Dortsman. Consequently the museum's opening hours are limited.

Before visiting the Six Collection, visitors must first ask for a letter of introduction, which is obtainable upon presentation of a passport at the information desk of the Rijksmuseum *(see p130–33).*

Magere Brug ❺

Amstel. **Map** 5 B3. 🚋 *4.*

OF AMSTERDAM'S 1,400 or so bridges, the Magere Brug (Skinny Bridge) is the city's best-known. The original drawbridge was built in about 1670. Tradition relates that it was named after two sisters called Mager, who lived on either side of the Amstel. However, it appears more likely that the bridge acquired the name from its narrow *(mager)* design.

The present drawbridge was put up in 1969 and, though wider than the original, it still conforms to the traditional double-leaf style. Constructed from African azobe wood, it was intended to last for 50 years. About every 20 minutes, the bridge master has to let boats through the bridge. He then jumps on his bicycle and opens up the Amstelsluizen *(see p145)* and Hoge Sluis.

Magere Brug, a traditional double-leaf Dutch drawbridge

The Amstelkerk, built as a temporary church in the 17th century

Amstelkerk ❻

Amstelveld 10. **Map** 5 A3. ☎ *623 8138.* 🚋 *4.* ● *to the public except for monthly exhibitions.* 📷

DESIGNED by Daniel Stalpaert in 1668, the wooden Amstelkerk was only intended to be a temporary structure, while money was raised for a massive new church on the Botermarkt (now Rembrandtplein). Sufficient funds for the grand project were never forthcoming however, so the Amstelkerk was maintained. In 1825 the Protestant church authorities attempted to raise money to renovate the Amstelkerk's plain interior in a Neo-Gothic style. It was not until 1840, however, when Frederica Elisabeth Cramer donated 25,000 guilders to the project, that the renovation actually began. The interior walls, pulpit and pews, and the organ made by Jonathan Batz, all date from this period. The windows are older, dating from 1821.

In the late 1960s, the Amstelkerk underwent a substantial conversion, costing 4 million guilders. Glass-walled offices were installed inside the building. However, services are still held in the Amstelkerk, and the nave, which was preserved in all its Neo-Gothic glory, now houses the charming Kort restaurant and café *(see p235).*

How the Magere Brug Works

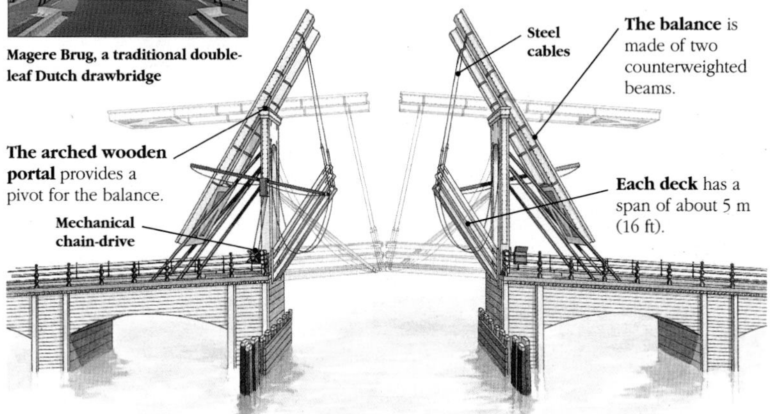

Museum Willet-Holthuysen ❷

Statue of Paris on stairway

NAMED AFTER its last residents, the museum allows the visitor a glimpse into the lives of the merchant class who lived in luxury along the *Grachtengordel* (Canal Ring). The house was built in 1685 and became the property of coal magnate Pieter Holthuysen (1788–1858) in 1855. It was passed to his daughter Sandrina and her art-connoisseur husband, Abraham Willet – both fervent collectors of paintings, glass, silver and ceramics. When Sandrina died childless in 1895, the house and its many treasures were left to the city. Some of the rooms remain unchanged, while others, such as the kitchen and Garden Room, have been restored in the style of the 18th century.

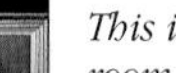

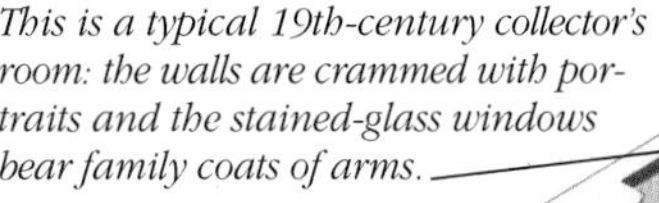

Collector's Room

This is a typical 19th-century collector's room: the walls are crammed with portraits and the stained-glass windows bear family coats of arms.

★ Silver Collection

A superb collection of silver was amassed by the Willet-Holthuysen family. This 17th-century silver spice holder is in the shape of a game bird.

★ Blue Room

Hung with heavy blue damask, the room boasts a chimney piece by Jacob de Wit (see p122)*, and was the exclusive preserve of the men of the house.*

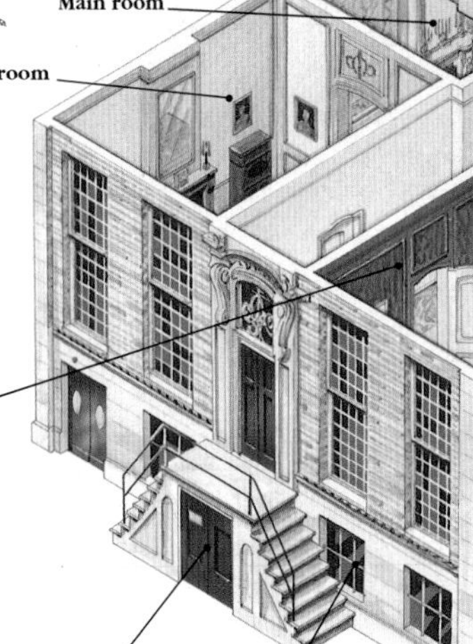

Garden Room
Now repainted in its original green, the Garden Room offers views over the intricate knot garden, laid out in 18th-century French style. It was used by the family to entertain guests for tea.

VISITORS' CHECKLIST

Herengracht 605. **Map** 8 D5.
523 1870. 4, 9, 14.
10am–5pm Mon–Fri, 11am–5pm Sat & Sun. Jan 1, Apr 30, Dec 25. 

The Antiquities Room was furnished in the last quarter of the 19th century in Dutch Renaissance style *(see p96)*, very popular at this time.

Bedroom

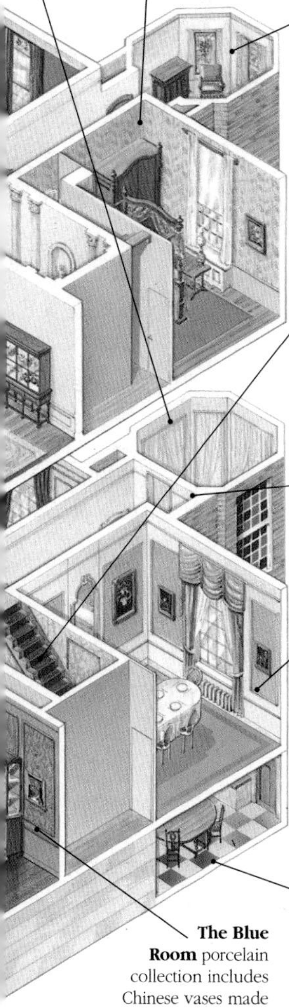

Staircase
The staircase was built in 1740 and has an elaborate gilded balustrade. The lower walls are painted to look like marble.

Hall

★ Dining Room
The wallpaper is a careful copy of the 18th-century silk original. The elaborate 275-piece Meissen dinner service provided up to 24 places.

Kitchen
The 18th-century kitchen has been restored using items salvaged from similar houses, including the sink and pump.

The Blue Room porcelain collection includes Chinese vases made during the Kangxi dynasty (1662–1722).

STAR FEATURES

- ★ **Blue Room**
- ★ **Dining Room**
- ★ **Silver Collection**

Albert Cuypmarkt 7

Albert Cuypstraat. **Map** 5 A5. *4, 16, 24, 25.* *10am–4:30pm Mon–Sat.*

THE MARKET running along Albert Cuypstraat began trading in 1904, shortly after the expansion of the city was completed. The wide street, once a canal, is named after the Dutch landscape painter Albert Cuyp (1620–91). It is located in the Pijp district, originally built for workers.

Described by the stallholders as "the best-known market in Europe," it attracts about 20,000 visitors on weekdays and often twice as many on Saturdays. Goods for sale at the 325 stalls range from fish, poultry, cheese, fruit and vegetables to clothes, and prices are among the best in town.

Smoked fish in Albert Cuypmarkt

Heineken Brouwerij 8

Stadhouderskade 78. **Map** 4 F3. *523 9666.* *6, 7, 10, 16, 24, 25.* *Jun–mid-Sep: 9:30am, 11am, 1pm, 2:30pm Mon–Fri; Jul–Aug: also noon, 2pm Sat; mid-Sep–end May: 9:30am, 11am.*

GERARD ADRIAAN HEINEKEN founded the Heineken company in 1864 when he bought the 16th-century Hooiberg (haystack) brewery on the Nieuwezijds Voorburgwal. His readiness to adapt to new methods and bring in foreign brewers established him as a major force in Amsterdam's profitable beer industry.

In 1988, the company finally stopped producing beer in its massive brick brewery on Stadhouderskade, because it was unable to keep up with the demand. Production is now concentrated in two breweries, one in Zoeterwoude, near Den Haag, the other in Den Bosch. Today, Heineken produces around half of the beer sold in Amsterdam, has production facilities in dozens of countries and exports all over the world.

The Stadhouderskade building now houses the Heineken Reception Center, open since 1991. The tour takes visitors through the tiled brewery, with its enormous brewing coppers, and on through the renovated stables where the splendid dray horses are on display again. Visitors to the museum can learn about the history of the company and of beer-making in general, a tradition that can be traced back to the Sumerians, who lived as long ago as 4000 BC. The offer of free beer makes a popular end to the tour, which is open to anyone over 18 years old.

Dray horse and beer wagon at the Heineken Brouwerij

Formal rose garden at Museum van Loon

Museum van Loon 9

Keizersgracht 672. **Map** 5 A3. *624 5255.* *16, 24, 25.* *10am–5pm Mon, 1–5pm Sun.*

VAN LOON was the name of one of Amsterdam's most prestigious families in the 17th century. They did not move into this house on the Keizersgracht, however, until 1884. Designed by Adriaan Dortsman, No. 672 is one of a pair of symmetrical houses built in 1672 for the Flemish merchant Jeremias van Raey. It was redecorated in 1752 when Dr. Abraham van Hagen and his wife Catharina Elisabeth Trip moved in. Their last names are incorporated in the copper staircase railing.

The house was opened as a museum in 1974, after 11 years of extensive restoration. It is now one of the most delightful canalside museums, managing to retain the original charming character of the house. It contains a collection of Van Loon family portraits, stretching back to the early 1600s. The period rooms are adorned with fine pieces of furniture, porcelain and sculpture. Some of the upstairs rooms contain sumptuous illusionistic wall paintings, which are known as *witjes* after their famous creator, Jacob de Wit (1695–1754). Outside, the formal rose garden contains a beautiful 18th-century Neo-Classical coach house, now used as a private residence.

Tuschinski Theater ⑩

Reguliersbreestraat 26–28. **Map** 7 C5. *626 2633.* *4, 9, 14.* **Box office** *noon–10pm.* *Jul–Aug: 10:30am Sun & Mon.*

ABRAHAM TUSCHINSKI'S movie and variety theater caused a sensation when it opened in 1921. Until then, Amsterdam's movie theaters had been somber places, but this was an exotic blend of Art Deco and Amsterdam School architecture *(see pp96–7)*. Its twin towers are 26 m (85 ft) tall. Built in a slum area known as the Duivelshoek (Devil's Corner), it was designed by Heyman Louis de Jong and decorated by Chris Bartels, Jaap Gidding and Pieter de Besten. In its heyday, Marlene Dietrich and Judy Garland performed here.

Converted into a six-screen movie theater, the building has been meticulously restored, both inside and out. The carpet in the entrance hall, replaced in 1984, is an exact copy of the original. Visitors may take a guided tour, but the best way to appreciate the opulence of the Tuschinski Theater is to go and see a movie. For just a few extra guilders, you can take a seat in one of the exotic boxes that make up the back row of the huge semicircular, 1,472-seat main auditorium.

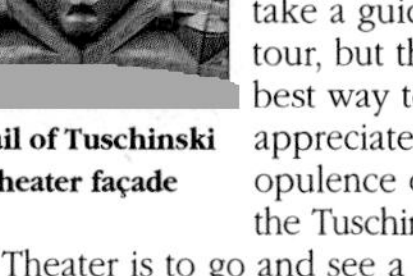

etail of Tuschinski Theater façade

View of the Munttoren at the base of Muntplein

Munttoren ⑪

Muntplein. **Map** 7 B5. *4, 9, 14, 16, 24, 25.* **Munttoren** *to the public.* **Shop** *10am–5pm daily.*

THE POLYGONAL BASE of the Munttoren (mint tower) formed part of the Reguliers-poort, a gate in Amsterdam's medieval city wall. The gate was destroyed by fire in 1618, but the base survived. In the following year, Hendrick de Keyser *(see p90)* added the clock tower, topped with a steeple and openwork orb. The carillon was designed by François Hemony *(see p68)* in 1699, and rings every 15 minutes. The tower acquired its name in 1673, during the French occupation of Amsterdam, when the city mint was temporarily housed here. An upscale gift shop is now located in the base of the tower.

Bloemenmarkt ⑫

Singel. **Map** 7 B5. *1, 2, 4, 5, 9, 11, 14, 16, 24, 25.* *9am–5pm Mon–Sat.*

ON THE SINGEL, west of Muntplein, is the last of the city's floating markets. In the past, nurserymen sailed up the Amstel from their smallholdings and moored here to sell cut flowers and plants directly from their boats. Today, the stalls are still floating but are permanent. Despite the sellers' tendency to cater purely to tourists, the displays of fragrant seasonal flowers and bright spring bedding-plants are always beautiful to look at.

Florist arranging his display at the Bloemenmarkt

MUSEUM QUARTER

UNTIL THE LATE 1800s, the Museum Quarter was little more than an area of farms and smallholdings. At this time, the city council designated it an area of art and culture, and plans were conceived for constructing Amsterdam's great cultural monuments: the Rijksmuseum, the Stedelijk Museum and the Concertgebouw. The Van Gogh Museum followed in 1973. The Museumplein has several memorials to the victims of World War II and there is a plaque commemorating the 1981 anti-nuclear campaign. The *plein* is still used as a site for political demonstrations. To the south is an area of turn-of-the-century houses, where the streets are named after artists and intellectuals, such as the 17th-century poet Roemer Visscher. To the west, the Vondelpark offers a pleasant break from all the museums.

"Russia" gablestone in Roemer Visscherstraat

SIGHTS AT A GLANCE

Museums and Workshops
Rijksmuseum pp130–33 ❶
Coster Diamonds ❷
Van Gogh Museum pp134–5 ❸
Stedelijk Museum pp136–7 ❹
Nederlands Filmmuseum ❾

Concert Halls
Concertgebouw ❺

Historic Buildings
Hollandse Manège ❼
Vondelkerk ❽

Parks
Vondelpark ❻

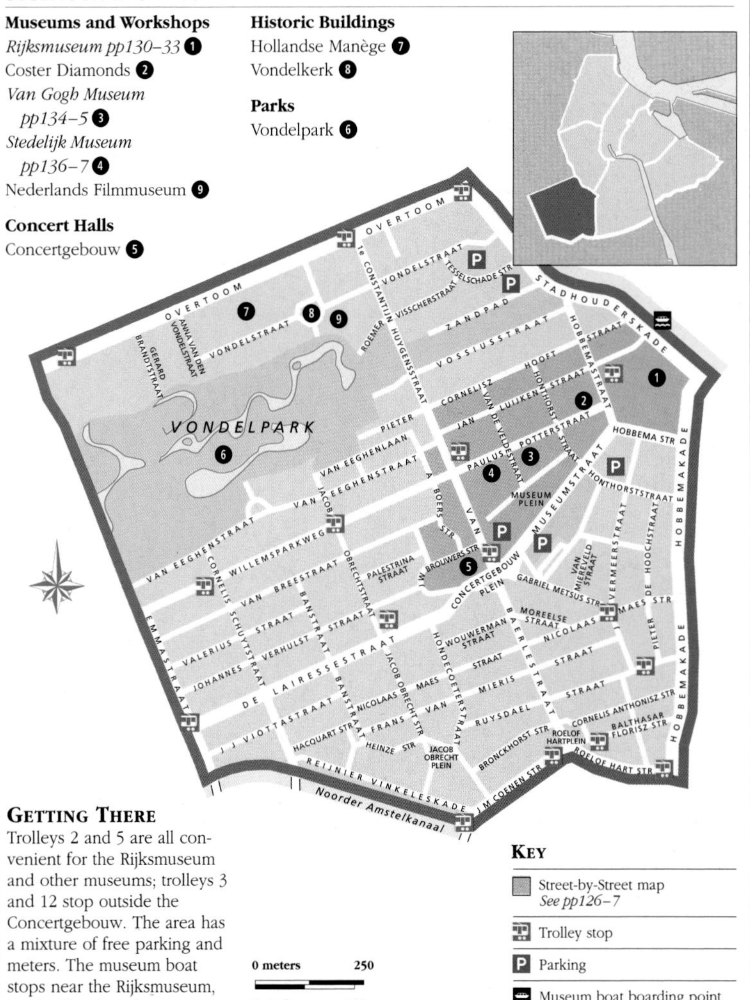

GETTING THERE

Trolleys 2 and 5 are all convenient for the Rijksmuseum and other museums; trolleys 3 and 12 stop outside the Concertgebouw. The area has a mixture of free parking and meters. The museum boat stops near the Rijksmuseum, on the Singelgracht.

0 meters 250
0 yards 250

KEY

- Street-by-Street map *See pp126–7*
- Trolley stop
- Parking
- Museum boat boarding point

◁ **Statue of the painter Pieter Aertsen (1509–75) on the façade of the Stedelijk Museum**

Street-by-Street: Museum Quarter

Statue on façade of Stedelijk

THE WELL-WORN green expanse of the Museumplein is bisected by a busy main road known locally as the "shortest highway in Europe." Although it is bordered by Amsterdam's major cultural centers, the square has a desolate feel and is largely used as a coach parking lot. Even so, the district is one of the wealthiest in the city, with wide streets lined with grand houses. After the heady delights of the museums, it is possible to window-shop at the upscale boutiques along the PC Hoofstraat and Van Baerlestraat, or watch the diamond polishers at work in Coster Diamonds.

★ Van Gogh Museum
Opened in 1973, in a building designed by Gerrit Rietveld (see p136), *this collection of Van Gogh's paintings also contains contemporary works from the artist's own collection* ❸

★ Stedelijk Museum
Housing the civic collection of modern art, this museum also stages controversial contemporary art exhibitions. A sculpture garden is behind the building ❹

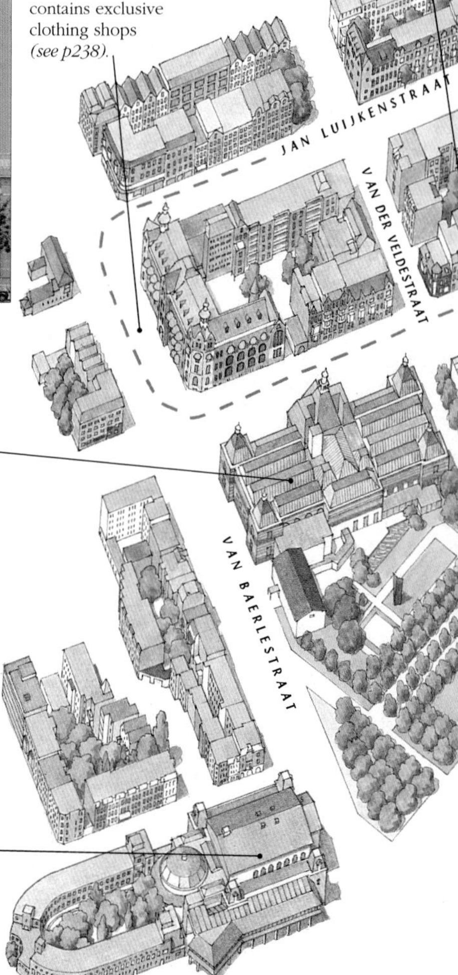

Van Baerlestraat contains exclusive clothing shops *(see p238).*

Concertgebouw
Designed by AL van Gendt, the building has a Classical façade and a concert hall with near-perfect acoustics ❺

Coster Diamonds
Diamonds have been cut, polished and sold at Coster since 1840. The firm now occupies three splendid adjoining villas, built on Museumplein in 1896 ❷

Locator Map
See Street Finder, map 4

The Rijksmuseum is surrounded by gardens that contain statuary. This weathered bronze of Mercury, designed by Ferdinand Leenhoff (1841–1914), is found in the southeast garden.

The Ravensbruck monument commemorates women victims of the Holocaust.

★ Rijksmuseum
The heavily ornamented Neo-Gothic Rijksmuseum holds the magnificent Dutch national art collection of some 5,000 paintings, 30,000 pieces of applied art and 17,000 historical artifacts ❶

Sculptures throughout Museumplein mark the city's anti-nuclear past. The Kernwarpen Monument stood here until 1995.

0 meters 50

0 yards 50

Star Sights

★ Rijksmuseum

★ Van Gogh Museum

★ Stedelijk Museum

Key

– – – Suggested route

Rijksmuseum ❶

See pp130–33.

Coster Diamonds ❷

Paulus Potterstraat 2–6. **Map** 4 E3. *676 2222.* *2, 4, 5, 6, 7, 10.* *9am–5pm.* *Jan 1, Dec 25.*

One of Amsterdam's oldest diamond factories, Coster was founded in 1840. Twelve years later, Queen Victoria's consort, Prince Albert, honored the company by giving them the task of repolishing the enormous *Koh-i-Noor* (mountain of light) diamond. This blue-white stone is one of the treasures of the British crown jewels and weighs in at 108.8 carats. A replica of the coronation crown, which incorporates a copy of the fabulous stone, is found in Coster's spacious entrance hall.

More than 2,000 people visit the factory each day to witness the processes of grading, cutting and polishing diamonds. The goldsmiths and diamond-cutters work together in the factory to produce customized items of jewelry, in a range of styles, which are available over the counter. For serious diamond-buyers, such as the jewelers who come here from all over the world, there is a series of private sales rooms where discretion is assured.

A potential sale under discussion at Coster Diamonds

Museum Vincent van Gogh ❸

See pp134–5.

Stedelijk Museum ❹

See pp136–7.

Façade of the award-winning Concertgebouw (1881) by AL van Gendt

Concertgebouw ❺

Concertgebouwplein 2–6. **Map** 4 D4. *675 4411 or 671 8345.* *2, 3, 5, 12, 16.* **Box office** *10am–7pm Mon–Sat.* *by arrangement.*

Following an open architectural competition held in 1881, AL van Gendt (1835–1901) was chosen to design a vast new concert hall for Amsterdam. The resulting Neo-Renaissance building boasts an elaborate pediment and colonnaded façade, and houses two concert halls. Despite Van Gendt's lack of musical knowledge, he managed to produce near-perfect acoustics in the Grote Zaal (main concert hall), which is renowned the world over.

The inaugural concert at the Concertgebouw was held on April 11, 1888, complete with an orchestra of 120 musicians and a choir of 600. A resident orchestra was established at the hall seven months later.

The building has been renovated several times over the years, most recently in 1983, when some serious subsidence threatened the building's entire foundation. To remedy this, the whole superstructure had to be lifted up off the ground while the original supporting piles, which rested on sand 13 m (43 ft) underground, were removed and replaced by concrete piles sunk into the ground to a depth of 18 m (59 ft). A glass extension and new entrance were added by Pi de Bruijn in 1988. The original entrance was then relocated around to the side of the building. Though primarily designed to hold concerts, the Concertgebouw has become a multi-functional building. It has played host to business meetings, exhibitions, conferences, political meetings and occasional boxing matches.

Bandstand in Vondelpark

Vondelpark ❻

Stadhouderskade. **Map** 4 E2. *2, 3, 5, 12.* **Park** *dawn–dusk.* **Open-air theater** *Jun–mid-Aug: Wed–Sun.*

In 1864, a group consisting of prominent Amsterdammers formed a committee with the aim of founding a public park, and they raised enough money to buy 8 hectares (20 acres) of land. JD and LP Zocher, a father-and-son team of landscape architects, were then commissioned to design the park in typical English landscape style. They used vistas, pathways and ponds to create the illusion of a large natural area. The park was opened to the public on June 15, 1865, as the Nieuwe Park. Its present name was adopted in 1867, when a statue of Dutch poet Joost van den Vondel

(1586–1679) was erected on the grounds. The committee soon began to raise money to enlarge the park, and by June 1877 it had reached its current dimensions of 45 hectares (110 acres). The park now supports about 100 plant species and 127 types of tree. Squirrels, hedgehogs, ducks and garden birds mix with a huge colony of greedy, bright green parakeets, which gather in front of the pavilion every morning to be fed. Herds of cows, sheep, goats and even a lone llama graze in the pastures.

Vondelpark welcomes about 8 million visitors a year, and is popular with the locals for dog-walking, jogging, playing music, or for just enjoying the view. Free concerts are given at the *openluchttheater* (open-air theater) in the summer.

Façade of the Hollandse Manege

Hollandse Manege ❼

Vondelstraat 140. **Map** 3 C2.
618 0942. *1, 6, 11.*
8:30–1am Mon–Fri, 8:30am–6pm Sat & Sun.

THE DUTCH RIDING SCHOOL was originally located on the Leidsegracht *(see p111)*, but in 1882 a new building was opened, designed by AL van Gendt and based on the Spanish Riding School in Vienna. The riding school was threatened with demolition in the 1980s, but was saved after a public outcry. Reopened in 1986 by Prince Bernhard, it has been restored to its former glory. The Neo-Classical indoor arena boasts gilded mirrors and molded horses' heads on its elaborate plaster walls. Some of the wrought-iron stalls remain and sound is muffled by sawdust. At the top of the staircase, one door leads to a balcony overlooking the arena, another to the café.

Vondelkerk ❽

Vondelstraat 120. **Map** 3 C2.
689 0416. *1, 3, 6, 11, 12.*
Church *to the public.*
Gallery *9am–5pm Mon–Fri.*
public and summer hols.

THE VONDELKERK was the largest church designed by PJH Cuypers, architect of the Centraal Station *(see pp30–31)*. Work began on the building in 1872, but funds ran out by the following year. Money gathered from public donations and lotteries allowed the building to be completed by 1880. When fire broke out in November 1904, firefighters saved the nave of the church by forcing the burning tower to fall into Vondelpark. A new tower was added later by the architect's son, JT Cuypers. The church was deconsecrated in 1979 and converted into offices in 1985.

Nederlands Filmmuseum ❾

Vondelpark 3. **Map** 4 D2.
589 1400. *1, 3, 6, 11, 12.*
Library *11am–5pm Tue–Sat.*
Jan 1, Dec 25. **Box Office**
10am–9:30pm Mon–Fri, 1–9:30pm Sat & Sun. **Screenings**: *approx. 7pm, 8pm & 9:30pm daily; plus 1pm & 3pm Sun.* *for movies.*

VONDELPARK'S pavilion was designed by the architects PJ Hamer (1812–87), and his son, W Hamer (1843–1913), and opened on May 4, 1881 as a café and restaurant. After World War II, it was restored and then reopened in 1947 as an international cultural center. In 1991, the pavilion was renovated once more. The Art Deco interior of the Cinema Parisien, Amsterdam's first movie theater, built in 1910, was moved into one of the rooms. It is now an important national film museum, showing more than 1,000 films a year. The museum owns a movie poster collection, runs a public film library at Nos. 69–71 Vondelstraat and holds free outdoor screenings during summer.

Café Vertigo at the Filmmuseum

Rijksmuseum ❶

THE RIJKSMUSEUM is a familiar Amsterdam landmark and possesses an unrivaled collection of Dutch art, begun in the early 19th century. The huge museum opened in 1885 to bitter criticism from Amsterdam's Protestant community for its Neo-Gothic style. Architect PJH Cuypers *(see p31)* had covertly incorporated more ornate detail, modifying his prize-winning plan during construction to reduce the Classical elements.

Winter Landscape with Skaters *(1618)*
Deaf painter Hendrick Avercamp specialized in intricate icy winter scenes.

First floor

The Gothic façade of Cuypers' building is red brick with elaborate decoration, including colored tiles.

★ The Kitchen Maid *(1658)*
The light falling through the window and the stillness of this domestic scene are typical of Jan Vermeer (see p194).

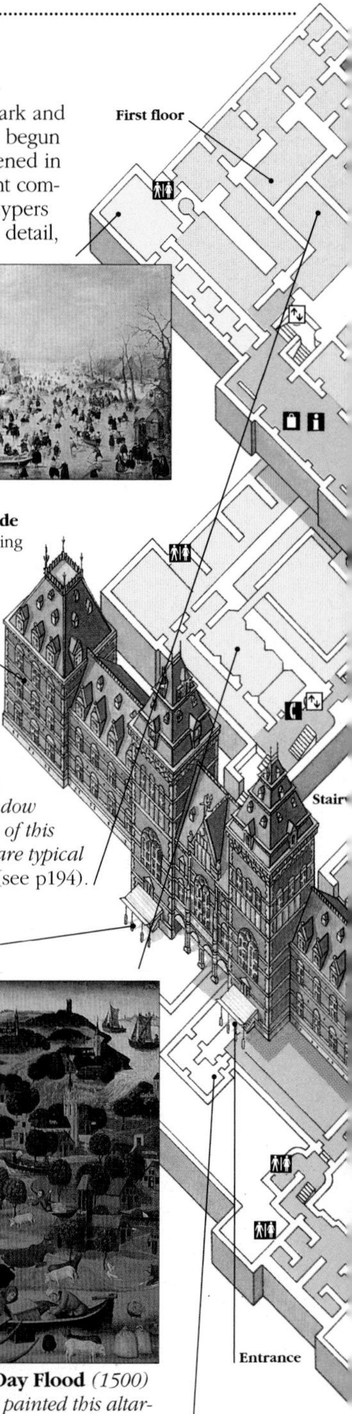

Stair

Entrance

KEY TO FLOORPLAN

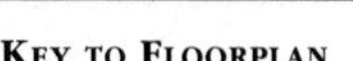

- Dutch history
- Early painting and foreign schools
- 17th-century painting
- 18th- and 19th-century painting
- Hague School and Impressionists
- Sculpture and applied art
- Prints and drawings
- Asiatic art
- Nonexhibition space

★ St. Elizabeth's Day Flood *(1500)*
An unknown artist painted this altarpiece, showing a disastrous flood in 1421. The dikes protecting Dordrecht were breached, and 22 villages were swept away by the flood waters.

Entrance

Study collections

STAR PAINTINGS

- **★ The Night Watch by Rembrandt**
- **★ St. Elizabeth's Day Flood**
- **★ The Kitchen Maid by Vermeer**

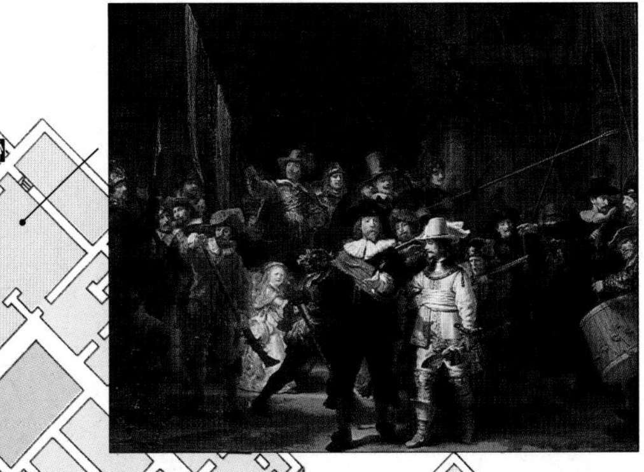

Visitors' Checklist

Stadhouderskade 42. **Map** 4 E3. *673 2121.* *2, 5, 6, 7, 10.* *10am–5pm daily (last adm 4:45pm).* *Jan 1.*

★ The Night Watch *(1642)*
Long regarded as the showpiece of Dutch 17th-century art, this vast, dramatic canvas was commissioned as a group portrait of an Amsterdam militia company.

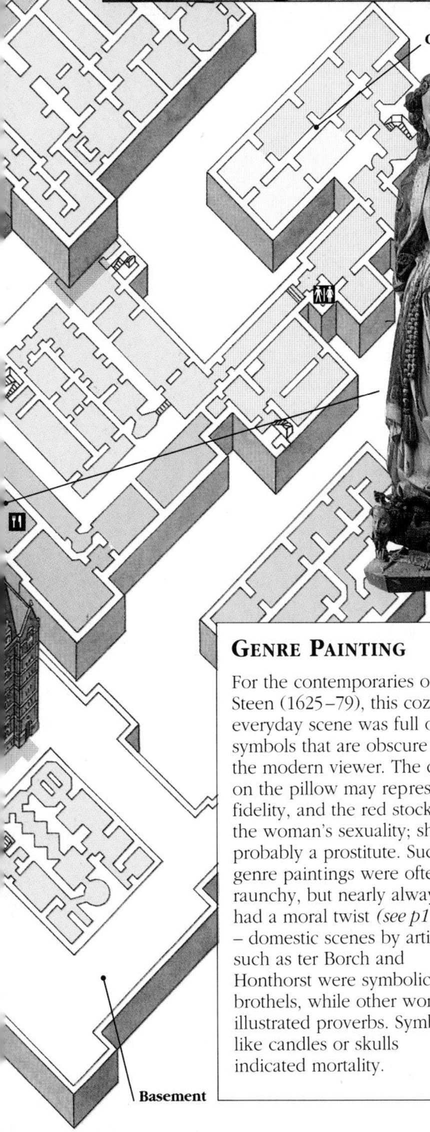

Ground floor

Gallery Guide

There are entrances on either side of the driveway under the building – the left leads into the Dutch history section, the right to prints and drawings, sculpture and applied art. The entrance on the right continues on up the stairs. On the first floor is a huge antechamber, with a shop and information desk. The entrance on the left begins with early Dutch painting, leading to the acclaimed 17th-century collection. The Asiatic art, 18th- and 19th-century paintings and Hague School sections are closed until 1996.

St. Catherine *(c.1465)*
This sculpture by the Master of Koudewater shows the saint stamping on Emperor Maxentius, who allegedly killed her with his sword.

Genre Painting

For the contemporaries of Jan Steen (1625–79), this cozy everyday scene was full of symbols that are obscure to the modern viewer. The dog on the pillow may represent fidelity, and the red stockings the woman's sexuality; she is probably a prostitute. Such genre paintings were often raunchy, but nearly always had a moral twist *(see p189)* – domestic scenes by artists such as ter Borch and Honthorst were symbolic of brothels, while other works illustrated proverbs. Symbols like candles or skulls indicated mortality.

Jan Steen's *Woman at her Toilet* was painted in about 1660

Basement

Exploring the Rijksmuseum

THE RIJKSMUSEUM is almost too vast to be seen in a single visit. It is famous for owning probably the best collection of Dutch art in the world, from early religious works to the masterpieces of the Golden Age. However, the applied art and sculpture sections, and the Asiatic artifacts, are equally wonderful, and the Dutch history section only slightly less rewarding. Those with just one chance to visit the museum should definitely start with the incomparable 17th-century paintings, taking in Frans Hals, Vermeer and scores of other Old Masters, to arrive finally at Rembrandt's *The Night Watch*.

Feeding the Hungry **from a series of seven panels by the Master of Alkmaar**

DUTCH HISTORY

THE TURBULENT HISTORY of the Netherlands is encapsulated in this section. In the opening room is the medieval altar painting of *St. Elizabeth's Day Flood (see p130)*. The central room has 17th-century models of ships, artifacts salvaged from shipwrecks and paintings of factories and townscapes from the days of the Dutch Empire. Later displays recall battles in naval history; exhibits from the 18th century deal with the impact of revolutionary France on Amsterdam, ending in 1815 after the Napoleonic Wars.

EARLY PAINTING AND FOREIGN SCHOOLS

ALONGSIDE a small collection of Flemish and Italian art, including portraits by Piero di Cosimo (1462–1521), are the first specifically "Dutch" paintings. These works are mostly religious, such as *The Seven Works of Charity* (1504) by the Master of Alkmaar, Jan van Scorel's quasi-Mannerist *Mary Magdalene* (1528) and Lucas van Leyden's triptych, *Adoration of the Golden Calf* (1530). As the 16th century progressed, religious themes were superseded by pastoral subjects; by 1552, paintings like Pieter Aertsen's *The Egg Dance* were full of realism, by then the keystone of much Dutch art.

17TH-CENTURY PAINTING

BY THE ALTERATION in 1578 *(see pp22–3)*, Dutch art had moved away completely from religious to secular themes. Artists turned to realistic portraiture, landscapes, still lifes, seascapes, domestic interiors, including genre work *(see p131)*, and animal portraits. Rembrandt *(see p62)* is the most famous of many artists who lived and worked around Amsterdam at this time. Examples of his work hanging in the Rijksmuseum include *Portrait of Titus in a Monk's Habit* (1660), *Self Portrait as the Apostle Paul* (1661), *The Jewish Bride (see p40)* and, inevitably, *The Night Watch (see p131)*.

In his lifetime, Rembrandt had many pupils, including Nicolaes Maes (1634–93) whose somber *Old Woman in Prayer* (1655) contrasts with the light-filled interior of Jan Vermeer's *The Kitchen Maid*, painted in 1658 *(see p130)*, or *The Woman Reading a Letter* (1662). Of several portraits by Frans Hals *(see pp178–9)* the best known are *The Wedding Portrait* and *The Merry Drinker* (1630). *The Windmill at Wijk* by Jacob van Ruisdael (1628–82) is a great landscape by an artist at the very height of his power. Other artists whose works contribute to making this an unforgettable collection include Pieter Saenredam, Jan van de Capelle, Jan Steen *(see p131)* and Gerard ter Borch.

The Wedding Portrait **(c. 1622) by Frans Hals**

18TH- AND 19TH-CENTURY PAINTING

IN MANY WAYS, 18th-century Dutch painting merely continued the themes and quality of 17th-century work.

This is particularly true of portraiture and still lifes, with the evocative *Still Life with Flowers and Fruit* by Jan van Huysum (1682–1749) standing out. A trend developed later for elegant "conversation pieces" by artists such as Adriaan van der Werff (1659–1722) and Cornelis Troost (1696–1750). Most had satirical undertones, like *The Art Gallery of Jan Gildemeester Jansz* (1794) by Adriaan de Lelie (1755–1820), showing an 18th-century salon whose walls are crowded with 17th-century masterpieces.

Hague School and the Impressionists

Artists of the Hague School came together around 1870 in Den Haag. Their landscape work captures the gentle, atmospheric quality of subdued Dutch sunlight. One of the prizes of the Rijksmuseum's collection is *Morning Ride on the Beach* (1876) by Anton Mauve (1838–88), painted with soft colors. Alongside hang the beautiful polder landscapes, *View near the Geestbrug* by Hendrik Weissenbruch (1824–1903), *A Windmill on a Polder Waterway* by Paul Gabriël (1828–1903), and the adorable, naturalistic *Ducks* by Willem Maris (1844–1910). Although the popularity of the Hague School ebbed with the advent of Impressionism, *The Bridge over the Singel at Paleisstraat, Amsterdam* (1890) by George Hendrik Breitner (1857–1923) ranks with the best work of the French Impressionists.

Sculpture and Applied Arts

Beginning with religious medieval sculpture, this section moves on to the splendor of Renaissance furniture and decoration. Highlights that capture the wealth of the Golden Age include an exquisite collection of glassware, delftware (*see p195*) and diamond-encrusted jewelry. A late 17th-century 12-leaf Chinese screen incorporates European figures on one side, a phoenix on the other; and two dollhouses are modeled on contemporary town houses. Some outstanding 18th-century Meissen porcelain and Art Nouveau glass complete the collection.

***Still Life with Flowers and Fruit* (c. 1730) by artist Jan van Huysum (1682–1740), one of many still lifes exhibited in the Rijksmuseum**

Prints and Drawings

The Rijksmuseum owns about a million prints and drawings. Although the emphasis is on Dutch works (most of Rembrandt's etchings as well as rare works by Hercules Seghers (c. 1589–1633) are here), there are prints by major European artists, including Dürer, Tiepolo, Goya, Watteau and Toulouse-Lautrec as well as a set of colored Japanese woodcuts. Small exhibitions are held on the ground floor of the museum, but particular prints can be viewed with special permission from the Study Collection in the basement.

Late 7th-century Cambodian *Head of Buddha*

Asiatic Art

Rewards of the Dutch imperial trading past are displayed in this department, which has a separate entrance at the rear of the museum. Some of the earliest artifacts are the most unusual: tiny bronze Tang dynasty figurines from 7th-century China and gritty, granite rock carvings from Java (c. 8th century). Later exhibits include a lovely – and extremely explicit – Hindu statue titled *Heavenly Beauty*, luscious Chinese parchment paintings of tigers, inlaid Korean boxes and Vietnamese dishes painted with curly-tailed fish. This is a veritable hoard of delights and, above all, a monument to the sophistication and skill of craftsmen and artists in early Eastern cultures.

Van Gogh Museum ❸

THE VAN GOGH MUSEUM is based on a design by De Stijl architect Gerrit Rietveld *(see p136)* that dates from 1963; it eventually opened in 1973. When Van Gogh died in 1890, he was on the verge of being acclaimed. His beloved younger brother Theo, a Paris art dealer, amassed a collection of 200 of his paintings and 500 drawings. These, combined with about 850 letters by Van Gogh to Theo, and selected works by his friends and contemporaries, form the core of the museum's outstanding permanent collection.

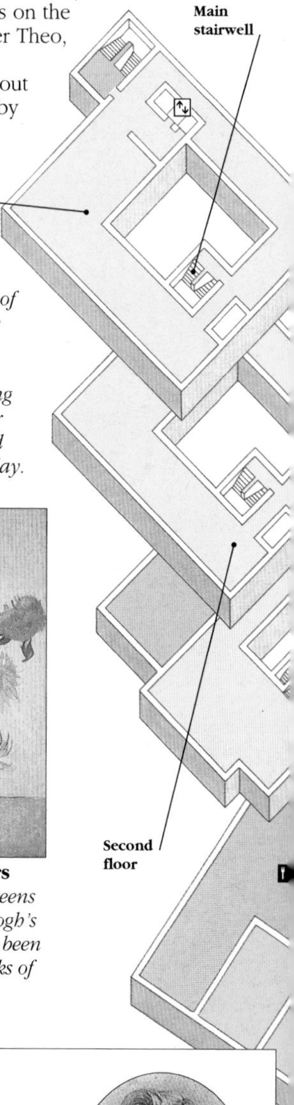

The Potato Eaters *(1885)*
The summation of Van Gogh's time in Nuenen, this painting shows peasants enjoying the fruits of their labors at the end of the working day.

STAR PAINTINGS

- ★ **Vase with Sunflowers**
- ★ **The Bedroom at Arles**
- ★ **Crows in the Wheatfield**

★ Vase with Sunflowers
The vivid yellows and greens in this version of Van Gogh's Sunflowers *(1889) have been enriched by broad streaks of bright mauve and red.*

Japonaiserie: the Courtesan *(1887)*
Van Gogh was influenced by Japanese art and attempted to emulate its form, vitality and clarity of color.

AN ARTIST'S LIFE

Vincent van Gogh (1853–90), born in Zundert, began painting in 1880. He worked in the Netherlands for five years before moving to Paris, later settling at Arles in the south of France. After a fierce argument with Gauguin, he cut off part of his own ear and his mental instability forced him into an asylum in Saint-Rémy. He sought help in Auvers, where he shot himself and died two days later.

Van Gogh in 1871

★ **The Bedroom at Arles** *(1888)*
One of Van Gogh's best-known works, this was painted to celebrate his achievement of domestic stability at the Yellow House in Arles. He was so delighted with the colorful painting that he did it twice.

Visitors' Checklist

Paulus Potterstraat 7. **Map** 4 E3. *570 5200.* *2, 3, 5, 12.* *10am–5pm (last adm 4:30pm).* *Jan 1.*

Museum Guide

Works by other 19th-century artists are on the ground floor, along with the bookstore and café. Paintings from Van Gogh's somber Dutch period and from his time in Paris, Arles, Saint-Rémy and Auvers are on the first floor. The study collection, occasional exhibits of Van Gogh's drawings and other temporary exhibitions are on the top two floors.

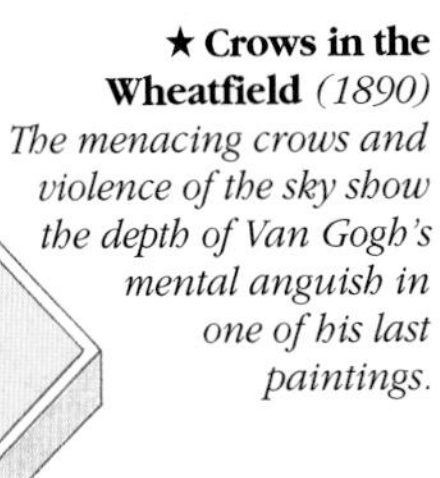

★ **Crows in the Wheatfield** *(1890)*
The menacing crows and violence of the sky show the depth of Van Gogh's mental anguish in one of his last paintings.

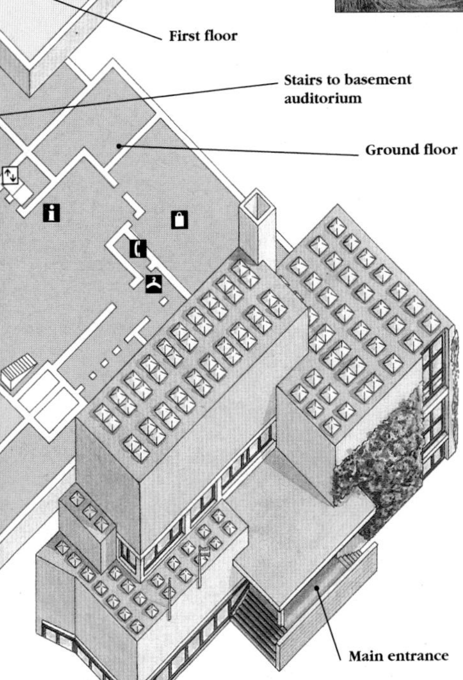

Pietà (after Delacroix) *(1889)*
Van Gogh painted this work while in the asylum at Saint-Rémy. The figure of Christ is thought to be a self-portrait.

Key to Floorplan

- Works by Van Gogh
- Study collection
- Other 19th-century paintings
- Temporary exhibitions
- Nonexhibition space

Stedelijk Museum ❹

THE STEDELIJK MUSEUM was built to house a personal collection bequeathed to the city in 1890 by art connoisseur Sophia de Bruyn. In 1938, the museum became the national museum of modern art, displaying works by artists such as Picasso, Matisse, Mondriaan, Cézanne and Monet. Exhibitions change constantly, with recent acquisitions reflecting the latest developments not only in painting and sculpture but also in printing, drawing, photography, video and industrial design.

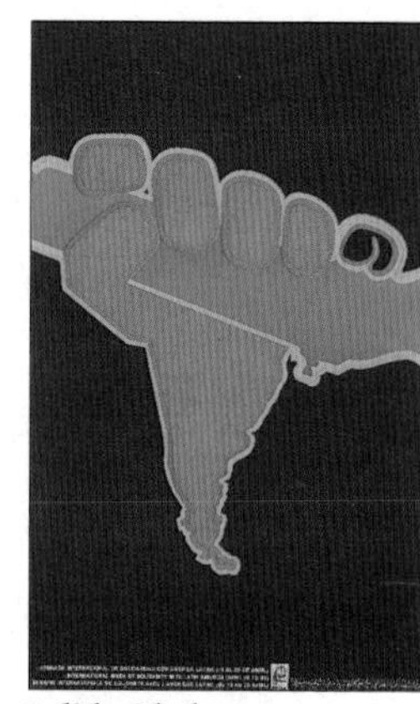

Solidaridad con America Latina *(1970)*
The Stedelijk's collection of rare posters comprises some 17,000 works, including this graphic image by the Cuban human rights campaigner Asela Perez.

Portrait of the Artist with Seven Fingers *(1912)*
Marc Chagall's self-portrait is heavily autobiographical; the seven fingers of the title allude to the seven days of Creation and the artist's Jewish origins. Paris and Rome, the cities Chagall lived in, are inscribed in Hebrew above his head.

The Museum Building

The Neo-Renaissance building was designed by AW Weissman (1858–1923) in 1895. The façade is adorned with turrets and gables and with niches containing statues of artists and architects. In contrast, the interior is ultramodern. There are plans for an extension.

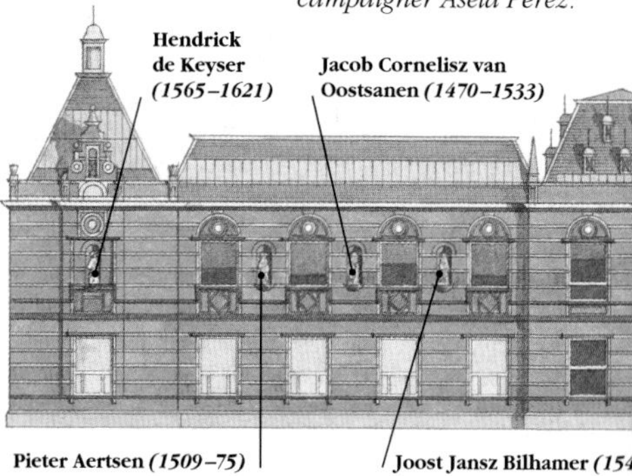

Hendrick de Keyser ***(1565–1621)***

Jacob Cornelisz van Oostsanen ***(1470–1533)***

Pieter Aertsen ***(1509–75)***

Joost Jansz Bilhamer ***(154***

De Stijl Movement

The Dutch artistic movement known as De Stijl (The Style) produced startlingly simple designs which have become icons of 20th-century abstract art. These include Gerrit Rietveld's famous *Red Blue Chair* and Pieter Mondriaan's *Composition in Red, Black, Blue, Yellow and Grey* (1920). The movement was formed in 1917 by a group of artists who espoused clarity in their work, which embraced the mediums of painting, architecture, sculpture, poetry and furniture design. Many De Stijl artists, like Theo van Doesburg, split from the founding group in the 1920s, and their legacy can be seen in the work of the Bauhaus and Modernist schools which followed.

Gerrit Rietveld's ***Red Blue Chair*** **(1918)**

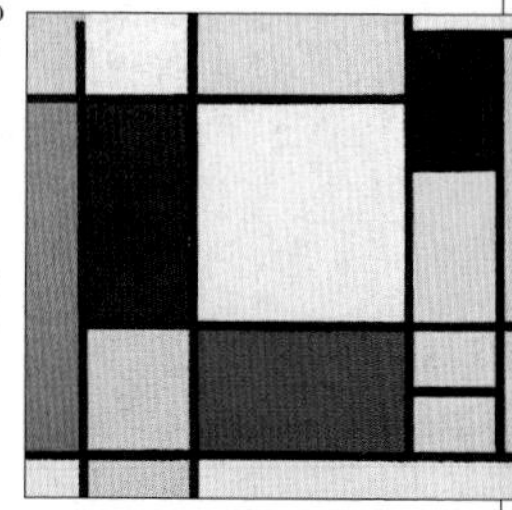

Composition in Red, Black, Blue, Yellow and Grey **by Mondriaan**

Dancing Woman *(1911)*
Ernst Ludwig Kirchner (1880–1938) was inspired by the primitive art of African and Asian cultures, and by the natural qualities of the materials he worked with.

Man and Animals *(1949)*
Karel Appel (born 1921) was a member of the short-lived, experimental Cobra movement. The human figure, dog, fish and mythical creature are painted in the naive style of a child.

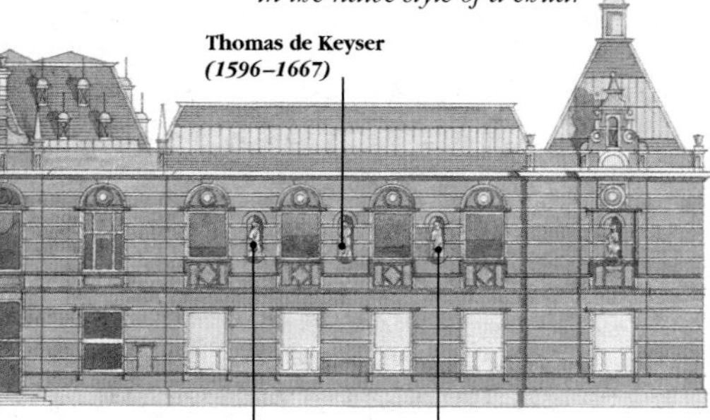

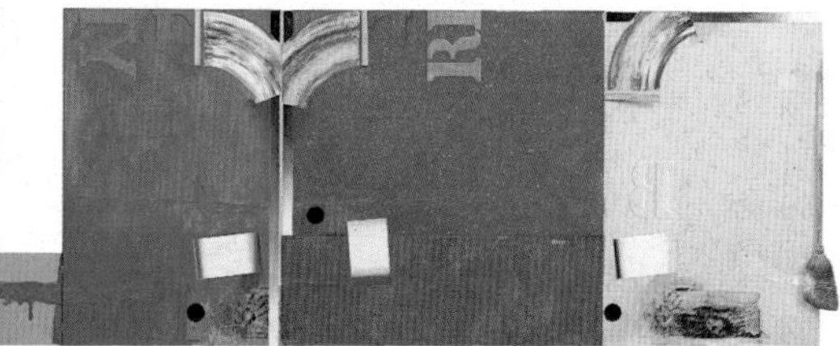

Untitled *(1965)*
Jasper Johns (born 1930) believed viewers should draw their own conclusions from his work. This huge canvas, with its bold rainbow (red, blue and yellow streaks and slabs), invites the viewer to think about the symbolism of color.

STAR COLLECTIONS

★ **Works by Mondriaan**

★ **Cobra Collection**

★ **Works by Malevich**

VISITORS' CHECKLIST

Paulus Potterstraat 13. **Map** 4 D3.
573 2737 or 573 7911
2, 3, 5, 12, 16. *11am–5pm (last admission: 4:45pm).*
Jan 1, Dec 25 & 26.

PERMANENT ARTISTS

Works by inventive photographer Man Ray, Russian artist Kazimir Malevich and sculptor Jean Tinguely are usually on show in the museum.

Man Ray *(1890–1977) elevated photography to an art form, and was a major influence on the Surrealists.*

Kazimir Malevich *(1878–1935) founded Suprematism, an abstract movement that experimented with color.*

Jean Tinguely *(born 1925) creates humorous, moving sculptures, welded together from junk and recycled metal.*

AMSTERDAM

PLANTAGE

Known as the "plantation," this area was once green parkland beyond the city wall, where 17th-century Amsterdammers spent their leisure time. From about 1848, it became one of Amsterdam's first suburbs. The tree-lined streets around Artis and Hortus Botanicus are still popular places to live. In the 19th century, many middle-class Jews prospered in the area, mainly in the diamond-cutting industry. They formed a large part of the Diamond Workers' Union, whose history is recorded at the Nationaal Vakbondsmuseum. From the Werf 't Kromhout, once a thriving shipyard, there is a fine view of De Gooyer Windmill, one of the few in Amsterdam to survive. The national maritime collection is kept at the Scheepvaart Museum, a former naval storehouse.

Pillar decoration on Theater Carré

SIGHTS AT A GLANCE

Museums

Nationaal Vakbondsmuseum 2
Hollandse Schouwburg 3
Geologisch Museum 5
Werf 't Kromhout Museum 11
Nederlands Scheepvaart Museum pp146–7 12

Historic Buildings and Structures

Entrepotdok 8
Muiderpoort 9
De Gooyer Windmill 10
Amstelsluizen 14

Sights of Scientific Interest

Artis 4
Aquarium 7
Planetarium 6

Botanical Gardens

Hortus Botanicus Plantage 1

Theaters

Koninklijk Theater Carré 13

GETTING THERE

Trolleys 9 and 14 pass Artis and Hortus Botanicus, while buses 22 and 28 stop at the Scheepvaart Museum. Weesperplein metro station is located in the southwest of Plantage. It can be intimidating at night, so use the nearby Waterlooplein station.

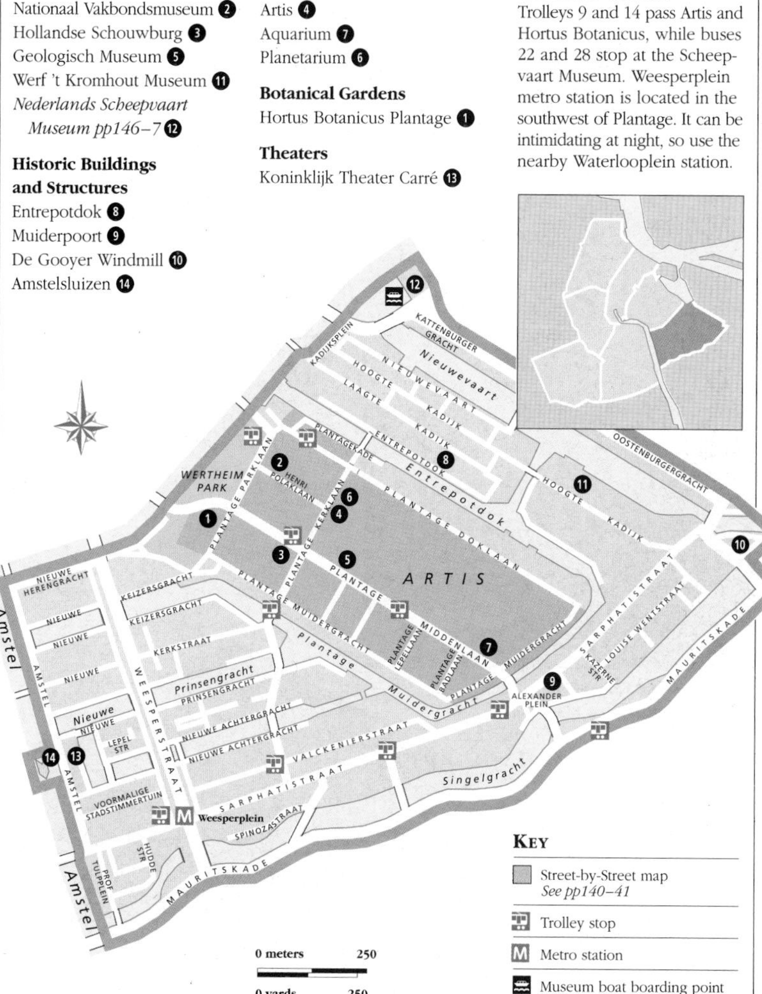

◁ **Replica of the *Amsterdam*, an East Indiaman, moored alongside the Scheepvaart Museum**

Street-by-Street: Plantage

Elephant from Artis zoo

With its wide, tree-lined streets and painted, sandstone buildings, the Plantage is a graceful and often overlooked part of the city. Though it seems like a quiet part of town, there is a lot to see and do. The area is dominated by the Artis complex. It has a diverse range of popular attractions which can get very busy on sunny days. The area has a strong Jewish tradition, and several monuments commemorate Jewish history in Amsterdam, including a basalt memorial in the Hollandse Schouwburg. The cafés of the Entrepotdok offer a pleasant setting for a relaxing coffee, within earshot of the zoo.

Nationaal Vakbondsmuseum
Berlage's building was inspired by an Italian palazzo, *and its small museum displays trade-union memorabilia* ❷

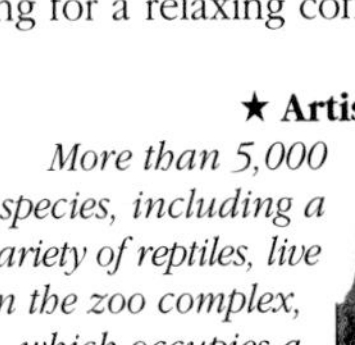

★ Artis
More than 5,000 species, including a variety of reptiles, live in the zoo complex, which occupies a beautifully laid out garden site ❹

PLANTAGE PARKLAAN

PLANTAGE KERKLAAN

★ Hortus Botanicus Plantage
The old greenhouses have been restored, and this new one built to hold tropical and desert plants ❶

Moederhuis, Aldo van Eyck's refuge for pregnant women, has a colorful, modern façade intended to draw people inside.

★ Hollandse Schouwburg
Little remains of this former theater, now a somber monument to the deported Jews of World War II ❸

Star Sights

- **★ Artis**
- **★ Hollandse Schouwburg**
- **★ Hortus Botanicus Plantage**

Entrepotdok
This was the largest warehouse development in Europe during the 19th century. It has recently been redeveloped and transformed into an attractive quayside housing, office and leisure complex ❽

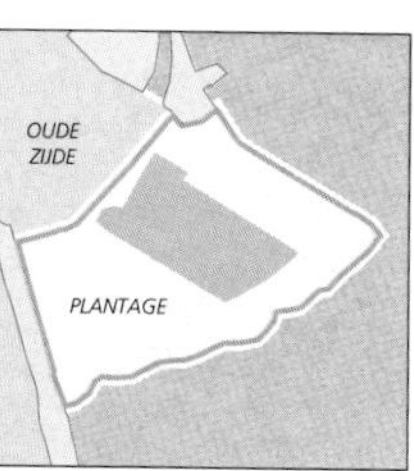

Locator Map
See Street Finder maps 5 & 6

Planetarium
Part of the Artis complex, the domed Planetarium explores man's relationship with the stars. Stellar maps plot the night sky, while interactive displays show the positions of the planets. Model spacecraft are on display in the hall around the auditorium ❻

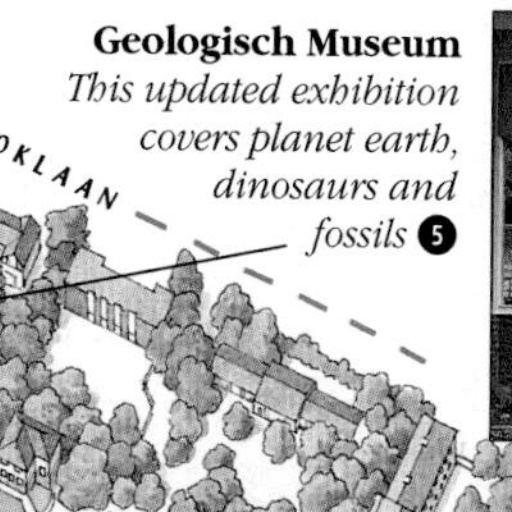

Geologisch Museum
This updated exhibition covers planet earth, dinosaurs and fossils ❺

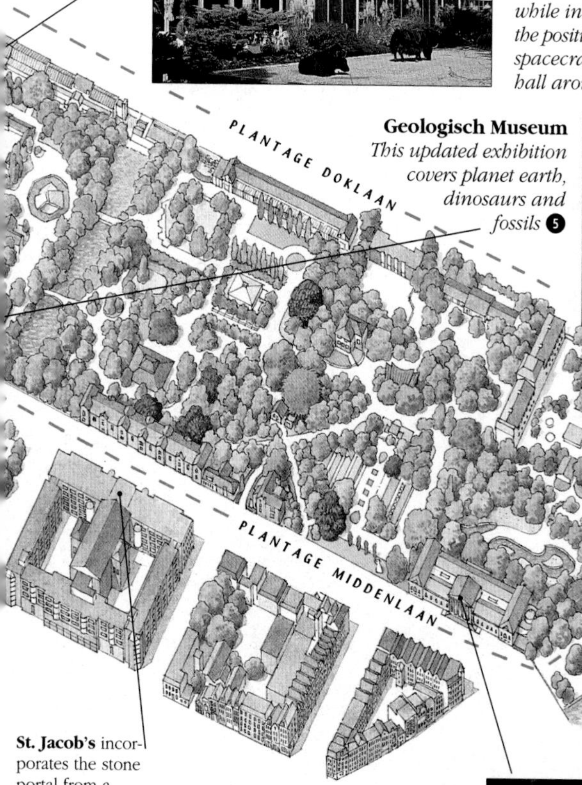

St. Jacob's incorporates the stone portal from a nursing home formerly on this site.

Aquarium
The fine Neo-Classical building is home to thousands of aquatic species, ranging from tiny, fluorescent tropical fish to gigantic European moray eels ❼

0 meters 100

0 yards 100

Key

– – – Suggested route

Tropical plants in the Hortus Botanicus

Hortus Botanicus Plantage ❶

Plantage Middenlaan 2a. **Map** 6 D2. *625 8411. 9, 14. Apr–Sep: 9am–5pm Mon–Fri, 11am–5pm Sat, Sun & public hols; Oct–Mar: 9am–4pm Mon–Fri, 11am–4pm Sat, Sun & public hols. Jan 1.*

THIS NEAT botanical garden began as a small apothecaries' herb garden in 1682, and now contains one of the world's largest botanical collections. Its range of flora expanded when tropical plants were brought back by the Dutch East India Company *(see pp26–7)*. In 1706, it became the first place outside Arabia to succeed in cultivating the coffee plant *(Coffea arabica)*.

The glass-domed Palm House, built in 1913, contains a 400-year-old cycad (palm fern), the world's oldest potted plant. Art shows with a botanical theme are also held here.

A modern glass and aluminum structure, designed by Moshé Zwarts and Rein Jansma, was opened in 1993 to make room for the tropical, subtropical and desert plants. There is also a greenhouse for carnivorous plants.

Nationaal Vakbondsmuseum ❷

Henri Polaklaan 9. **Map** 5 C2. *624 1166. 7, 9, 14. 11am–5pm Tue–Fri, 1–5pm Sun. public hols.*

THIS SMALL MUSEUM, housed in the headquarters of the General Dutch Diamond Workers' Union (ANDB), outlines the history of the Dutch trade union movement. The ANDB was the first, largest and wealthiest union in the Netherlands. Founded in 1894, its membership had grown to more than 10,000 by 1910.

The redbrick crenellated building, known locally as "the castle," was designed by HP Berlage *(see p79)* in 1900. It has a beautiful interior, with murals by the socialist artist Rik Roland Holst of the Amsterdam School *(see p97)*, and a spectacular arched foyer. But the material on show will be best enjoyed by Dutch speakers.

Hollandse Schouwburg ❸

Plantage Middenlaan 24. **Map** 5 C2. *626 9945. 7, 9, 14. 11am–4pm. Yom Kippur.*

FORMERLY A THEATER, this is now a memorial to the 104,000 Dutch Jewish victims of World War II. More than 60,000 of them were detained here before being deported to concentration camps. After the war, the building was abandoned until 1962 when a garden was laid out in the former auditorium. A basalt column with a base in the shape of the Star of David was erected on the site of the stage and behind it is written: "To the memory of those taken from here."

The façade and foyer were restored in 1993, and became an education center. On the ground floor, a candle illuminates the names of the war victims. Upstairs, exhibits especially for children explain the fate of the city's Jewish community and the dark role played by the theater.

Artis ❹

Plantage Kerklaan 40. **Map** 6 D2. *523 3400. 7, 9, 14. 9am–5pm daily.*

ARTIS IS the oldest surviving zoological complex in the Netherlands. It was founded in 1838 by Dr. GF Westerman, president of the Natura Artis Magistra (Nature the Teacher

Decorative tiles on the staircase of the Vakbondsmuseum

Seals basking in their pool in Artis zoo complex

of Art) association. Since its inception, leading biologists have worked here and later the general public were allowed in to admire the zoo's rich collection of plants, trees and animals.

The complex has more than 900 animal species, in addition to three spacious exotic greenhouses, the Planetarium, Geologisch Museum, Aquarium, Amfibarium and Zoölogisch Museum. Numerous footpaths weave past a good selection of mature trees, ponds, sculptures and animal enclosures.

While some of the spaces for the animals are cramped, the zoo's attractions include big cats, giraffes, polar bears, penguins, hippos and seals. It also contains a steamy reptile house, nocturnal house, aviary, ape house and flamingo lake. Children can clamber around on model animals in the playground or pet the sheep and goats in the farmyard.

Geologisch Museum 5

Plantage Kerklaan 40. **Map** 6 D2.
523 3400. 7, 9, 14.
9am–5pm daily.

LOCATED AT the southwest corner of the Artis complex, the Geologisch Museum offers an entertaining introduction to planet earth. The admission charge is automatically covered by the entry ticket to Artis.

The first gallery on the ground floor is devoted to the evolution of life on earth. Displays trace the gigantic leap from single-cell life forms, via dinosaurs, to mammals. The second gallery on the ground floor deals imaginatively with the interacting elements of the earth and the forces which control it. The gallery's central attraction is the Earth Machine, which features rotating components to represent the biosphere (the area inhabited by living things), hydrosphere (water), atmosphere (air) and geosphere (the earth's solid crust). Upstairs, there is an extensive display of fossils, minerals and stones.

Ammonite fossil at the Geologisch Museum

Planetarium 6

Plantage Kerklaan 40. **Map** 6 D2.
523 3400. 7, 9, 14.
12:30–5pm Mon, 9am–5pm Tue–Sun.

THE ONLY supplementary exhibition charge within the Artis complex is for the hourly shows at the Planetarium. In this large, domed building, close to the zoo's main entrance, a powerful projector reproduces the night sky and shows how the planets constantly change positions in relation to the constellations. Adult and children's programs are shown alternately and, although the commentary is in Dutch, there are summaries in English, French and German.

Around the edge of the Planetarium, stellar and planetary systems are mapped out using models, photographs, videos and push-button exhibits. There are also educational computer games and displays on space exploration and astronomy.

Aquarium 7

Plantage Kerklaan 40. **Map** 6 D3.
523 3400. 7, 9, 14.
Aquarium *9am–5pm daily.*
Zoölogisch Museum *9am–5pm Tue–Sun.*

PERHAPS THE best feature of the Artis complex is its Aquarium, which opened in 1882 in a grand Neo-Classical building. Mainly housed on the first floor, there are now four separate aquatic systems: one freshwater and three saltwater. Together they hold almost a million liters (260,000 gallons) of water. These tanks, each kept at a different temperature, contain almost 500 species of fish and marine animals that can all be viewed close up. They range from simple invertebrates to piranhas, sharks and massive marine turtles. Look out for the vivid coral fish and charming sea horses housed at the far end of the gallery.

The Amfibarium is housed in the basement of the Aquarium building. This hall contains a substantial collection of frogs, toads and salamanders in all shapes, sizes and colors.

The building also houses the small Zoölogisch Museum, which is as old as the park itself. The museum has a more academic flavor, and its exhibition halls hold temporary shows on such themes as the history of the dodo or aspects of animal behavior.

Tropical fish at the Aquarium, home to almost 500 marine species

Entrepotdok ❽

Map 6 D2. [tram] *7, 9, 14.*

THE REDEVELOPMENT of the old VOC *(see pp26–7)* warehouses at Entrepotdok has revitalized this dockland area since the 1980s. The buildings formed the greatest warehouse complex in Europe during the mid-19th century, following its designation, in 1827, as a customs-free zone for goods in transit. The pedimented Neo-Classical entrance on Kadijksplein, where goods came in to be checked off at the customs halls, provided the only access to the warehouses at that time.

Now easily accessible from all sides, the quayside buildings of Entrepotdok form a lively complex of offices (many occupied by designers and architects), residential dwellings, cafés and restaurants. Some of the original façades of the warehouses have been preserved, unlike the interiors, which have been opened up to provide an attractive inner courtyard at first-floor level.

Café tables are often set out on the street, alongside the Entrepotdok canal. On the other side of the water, brightly colored houseboats are moored side by side, herons doze at the water's edge and the calls of apes reverberate from the Artis zoo *(see pp142–3)*, making the Entrepotdok area a very pleasant place to visit.

The grand dome and clock tower of the Muiderpoort

Muiderpoort ❾

Alexanderplein. **Map** 6 E3. [tram] *6, 9, 10, 14.* [closed] *to the public.*

FORMERLY A CITY GATE, the freestanding Muiderpoort was designed by Cornelis Rauws in about 1770. It now houses the specialist library of the International Tax Academy.

The central archway of this rather grand and forbidding Classical structure is crowned with a dome and clock tower. Above the banded Doric columns, the pediment is adorned with a relief carving of the Amsterdam coat of arms by A Ziesenis. Napoleon entered the city through this gate in 1811 and, according to legend, forced the citizens to feed and house his ragged troops.

De Gooyer Windmill ❿

Funenkade 5. **Map** 6 F2. [tram] *6, 10.* [closed] *to the public.*

OF THE SIX remaining windmills within the city's boundaries, De Gooyer, also known as the Funenmolen, is the most central. Dominating the view down the Nieuwevaart, the mill was built around 1725 to grind grain, and was the first grain mill in the Netherlands to utilize newly developed, streamlined sails.

It first stood to the west of its present site, but the Oranje Nassau barracks, built in 1814, acted as a windbreak, and the mill was then moved piece by piece to the Funenkade. The octagonal wooden structure was rebuilt on the stone foot of an earlier water-pumping mill, demolished in 1812.

By 1925, De Gooyer was in a very poor state of repair and was bought by the city council, which fully restored it. The work included replacing the wooden balcony, which had completely crumbled away. Since then, the lower part of the mill, with its neat thatched roof and tiny windows, has been a private home, though

Spout-gable façades of former warehouses along Entrepotdok

The 18th-century De Gooyer windmill, with its renovated balcony

its massive sails still creak into action sometimes. Next to the mill is the IJ brewery *(see p48)*, one of two independent breweries in the city.

Werf 't Kromhout Museum ⓫

Hoogte Kadijk 147. **Map** 6 D1. *627 6777.* 7. 22, 28. *Oosterdok or Kattenburgergracht.* *10am–4pm Mon–Fri.* *public hols.*

WERF 'T KROMHOUT is one of the oldest working shipyards in Amsterdam, and is also a museum. Ships were built here as early as 1757. In the second half of the 19th century, production changed from sailing ships to steamships. The yard was therefore one of the first to acquire such innovations as a covered awning, a steam slipway, electric lighting and a workshop capable of producing boilers and steam engines.

As ocean-going ships became bigger, the yard, because of its relatively small size, turned to building lighter craft for inland waterways. It is now used only for restoration and repair work. Houseboats, impressive historic barges and ships are moored outside.

The museum is largely dedicated to the history of marine engineering, concentrating on work carried out at the Kromhout shipyard. In the former workshop is a collection of historic Dutch engines. There are also displays of maritime photographs and ephemera, and a well-equipped forge.

Werf 't Kromhout Museum and working shipyard

Nederlands Scheepvaart Museum ⓬

See pp146–7.

Koninklijk Theater Carré ⓭

Amstel 115–125. **Map** 5 B3. *622 5225.* 6, 7, 10. *Weesperplein.* **Box office** *10am–7pm Mon–Sat, 1–7pm Sun. See* ***Entertainment*** *p246.* *3pm Wed & Sat.*

DURING the 19th century, the annual visit of the Carré Circus was a popular event. In 1868, Oscar Carré built wooden premises for the circus on the banks of the Amstel river. The city council considered the structure a fire hazard, so Carré persuaded them to accept a permanent building modeled on his other circus in Cologne.

Designed by the architects JPF van Rossem and WJ Vuyk, and built in 1887, the new building included both a circus ring and a stage. The Classical façade is richly decorated with sculpted heads of dancers, jesters and clowns. The Christmas circus is still one of the annual highlights at the theater, but for much of the year the recently enlarged stage is taken over by concerts and big-show musicals.

Carving on façade of the Koninklijk Theater Carré

Amstelsluizen ⓮

Map 5 B3. 6, 7, 10.

THE AMSTELSLUIZEN, a row of sturdy wooden sluice gates spanning the Amstel river, form part of a complex system of sluices and pumping stations that ensure Amsterdam's canals do not stagnate. Four times a week in summer and twice a week in winter, the sluices are closed while freshwater from large lakes north of the city, such as the IJmeer, is allowed to flow into Amsterdam's canals. Sluices to the west of the city are left open, allowing the old water to flow, or be pumped, into the North Sea.

The Amstelsluizen date from the 18th century, and were operated manually until 1994, when they were mechanized.

Nederlands Scheepvaart Museum ⓬

Ornate 17th-century brass sextant

ONCE THE ARSENAL of the Dutch Navy, this vast Classical sandstone building was built by Daniel Stalpaert in 1656. It was constructed around a massive courtyard and supported by 18,000 piles driven into the bed of the Oosterdok. The Navy stayed until 1973, when the building was converted into the National Maritime Museum, holding the largest collection of boats in the world. Displays of boats, models and maps give a chronological survey of Dutch naval history.

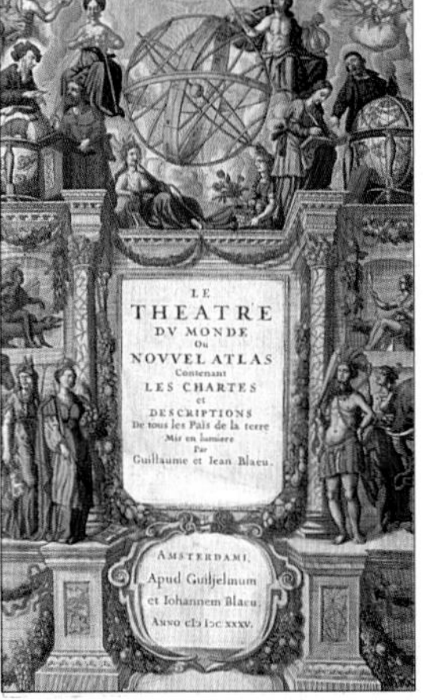

★ Blaeu's World Atlas
In the 17th century, Amsterdam led the world in marine cartography. The Blaeu family produced a nine volume atlas.

First floor

Ajax
This figurehead is from a ship built in 1832. It portrays Ajax, a hero of the Trojan War, who killed himself in despair when Achilles' armor was given to Odysseus.

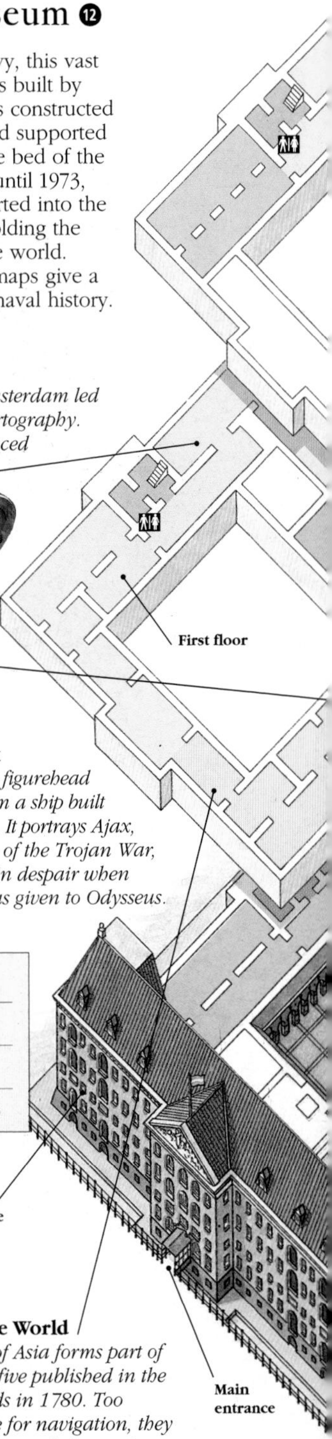

MUSEUM GUIDE
The museum is arranged chronologically. The first floor covers the early maritime history of the Netherlands. The second floor spans merchant shipping from the 19th century to date, including technical developments. An audiovisual theater is on the first floor, and a full-size model of the East Indiaman, Amsterdam, *is docked at the quayside.*

STAR EXHIBITS

★ Royal Barge

★ The Amsterdam

★ Blaeu's World Atlas

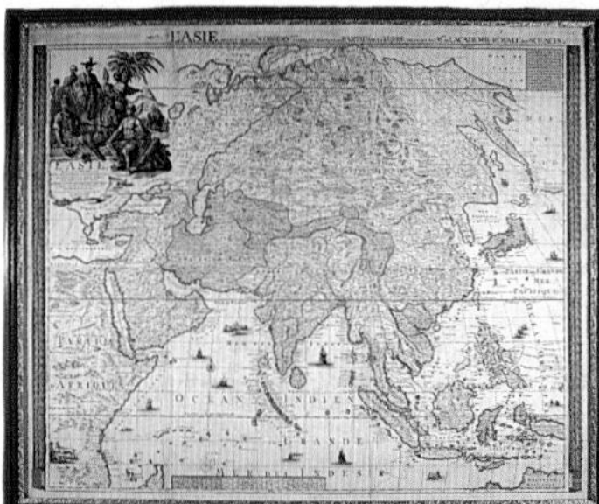

Classical sandstone façade

Map of the World
This map of Asia forms part of a series of five published in the Netherlands in 1780. Too inaccurate for navigation, they were used as wall decorations.

Main entrance

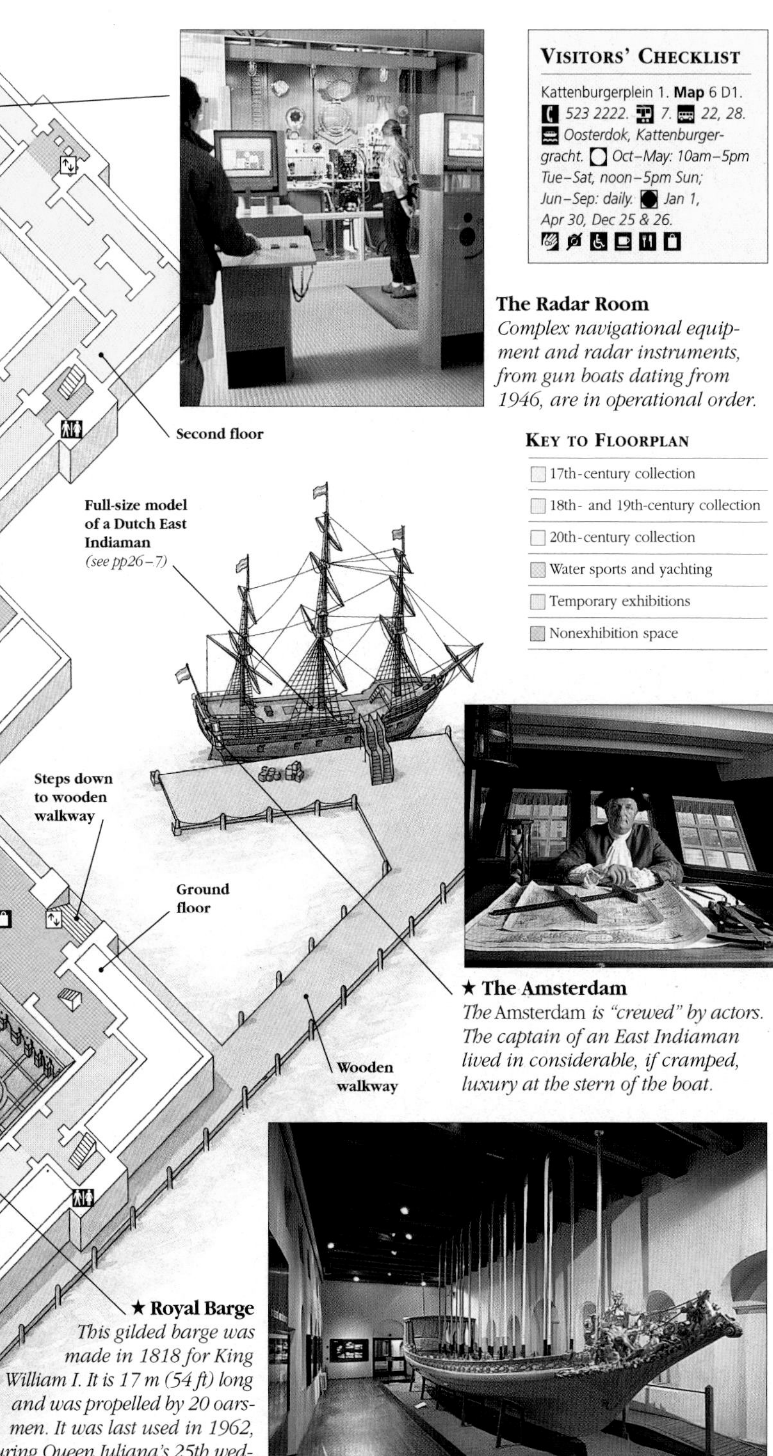

Visitors' Checklist

Kattenburgerplein 1. **Map** 6 D1. *523 2222.* *7.* *22, 28.* *Oosterdok, Kattenburgergracht.* *Oct–May: 10am–5pm Tue–Sat, noon–5pm Sun; Jun–Sep: daily.* *Jan 1, Apr 30, Dec 25 & 26.*

The Radar Room
Complex navigational equipment and radar instruments, from gun boats dating from 1946, are in operational order.

Key to Floorplan

- 17th-century collection
- 18th- and 19th-century collection
- 20th-century collection
- Water sports and yachting
- Temporary exhibitions
- Nonexhibition space

★ The Amsterdam
The Amsterdam *is "crewed" by actors. The captain of an East Indiaman lived in considerable, if cramped, luxury at the stern of the boat.*

★ Royal Barge
This gilded barge was made in 1818 for King William I. It is 17 m (54 ft) long and was propelled by 20 oarsmen. It was last used in 1962, during Queen Juliana's 25th wedding anniversary celebrations.

Farther Afield

Great architecture and good town planning are not confined to central Amsterdam. Parts of the Nieuw Zuid (New South) bear testament to the imagination of the innovative Amsterdam School architects *(see p97)* under the auspices of the Municipal Councils. Many fine buildings can be found in De Dagraad Housing complex and the streets around the Olympic Quarter. If you are seeking old-world charm, the historic small town of Ouderkerk aan de Amstel, nestling on the southern fringes of the city, prides itself on being older than Amsterdam. There are also fine parks a short trolley ride from the city center, which offer a whole host of leisure activities. Visitors can view the lakes, woods and parkland of the Amsterdamse Bos *(see pp32–3)* from the deck of an old trolley that tours the park from the Electrische Museumtramlijn. The formal horticulture of the Amstelpark can be viewed aboard a miniature train. There are also several instructive museums to be found in the suburbs of Amsterdam.

Sculpture on the fountain at Frankendael

Sights at a Glance

Historic Monuments, Buildings and Districts

Frankendael 1
De Dageraad Housing 5
Ouderkerk aan de Amstel 9
Olympic Quarter 10

Parks and Gardens

Amstelpark 8
Amsterdamse Bos 12

Museums and Exhibition Halls

Tropenmuseum see pp152–3 2
Technologie Museum NINT 3
Gemeentaerchief Amsterdam 4
Verzetsmuseum Amsterdam 6
Amsterdam RAI 7
Electrische Museumtramlijn 11
Nationaal Luchtvaartmuseum Aviodome 13

Key

Central Amsterdam
Greater Amsterdam
Airport
Major road
Minor road

0 kilometers 2
0 miles 2

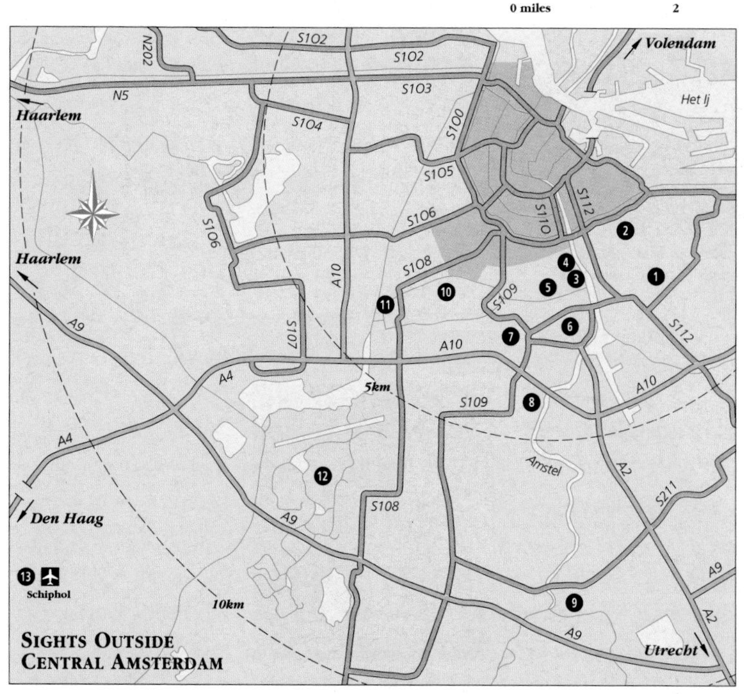

◁ **Moored sailing boat on the river at Ouderkerk aan de Amstel**

Frankendael ❶

Middenweg 72. **Map** 6 F5. 🚋 *9.* 🚌 *59, 120, 126, 136.* **Gardens** ☎ *596 2504.* ◯ *dawn–dusk.*

DURING THE early part of the 18th century, many of Amsterdam's wealthier inhabitants built country retreats south of Plantage Middenlaan on reclaimed land called the Watergraafsmeer. The elegant Louis XIV-style Frankendael, flanked by a stable and coach house, is the only one from this period to survive.

The house itself is closed to the public and the best views of the ornamented façade are from the busy Middenweg. This is also the best place to view the ebullient fountain, complete with reclining river gods, made by Ignatius van Logteren in 1714, which stands in the front garden.

The gardens behind the house, however, are open to the public, and offer a peaceful, if unkempt, refuge where overgrown shrubs and ancient trees line the footpaths. There are also large nurseries that visitors are free to wander in.

Ignatius van Logteren's fountain in the grounds of the Frankendael

Tropenmuseum ❷

See pp152–3.

Technologie Museum NINT ❸

Tolstraat 129. ☎ *570 8170.* 🚋 *3, 4.* ◯ *10am–5pm Mon–Fri, noon–5pm Sat & Sun.* ● *Jan 1, Apr 30, Dec 25.*

LOCATED IN a former diamond-cutting factory, the NINT (Nederlands Instituut voor Nijverheid en Techniek) is geared to presenting science and technology in a dynamic way to children. The ground floor is set up as an "Exploratorium" of scientific phenomena. Most of the displays are interactive and help children to understand forces such as electricity and magnetism, or the principles behind dams and dikes. Visitors can even stand inside a giant soap bubble. Upstairs, there is a computer section which runs both recreational and educational programs. An English-language guide to the exhibits is now available at the ticket office. A new national Science and Technology center (IMPULS) is being set up under NINT's guidance to raise the public's interest in technological innovation. Plans for the center include exhibition halls, a science theater, conference facilities and a movie theater.

The late-19th-century façade of the Gemeentearchief Amsterdam

Seeing the world through a soap bubble at the NINT

Gemeentearchief Amsterdam ❹

Amsteldijk 67. **Map** 5 B5. ☎ *572 0202.* 🚋 *3, 4.* ◯ *8:45am–4:45pm Mon–Fri; mid-Aug–mid-Jul: 9am–noon Sat.* ● *public hols.*

THIS ELABORATE 19th-century building, with its ornate Neo-Renaissance façade, used to be the town hall of Nieuwer Amstel, a small community partly annexed by Amsterdam in 1869. It has been home to the city's municipal archives since 1914 and major extensions have been added.

The oldest document in the archives is the Toll of Privilege of 1275, by which Floris V granted freedom from tolls "to the people living near the Dam in the river Amstel" *(see p19)*. The city records include a register of baptisms, marriages and burials dating back to 1550, and a collection of drawings, books, newspapers and audiovisual material. Good exhibitions are often held here.

De Dageraad Housing ❺

Pieter Lodewijk Takstraat. 🚋 *4, 12, 25.* ● *to the public.*

ONE OF THE best examples of Amsterdam School architecture *(see p97)*, De Dageraad housing project was developed for poorer families following the revolutionary Housing Act of 1901 by which the city council was forced to condemn slums and rethink housing policy.

Socialist architect HP Berlage *(see p79)* drew up ingenious plans for the suburbs, aiming to integrate rich and poor by juxtaposing their housing. After Berlage's death, Piet Kramer and Michel de Klerk of the Amsterdam School adopted his ideas. Between 1918 and 1923, they designed this complex for a housing association known as De Dageraad (the Dawn). They used a technique called "apron architecture" in which an underlayer of concrete allows for tucks, folds and rolls in the brick exterior that was then subtly colored and interspersed with decorative doors and windows. Each house mirrors the one opposite and there is a corner tower at the end of every block. The façades were built to give the impression of horizontal movement, an effect produced by the streamlined windows and the undulating roofs.

Imposing corner block of De Dageraad public housing

Interior of Amsterdam RAI with trade fair in progress

Verzetsmuseum Amsterdam ❻

Lekstraat 63. 📞 *644 9797.* 🚋 *4, 12, 25.* 🚌 *15, 69, 169.* ○ *10am–5pm Tue–Fri, 1–5pm Sat, Sun & most public hols.* ● *Jan 1, Apr 30, Dec 25.*

THE RESISTANCE MUSEUM, based in a former synagogue in Nieuw Zuid (New South), holds a fascinating collection of memorabilia recording the activities of Dutch Resistance workers in World War II. It is run by former members of the Resistance and focuses on the courage of the 25,000 people actively involved in the movement. There are gripping displays of false documents, weaponry, videos, film clips, slide shows, photographs and makeshift equipment.

By 1945, there were some 300,000 people in hiding in the Netherlands, including Jews and the Dutch who refused to work for the Nazis. The subsequent "safe house" operation and events organized by the Resistance, like the February Strike against deportation of the Jews *(see p33)*, are brought to life by exhibits showing where the refugees hid and how food was smuggled in. The museum complements the Anne Frankhuis *(see p90)* perfectly.

Amsterdam RAI ❼

Europaplein. 📞 *549 1212.* 🚋 *4.* M 🚆 *RAI.* 🚌 *15, 60, 69, 169.* ○ *depending on exhibition.* **Office & inquiries**: *9am–5pm Mon–Fri.* ♿ *with assistance.*

AMSTERDAM RAI is one of the largest exhibition and conference centers in the country. It hosts more than a thousand events annually, from cabaret to horse shows and trade fairs.

The first Amsterdam trade fair was a bicycle exhibition held in 1893. In subsequent years, the show expanded to include cars and became an annual event known as the "RAI" (Rijwiel Automobiel Industrie). The present complex on Europaplein opened in 1961, but since then has undergone several state-of-the-art expansions. It now boasts 11 exhibition halls, 22 meeting halls and seven restaurants.

Tropenmuseum ❷

BUILT TO HOUSE the Dutch Colonial Institute, this vast complex was finished in 1926 by architects MA and J Nieukerken. The exterior is decorated with symbols of imperialism, such as stone friezes of peasants planting rice. When the building's renovation was completed in 1978, the Royal Tropical Institute opened a museum, with a huge central hall and three levels of galleries. The institute's aims are to study and to help improve the lives of the indigenous populations of the tropics. The displays reflect development issues regarding education, economics and daily life.

Nomad's Felt Tent
Made of felt, with a homey interior, this is a re-created nomad's tent from Afghanistan.

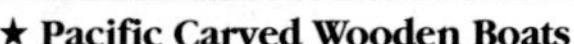

★ Pacific Carved Wooden Boats
The mythical figures in the carved boats, which were used in initiation ceremonies, represent the souls of dead villagers.

★ Bisj Poles
The roots of massive mangrove trees were used to make these exotic, painted ritual totem poles from New Guinea.

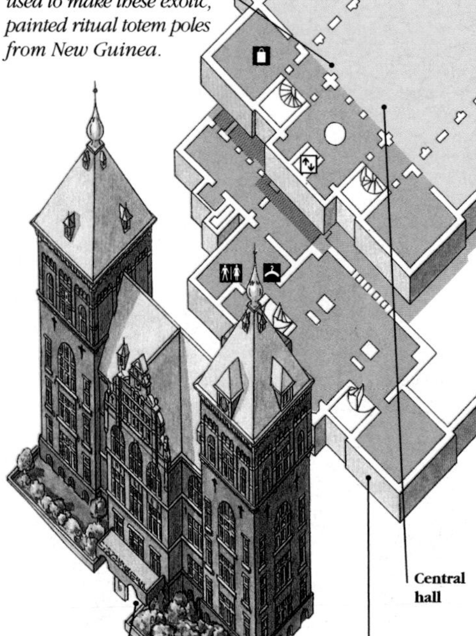

GALLERY GUIDE
The museum has permanent and temporary display areas, with major temporary exhibitions in the central hall on the ground floor. On the upper floors, the permanent exhibitions combine static and interactive displays covering diverse regional topics. The shop on the ground floor has a range of gifts from developing countries, and in the basement are a restaurant, café and theater. There is no guidebook and most of the information is in Dutch.

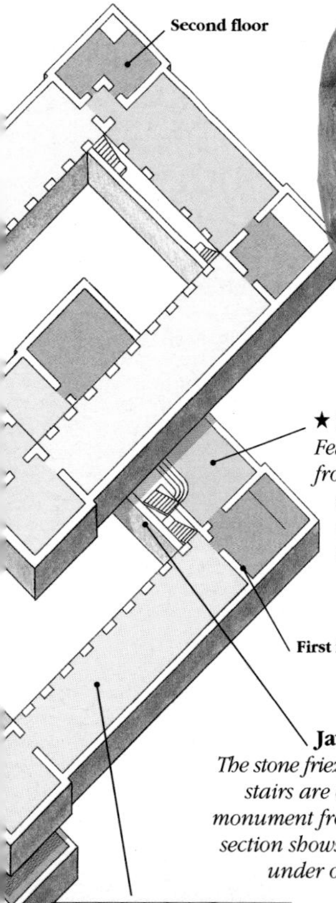

Second floor

First floor

Visitors' Checklist

Linnaeusstraat 2. **Map** 6 E3.
Tropenmuseum *568 8200.* *10am–5pm Mon–Fri, noon–5pm Sat & Sun.* *Jan 1, Apr 30, May 5, Dec 25.*
Kindermuseum *568 8233.* *11am–5pm Mon–Fri during school hols; 1:30–3pm Wed, noon–5pm Sat, Sun & public hols.* *Jan 1, Apr 30, May 5, Dec 25.* 6, 9, 10, 14. *Kindermuseum.*

★ Mask Collection
Feathered fertility masks from Zaire and this carved wooden mask from Central America are included in this collection.

Key to Floorplan

- Asia
- Southeast Asia and Oceania
- Africa
- Central and South America
- Kindermuseum
- Temporary exhibition
- Nonexhibition space

Javanese Stone Friezes
The stone friezes decorating the main stairs are copies from a Javanese monument from about AD 800. This section shows two Buddhas praying under ornate temple awnings.

Bombay Slums
Cramped shacks and street stalls recreate the claustrophobic atmosphere of a typical Indian slum.

Kindermuseum (Children's Museum)

Admission to the children's museum is by appointment only, and adults are not allowed in unless accompanied by a child. The museum, which is aimed at six- to 12-year-olds, takes a "hands-on" approach and young visitors can examine and explore the exhibits. Guides are available to help younger children gain the most from the collection, which is geared to bringing objects alive through their history and culture. Part of the exhibition is permanent, but much of the space is given over to temporary displays exploring specific topics.

Tiger protector mask and model from Bali

Star Exhibits

- **★ Bisj Poles**
- **★ Pacific Carved Wooden Boats**
- **★ Mask Collection**

Amstelpark's Rieker windmill

Amstelpark 8

Europaboulevard. 4. M RAI. 69, 169. dawn–dusk.

SITUATED in the suburb of Buitenveldert, southwest of Amsterdam, this large park was created in 1972. Among its attractions are a rose garden, rhododendron walk and model garden with nursery.

The park offers good facilities for children, including a playground, pony rides and miniature golf and football. The well-preserved Rieker windmill (1636) stands at the southern tip of the park, and art exhibitions are held in the Glazen Huis (Glass House) and the Papillon Gallery. From Easter to October, you can tour the park in a miniature train.

Ouderkerk aan de Amstel 9

M Oranjebaan 175. **Wester Amstel Garden** dawn–dusk.

THIS PRETTY VILLAGE at the junction of the Amstel and the Bullewijk rivers has been a favorite with Amsterdammers since the Middle Ages. They had no church of their own until 1330 *(see pp66–7)*, and worshipers had to travel to the 11th-century Ouderkerk that gave the village its name. The Old Church was destroyed in a tremendous storm in 1674, and a fine 18th-century church now stands on its site. Opposite is the Beth Haim Jewish cemetery, where more than 27,000 Jews from Amsterdam have been buried since 1615. The elders of the Jewish community bought this land to use as a burial ground because Jews were forbidden to bury their dead inside the city.

Today Ouderkerk aan de Amstel is popular with cyclists who come to enjoy the ambience of its waterfront cafés and restaurants. The skyline is dominated by the 50-m (160-ft) spire of the Urbanuskerk, a Catholic church designed by PJH Cuypers *(see pp30–31)* and consecrated in 1867.

A short walk upriver along Amsteldijk, there are two 18th-century country houses. While there is no access to the first, the restful wooded garden of the second house, Wester Amstel, is open to the public. The house, built in 1720, has a fine Louis XV-style gateway and was fully restored in 1989.

Olympic Quarter 10

6, 16, 24. 63, 170, 179.

DEVELOPMENT OF the western side of the Nieuw Zuid (New South) began during the run up to the Olympic Games, held here in 1928. Many of the streets and squares were given Grecian names, like Olympiaplein and Herculesstraat.

The Stadium was designed by J Wils and C van Eesteren. Its stark vertical lines and soaring torch tower recall the work of the American architect Frank Lloyd Wright. Unfortunately, it is obscured by the Citroën building in front, and is under threat of demolition.

The sturdy bridge across the Noorder Amstel Kanaal at Olympiaplein is typical Amsterdam School design. It is the work of PL Kramer and the sculptor H Krop. Beyond the bridge, the Amsterdams Lyceum (a secondary school) shows the style at its best.

The peaceful waterfront at Oudekerk aan de Amstel, south of Amsterdam

Paddleboats on a lake in the Amsterdamse Bos

Electrische Museumtramlijn ⓫

Amstelveenseweg 264.
673 7538. 6, 16. 15.
Apr–Oct: 10:30am–6pm Sun; also school and some public hols.

NOT A MUSEUM, as the name suggests, but a trolley ride with a difference that operates from Haarlemmermeerstation and the southern tip of the Amsterdamse Bos. The trolleys, which were built between 1910 and 1950, have been collected from all over the Netherlands, and from Vienna, Prague and Berlin. The fleet is run by a group of trolley enthusiasts along traditional lines and cars depart regularly from either terminus. A one-way journey takes about 20 minutes and provides a good view of the Olympic Stadium.

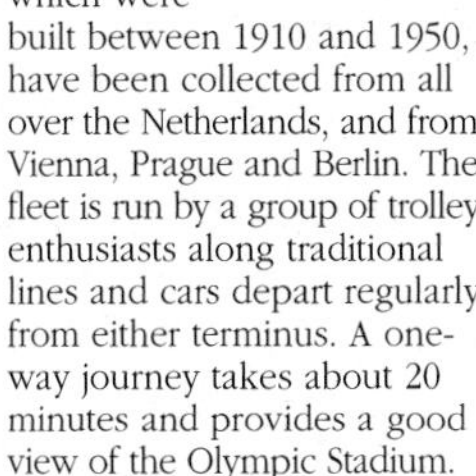

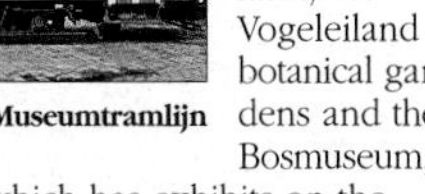

Classic tram from the Museumtramlijn

Amsterdamse Bos ⓬

Amstelveenseweg. Electrische Museumtramlijn (see entry 11).
170, 171, 172. **Theater**
638 3847 (May–Sep).

THIS WOODLAND PARK is the largest recreational area in Amsterdam. It was laid out in the 1930s, in a project to reduce unemployment in the city *(see p33)*. Extensive wooded areas, interspersed with grassy meadows, lakes, waterways and even a hill, were created on reclaimed land that lies 3 m (13 ft) below sea level. The park was enlarged periodically until 1967, when it reached its present size of more than 800 ha (2,000 acres).

Today, the marshy areas around Nieuwe Meer and the lakes at Amstelveense Poel and Kleine Poel are nature preserves. Other highlights include an animal enclosure with gigantic European bison, a goat farm, the Vogeleiland botanical gardens and the Bosmuseum, which has exhibits on the natural and social history of the park.

Among the facilities are a network of planned walks, cycle paths and bridle ways, as well as water sports and an open-air theater *(see p245)*.

Nationaal Luchtvaartmuseum Aviodome ⓭

Westelijke Randweg 1, Schiphol-Centrum. 604 1521. Schiphol. 68, 169, 174. Apr–Sep: 10am–5pm daily; Oct–Mar: 10am–5pm Tue–Fri, noon–5pm Sat & Sun. Jan 1, Dec 25, Dec 31.

THE NATIONAL Aerospace Museum is housed in the giant aluminum Aviodome at Schiphol Airport. On view are more than 30 aircraft as well as models and spacecraft, which trace the history of aviation and space exploration.

Exhibits include the American Wright Flyer of 1903, and the Spider, brainchild of the famous Dutch engineer Anthony Fokker. His Triplane, flown by the famous Red Baron, was the best-known German airplane in World War I. British designs, such as the Spitfire, are also on view.

Many of the exhibits deal with space exploration, from the first unmanned Russian satellite launch in 1957 to recent American space shuttles. Outside the Aviodome there is a 1:10 scale model of Saturn 5, the rocket that took the astronauts Neil Armstrong, Michael Collins and Edwin "Buzz" Aldrin to the moon in 1969.

In the amphitheater at the center of the museum you can see videos about flight, and try your hand at the controls of coin-operated flight-simulators.

The Fokker Triplane from World War I, on view in the Aviodome

Two Guided Walks

Many of Amsterdam's most important historical landmarks, and several fine examples of 16th- and 17th-century architecture, can be enjoyed on both of these walks. The first takes the visitor through the streets of the Jordaan, a peaceful quarter known for its narrow, pretty canals, houseboats and traditional architecture. The route winds through to the man-made Western Islands of Bickerseiland, Realeneiland and Prinseneiland, built in the 17th century to accommodate the expansion in Amsterdam's overseas trade. The area, with its rows of warehouses and wharves, is a reminder of the city's former supremacy at sea. The city's maritime heritage is also evident on the second walk, which starts off from the Schreierstoren, where women waved their husbands off to sea in the 17th century, and finishes at the Nederlands Scheepvaart Museum. On the way, the walk passes the original city boundaries, countless converted warehouses and along streets named after the spices brought in by the East India Company (VOC). On any weekday, there is also the opportunity to spend a few pleasurable hours browsing round the Waterlooplein flea market.

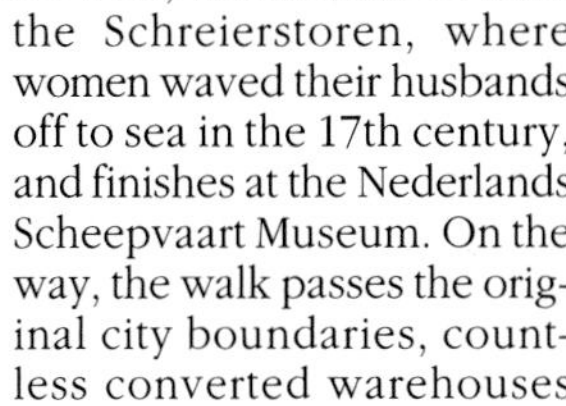

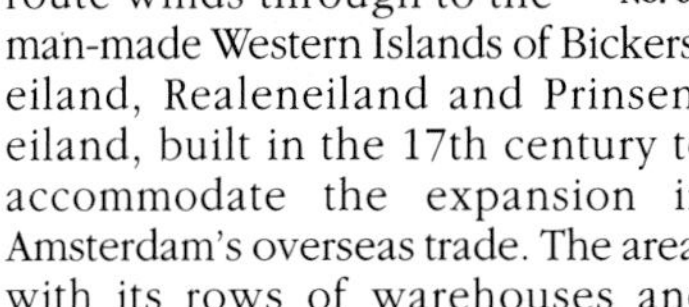

H. WAPEN VAN ESSENDELFT 1657

Wall plaque at No. 6 Zandhoek

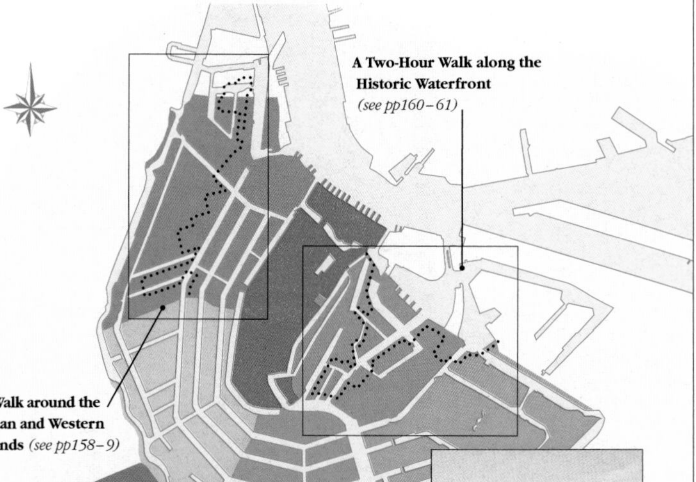

A Two-Hour Walk along the Historic Waterfront *(see pp160–61)*

A Walk around the Jordaan and Western Islands *(see pp158–9)*

Houses on the Amstel near the Stopera *(see pp160–61)*

The Drieharingenbrug across Prinsengracht *(see pp158–9)*

Key

··· Walk route

0 kilometers 1

0 miles 0.5

◁ **View from the tower of the Westerkerk across the Jordaan, with Prinsengracht in the foreground**

A Walk around the Jordaan and Western Islands

THE JORDAAN is a tranquil part of the city, crammed with canal houses, old and new galleries, restaurants, craft shops and sidewalk cafés. The walk route meanders through narrow streets and along enchanting canals. It starts from the Westerkerk and continues past Brouwersgracht, up to the IJ river and on to the Western Islands. These islands have now been adopted by the bohemian artistic community as a fashionable area to live and work.

Plaque on No. 8 Zandhoek, a former sailors' hostel

Prinsengracht to Westerstraat

Outside Hendrick de Keyser's Westerkerk ① *(see p90)* turn left up Prinsengracht, past the Anne Frankhuis ② *(see p90)*, and cross over the canal. Turn left down the opposite side of Prinsengracht and walk along Bloemgracht – the prettiest, most peaceful canal in the Jordaan. Crossing the second bridge, look for the three identical mid-17th-century canal houses called the Drie Hendricken (the three Henrys) ③ *(see p91)*. Continue up 3e Leliedwarsstraat, with its cafés and old shops, turn right and walk past the St. Andrieshofje ④, one of the numerous well-preserved poorhouses in the city. It is worth pausing to take a look across Egelantiersgracht at No. 360, a rare example of an Art Nouveau canal house.

Follow the bank to the end, turn left on to Prinsengracht, passing the Café 't Smalle, and turn left into Egelantiersstraat. In 1e Egelantiersdwarsstraat can be found a group of 17th-century poorhouses, known as the Claes Claeszhofje ⑤ *(see p92)*. Follow this tiny street past several cafés as well as many unusual shops selling clothes, bric-a-brac, pottery and paintings, to Westerstraat.

Ornate step gables (1642) at Nos. 89 and 91 Bloemgracht

Simple wooden gable with hoisting hook on Westerstraat

Westerstraat to Bickerseiland

Cross the street – Westerstraat originally bordered a canal, now filled in – and turn right. The gabled houses are typical of the late-17th-century style of the Jordaan. Walk along for one block and take the first left into 1e Boomdwarsstraat, then right to the Noorderkerk ⑥ *(see p92)*. Each Monday morning a lively flea market takes place in the Noordermarkt *(see p92)*.

Continue on to the south side of the Lindengracht and turn right, passing the Suyckerhofje ⑦ at Nos. 149–163, a former refuge for abandoned women. There is a wall plaque on No. 55 Lindengracht depicting fish swimming in trees and echoing an inverted view of houses reflected in the city's canals. The statue on Lindengracht is of the writer and educationalist Theo Thijssen. Turn left down Brouwersgracht *(see p93)*, which is lined with brightly painted houseboats. Cross the first drawbridge and go into Binnen Oranjestraat, then walk under the railroad bridge onto Bickerseiland, which is named after one of Amsterdam's most wealthy 17th-century families.

KEY

••• Walk route

0 meters 200

0 yards 200

A view of houseboats and gabled houses from Galgenstraat ⑨

The Western Islands

The Western Islands are made up of Bickers-, Prinsen- and Realeneiland *(see p93)*. They were created in the early 17th century to cope with the city's need for warehouses as a result of Amsterdam's maritime trading success. Their quays were lined with ships and barges, while sailors and dock-workers lived in nearby canal houses.

Cross the Hendrik Jonkerplein ⑧ and go on to Bickersgracht where the boatyards are still operational. The first bridge to the left leads on to Prinseneiland and then into Galgenstraat (gallows street) ⑨, so called because the view from here in the 17th century was of the gallows across the IJ. Turning right, follow the bend and cross the wooden drawbridge on to Realeneiland. Turn right along Realengracht, take the first left, then right into Taanstraat, first looking back along Vierwindenstraat where there stands a series of somber old warehouses, once used for storing grain, hemp and flax. At the end, turn right down Zandhoek (sand corner) ⑩ *(see p93)*, with its rows of charming 17th-century houses. The name originates from the sand market that once took place here.

Follow Zandhoek and cross the wooden bridge (a 1983 replica of the original). Stay on the canal and follow the footpath that runs along Bickersgracht. Keep your eyes on the water and you might see a blue-gray heron looking for fish. Walk along Grote Bickersstraat and you will find yourself back where you started, at the bridge leading on to Prinseneiland. To leave the islands and return to the city center, retrace your steps to Haarlemmerdijk and turn left.

The tranquil, tree-lined Egelantiersgracht

Tips for Walkers

***Starting point**: Outside the Westerkerk on the Prinsengracht.*
***Length**: 4.5 km (2.8 miles).*
***Duration**: One and a half hours.*
***Getting there**: Buses 21, 47, 67, 170, 171 and 172. Trolleys 13, 14 and 17 from Centraal Station.*
***Stopping off points**: The Jordaan is packed with cafés and bars. On the Egelantiersgracht, 't Smalle is particularly atmospheric, and there are bars in Noordermarkt, Haarlemmerdijk and Hendrik Jonkerplein. De Gouden Reaal café in Zandhoek is ideal to rest in before the trip home.*

A Two-Hour Walk along the Historic Waterfront

BEGIN THE WALK at the Schreierstoren *(see p67)*, once a defense tower in the medieval town wall. The route follows the development of Amsterdam as a great trading city, as wharves, warehouses and houses were built to accommodate the boom in overseas trade and in population. The city's expansion was carefully planned; as existing waterfronts became overcrowded, more islands were created to the east, slowly reclaiming the surrounding marshy countryside. The walk takes in a number of reminders of the Dutch East India Company (VOC) *(see pp26–7)*, such as the streets named after spices, and ends up at the imposing Nederlands Scheepvaart Museum.

16th-century stone tablet near the main door, Schreierstoren ①

Gables and façades along the right bank of Krommewaal

Schreierstoren to St. Antoniesbreestraat

From the Schreierstoren ①, walk along Prins Hendrikkade, turning at Krommewaal and following the right bank, with its series of rich façades and gables, to Lastageweg ②. Lastage is an area that was developed for trade after the fire of 1452 *(see p21)*. The expansion that followed in the 16th century *(see p23)* brought Lastage within the city walls.

Continue to Rechtboomsloot and turn right and keep going until you reach Geldersekade, which was one of the town boundaries in the 15th century. Follow along Rechtboomsloot, then along the side of Kromboomsloot, until you reach the Schottenburg warehouses ③ at Nos. 18–20. Built in 1636, these are among the oldest in the city and are now converted into apartments. Next door is a former Armenian church, converted from a warehouse in the mid-18th century. Then follow Snoekjesgracht, turning right into St. Antoniesbreestraat ④.

St. Antoniesbreestraat to Uilenburg Island

On St. Antoniesbreestraat, cross the road opposite Elias Bouwman's Pintohuis ⑤ *(see p66)*, the only surviving building from the original street. Enter the Zuiderkerk ⑥ yard opposite through its skull-adorned gateway. The church was built by Hendrick de Keyser *(see p90)* in 1603 and now hosts a permanent exhibition on various aspects of urban renewal. Cross the square and take the exit to

Drawbridge on Staalstraat, crossing Groenburgwal

0 meters 200

0 yards 200

KEY

••• Walk route

M Metro station

Zanddwarstraat, turning right at Zandstraat. Continue to Kloveniersburgwal and turn left along the canal to Staalstraat, where another left turn takes you past the Saaihal ⑦ (the draper's hall), with its unusual trapezoid gable. The first bridge crosses the Groenburgwal, with splendid views of the Amstel to the right. The next bridge leads to the Stopera ⑧ *(see p63)*, and the bustle of Waterlooplein flea market ⑨ *(see p63)*. Follow the market stalls along to Jodenbreestraat, transformed since it was the heart of Jewish Amsterdam. Cross over the road and, with the Museum Het Rembrandthuis ⑩ *(see p62)* to the left, continue to Nieuwe Uilenburgerstraat and on to the island of Uilenburg, built in the late 16th century to take housing for the poor. On the right can be seen the vast Gassan Diamonds factory ⑪, with two synagogues in the yard, a reminder of the time when diamond polishing was one of the few trades open to Jews *(see p64)*.

Wall plaque at Museum Het Rembrandthuis

Uilenburg to the Eastern Islands

Turn left into Nieuwe Batavierstraat and then right at Oude Schans, a broad canal with former warehouses and quays full of eccentric-looking houseboats. On the opposite bank of the canal is the Montelbaanstoren ⑫ *(see p66)*, a defense tower that originates from the 16th century.

At the bend, cross over the Rapenburgwal bridge until you reach Peperstraat. Like other streets on these man-made islands, Peperstraat was named after a commodity imported by the VOC *(see pp26–7)* in the 17th century. From here, turn right onto the main road of Prins Hendrikkade and then into Nieuwe Foliestraat (new mace street). The warehouses on the corner, at No. 176, were once used to store Cape wine and the liqueur, arrack. In Rapenburgerplein, turn left and left again up Schippersgracht, and take the bridge across Nieuwe Herengracht to the gateway of the Entrepotdok ⑬ *(see p144)*. Turn left to Kadijksplein, go along Prins Hendrikkade and across Nieuwevaart bridge where you can see Daniel Staelpart's Oosterkerk, built in the shape of a Greek cross. Continue on to the Eastern Islands, built in 1658 to create more shipyards. The Nederlands Scheepvaart Museum ⑭ *(see pp146–7)* dominates the Oosterdok to the left. To return to the center, follow Prins Hendrikkade westward.

The 16th-century Montelbaanstoren, part of the city defenses ⑫

Antiques at Waterlooplein flea market ⑨

Tips for Walkers

***Starting point**: The Schreierstoren on Prins Hendrikkade.*
***Length**: 6 km (4 miles).*
***Duration**: Two hours.*
***Getting there**: Some buses go along Prins Hendrikkade, but it is easier to take a trolley to Centraal Station (see p79) and walk along the IJ. To join the walk halfway, trolley 9 goes to Waterlooplein.*
***Stopping-off points**: There are cozy brown cafés (see pp 48 and 236) along the start of the walk and at the Stopera (see p63). There are also bars on Schippersgracht and within the Entrepotdok.*

Beyond Amsterdam

BEYOND AMSTERDAM

AMSTERDAM IS AT THE HEART *of a region known as the Randstad, the economic powerhouse of the Netherlands. The city is a haven for tourists; within easy reach are the ancient towns of Leiden and Utrecht, as well as Den Haag and Haarlem with their exceptional galleries and museums. The Randstad extends south as far as Rotterdam, a thriving modern city full of avant-garde architecture.*

Much of the land comprising the Randstad has been reclaimed from the sea during the last 300 years, and the fertile soil is farmed intensively. Production is centered around early season greenhouse crops, like tomatoes and cucumbers and the incomparable Dutch bulbs. Spreading to the southwest in spring, dazzling colors carpet the fields, and the exquisite gardens at Keukenhof *(see p181)* are the showcase of the bulb industry.

Reclamation continues at a quick pace, and Flevoland, the Netherlands' newest province, consists entirely of polder. This flat marshy land, interspersed with drainage channels, has been created since 1950 by draining 1,800 sq km (695 sq miles) of the IJsselmeer. The flat terrain provides shelter for wild birds such as herons, swans and grebes, which nest along the reed-fringed canals. The area beyond Utrecht, to the east of Amsterdam, is much less populated than the Randstad, with vast tracts of unspoiled forest, moorland and peat bog, home to red deer and wild boar.

North of Amsterdam, the traditional fishing communities that depended on the Zuiderzee before it was closed off from the sea in 1932 *(see p170–71)*, have now turned to tourism for their income.

The coast around Zandvoort, lying to the west of Amsterdam, takes the full brunt of vicious North Sea storms in winter, but maritime vegetation and wild birds find shelter among the sandbanks of the exposed coastline.

Drawbridge and canalside café at Enkhuizen – popular with visitors to the Zuiderzee Museum

◁ Traditional working smock mills *(see p173)* at Zaanse Schans

Exploring the Netherlands

AMSTERDAM IS AT THE CENTER of a part of the Netherlands where there are many places of interest within easy reach. Haarlem is just 15 minutes away, and it takes less than half an hour to get to the cheese markets of Edam and Gouda. To the north, the Zuiderzee Museum re-creates an old fishing community, and to the south lies historic Utrecht. The east offers the wilderness of the Nationaal Park de Hoge Veluwe, and the stately Paleis Het Loo, a hunting lodge and summer residence of the Dutch royal family since 1692.

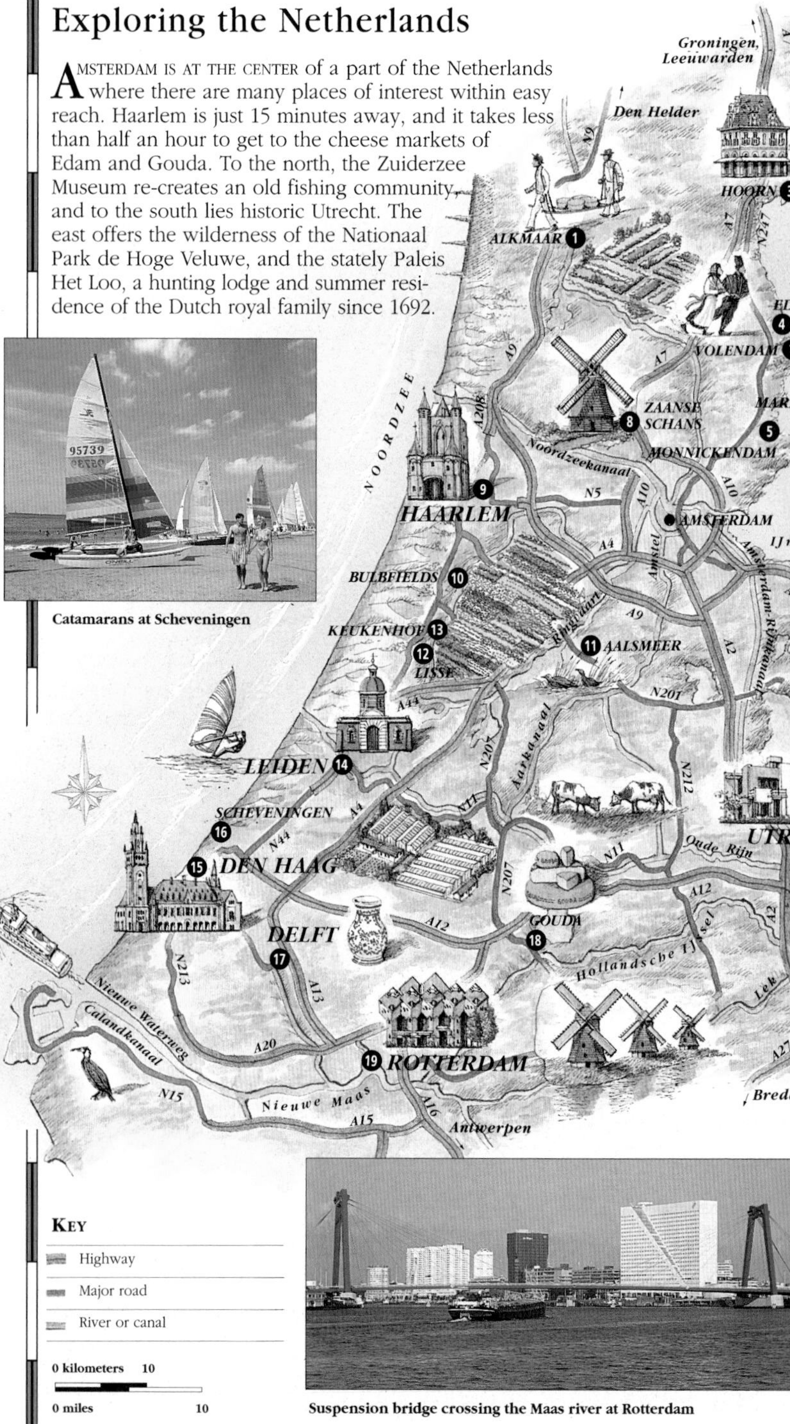

Catamarans at Scheveningen

Suspension bridge crossing the Maas river at Rotterdam

KEY

- Highway
- Major road
- River or canal

0 kilometers 10

0 miles 10

Traditional wooden fishing boats in the harbor at Hoorn

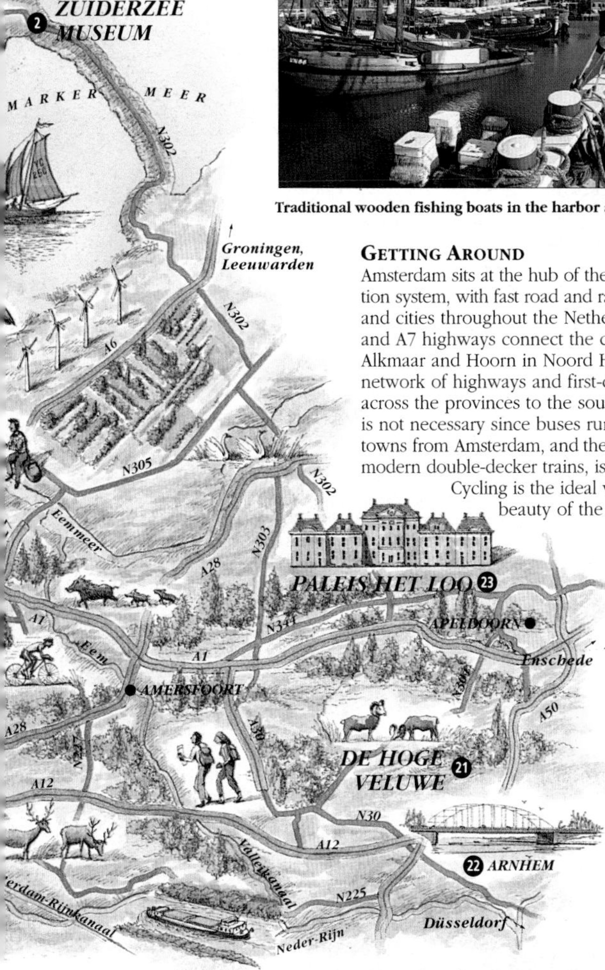

Getting Around

Amsterdam sits at the hub of the Dutch transportation system, with fast road and rail links to towns and cities throughout the Netherlands. The A9 and A7 highways connect the capital with Alkmaar and Hoorn in Noord Holland, and a network of highways and first-class roads cuts across the provinces to the south and east. A car is not necessary since buses run to all major towns from Amsterdam, and the rail service, using modern double-decker trains, is even better.

Cycling is the ideal way to take in the beauty of the spring bulbfields.

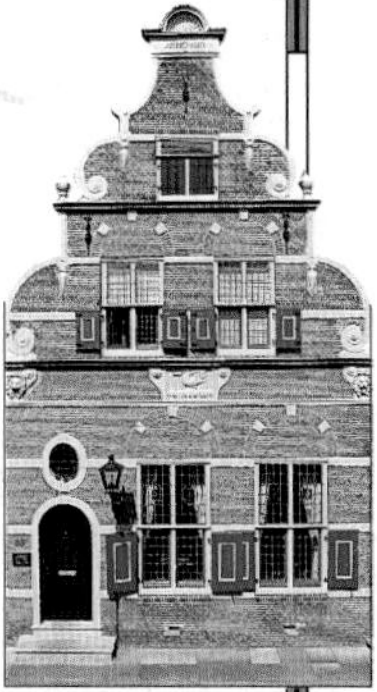

An elaborate gabled façade in Monnickendam

Sights at a Glance

Aalsmeer 11
Alkmaar 1
Arnhem 22
Delft 17
Den Haag 15
Edam 4
Gouda 18
Haarlem 9
Hoorn 3
Keukenhof 13
Leiden 14
Lisse 12
Marken 6
Monnickendam 5
Nationaal Park de Hoge Veluwe 21
Paleis Het Loo 23
Rotterdam 19
Scheveningen 16
Utrecht 20
Volendam 7
Zaanse Schans 8
Zuiderzee Museum 2

Tour

Tour of the Bulbfields 10

Children in national costume at the Zuiderzee Museum

Renaissance façade and bell tower of Alkmaar's Waaggebouw (1582)

Alkmaar ❶

40 km (25 miles) NW of Amsterdam. *90,000.* *Waaggebouw, Waagplein 2. (072) 5114 284.* *cheese market: mid-Apr–mid-Sep: 10am–noon Fri; general market: Sat.*

ALKMAAR is an attractive old town with tree-lined canals and an historic center, scene of an unsuccessful siege by the Spanish in 1573. It is one of the few Dutch towns to maintain its traditional cheese market, which is held every Friday morning in summer. Local producers lay out Gouda cheeses and some rounds of Edam in the Waagplein, and from here porters take them off on sleds for weighing. The porters, who sport colorful straw hats, belong to an ancient guild and indulge in good-natured rivalry for the benefit of onlookers. The streets around the Waagplein are packed with stands that sell everything from cheese to locally made pottery.

Waaggebouw

Waagplein 2. *(072) 5114 284.* **Waaggebouw** *mid-Apr–mid-Sep: 9:30am–1pm Fri.* **Hollandse Kaasmuseum** *Apr–Oct: Mon–Sat.*

The focal point of the cheese market is the imposing Waaggebouw (weigh house), which was altered in 1582 from a 14th-century chapel. It now contains the Hollandse Kaasmuseum, where local cheesemaking techniques are revealed. Each day on the hour, mechanical knights, situated under the clock of the Waaggebouw, stage a short jousting tournament while a clarion blower sounds his trumpet.

Grote Kerk

Kerk Plein, Koor Straat. *(072) 5159 979.* *until 1996 for restoration.*

This imposing Gothic church contains the tomb of Floris V *(see p19)*, whose body was exhumed and brought here when the building was completed in 1520. The 17th-century organ, built by Jacob van Campen *(see p74)* and painted by Cesar van Everdingen, dominates the Grote Kerk's nave.

Porters carrying cheese on sleds in Alkmaar's traditional market

Zuiderzee Museum ❷

See pp170–71.

Hoorn ❸

40 km (25 miles) N of Amsterdam. *60,000.* *Veemarkt 4. (0229) 231 055.* *Wed.*

HOORN WAS the capital of the ancient province of West Friesland and one of the great seafaring towns of the Golden Age *(see pp24–7)*. The collection of ornate patrician houses in the streets around Rode Steen, Hoorn's main square, attest to the town's prosperous history. Several famous maritime heroes were born here, including Willem Schouten (1580–1625), who named the tip of South America Cape Horn after his birthplace, and Abel Tasman *(see pp26–7)*. A statue in Rode Steen commemorates Jan Pietersz Coen (1587–1629), a famous explorer who went on to found Batavia, now known as Jakarta, the capital of Indonesia *(see pp26–7)*.

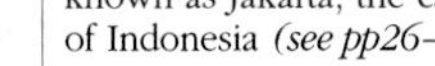

ANNO 1609

Painted unicorn, Westfriies Museum

Westfriies Museum

Rode Steen 1. *(0229) 215 783.* *daily.* *Jan 1, Apr 30, Aug 15, Dec 25.*

The building that houses the Westfriies Museum in Rode Steen was built in 1632 as a prison – indeed the square took its name, "red stone," from the blood spilled at public executions held there.

The three-tiered gable of this splendid building is decorated with heraldic figures carrying the coats of arms of the towns that made up the province of West Friesland. Inside, the museum is little changed since Aldous Huxley, the English writer, described it affectionately in 1925 as "filled with mixed rubbish." There is much to enjoy here, from the archaeological displays in the basement to the 17th-century period rooms filled with rich furniture and antique clocks.

Wooden clogs outside a restored fisherman's cottage in Monnickendam

Edam ❹

22 km (14 miles) N of Amsterdam. 7,000. Damplein 1. (0299) 371 727. cheese market: Jul–Aug: 10am–noon Wed; general market: every Wed.

The name of Edam is known throughout the world for its ball-shaped cheeses that are wrapped in wax – red for export, and yellow for local consumption. In the summer, cheese lovers should head for the *kaasmarkt* (cheese market), held in the main square, which is called Damplein. The *kaasmarkt's* single-gabled weigh house dates from 1592 and has a gaudy painted façade. Nowadays, cheesemaking is an automated process and some of the factories around the outskirts of the town offer guided tours for visitors.

Edam itself is exceptionally pretty, full of narrow canals bordered by elegant, gabled Golden Age canal houses and crossed by drawbridges. The imposing Grote Kerk is noted both for its 16th-century carillon, and its stained-glass windows (1606–24), which are among the most beautiful in the Netherlands. The harbor to the east of the town was built in the 17th century, in the days when Edam was a prominent whaling center.

Edams Museum

Damplein 8. (0299) 372 644. Apr–Oct: daily. Apr 30, May 1.

This amazing Gothic building (1530) is home to an eccentric museum of local history. The peculiar, timbered interior and steep, narrow stairs look like the inside of a ship. According to some, the house was built for a retired sea captain who could not bear sleeping on dry land. Adding credence to this story is the unusual floating cellar, where the floor rises and falls with fluctuations in the water table. Just as strange are the 17th-century portraits of odd-looking locals, such as Trijntje Kever, who was said to be almost 2.8 m (9 ft) tall.

Monnickendam ❺

16 km (10 miles) N of Amsterdam. 10,000. De Zarken 2. (0299) 651998. Sat.

Visitors flock to this beautifully preserved little port to admire the gabled houses and wander past the renovated fishermen's cottages in the narrow, winding streets around the harbor. Freshly smoked local eel can be bought from the smokehouses along the harbor walls, and here the fish restaurants have become a popular draw for tourists.

The **Museum de Speeltoren** is dedicated to the history of Monnickendam. It is housed in the clock tower of the Stadhuis, which has a rather ornate, arched 15th-century carillon. When the bells chime on the hour, the clockwork knights in armor parade around the exterior of the tower.

Museum de Speeltoren

Noordeinde 4. (0299) 652203. May–Aug: daily.

Drawbridge on one of the canals at Edam

Zuiderzee Museum ❷

ENKHUIZEN WAS one of several villages around the edge of the Zuiderzee whose fishing-based economy was devastated when access to the North Sea was blocked by construction of the Afsluitdijk in 1932 *(see p165)*. The village's fortunes were revived with the opening of this museum complex and the conversion of the old fishing harbor into a yachting marina. A permanent display of local boats is housed in the Binnenmuseum (indoor museum). The Buitenmuseum (open air museum) consists of rescued buildings, reconstructed to characterize a typical Zuiderzee village.

★ Houses from Urk
Buildings from the little island of Urk have been rebuilt in the open air museum. Daily life on the island in 1905 is re-created by actors in role play.

★ Marine Hall
Housed in an old warehouse of the Dutch East India Company (see pp26–7), *the indoor museum's Marine Hall contains sailing and fishing boats. A small pleasure boat is rigged up for children to play in.*

Smoke-houses from Monnickendam

Reconstruction of Marken harbor

Sail-maker's Shop
Until the early 20th century, most Dutch ships and fishing boats had sails. The ancient craft of sailmaking is kept alive in this workshop.

Barges carry visitors to the open air museum.

★ Lime Kilns
Bottle-shaped kilns were used to burn shells dredged from the sea bed. The resulting quicklime was used as an ingredient in mortar for bricklaying. These kilns are from Akersloot in Noord Hollan

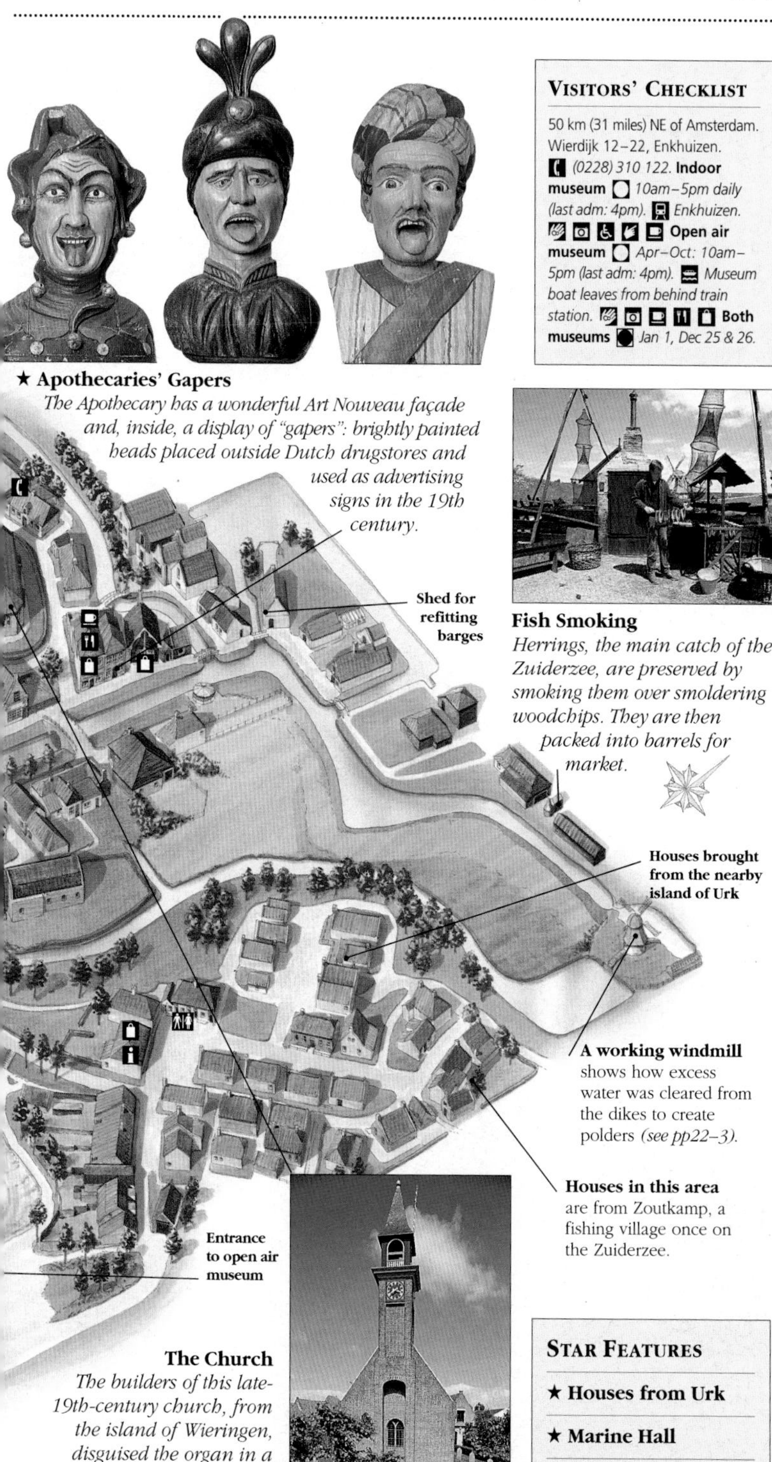

Visitors' Checklist

50 km (31 miles) NE of Amsterdam. Wierdijk 12–22, Enkhuizen. *(0228) 310 122.* **Indoor museum** *10am–5pm daily (last adm: 4pm).* *Enkhuizen.* **Open air museum** *Apr–Oct: 10am–5pm (last adm: 4pm).* *Museum boat leaves from behind train station.* **Both museums** *Jan 1, Dec 25 & 26.*

★ Apothecaries' Gapers

The Apothecary has a wonderful Art Nouveau façade and, inside, a display of "gapers": brightly painted heads placed outside Dutch drugstores and used as advertising signs in the 19th century.

Fish Smoking

Herrings, the main catch of the Zuiderzee, are preserved by smoking them over smoldering woodchips. They are then packed into barrels for market.

A working windmill shows how excess water was cleared from the dikes to create polders *(see pp22–3).*

Houses in this area are from Zoutkamp, a fishing village once on the Zuiderzee.

The Church

The builders of this late-19th-century church, from the island of Wieringen, disguised the organ in a cupboard to avoid the tax then levied on church organs.

Star Features

- ★ Houses from Urk
- ★ Marine Hall
- ★ Apothecaries' Gapers

Marken 6

16 km (10 miles) NE of Amsterdam. 2,000. *De Zarken 2. (0299) 651998.*

UNTIL RECENTLY, Marken was an island fishing community that had changed very little over 200 years. However, the construction of a causeway link between the village and the mainland in 1957 brought an abrupt end to its isolation.

Though the appearance of the village may seem slightly artificial, it is extremely popular with tourists, who are drawn here by its old-world character. The local inhabitants still wear traditional dress and the gabled timber houses are painted in the rather somber shades of black and green.

Marken's transition from fishing community to tourist center is neatly symbolized by the local heritage center, the **Marker Museum** – a cramped fisherman's house packed with brightly painted furniture.

Marker Museum
Kerkbuurt 44. *(0299) 651904.*
Apr–Oct: daily.

Yachts and pleasure boats in Volendam's marina

Volendam 7

18 km (11.5 miles) NE of Amsterdam. 18,000. *Zeestraat 37. (0299) 363747. Sat.*

THE HARBOR in Volendam is now overrun with tourists and souvenir shops, but the village is still worth exploring for the narrow canals and streets behind the main dikes, an area known as the Doolhof. The residents wear traditional costume: tight bodices, winged lace caps and striped aprons for the women; baggy trousers and sweaters for the men.

Artists flocked to Volendam in the late 19th century to paint views of this pretty town. Many stayed at the Spaander Hotel at No. 15 Haven, and the walls of the hotel's café are covered with paintings accepted by the owners in lieu of payment.

A typical 17th-century gabled timber house in Marken

Zaanse Schans 8

13 km (8 miles) N of Amsterdam. 130,000. *1509 AV Zaandam, Zaandijk. (075) 6168 218.*

ZAANSE SCHANS is a small village, newly created in 1960 as a monument to local life in the 17th century. Stores, cottages, windmills, houses and historic buildings from all over the Zaan region have been relocated here to create a museum village in which people can live and work.

The village community is dedicated to preserving the traditional Dutch way of life, and Zaanse Schans is run as a piece of living history. The villagers operate the carefully restored windmills themselves; these include a mustard mill, the last working oil mill still in existence, and mills that generate power. The energy they produce goes to sawing logs for building timber, and to grinding minerals to make pigments used in paint.

Although the village is very crowded in summer, visitors still flock to Zaanse Schans. Attractions include the clock museum and craft workshops, and there are several restaurants catering exclusively to tourists. In summer, cruises can be taken in open-topped boats along the surrounding dikes.

Windmill Technology

WINDMILLS HAVE been a familiar feature of the Dutch landscape since the 13th century. They had many uses, including grinding corn, crushing seed to make oil and driving sawmills. However, since much of the Netherlands lies below sea level, their most vital function was to drain the land of lakes and marshes, and extend the shoreline to create fertile farmland called *polder*. Subsequently, the windmills have had to cope with the constant threat of flooding. To help prevent this, canals were dug to drain water from the soil; the mills then pumped excess water via a series of stepped canals until it drained into the main river system. Today, most land drainage is carried out by electric pumps driven by wind turbines. Of the thousands of windmills that once dotted the Dutch countryside, about 950 survive, many preserved in working order.

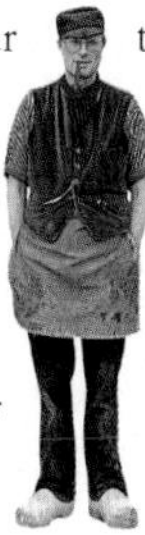

Miller in cap and apron

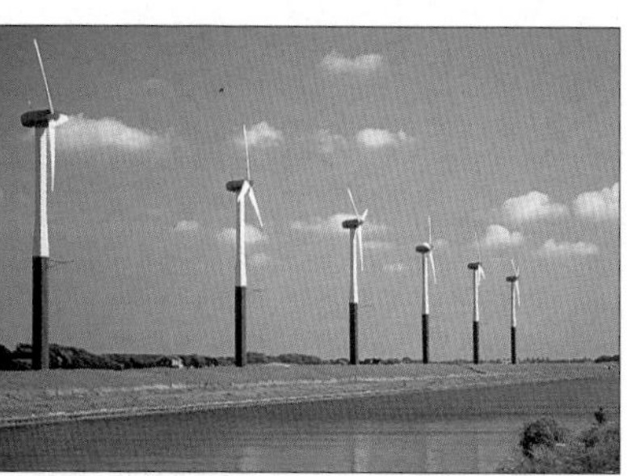

***Modern aerogenerators**, or wind turbines, are widely used in the Netherlands. They harness strong gusts of wind to create electricity without the pollution caused by burning fossil fuels such as gas or coal.*

Trelliswork and canvas sail
Drive shaft
Archimedes' screw
Upper channel

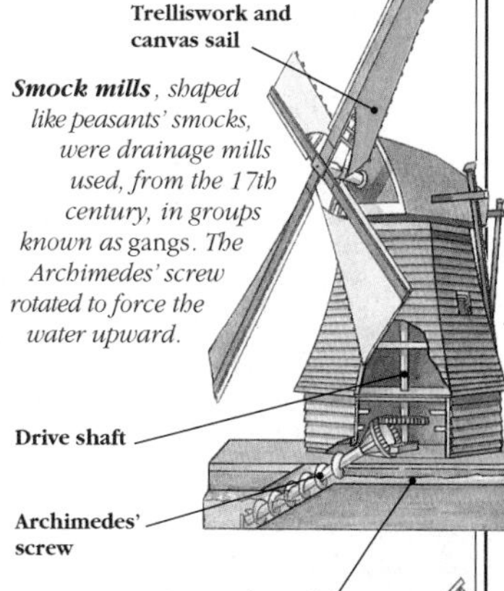

***Smock mills**, shaped like peasants' smocks, were drainage mills used, from the 17th century, in groups known as* gangs. *The Archimedes' screw rotated to force the water upward.*

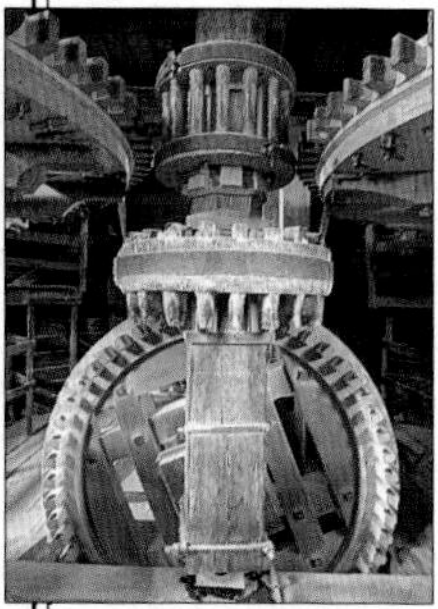

***The sails** of this traditional windmill transmit power via mechanical gears. A rotating cog operates an adjacent wheel to drive the water pump.*

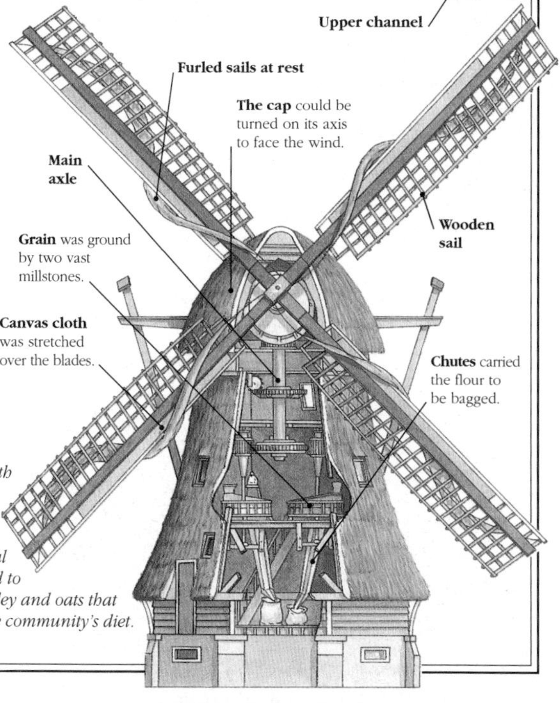

Furled sails at rest
The cap could be turned on its axis to face the wind.
Main axle
Wooden sail
Grain was ground by two vast millstones.
Canvas cloth was stretched over the blades.
Chutes carried the flour to be bagged.

***Flour mills**, thatched with reeds and shaped like giant pepperpots, were vital to Dutch daily life. Sophisticated internal mechanisms were used to grind the wheat, barley and oats that formed the basis of the community's diet.*

Street-by-Street: Haarlem ❾

Misericord in the Grote Kerk

HAARLEM is the commercial capital of Noord Holland province and the eighth largest city in the Netherlands. It is the center of the Dutch printing, pharmaceutical and bulb-growing industries, but there is little sign of this in the delightful pedestrianized streets of the historic heart of the city. Most of the sites of interest are within easy walking distance of the Grote Markt, a lively square packed with ancient buildings, cafés and restaurants. Old bookstores, antique dealers and traditional food stores are all to be discovered in nearby streets.

Statue of Laurens Coster
According to local legend, Haarlem-born Laurens Jansz Coster (1370–1440) invented printing in 1423, 16 years before Gutenberg. The 19th-century statue in the Grote Markt celebrates the claim.

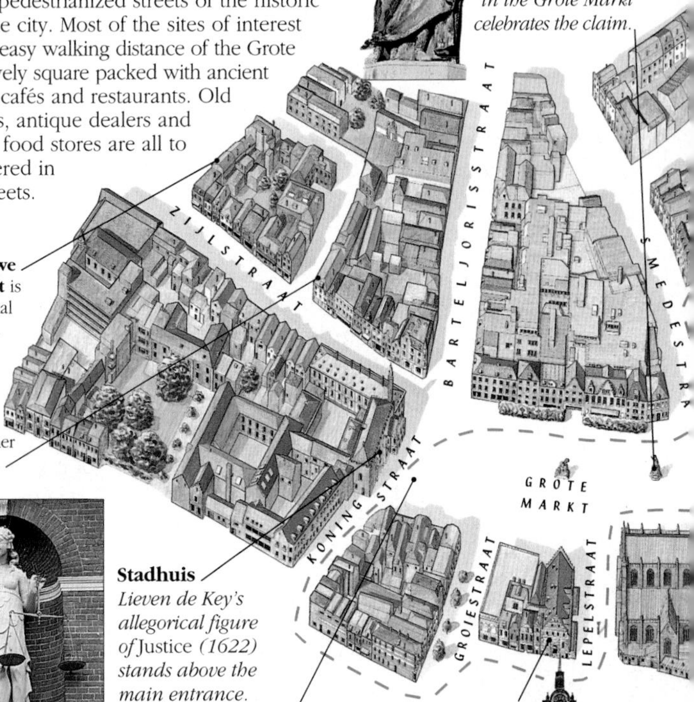

ZIJLSTRAAT
BARTELJORISSTRAAT
SMEDESTRAAT
KONINGSTRAAT
GROTE MARKT
GROIESTRAAT
LEPELSTRAAT

No. 39 Nieuwe Groenmarkt is an exceptional cheese shop.

The Hoofdwacht is a 17th-century, former guard house.

Stadhuis
Lieven de Key's allegorical figure of Justice (1622) stands above the main entrance. She carries a sword and the scales of justice.

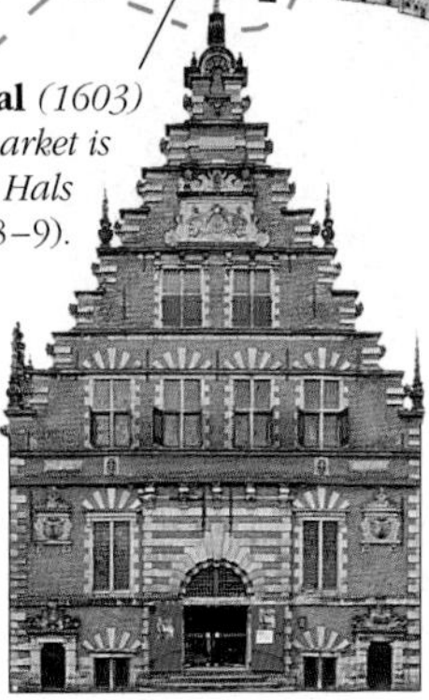

Vleeshal *(1603)*
The old meat market is part of the Frans Hals Museum (see pp178–9).

Grote Markt
The tree-lined market square is bordered with busy pavement restaurants and cafés. It has been the meeting point for the townspeople for centuries.

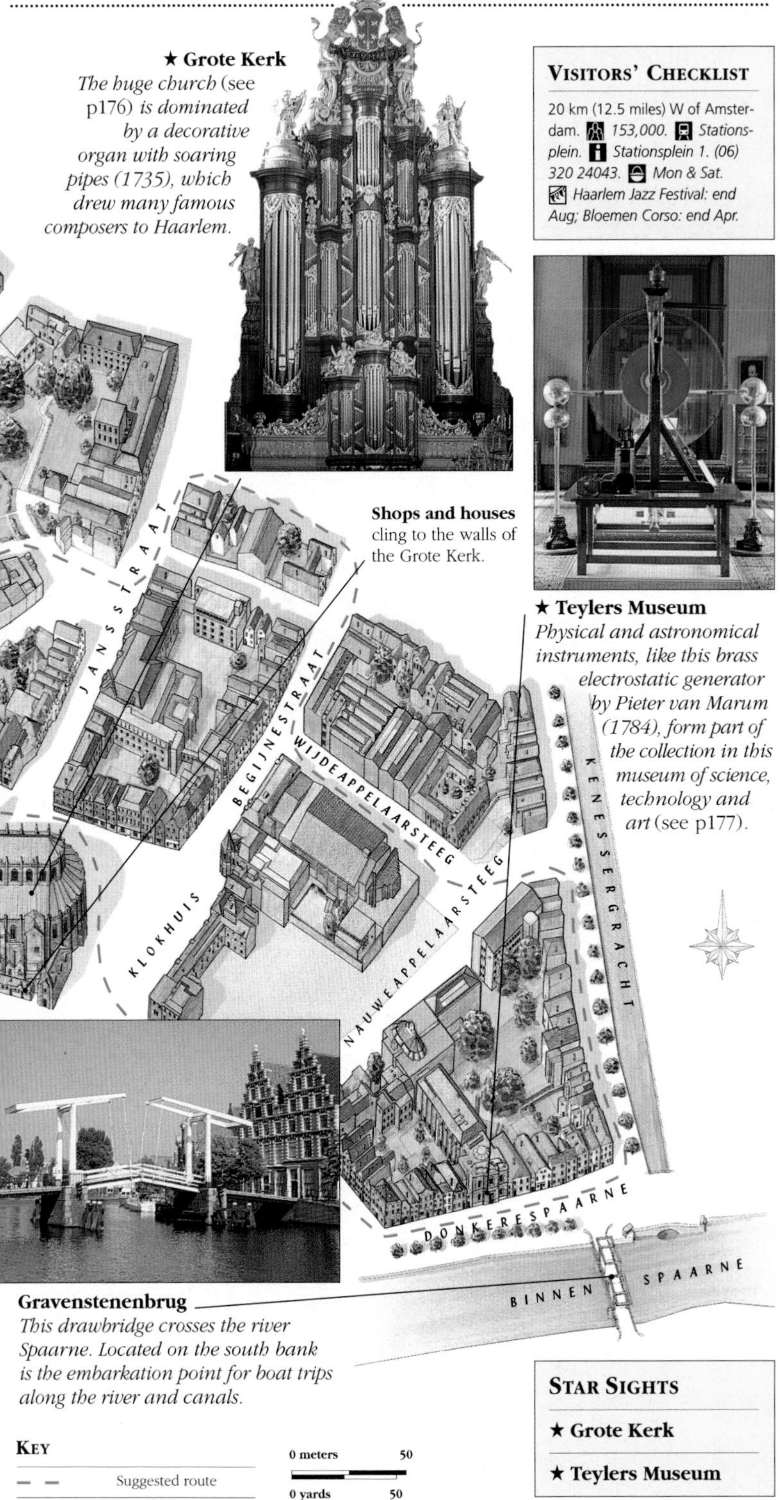

★ Grote Kerk
The huge church (see p176) *is dominated by a decorative organ with soaring pipes (1735), which drew many famous composers to Haarlem.*

Visitors' Checklist

20 km (12.5 miles) W of Amsterdam. *153,000.* *Stationsplein.* *Stationsplein 1. (06) 320 24043.* *Mon & Sat.* *Haarlem Jazz Festival: end Aug; Bloemen Corso: end Apr.*

Shops and houses cling to the walls of the Grote Kerk.

★ Teylers Museum
Physical and astronomical instruments, like this brass electrostatic generator by Pieter van Marum (1784), form part of the collection in this museum of science, technology and art (see p177).

Gravenstenenbrug
This drawbridge crosses the river Spaarne. Located on the south bank is the embarkation point for boat trips along the river and canals.

Key

– – Suggested route

0 meters 50

0 yards 50

Star Sights

- **★ Grote Kerk**
- **★ Teylers Museum**

Exploring Haarlem

HAARLEM BECAME A CITY in 1245, and had grown into a thriving clothmaking center by the 15th century. But in the Spanish siege of 1572–3 the city was sacked, and a series of fires wreaked further destruction in 1576. The town's fortunes changed in the 17th century, when industrial expansion ushered in a period of prosperity lasting throughout the Golden Age *(see pp24–7)*. The center was largely rebuilt by Lieven de Key (1560–1627) and still retains much of its character. The Grote Kerk continues to overlook the city's *hofjes* (poorhouses), and the brick-paved lanes around the Grote Markt are little changed.

***Grote Markt, Haarlem* (c.1668) by Berckheyde, showing the Grote Kerk**

Frans Hals Museum

See pp178–9.

Grote Kerk

Oude Groenmarkt. *(023) 5324 399.* *Mon–Sat.*

The enormous Gothic edifice of Sint Bavo's great church, often referred to simply as the Grote Kerk, was a favorite subject of the 17th-century Haarlem School artists Pieter Saenredam (1597–1665) and Gerrit Berckheyde (1639–98). Built between 1400 and 1550, the church and its ornate bell tower dominate the market square. Clinging to the exterior of the south wall is a jumble of 17th-century stores and houses. The rents raised from these ramshackle, untidy buildings contributed to the maintenance of the church.

Today, the entrance to the Grote Kerk is through one of the surviving stores, a tiny antechamber that leads straight into the enormous nave. The church has a high, delicately patterned, vaulted cedarwood ceiling, white upper walls, and 28 supporting columns painted in greens, reds and golds. The intricate choir screen, like the magnificent brass lectern in the shape of a preening eagle, was made by master metal worker Jan Fyerens in about 1510. The choirstalls (1575) are painted with coats of arms, and the armrests and misericords are carved with caricatures of animals and human heads. Nearby is the simple stone slab covering the grave of Haarlem's most famous artist, Frans Hals.

The Grote Kerk boasts one of Europe's finest and most flamboyant organs, built in 1735 by Christiaan Müller. In 1738 Handel tried the organ and pronounced it excellent. It also found favor with the child prodigy Mozart, who shouted for joy when he gave a recital on it in 1766. The organ continues to contribute to the city's civic pride, and is often used for concerts, recordings and teaching.

Detail on Vleeshal façade by Lieven de Key

Stadhuis

Grote Markt 2. *(023) 5113 000.* *by appt only.*

Haarlem's Stadhuis (town hall) has grown rather haphazardly over the centuries and is an odd mixture of architectural styles dating from 1250. The oldest part of the building is the beamed medieval banquet hall of the counts of Holland *(see p19)*, originally known as the Gravenzaal. Much of this was destroyed in two great fires in 1347 and 1351, but the 15th-century panel portraits of the counts of Holland can still be seen.

The wing of the town hall bordering the Grote Markt was designed by Lieven de Key in 1622. It is typical of Dutch Renaissance architecture, combining elaborate gables, ornate painted detail and Classical features, such as pediments over the windows.

In a niche above the main entrance is a plump allegorical figure of Justice, bearing a sword in one hand and scales in the other as she smiles benignly upon the pavement cafés in the market below. To the left, in Koningstraat, an archway leads to the university buildings behind the Stadhuis, where there is a 13th-century cloister and library.

De Hallen (Vleeshal and Verweyhal)

Grote Markt 16. *(023) 5164 200.* *daily.* *Jan 1, Dec 25.*

De Hallen (the halls) is the collective name for two buildings in the Grote Markt that have recently been acquired by the Frans Hals Museum *(see pp178–9)*. They have each been remodeled inside to accommodate exhibitions of Dutch Expressionism, the Cobra School, Impressionists and contemporary works by Dutch artists and sculptors. The heavily ornamented Vleeshal (meat market) is situated just to the west of the church. It was built in 1602 by the city surveyor, Lieven de Key, and has a steep step gable that

The west gate of the Amsterdamse Poort (1355)

disguises the roof line. The extravagantly overdecorated miniature gables above each dormer window bristle with pinnacles. A giant painted ox's head on the building's façade signifies its original function.

The more recent Verweyhal is named after the Impressionist painter Kees Verwey, whose still lifes are an important feature in this modern art museum.

Amsterdamse Poort

Nr Amsterdamsevaart. *to public.*

The imposing medieval gateway that once helped protect Haarlem lies close to the west bank of the river Spaarne. The Amsterdamse Poort was one of a complex of 12 gates guarding strategic transport routes in and out of Haarlem. The gate was built in 1355, though much of the elaborate brickwork and tiled gables date from the late 15th century.

The city defenses were severely tested in 1573, when the Spanish, led by Frederick of Toledo, besieged Haarlem for eight months during the Dutch Revolt *(see pp22–3).* The city fathers agreed to surrender the town on terms that included a general amnesty for all its citizens. The Spanish appeared to accept, but once the city gates were opened, they marched in and treacherously slaughtered nearly 2,000 people – almost the entire population of the city.

Teylers Museum

Spaarne 16. *(023) 5319 010.* *Tue–Sun.* *Jan 1, Dec 25.*

This was the first major public museum to be founded in the Netherlands. It was established in 1778 by the wealthy silk merchant Pieter Teyler van der Hulst to encourage the study of science and art. The museum's eccentric collection of fossils, drawings and scientific paraphernalia is displayed in considerable Neo-Classical splendor in a series of 18th-century rooms. The two-story Oval Hall was added in 1779, and contains bizarre glass cabinets full of minerals and cases of intimidating medical instruments. A significant collection of sketches by Dutch and Italian masters, including Rembrandt and Michelangelo, are shown a few at a time.

St. Elisabeth's Gasthuis

Groot Heiligland. *(023) 5340 584.* *Tue–Sun.* *Jan 1, Dec 25.*

Haarlem is well known for its *hofjes* (almshouses) that were set up to minister to the poor and sick *(see p93).* Almshouses began to appear in the 16th century, and were run by rich guild members, who took over the role traditionally filled by the monasteries until the Alteration of 1578 *(see pp22–3).*

St. Elisabeth's Gasthuis was built in 1610, around a pretty courtyard opposite what is now the Frans Hals Museum. A stone plaque carved above the main doorway in 1612 depicts an invalid being carried off to the hospital, with distraught relatives following. This almshouse has recently undergone extensive restoration and opens in 1995 as Haarlem's principal historical museum.

Haarlem Station

Stationsplein. *(023) 5319 059.*

The first railway line in the Netherlands opened in 1839 and ran between Haarlem and Amsterdam *(see pp30–31).* The original station, built in 1842, was reworked in Art Nouveau style between 1905–8. It is a grandiose brick building with an arched façade and square towers. The green and beige interior is decorated with brightly colored tiles depicting modes of transportation. Other highlights are the timberwork of the offices and highly decorative wrought-iron staircases.

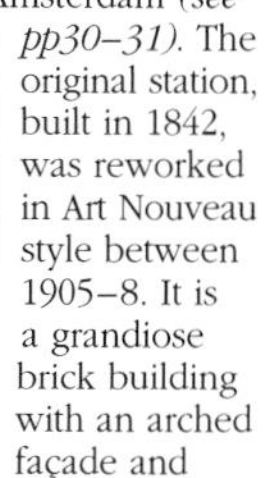

Tiles in Haarlem Station

17th- and 18th-century gabled houses along the Spaarne in Haarlem

Frans Hals Museum

HAILED AS the first "modern" artist, Frans Hals (1580–1666) introduced a new realism into painting. While contemporary painters aimed for an exact likeness, Hals captured the character of his sitters through a more impressionistic technique. In his eighties, he was still able to paint impressive portraits, such as *The Lady Governess of the Old Men's Home in Haarlem* (1664). His last years were spent in the Old Men's Home, which became the Frans Hals Museum in 1913. Besides his work, there is a selection of Dutch art from the 16th century to the present day.

Mother and Child
Following the Alteration (see pp22–3), *artists like Pieter de Grebber (1600–53) often painted secular versions of religious themes. This painting (1622) of a woman suckling her baby recalls the Virgin Mary with Jesus.*

STAR PAINTINGS

- ★ **Banquet of the Officers by Frans Hals**
- ★ **Still Life by Floris van Dijck**
- ★ **Mercury by Hendrick Goltzius**

KEY TO FLOORPLAN

- Works by Frans Hals
- Renaissance Gallery
- Old Masters
- Applied art and design
- Modern art
- Temporary exhibitions
- Nonexhibition space

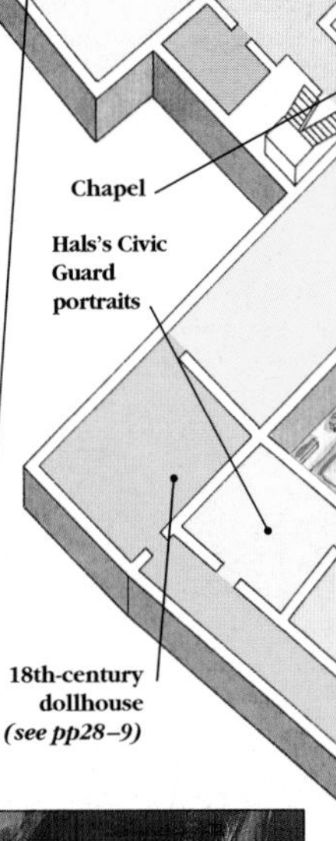

★ Banquet of the Officers of the Civic Guard of St. George *(1616)*
The characteristics of each of the 12 Civic Guards and the opulence of their banqueting hall are superbly portrayed in this formal group portrait by Frans Hals.

Delft Dish *(1662)*
This blue-and-white earthenware dish by M Eems shows the Grote Kerk and Grote Markt in Haarlem (see p176).

Portrait of Else Berg
Leo Gestel (1881–1941) was instrumental in the introduction of Cubism to the Netherlands. This vivid portrait of his fellow artist, wearing a flamboyant hat, was painted in 1913.

Visitors' Checklist

Groot Heiligland 62, Haarlem. *(023) 5164 200.* *Haarlem.* *11am–5pm Mon–Sat (last adm 4:30pm); 1–5pm Sun & public hols.* *Jan 1, Dec 25.* *1:30pm Sun.*

★ Mercury *(1611)*
Hendrick Goltzius (1558–1617) was best known for his studies of Classical nudes. This canvas was commissioned by a wealthy Haarlem burgomaster as one of a series of three.

Museum Guide
The entrance leads into a modern wing housing temporary exhibits. Walk around the museum counter-clockwise; displays of Frans Hals' work, portraits, still life and modern paintings are in rough chronological order. Exhibits are also held in De Hallen (Vleeshal and Verweyhal) which are in the Grote Markt (see p176).

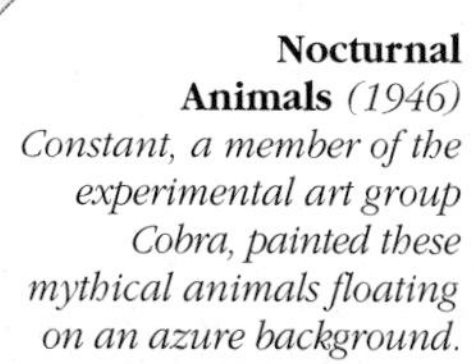

Small courtyard

Main entrance

Nocturnal Animals *(1946)*
Constant, a member of the experimental art group Cobra, painted these mythical animals floating on an azure background.

★ Still Life *(1613)*
Precise attention to detail and texture was the hallmark of Floris van Dijck (1575–1651). The damask tablecloth shown in the painting was a product of Haarlem's thriving linen industry.

A Tour of the Bulbfields ⑩

Occupying a 30-km (19-mile) strip between Haarlem and Leiden, the Bloembollenstreek is the most important bulb-growing area in the Netherlands. From late January, the polders bloom with a succession of vividly colored bulbs, beginning with early crocuses and building to a climax around mid-April when the tulips flower. These are followed by late-blooming flowers like lilies, which extend the season into late May. If you don't have a car, the VVV *(see p256)* has details on a variety of tours. Alternatively, you can rent a bicycle at Haarlem railroad station and drop it off at Leiden station.

Tips for Drivers

Starting point: *Haarlem.*
Length: *Approx 30 km (19 miles).*
Stopping-off points: *In addition to the places named below, all of which have a selection of restaurants, cafés and bars, it is worth diverting to Noordwijk aan Zee. This lively seaside town, with its lovely dune-backed beach, is a perfect picnic spot. Good viewpoints en route are marked on the map.*

Sand dunes lining the coast

De Cruquius Museum ①
The museum contains a mass of exhibits that explain how polders and dams are created and how the Dutch have kept sea and flood water at bay .

Linnaeushof ②
Named after an 18th-century botanist, this huge park contains one of Europe's largest adventure playgrounds.

Vogelenzang ③
The Frans Rozen nurseries were established in Vogelenzang as far back as 1789 and demonstrate every stage of bulb cultivation.

Keukenhof ④
Visitors to this park are greeted by the heady scents and brilliant colors of millions of bulbs in bloom.

Lisse ⑤
There is a small bulb-museum in Lisse and boat trips are available on Kager Plassen lake, nearby.

0 kilometers 5
0 miles 2.5

Key

Tour route
Roads
Viewpoint

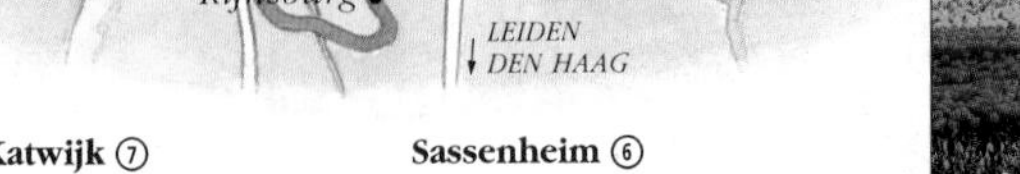

A tulip field in the Bloembollenstreek

Katwijk ⑦
A rare, early-17th-century lighthouse is located just to the north of this seaside town, which stands at the mouth of the Oude Rijn.

Sassenheim ⑥
West of the town lie the remains of Burcht Teilingen, an 11th-century castle where Jacqueline of Bavaria, the deposed Countess of Holland, died in 1436.

)UTCH BULBS

he most cultivated bulbs in ıe Netherlands include glad-ıli, lilies, daffodils, hyacinths, ises, crocuses and dahlias. ulips, however, are still far nd away the country's iggest flower crop. Originally om Turkey, the tulip was rst grown in Dutch soil by arolus Clusius in 1593.

laddin tulips

hina pink tulips

ahiti daffodils

linnow daffodils

lue jacket hyacinths

An array of bulbs in bloom in the wooded Keukenhof park

Aalsmeer ⓫

10 km (6 miles) south of Amsterdam. 22,000. *Driekolommen-plein 1. (02977) 25374.* *Mon-Fri.*

AALSMEER IS HOME to the largest flower auction in the world, the Bloemenveiling. Visitors can watch the proceedings from a viewing gallery, suspended above the frenetic activity on the trading floors. Since the 3.5 billion cut flowers and 400 million potted plants sold here annually all have a short shelf life, speed is of the essence. A clock above the auctioneer's head shows the prices falling as the hand sweeps around, from 100 to 1. When it reaches the price that bidders are willing to pay, the clock stops.

Lisse ⓬

35 km (22 miles) west of Amsterdam. 25,000. *Grachtweg 53a. (02521) 14262.* *Mon.*

THE BEST TIME to visit Lisse is at the end of April, when the town mounts a series of colorful flower parades.

The **Museum voor Bloembollenstreek** (the Bulb-growing District Museum), has displays on the history and life cycle of bulbs. The most astonishing aspect of "tulip mania" occurred between 1634 and 1637 *(see pp24–5)*, when such a demand for rare tulip bulbs was created by eager investors that they were sold for their actual weight in gold.

Museum voor Bloembollenstreek
Heereweg 219. *(02521) 17900.* *Tue–Sun.*

Keukenhof ⓭

Stationsweg, Lisse. *(02521) 19034.* *Mar 23–May 25: daily.*

SET IN 28 ha (70 acres) of wooded park on the outskirts of Lisse, Keukenhof is one of the most spectacular flower gardens in the world. It was set up in 1949 as a showcase for Dutch bulb growers and is now planted with some 7 million bulbs. The park is at its most spectacular from late March to late May, when great drifts of dazzlingly colored daffodils, hyacinths or tulips are in bloom. The array of flowers is complemented by the snowy blossoms of Japanese cherry trees early in the season, and by showy splashes of azaleas and rhododendrons later on during the year.

Street-by-Street: Leiden 14

LEIDEN IS A PROSPEROUS university town, with its origins in Roman times. It grew due to its location on a branch of the Rijn (Rhine) and is still an important commercial crossroads. During the school year the streets are crowded with students cycling to classes or packing the cafés and bookstores. A number of exceptional museums document Leiden's turbulent history, including the Golden Age, when the town was a center for world-wide trade *(see pp24–5)*. The wall plaque on the façade of Rembrandt's house in Weddesteeg marks his birthplace in June 1606 *(see p62)*.

Statue of Justice on Stadhuis wall

★ Rijksmuseum van Oudheden
This squat statue of a kneeling treasury scribe is among the many Egyptian artifacts in the museum.

John Robinson *(see p185)* lived in the Jan Pesijnshofje.

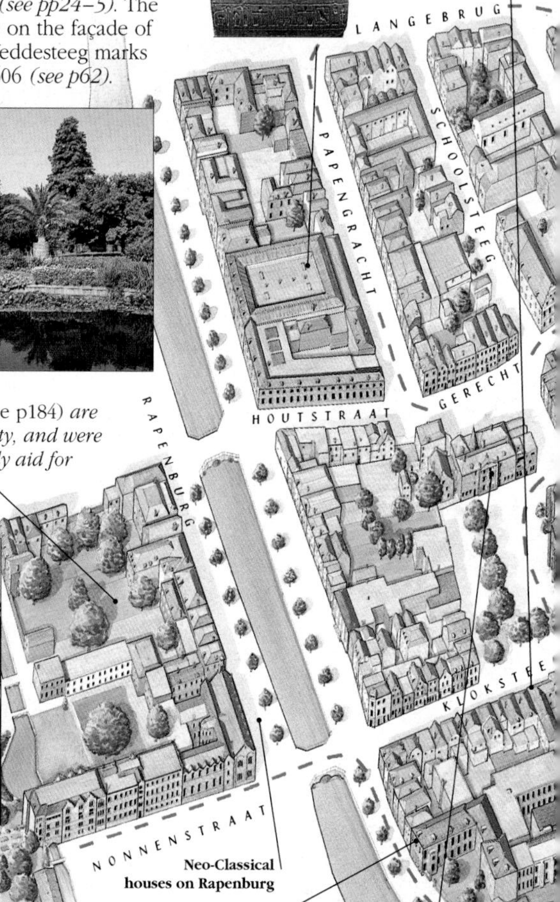

★ Hortus Botanicus
The botanical gardens (see p184) *are owned by Leiden University, and were laid out initially as a study aid for botany students in 1587.*

Oude Rijn
Many of the gabled houses along Leiden's canals have stores and cafés on the ground floor.

LANGEBRUG
PAPENGRACHT
SCHOOLSTEEG
HOUTSTRAAT
GERECHT
RAPENBURG
KLOKSTEEG
NONNENSTRAAT

Neo-Classical houses on Rapenburg

University library

Het Gravensteen
The university's law school lies behind the Classical façade of this complex of buildings, which grew up between the 13th and 17th centuries.

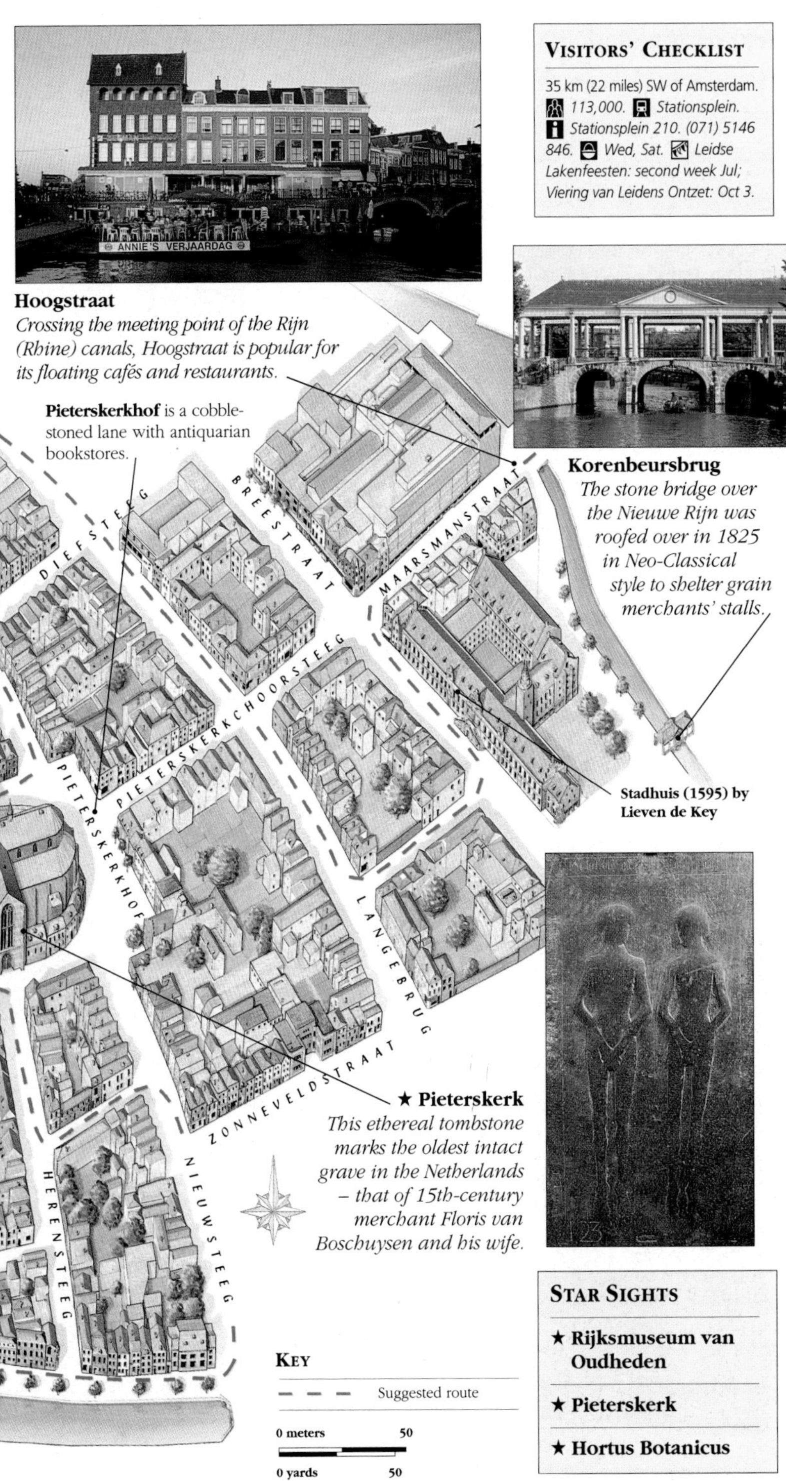

Hoogstraat
Crossing the meeting point of the Rijn (Rhine) canals, Hoogstraat is popular for its floating cafés and restaurants.

Pieterskerkhof is a cobblestoned lane with antiquarian bookstores.

Korenbeursbrug
The stone bridge over the Nieuwe Rijn was roofed over in 1825 in Neo-Classical style to shelter grain merchants' stalls.

Stadhuis (1595) by Lieven de Key

★ Pieterskerk
This ethereal tombstone marks the oldest intact grave in the Netherlands – that of 15th-century merchant Floris van Boschuysen and his wife.

Visitors' Checklist

35 km (22 miles) SW of Amsterdam. *113,000.* *Stationsplein.* *Stationsplein 210. (071) 5146 846.* *Wed, Sat.* *Leidse Lakenfeesten: second week Jul; Viering van Leidens Ontzet: Oct 3.*

Star Sights

- ★ **Rijksmuseum van Oudheden**
- ★ **Pieterskerk**
- ★ **Hortus Botanicus**

Key

Suggested route

0 meters 50

0 yards 50

Exploring Leiden

LEIDEN IS FAMOUS for its university, the oldest and most prestigious in the Netherlands. It was founded in 1575 by William of Orange, a year after he rescued the town from a yearlong siege by the Spanish *(see pp22–3)*. As a reward for their endurance, William offered the citizens of Leiden a choice of the building of a university or the abolition of tax. They chose wisely, and the city's reputation as a center of intellectual and religious tolerance was firmly established. English Puritan dissidents, victims of persecution in their homeland, were able to settle here in the 17th century before undertaking their epic voyage to the New World.

Arched gazebo within a walled garden in the Hortus Botanicus

Stedelijk Museum De Lakenhal

Oude Singel 28–32. *(071) 5165 360.* *Tue–Sun.* *Mon, Jan 1, Oct 3, Dec 25.*

The Lakenhal (cloth hall) was the 17th-century headquarters of Leiden's cloth trade. It was designed in Dutch Classical style in 1640 by Arent van 's Gravesande. It now houses the municipal museum, with temporary exhibitions of modern art and furniture from the 16th century onward.

The pride of the collection is Lucas van Leyden's Renaissance triptych of *The Last Judgment* (1526–7), rescued from the Pieterskerk during the religious struggles of 1566 *(see pp22–3)*.

A wing built in the 1920s houses a silver collection, furniture and exhibits covering the local weaving industry. Not to be missed is a big bronze *hutspot*, or cauldron, allegedly left behind by the Spanish when William of Orange broke the siege in 1574. The cauldron contained a spicy stew, which the starving people ate. This meal is now cooked every year on October 3, to commemorate Dutch victory over the Spanish.

Hortus Botanicus der Rijksuniversiteit Leiden

Rapenburg 73. *(071) 5277 249.* *daily.* *Feb 8, Oct 3, Dec 25, first Mon in Jan.* *partial.*

Leiden's botanical garden was founded in 1587 as part of the university. Some of the trees and shrubs are very old, including a 350-year-old laburnum planted shortly after the gardens were initially set up. Carolus Clusius, who was responsible for introducing the tulip to the Netherlands in 1593 *(see pp24–5)*, became the first professor of botany at Leiden University. Today the Hortus Botanicus contains a modern reconstruction of his original walled garden, called the Clusiustuin. Other delights include hothouses full of exotic orchids, rose gardens and colorful beds of tulips planted around ponds.

Museum Boerhaave

Lange St. Agnietenstraat 10. *(071) 5214 224.* *Tue–Sun.* *Jan 1, Oct 3.*

The Leiden physician, Herman Boerhaave (1668–1738), wrote the definitive 18th-century medical textbook, called *Institutiones Medicae*. The museum named after him is devoted to

Lucas van Leyden's triptych of *The Last Judgment* in the Stedelijk Museum de Lakenhal

the development of science in the Netherlands and contains reconstructions of an anatomy theater and hospital wards. The displays are arranged chronologically and include pendulum clocks made by Christiaan Huygens (1629–95), the discoverer of Saturn's rings, and thermometers by Gabriel Fahrenheit (1686–1736). The macabre display of grotesque surgical instruments is only for those with strong stomachs.

THE PILGRIM FATHERS

The Netherlands was proudly Protestant by the 17th century, giving refuge to Puritans fleeing persecution in England. Preacher John Robinson (1575–1625) established a church in Leiden in 1609, inspiring his congregation with visions of a new Jerusalem in the New World. The Pilgrim Fathers set sail from Delfshaven in 1620 in the *Speedwell*, which proved unseaworthy. Putting in at Plymouth, England, they crossed the Atlantic in the *Mayflower* to found Plymouth, Massachusetts. Robinson was too ill to travel, dying in Leiden in 1625.

The *Mayflower* crossing the Atlantic Ocean

Rijksmuseum voor Volkenkunde

Steenstraat 1. *(071) 5168 800.* *Tue–Sun.* *Mon, Jan 1, Oct 3.*

This outstanding ethnological museum, founded in 1837, houses collections from many non-western cultures. It is currently undergoing restoration work, which is likely to continue until early 1996. There is still much to see, however, as temporary exhibitions are mounted to show living conditions around the world, from the Arctic wastes to the hills of China. Informative and entertaining displays add to the eclectic museum's wide appeal to people of all age groups.

Heraldic lion at De Burcht

Stedelijk Molenmuseum de Valk

2e Binnenvestgracht 1. *(071) 5165 353.* *Tue–Sun.* *Jan 1, Oct 3, Dec 25.*

This towering grain mill, built in 1743, is Leiden's last remaining mill. It is an imposing seven stories high, and now restored to its original working state. A tour takes in the living quarters on the ground floor, the repair workshop and a retrospective exhibition on the history of Dutch windmills.

Pieterskerk

Pieterskerkhof 1a. *(071) 5124 319.* *daily.* *Good Friday, Oct 3.*

The magnificent Gothic church was built in the 15th century in rose-pink brick, and stands in a leafy square surrounded by elegant houses. Now a community center, the church is worth visiting for its austere interior and its organ, built by the Hagenbeer brothers in 1642 and enclosed in gilded woodwork. The floor of the nave is covered with worn slabs marking the burial places of 17th-century intellectuals like Puritan leader John Robinson, physician Herman Boerhaave and Golden Age artist, Jan Steen *(see p133)*.

De Burcht

Nieuwe Rijn. **Battlements** *daily.*

De Burcht is an odd 12th-century fortress with crenellated battlements. It sits between two channels of the Rijn (Rhine) atop a grassy, man-made mound, thought to be of Saxon origin. The fortress is reached by a wrought-iron gate covered in heraldic symbols. The top of the citadel offers superb views over Leiden.

Rijksmuseum van Oudheden

Rapenburg 28. *(071) 5163 163.* *Tue–Sun.* *Jan 1, Oct 3, Dec 25.*

The Dutch museum of antiquities, established in 1818, is Leiden's main attraction. The centerpiece of the collection is the Egyptian Temple of Taffeh, reassembled in the main exhibition hall in 1978. It dates from the 1st century AD, and was dedicated to Isis, Egyptian goddess of fertility, from the 4th century AD.

The museum's collection of Egyptian artifacts is very rich indeed, and occupies much of the first two floors. Alongside there are impressive displays of musical instuments, textiles and shoes, expressive Etruscan bronzework and fragments of Roman mosaic and frescoes.

The upper floor of the museum holds an exhibition of Dutch archaeology, which begins in prehistoric times and runs to the Middle Ages.

A drawbridge across the Oude Rijn in Leiden

Den Haag ⓯

Statue in Binnenhof courtyard

DEN HAAG ('s-Gravenhage or The Hague) is the political capital of the Netherlands, home to prestigious institutions such as the Dutch Parliament and International Court of Justice, located in the Vredespaleis *(see p190)*. When Den Haag became the seat of government in 1586, it was a small town built around the castle of the counts of Holland. That same castle, much rebuilt, now stands at the heart of a city that is home to half a million people. It is surrounded by public buildings, such as the Mauritshuis *(see pp188–9)*, and protected to the north by the remains of a moat that forms the Hofvijver (lake). To the west is the seaside town of Scheveningen *(see p191)*.

Mauritshuis

See pp188–9.

Ridderzaal

Binnenhof 8a. (070) 364 6144. Mon–Sat. Jan 1, Dec 25.

Beside the Hofvijver is the Binnenhof courtyard. In the center of this stands the fairy-tale, double-turreted Gothic Ridderzaal (Hall of the Knights). This was the 13th-century dining hall of Floris V, Count of Holland *(see p19)*. Since 1904, the hall's function has been primarily ceremonial; it is used for the opening of the Dutch Parliament by the monarch, and for other state occasions. The hall is open to visitors when parliament is not sitting in its new premises in the complex. A guided tour includes the two former debating chambers and an exhibition charting the growth of democracy in the Netherlands.

Museum Bredius

Lange Vijverberg 14. (070) 362 0729. Tue–Sun. Jan 1, Dec 25.

Dr. Abraham Bredius was an art historian and collector as well as director of the Mauritshuis *(see pp188–9)* from 1895 to 1922. On his death in 1946, he bequeathed his vast collection of 17th-century art to the city of Den Haag. This bequest is displayed in a distinguished 18th-century merchant's house on the north side of the Hofvijver, and features about 200 Golden Age paintings – famous works by Dutch Masters such as Rembrandt *(see p66)* and Jan Steen *(see p133)*, and others by lesser-known artists.

The building itself has undergone considerable renovation, and now contains an equally impressive collection of antique furniture, delicate porcelain and elaborate silverware.

The Hofvijver and parliament buildings in Den Haag

Grote Kerk

Rond de Grote Kerk 10. (070) 365 8665. Jul–Aug: Mon–Sat.

In its present form, the Grote Kerk dates mainly from 1539, but has undergone major rebuilding between 1985 and 1987. Its most impressive feature is a stained-glass window that depicts Charles V, the Holy Roman Emperor *(see pp22–3)*, kneeling at the feet of the Virgin Mary. The church is at the center of Den Haag's shopping area, which is closed to traffic and has many upscale galleries selling works of art.

Coat of arms on façade of Rijksmuseum Gevangenpoort

Rijksmuseum Gevangenpoort

Buitenhof 33. (070) 346 0861. Sun–Fri. Jan 1, Dec 25, Dec 26. only.

The Gevangenpoort (prison gate) was originally the main gateway to the 14th-century castle of the counts of Holland. Later, it was turned into a jail, becoming infamous during a period of violent social unrest in the late 17th century when burgomaster Cornelis de Witt *(see p25)* was confined and tortured here. Both he and his brother Jan were subsequently tried for heresy, and torn limb from limb outside the prison gate by a rioting mob.

Appropriately, the building has now been converted into a prison museum. On display is a unique collection of torture instruments, which is accompanied by a stereo soundtrack of blood-curdling screams.

Paintings in Galerij Prins Willem V

🏛 Galerij Prins Willem V

Buitenhof 35. ☎ (070) 318 2486. ◯ *Tue–Sun.* ● *Jan 1, Dec 25.*

In his youth, Prince William V *(see p28)* was an enthusiastic collector of Golden Age paintings. His private collection was opened to the public in 1774, inside this former inn, which the prince had converted for use as his *kabinet* – the 18th-century Dutch word for an art gallery. The Galerij is the oldest art gallery in the Netherlands. The contemporary fashion for covering every available inch of wall space with paintings has been retained, and consequently several pictures are hung too high and too close together to be properly enjoyed. Not all are annotated, which may lead to some confusion for the viewer, but many of Prince William's original purchases are still to be seen. Old Master paintings by Rembrandt, Jan Steen and Paulus Potter (1625–54) are included in a collection that consists principally of typically Dutch Golden Age landscapes, genre works, "conversation pieces" and re-creations of historical events *(see p132).*

🏛 Haags Historisch Museum

Korte Vijverberg 7. ☎ (070) 364 6940. ◯ *daily.* ● *Jan 1, Dec 25.*

Den Haag's history museum is housed in the Sebastiaansdoelen, a Dutch Classical mansion built in 1636 and the former headquarters of the Civic Guard of St. Sebastian.

Exhibitions tell the story of Den Haag's development and growth since the Middle Ages. The displays change periodically and are drawn from the city's collection of landscapes, portraits and genre paintings *(see pp132–3)* as well as 17th- and 18th-century furnishings. A luxuriously fitted-out doll-house from the 19th century is on permanent display.

Visitors' Checklist

56 km (35 miles) SW of Amsterdam. *450,000.* *Koningin Julianaplein 10; Stationsplein 25.* *Koningin Julianaplein 30. 06 340 35051.* *Mon, Wed, Fri, Sat.* *Vlaggetjesdag Scheveningen: last Sat in May; North Sea Jazz Festival: second weekend of Jul; Swinging Scheveningen: third weekend of Jul.*

The 17th-century façade of the Haags Historisch Museum

Den Haag City Center

Galerij Prins Willem V ③
Grote Kerk ①
Haags Historisch Museum ⑥
Mauritshuis ⑦
Museum Bredius ④
Ridderzaal ⑤
Rijksmuseum
Gevangenpoort ②

Scheveningen · Centraal Station · Delft · Rotterdam

0 meters 250
0 yards 250

Key

Parking
Church

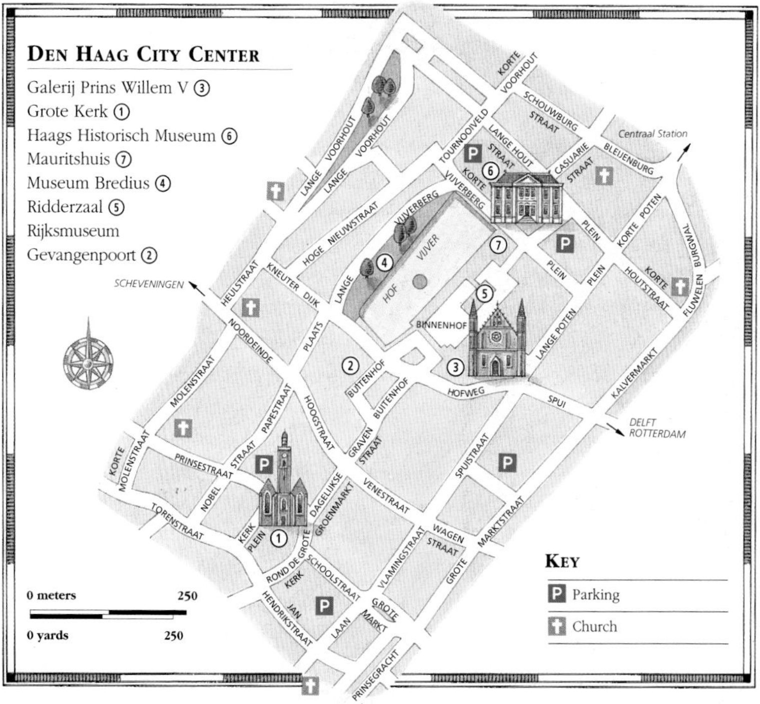

The Mauritshuis

THE COUNT OF NASSAU, Johann Maurits, commissioned this graceful house after he retired as the governor of Brazil. It was completed in 1644 by Pieter Post in Dutch Classical style with influences from Italian Renaissance architecture, and enjoys wonderful views across the Hofvijver *(see p186)*. The mansion was bequeathed to the state after Maurits's death in 1679, and has been the home of the Royal Picture Gallery since 1821. The collection is small, but almost every painting is a superb work by one of the Old Masters. This, combined with the exquisite presentation in elegant period rooms, makes the Mauritshuis one of the finest galleries in the Netherlands.

★ **The Anatomy Lesson of Dr. Nicolaes Tulp** *(1632)*
Rembrandt's painting of surgeons examining a corpse reflects the burgeoning contemporary interest in anatomy and science.

Gallery Guide

The Mauritshuis, a small art gallery set on three floors, is packed with paintings crowded on to all available wall space. The displays are changed constantly in order to cover all aspects of the collection. Information sheets are available in English, listing the principal works. The arrangement of the paintings is delightfully jumbled, and many of the pictures are not labeled. If in doubt, ask for help from one of the well-informed gallery attendants.

Portrait of Cornelis Schellinger *(1584)*
The verse on Pieter Pietersz's portrait refers to William of Orange's murder (see p195).

Vase with Flowers *(1618)*
Ambrosius Bosschaert captured the beauty of early summer flowers, but the flies buzzing around them are there to remind us of our mortality.

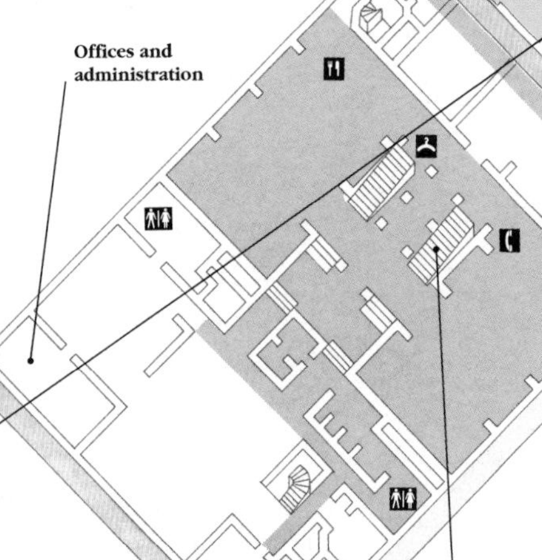

The Goldfinch *(1654)*
This tiny, delicate painting is by Carel Fabritius (1622–54), who was a pupil of Rembrandt.

First floor

Main stairs (first floor)

Visitors' Checklist

Korte Vijverberg 8, Den Haag. *(070) 365 4779. Stationsplein 25. 10am–5pm Tue–Sat, 11am–5pm Sun & public hols (last adm 4:45pm). Jan 1, Dec 25.*

Key to Floorplan

- Portrait Gallery
- 15th- and early-16th-century work
- Late-16th- and 17th-century work
- Golden Room
- 17th-century painting
- 17th-century Flemish painting
- 18th-century painting
- Nonexhibition space

The Way You Hear It is the Way You Sing It *(1665)*
A serious moral is implicit in Jan Steen's allegorical genre painting (see p131) *warning adults not to set a bad example for their offspring.*

★ The Louse Hunt *(1653)*
Gerard ter Borch's painting is a scene of obsessive domesticity. It reflects the preoccupation of the 17th-century Dutch with order, cleanliness and social respectability.

Main entrance

★ Girl with a Turban *(1660)*
This haunting portrait was painted during the most successful middle period of Jan Vermeer's career. The model may have been his daughter, Maria.

Star Paintings

- ★ **Girl with a Turban by Jan Vermeer**
- ★ **The Louse Hunt by Gerard ter Borch**
- ★ **The Anatomy Lesson of Dr. Nicolaes Tulp by Rembrandt**

Vredespaleis

Carnegieplein 2. *(070) 302 4242.* *Mon–Fri.* *by appt.* *public hols and when court is in session.*

In 1899, Den Haag played host to the first international peace conference. This then led to the formation of the Permanent Court of Arbitration, which had the aim of maintaining world peace. To provide a suitably august home for the court, the Scottish-born philanthropist, Andrew Carnegie (1835–1918) donated £1 million towards the building of the mock-Gothic Vredespaleis (peace palace), which was designed by French architect Louis Cordonnier.

The enormous palace was completed in 1913, and many of the member nations of the Court of Arbitration contributed to the interior's rich decoration. Today the Vredespaleis is the seat of the United Nations' International Court of Justice, which was formed in 1946 as successor to the Permanent Court of Arbitration.

Vredespaleis, home to the International Court of Justice

Haags Gemeentemuseum

Stadhouderslaan 41. *(070) 338 1111.* *Tue–Sun.* *Jan 1, Dec 25.*

The Gemeentemuseum is one of the town's finest museums. The building was the last work of HP Berlage, the father of the architectural movement known as the Amsterdam School *(see p97)*. The museum was completed in 1935, a year after his death, and is built in sandy-colored stone on two levels round a central courtyard.

Exhibits from several other museums have been collected to form three sections. Highlights of the superb applied arts section include antique delftware, Islamic and Oriental porcelain and the world's largest collection of paintings by Piet Mondriaan *(see p136)*. An annex to the main building houses an exhibition of everyday costume worn in the 18th century onward, including showcases on jewelry and fashion photography.

Probably the museum's main attraction is the collection of musical instruments which date from the 15th to 19th centuries. European instruments include harpsichords and pocket-size fiddles; more exotic is a Javanese *gamelan*, which consists of gongs and drums.

Haags Gemeentemuseum (1935), designed by HP Berlage

Panorama Mesdag

Zeestraat 65. *(070) 364 2563.* *daily.* *Dec 25.*

This painted cyclorama is important both as a work of Dutch Impressionism and as a rare surviving example of 19th-century entertainment. The vast painting is 120 m (400 ft) around, and lines the inside wall of a circular, canopied pavilion. It shows the old fishing village of Scheveningen, 10 km (6 miles) north of Den Haag.

The realistic effect of the painting is achieved through the brilliant use of perspective, enhanced by the natural daylight, which falls onto the canvas from above. Real sand and drift-wood piled at the foot of the painting add to the illusion. The canvas was painted in 1881 by members of the Dutch Impressionist School, led by HW Mesdag (1831–1915) and his wife, Sientje (1834–1909). George Hendrik Breitner (1857–1923) later added his personal touch by painting a group of cavalry officers charging along the beach on horseback.

Omniversum

President Kennedylaan 5. *(070) 354 5454.* *Apr–Sep: daily; Oct–Mar: Tue–Sun.*

The Omniversum is a cross between a planetarium and a space-age movie theater, and is especially appealing to children. It has a high-tech sound system and a massive dome-shaped screen, on to which films and lasers are projected. These are combined to create stunning three-dimensional images of space, volcanic eruptions and life beneath the ocean's surface.

Madurodam

Haringkade 175. *(070) 355 3900.* *daily.*

Madurodam is a model of a composite Dutch city, built to a scale of 1:25. It incorporates replicas of the Vredespaleis and Binnenhof in Den Haag, the canal houses of Amsterdam, Rotterdam's Europoort *(see p199)* and Schiphol Airport *(pp266–7)*, along with windmills, polders, bulbfields and a nudist beach. At night the streets and buildings are illuminated by 50,000 tiny lights.

The model city was opened by Queen Juliana in 1952. It was conceived by JML Maduro as a memorial to his son George, who died at Dachau concentration camp in 1945. All profits go to children's charities.

Scale models in the miniature town of Madurodam

Scheveningen ⓰

45 km (28 miles) SW of Amsterdam. *17,800.* *Gevers Deyjnootweg 1134. (06) 3403 5051.* *Thu.*

THE RESORT of Scheveningen is only a 15-minute trolley ride from the center of Den Haag. Like many Dutch seaside towns, it had its heyday in the 19th century, and is now a mixture of faded gentility and seediness. Even so, it has retained its popularity as a vacation destination, mainly due to stretches of clean, sandy beaches as well as a pier, built earlier this century, which is currently being restored. There is no shortage of places to eat, including some good seafood restaurants. The imposing French Empire-style Kurhaus, now a luxury hotel with its own casino, was built in 1885 when Scheveningen was still an important spa town.

Modern amenities include the **Sea Life Center**, nearby, where visitors can walk in see-through tunnels for underwater views of stingrays, sharks and other forms of sea life. It is also a sanctuary for all kinds of wounded marine creatures.

The town has swallowed up the original fishing village of Scheveningen Haven, which has still managed to maintain some of its traditional fishing industry. The south side of the harbor is the departure point for tourists' fishing trips.

Close by is the small **Zee Museum** of marine biology. It is found in the former auction hall of the fish market and looks out across the marina. It houses exhibits of marine life from around the world.

Sea Life Center

Strandweg 13. *(070) 354 2100.* *daily.* *Dec 25.*

Zee Museum

Dr. Lelykade 39. *(070) 350 2528.* *daily.*

Vacationers on Scheveningen's popular sandy beach

Street-by-Street: Delft ⑰

19th-century Delft tile showing a church and barges

The origins of Delft date from 1075 and its prosperity was based on weaving and brewing. However, a massive explosion at the national arsenal destroyed much of the medieval town in October 1645. The center was rebuilt in the late 17th century and the sleepy old town has changed little since then – gabled Gothic and Renaissance houses still line the tree-shaded canals. Activity centers on the market square, bordered by the landmarks of the Stadhuis and Nieuwe Kerk. Visitors can dip into the scores of stores selling antiques and expensive, hand-painted delftware. Tours of local factories are available, and their stores are often reasonably priced.

★ Stedelijk Museum Het Prinsenhof
Here you can see bullet holes where William of Orange was murdered in 1584.

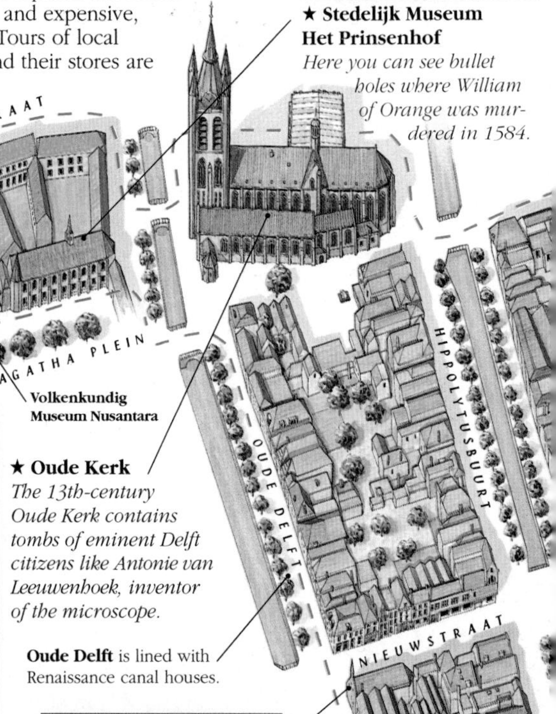

SCHOOLSTRAAT
ST AGATHA PLEIN
HIPPOLYTUSBUURT
OUDE DELFT
NIEUWSTRAAT
BOTER BRUG
PEPERSTR

Volkenkundig Museum Nusantara

★ Oude Kerk
The 13th-century Oude Kerk contains tombs of eminent Delft citizens like Antonie van Leeuwenhoek, inventor of the microscope.

Oude Delft is lined with Renaissance canal houses.

Chapel of St. Hippolytus
This simple, redbrick Gothic chapel (1396) was used for storage during the Alteration (see pp22–3).

Star Sights

- ★ **Oude Kerk**
- ★ **Nieuwe Kerk**
- ★ **Stedelijk Museum Het Prinsenhof**

0 meters 50
0 yards 50

Key

– – – Suggested route

VISITORS' CHECKLIST

50 km (31 miles) SW of Amsterdam. *90,000.* *Stationsplein.* *Markt 85. (015) 2126 100.* *Thu, Sat.* *Jazz Festival: end Aug; Delft Dag: last Sat in Aug.*

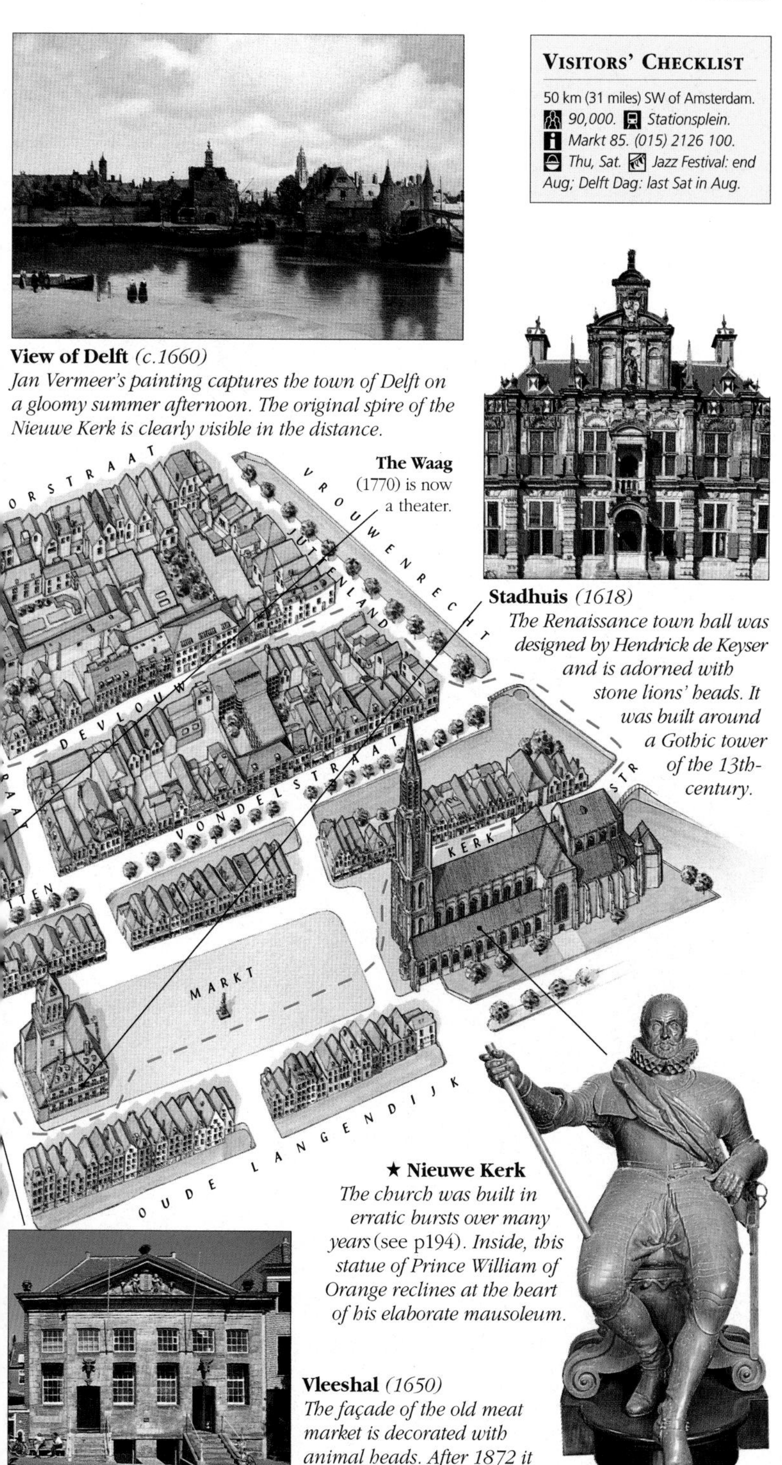

View of Delft *(c.1660)*
Jan Vermeer's painting captures the town of Delft on a gloomy summer afternoon. The original spire of the Nieuwe Kerk is clearly visible in the distance.

The Waag (1770) is now a theater.

Stadhuis *(1618)*
The Renaissance town hall was designed by Hendrick de Keyser and is adorned with stone lions' heads. It was built around a Gothic tower of the 13th-century.

★ Nieuwe Kerk
The church was built in erratic bursts over many years (see p194). *Inside, this statue of Prince William of Orange reclines at the heart of his elaborate mausoleum.*

Vleeshal *(1650)*
The façade of the old meat market is decorated with animal heads. After 1872 it was used as a grain exchange.

Exploring Delft

THE CHARMING TOWN of Delft is known the world over for its blue-and-white pottery, but is equally famous as the resting place of William of Orange (1533–84), one of the most celebrated figures in Dutch history. He commanded the Dutch Revolt against Spanish rule from his headquarters in Delft, and his victory resulted in religious freedom and independence for the Dutch people *(see pp22–3)*. Delft was also the birthplace of artist Jan Vermeer (1632–75), whose talent was so underrated during his lifetime that he died in extreme poverty.

The imposing Renaissance pulpit (1548) of the Oude Kerk

Oude Kerk

Oude Delft. (015) 2123 015.
Apr–Oct: Mon–Sat.

A church has existed on this site since the 13th century, but the original building has since been added to many times. The ornate clock tower, which now has a pronounced list, was built in the 14th century, and the flamboyant Gothic north transept was added by Belgian architect Anthonis Keldermans in the early 16th century. The focal point of the interior is the elaborately carved wooden pulpit with an overhanging canopy. The floor is paved with 17th-century tomb slabs, many carved with skeletons and coats of arms. The simple stone tablet at the east end of the north aisle marks the burial place of Jan Vermeer. In the north transept is the tomb of Admiral Maarten Tromp (1598–1653), who routed the English fleet in 1652. Admiral Piet Heyn (1577–1629), who captured the Spanish silver fleet in 1628, is buried in the chancel.

The Nieuwe Kerk in Delft's market square

Nieuwe Kerk

Markt. (015) 2123 025.
Mon–Sat.

The Nieuwe Kerk was built between 1383 and 1510, but much of the original structure was restored following a fire in 1536 and an explosion at the national arsenal in 1654. Work on the church continued for many years, and it was not until 1872 that PJH Cuypers *(see pp30–31)* added the statuesque 100 m (320 ft) tower to the Gothic façade.

The burial vaults of the Dutch royal family are in the crypt of this empty, cavernous church, but the most prominent feature of the interior is the stately mausoleum of William of Orange. Set in the vast arched choir, the richly decorated tomb was designed by Hendrick de Keyser *(see p90)* in 1614 and is carved from black and white marble, with heavy gilded detailing. At its heart is a sculpture of William, resplendent in his battle dress, and at each corner stand bronze figures representing the Virtues. Close to William is the forlorn figure of his dog, who died days after him, and at the foot of the tomb is a trumpeting angel – symbol of Fame.

DELFTWARE

The blue-and-white tin-glazed pottery, known as delftware, was developed from majolica and introduced to the Netherlands by immigrant Italian potters in the 16th century. Settling around Delft and Haarlem, the potters made wall tiles, adopting Dutch motifs such as animals and flowers as decoration. Over the next hundred years, trade with the east brought samples of delicate Chinese porcelain to the Netherlands, and the market for coarser Dutch majolica crashed. By 1650, local potters had adopted the Chinese model and designed fine plates, vases and bowls decorated with Dutch landscapes, and biblical and genre scenes. In 1652, De Porceleyne Fles was one of 32 thriving potteries in Delft. Today, it is the only original delftware factory still in production, and is open for guided tours.

Handpainted 17th-century delft tiles

Koninklijk Nederlands Legermuseum

Korte Geer 1. *(015) 2150 500.* *Tue–Sun.* *Jan 1, Dec 25.*

The Legermuseum (army museum) is housed in the Armamentarium, formerly the arsenal of the old provinces of West Friesland and Holland. The bluff, square armory was built in 1692 and is still full of weaponry, now displayed with military uniforms, battle models and armored vehicles. These exhibits trace developments in Dutch military history since the Middle Ages up to the present peacekeeping role of the Netherlands in the service of the United Nations.

Coat of arms on façade of the Legermuseum

Stedelijk Museum Het Prinsenhof

St. Agathaplein 1. *(015) 2602 358.* *Tue–Sun.* *Jan 1, Dec 25.*

This tranquil Gothic building, formerly a convent, now houses Delft's historical museum, but is better known as the place where William of Orange was assassinated. He requisitioned the convent in 1572 for use as his headquarters during the Dutch Revolt. In 1584, by order of Philip II of Spain *(see pp22–3)*, William was shot by Balthasar Geraerts, a fanatical Catholic. The bullet holes in the main staircase wall can still be seen today.

The crooked tiled floors and leaded windows of the convent provide the perfect backdrop for a rare collection of antique delftware. This is displayed alongside tapestries, silverware, medieval sculpture and a series of portraits of the Dutch royal family, from William of Orange to today.

Fine gabled façades along Binnenwaterslot in the center of Delft

Volkenkundig Museum Nusantara

St. Agathaplein 4. *(015) 2602 358.* *Tue–Sun.* *Jan 1, Dec 25.*

When William of Orange took over the Prinsenhof in 1572, the nuns moved into one of its wings across the square. This is now the home of the Nusantara ethnological museum. It is small, but has a wonderful collection of masks, carvings, textiles, jewelry, and musical instruments brought back from Indonesia by traders working for the Dutch East India Company *(see pp26–7)*. The museum shop sells unusual, but rather expensive, modern Indonesian crafts.

Museum Lambert van Meerten

Oude Delft 199. *(015) 2602 358.* *Tue–Sun.* *Jan 1, Dec 25.*

This small museum is located in an elegantly furnished 19th-century mansion, with paintings and architectural details recently salvaged from local 17th- and 18th-century buildings. Its main attraction is the antique hand-painted delftware tiles and tile pictures from around the world.

St. Janskerk, Gouda

Donor's coat of arms (1601)

The original Catholic church of 1485 was rebuilt in Gothic style after it was razed by fire in 1552. Between 1555 and 1571, a series of remarkable stained-glass windows were donated to the church by wealthy Catholic benefactors such as Philip II of Spain. After the Alteration *(see pp22–3)* the church became Protestant, but even the iconoclasts could not bring themselves to destroy the windows – in fact Protestant patrons, such as the aldermen of Rotterdam, continued to donate windows until 1603. Depicting contemporary figures and events, the stained glass is rich in political symbolism, using biblical stories to make coded reference to the conflict between Catholic and Protestant, and Dutch and Spanish, that led to the Dutch Revolt in 1572.

The Nave
At 123 m (403 ft), the nave is the longest in the Netherlands. Memorial slabs cover the floor.

The Adulterous Woman *(1601)*
Dressed as a Franciscan monk, Jesus begs the people in the temple to forgive the adulterous wife, who is heavily guarded by Spanish soldiers.

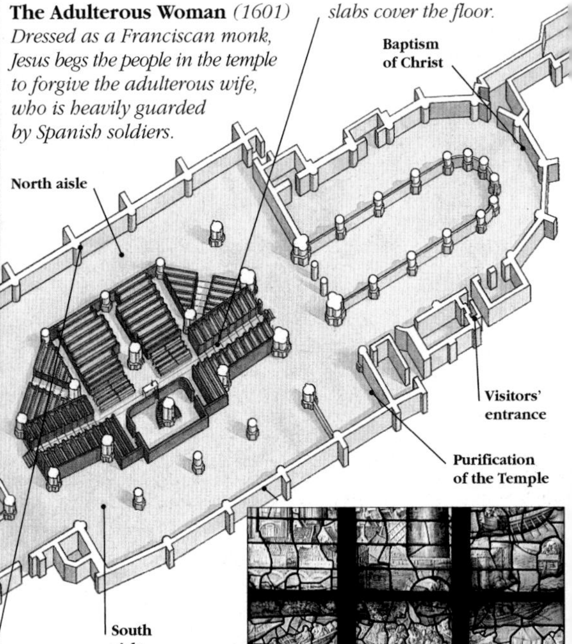

Baptism of Christ

North aisle

Visitors' entrance

Purification of the Temple

South aisle

Judith Slays Holofernes
This detail is taken from a window that portrays the biblical story of the slaying of Holofernes by Judith. The glazier, Dirck Crabeth, shows John the Baptist holding a lamb. Next to him is the kneeling figure of Jean de Ligne, Count of Aremberg, who commissioned the window.

The Relief of Leiden *(1603)*
William of Orange is pictured here directing Leiden's heroic resistance to the Spanish siege of 1574 (see p184).

VISITORS' CHECKLIST

Achter de Kerk 15. *(01 825) 126 84.* *Mar–Oct: 9am–5pm Mon–Sat; Nov–Feb: 10am–4pm Mon–Sat.* *Jan 1, Dec 25 & 26.*

Purification of the Temple
The window was donated by William of Orange (see p22) *in 1567. The detail shows dismayed traders watching Jesus drive the moneylenders from the temple. It represents the Dutch desire to expel the Spanish from their country.*

Baptism of Christ *(1555)*
John the Baptist is shown baptizing Christ in the river Jordan. The window was donated by the Bishop of Utrecht.

View over Gouda with St. Janskerk in the background

Gouda ⓲

50 km (33 miles) S of Amsterdam. *70,000.* *Markt 27. (01 825) 136 66.* *cheese market: Jul & Aug: 10am–noon Thu; general market: Thu & Sat.*

GOUDA received its charter from Count Floris V *(see p19)* in 1272. Situated at the confluence of two rivers, the town became the center of a successful brewing industry in the 15th century. The growth of the cheese trade during the 17th century brought more prosperity. Today, the name of Gouda is synonymous with its famous full-bodied cheese. There is a cheese market in summer, and the twice-weekly market offers the chance to buy local cheeses and crafts. Carols are sung at the special candelit Christmas market.

These markets take place in the huge square around the Stadhuis which, dating from 1450, is one of the oldest town halls in the Netherlands. The building bristles with pinnacles and miniature spires in Flemish Gothic style. Statues in niches seen on the elaborate façade represent Gouda's former rulers. However, the principal attraction of the town is the set of superb stained-glass windows found in St. Janskerk.

Stedelijk Museum Het Catharina Gasthuis

Oosthaven 10. *(01 825) 884 40.* *daily.* *Jan 1, Dec 25.*

An arched gatehouse (1609) leads into the leafy courtyard of this delightful museum. The Catharina Gasthuis was built in the 14th century as a hospice for travelers, later becoming an almshouse for the elderly. Converted into a museum in 1910, it has a series of Civic Guard portraits and landscapes by Dutch Impressionists. The more eccentric elements of the collection include rather gruesome surgical instruments and a torture chamber.

Stedelijk Museum De Moriaan / The Blackamoor

Westhaven 29. *(01 825) 884 44.* *daily.* *Jan 1, Dec 25.*

This little tobacco museum was once a sugar refinery and later a coffee and tobacco shop. Behind the 1617 façade it is packed with tobacco jars and traditional clay pipes with long stems and tiny bowls.

Gatehouse of the Stedelijk Museum Het Catharina Gasthuis

Rotterdam ⓳

ROTTERDAM OCCUPIES a strategic position where the Rijn (Rhine), Europe's most important river, meets the North Sea. Barges from Rotterdam transport goods deep into the continent, and ocean-going ships carry European exports around the world. This made Rotterdam a prime target for aerial bombardment during World War II, and the city's ancient heart was destroyed. Much of the city has been rebuilt in experimental styles, resulting in some of Europe's most original and innovative architecture. The Europoort is now the world's largest container port, stretching for 37 km (23 miles) along the river banks.

Oudehaven, with the futuristic Kijk-Kubus houses in the background

Exploring Rotterdam

Much of Oudehaven, the old harbor area of Rotterdam, was destroyed in bombing raids during World War II. It has largely been rebuilt in daring and avant-garde styles. The pyramid-shaped **Gemeentebibliotheek** (public library) is similar to the Pompidou Center in Paris: its yellow ventilation ducts and service piping are on the exterior of the building.

Piet Blom's **Kijk-Kubus** (cube houses) of 1956 are extraordinary apartments, set on concrete stilts and tilted at a crazy angle. Residents have specially designed furniture to fit the sloping rooms. Sidewalk cafés have sprung up along the harbor quayside, and apartment blocks with covered shopping arcades have now replaced the old wooden warehouses.

In the Golden Age, maritime trade brought wealth to Dutch towns with access to the sea. Delft *(see pp192–5)* lacked a harbor, so its citizens built a 12-km (7.5-mile) canal from the town to the Nieuwe Maas river, and constructed **Delfshaven** – a specially designed village complete with harbor. This has long been swallowed up by Rotterdam, but remains a pretty corner of the city, with 18th-century warehouses converted into apartments, galleries, restaurants and cafés.

Museum Boymans-van Beuningen

See pp200–201.

Cabin on the warship *De Buffel*

Maritiem Museum Prins Hendrik

Leuvehaven 1. *(010) 413 2680.* *daily (Sep–May: Tue–Sun).* *Jan 1, Apr 30, Dec 25.*

Prince Hendrik, brother of King William III *(see pp30–31)*, founded this maritime museum in 1873. Its main highlight is an iron-clad warship called *De Buffel*, built in 1868. The ship boasts lavish fittings in the officers' quarters, which have the staid atmosphere of a gentleman's club. Other exhibits include a small fleet of barges and steamships.

Historisch Museum het Schielandshuis

Korte Hoogstraat 31. *(010) 217 6767.* *daily.* *Jan 1, Apr 30, Dec 25.*

Rotterdam's historical museum is in the Schielandshuis, a gracious town house built in 1665 by Jacob Lois. It is one of few 17th-century buildings to survive the war and has now been restored. The museum charts the development of the city, and the urbane lifestyles of its people, through displays of paintings, silverware and furniture in elegant rooms.

Peaceful canal houses in a quiet corner of Delfshaven

Museum de Dubbelde Palmboom

Voorhaven 12. *(010) 477 2664.* *Tue–Sun.* *Jan 1, Apr 30, Dec 25.*

The museum "of the double palm tree" is in a twin-gabled, wooden warehouse dating to 1825. Now converted, its five stories are open-plan with vast, beamed rooms. These display a variety of arts and crafts, photographs and scale models depicting life at the mouth of the Nieuwe Maas river, from the earliest Iron Age fishing settlements to the booming industrial port of present day.

Museum voor Volkenkunde

Willemskade 25. *(010) 411 1055.* *Tue–Sun.* *Jan 1, Apr 30, Dec 25.*

During the 17th century, Rotterdam's city fathers amassed a superb ethnological collection. It has been kept in a museum built in 1851, with a modern interior incorporating audio-visual displays of theater, film, dance and music. Permanent collections include Indonesian musical instruments, ancient folk art, masks and carvings.

Euromast against the skyline

Euromast

Parkhaven 20. *(010) 436 4811.* *daily.*

Visitors ride a high-speed lift up the first 100 m (328 ft) of the Euromast to enjoy sweeping views of Rotterdam. This lower section, built in 1960, has a viewing platform with a restaurant and exhibition area. In 1970 the Space Tower added another 85 m (272 ft) in height to make this the tallest structure in the Netherlands. A covered "space cabin" attached to the outside of the tower ascends 58 m (190 ft) up from the viewing platform.

Visitors' Checklist

65 km (40 miles) SW of Amsterdam. *580,000.* *Stationsplein.* *6 km (4 miles) NW.* *Coolsingel 67. (010) 402 3200.* *Tue, Sat.* *Rotterdam Film Festival: Feb; Jazz and Blues Festival: end of Aug; Uitgaansmarkt: first weekend of Sep.*

Europoort

Leuvehoofd 5. *(010) 413 5400.* **Europoort** *daily.* *See **Getting to Amsterdam By Ferry** p268.* **Boat tours** *Jul–Aug: Tue.*

The wharves and quays of the city's highly automated port service about 32,000 container ships a year. A boat tour is an ideal way of seeing the port, built between 1958 and 1975. Cyclists and motorists follow the 48-km (30-mile) Haven Route (harbor route) along the Nieuwe Mass, passing oil terminals, docks and tankers.

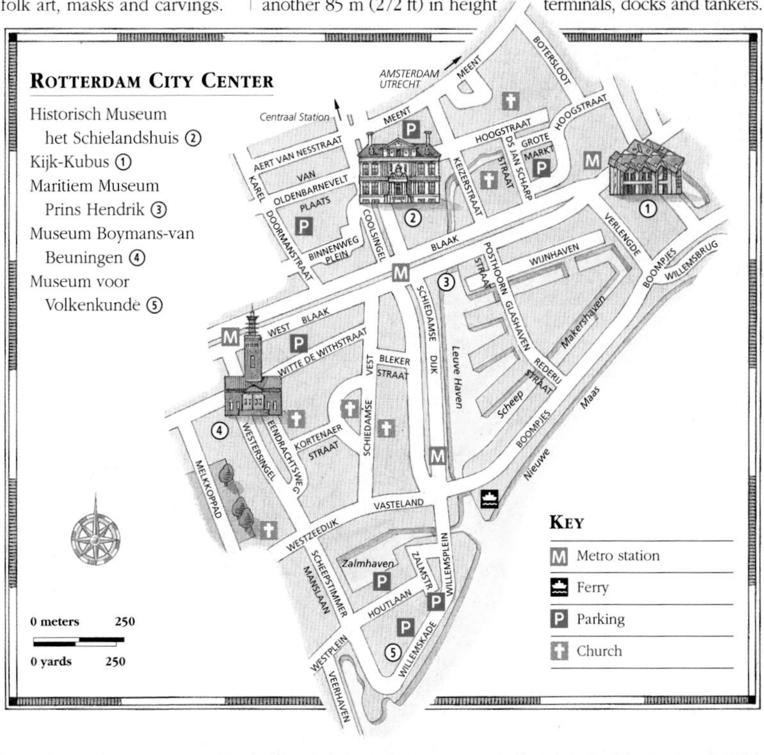

Rotterdam City Center

Historisch Museum het Schielandshuis ②
Kijk-Kubus ①
Maritiem Museum Prins Hendrik ③
Museum Boymans-van Beuningen ④
Museum voor Volkenkunde ⑤

Key

Metro station
Ferry
Parking
Church

0 meters 250
0 yards 250

Museum Boymans-van Beuningen

The museum is named after two art connoisseurs, FJO Boymans, who bequeathed his paintings to Rotterdam in 1847, and DG van Beuningen, who donated works between 1916 and 1954. The resulting collection is one of the Netherlands' finest. First displayed in the nearby Schielandshuis, the collection was moved to the present gallery in 1935. Known mainly for its supreme series of Old Master paintings, the collection also covers the whole spectrum of Dutch art, from the medieval works of Jan van Eyck to rare glassware and recent installations using laser technology.

La Méditerranée *(1905)*
Aristide Maillol's bronze was presented to the museum in 1961. He often used the female nude as a medium to express his philosophy of form.

Star Exhibits

- ★ **The Tower of Babel by Pieter Brueghel**
- ★ **Study of Two Feet by Albrecht Dürer**
- ★ **Titus at his Desk by Rembrandt**

★ **Titus at his Desk** *(1655)*
Rembrandt portrayed his sickly son in introspective mood, bathed in a tender light that heightens the ghostly pallor of his brooding features.

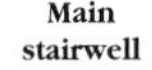

Main stairwell

First floor

Three Marys at the Open Sepulchre *(1430)*
Brothers Jan and Hubert van Eyck collaborated on this colorful work, which shows the three Marys at the tomb of the resurrected Christ.

Museum Guide

The museum is vast and can be confusing, especially since the displays change regularly. Directions to the museum's four main sections is clear and attendants are adept at directing visitors. For Brueghel and Rembrandt follow signs to the Old Masters Collection; for Dali and Magritte look for the Modern Art section.

Mother and Child *(1951)*
CJ Constant was a prominent member of the Cobra group. Here he explores the movement's fascination with primitive art.

Visitors' Checklist

Museumpark 18–20, Rotterdam. *(010) 441 9400. Centraal Station. 10am–5pm Tue–Sat, 11am–5pm Sun & public hols. Jan 1, Apr 30, Dec 25.*

Standing Clock *(1750)*
Lourens Eichelar designed this clock, which stands 215 cm (7 ft) high. It is made of walnut root wood and adorned with gilded cherubs blowing long horns.

Key to Floorplan

- Print Room
- Old Masters
- 19th- and 20th-century paintings
- Applied art and design
- Modern Art
- Nonexhibition space

Pavilion

Ground floor

Tower

Courtyard

Entrances to courtyard

Main entrance

★ **The Tower of Babel** *(c.1553)*
Pieter Brueghel took his theme from the Old Testament, and showed the elaborate ten-story edifice teeming with frenetic activity.

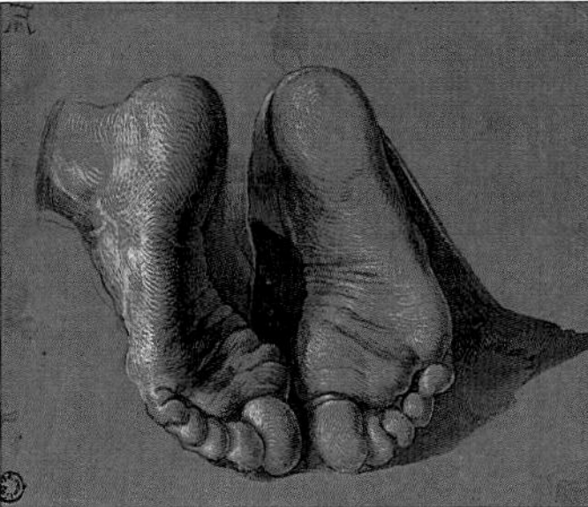

★ **Study of Two Feet** *(1507)*
Albrecht Dürer's study in gray and white ink is one of a series of preliminary sketches on the subject of the Assumption made for the Heller Altar in Frankfurt.

Utrecht 20

UTRECHT WAS FOUNDED by the Romans in AD 47 to protect an important river crossing on the Rijn (Rhine). The town was among the first in the Netherlands to embrace Christianity. In 700, St. Willibrord (658–739), a missionary from northern England, established a bishopric here, known as Het Sticht. Utrecht grew in importance as a religious center throughout the Middle Ages, extending its control over much of the Netherlands until 1527, when Bishop Hendrik of Bavaria was obliged to sell all his temporal powers to Charles V *(see pp22–3)*. The city center still retains many of its medieval churches and monasteries, but these now stand alongside modern blocks and a vast undercover shopping complex. The Oudegracht (old canal) threads its way through the city, flowing 5 m (16.5 ft) below ground level to prevent flooding. Today, it is lined with broad quays, cellar bars and cafés.

Domtoren

Domplein 1. (030) 2919 540. daily. public hols, except by prior appointment. hourly.

The Gothic Domtoren

The soaring Domtoren is a Gothic masterpiece and one of the tallest towers in the Netherlands at 112 m (367 ft) high. It was completed in 1382, on the site of the small, 8th-century church of St. Willibrord. The tower, which has always stood apart from the Domkerk, miraculously survived a massive hurricane in 1674 that destroyed the nave of the cathedral. The Domtoren continues to dominate Utrecht, and the viewing gallery in its spire still affords the best views across the city.

Domkerk

Achter den Dom 1. May–Oct: daily; Nov–Apr: Mon–Sat.

Construction of Utrecht's cathedral began in 1254. Today, only the north and south transepts, two chapels and the choir remain, along with the 15th-century cloisters and a chapter house (1495), which is now part of the university. It was here that the Union of Utrecht *(see p23)* was signed in 1579 by John, Count of Nassau, brother of William of Orange. Outside the church stands a giant boulder, dated 980 and covered with runic symbols. It was presented by the Danish people in 1936, to commemorate Denmark's early conversion to Christianity by missionaries from Utrecht.

Nederlands Spoorwegmuseum

Maliebaanstation. (030) 2306 206. Tue–Sun. public hols.

The headquarters of the Dutch railroads are based in Utrecht, so it is fitting that the town has a superb railroad museum. The Spoorwegmuseum is in the former 19th-century Maliebaan station. Inside the old building, there are specialized technical displays, engines and modern rail accessories.

Outside, children can explore steam engines, carriages, trolleys and signal boxes on the platforms. A high point for many visitors, young and old, is the simulated ride in the cab of a high-tech express train.

Organ in the Speelklok museum

Nationaal Museum van Speelklok tot Pierement

Buurkerkhof 10. (030) 2312 789. Tue–Sun. public hols.

This magical place – literally "from musical clock to street organ" – is located in the 13th-century Buurkerk, Utrecht's oldest church. The museum now houses an intriguing collection of mechanical musical instruments dating from the 18th century to the present day. Noisy fairground organs compete loudly with clocks, carillons, pianolas and the twittering of automated birds. These instruments are demonstrated on guided tours, during which visitors are encouraged to sing along and take partners for a spin on the dance floor.

Centraal Museum

Agnietenstraat 1. (030) 2362 362. Tue–Sun. Jan 1, Dec 25.

Housed in an old convent, Centraal Museum is only a ten-minute walk from the city center. The pride of the collection is a series of portraits by artist Jan van Scorel (1495–1562).

Steam engine and guard's box, Nederlands Spoorwegmuseum

Gerrit Rietveld's Schröderhuis (1924), part of the Centraal Museum

Van Scorel absorbed ideas from Italian Renaissance painting when he visited Rome, and he became the first Dutch artist to paint group portraits. These established the tradition leading to the magnificent 16th-century Civic Guard portraits *(see p81)*.

Six period rooms on the ground floor of the museum show changing styles of Dutch interiors from the Middle Ages through to the 18th century.

Gerrit Rietveld's Schröderhuis, designed in 1924, is regarded as the apogee of De Stijl architecture *(see p136)*. It is owned by the museum, and open to the public at Prins Hendriklaan 50.

Pieterskerk

Pieterskerkhof. *sporadically.*
Built of tufa (limestone) with red sandstone columns, the church was completed in 1048. It is a rare Dutch example of German Romanesque architecture, and set in a crescent of elegant Golden Age houses.

Museum Catharijneconvent

Nieuwegracht 63. *(030) 2313 835.* *Tue–Sun.* *Jan 1.*
The beautiful former convent of St. Catherine (1562) is home to this fascinating museum. It traces the troubled history of religion in the Netherlands and owns an award-winning collection of medieval art. Wooden and stone sculptures, gold and silver work, manuscripts, paintings and delicate jewel-encrusted miniatures are displayed in rooms around the cloister. On the upper floors of the museum is a series of model church interiors, highlighting the great variety of Dutch religious philosophies through the ages. These show the contrast between the lavish statues, paintings and altar in a Catholic church and the somber seating and plain wooden pulpit which characterizes most Protestant interiors.

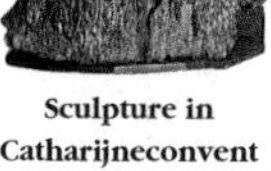

Sculpture in Catharijneconvent

Visitors' Checklist

57 km (35 miles) SE of Amsterdam. *232,000.* *Hoog Catharijne.* *Vredenburg 90. 06 340 340 85.* *Wed & Sat.* *Hollands Festival Oude Muziek: end Aug; Paper Note Jazz Route: beginning Sep; Nederlandse Filmdagen: end Sep.*

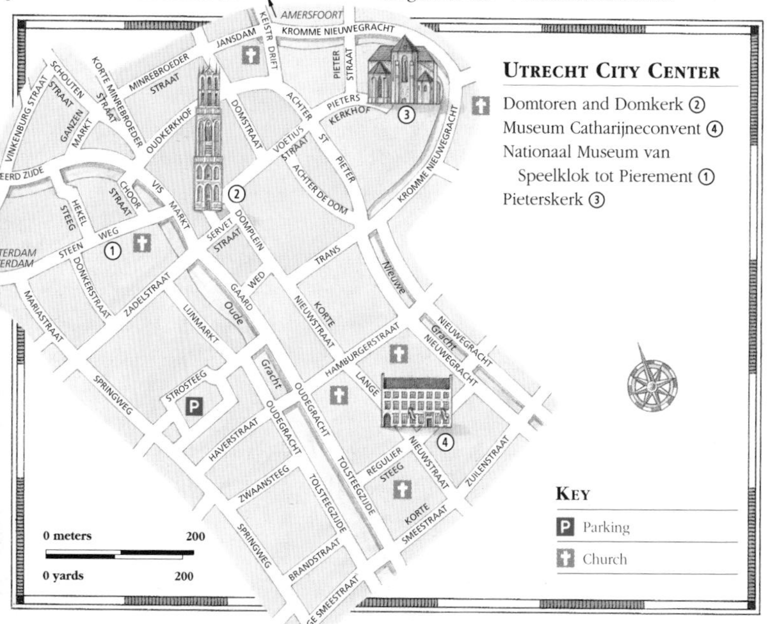

Utrecht City Center

Domtoren and Domkerk ②
Museum Catharijneconvent ④
Nationaal Museum van Speelklok tot Pierement ①
Pieterskerk ③

Key

Parking
Church

Nationaal Park de Hoge Veluwe ㉑

MADE UP OF MORE THAN 5,500 ha (13,750 acres) of woodland, fen, heath and sand drifts, the Netherlands' largest nature preserve is home to thousands of rare plants, wild animals and birds. In order to preserve the natural habitat, cars are banned from many sections. Also located in the park are the Museum Kröller-Müller, with 278 paintings by Van Gogh, and an outdoor sculpture garden, the Beeldenpark. Beneath the Visitors' Center is the Museonder, with audiovisual displays about the earth's subsurface, including an earthquake simulator.

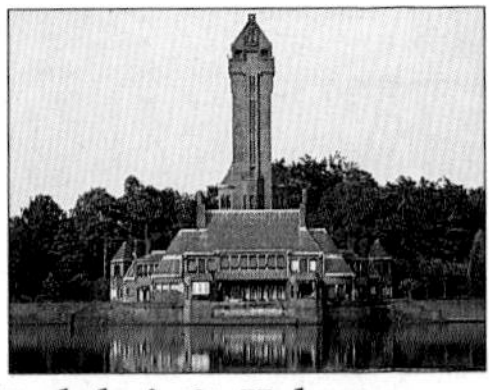

Jachthuis St. Hubertus
This hunting lodge was built in 1920 by HP Berlage (see p79) *for the park's wealthy patrons, the Kröller-Müllers.*

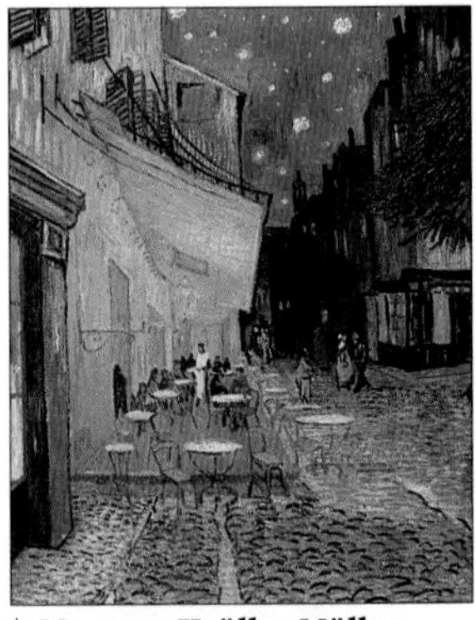

★ Museum Kröller-Müller
Besides Van Gogh's Café Terrace at Night *(1881), the museum has a collection of early Flemish masters and works by modern artists.*

Otterlo entrance

Visitors' Center and Museonder

Nieuwe Plijmen game observation post

Bosje van Staf game observation post

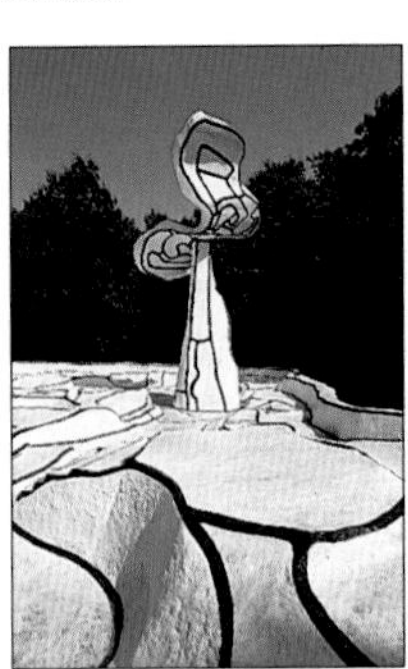

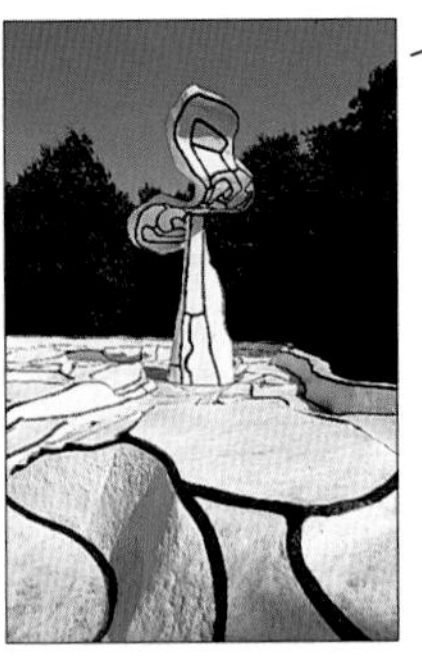

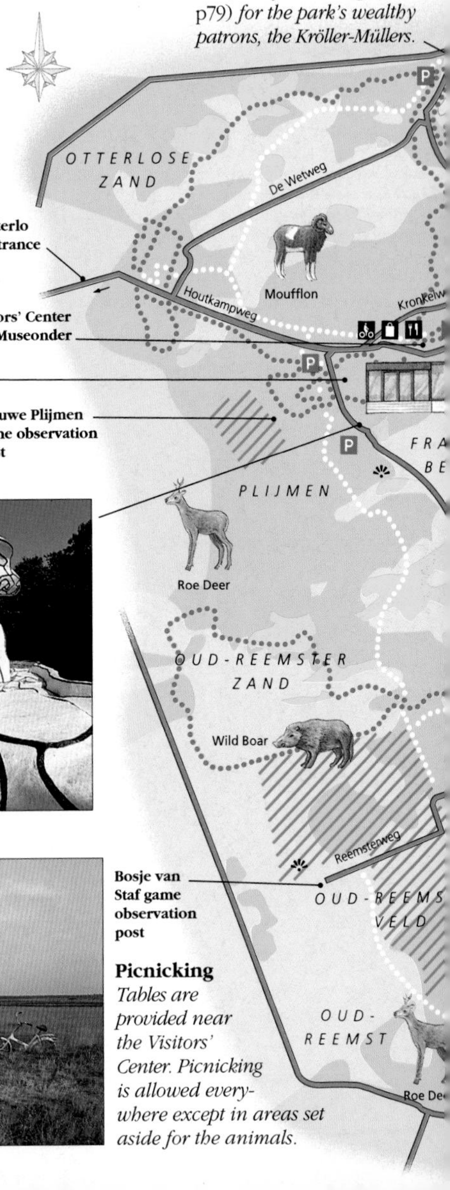

★ Beeldenpark
Jean Dubuffet's Jardin d'Emaille, *shown here, is one of the striking modern sculptures on display in this 11-ha (27-acre) sculpture park. The Beeldenpark also provides an elemental setting for works by Auguste Rodin, Alberto Giacometti and Barbara Hepworth.*

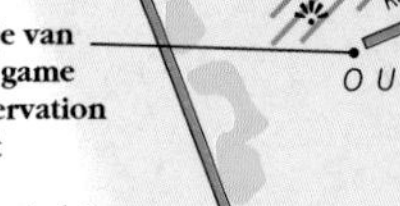

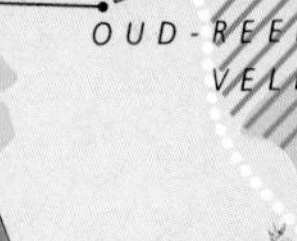

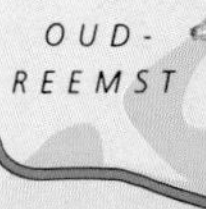

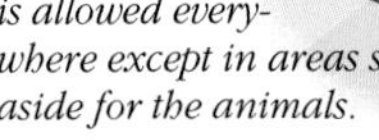

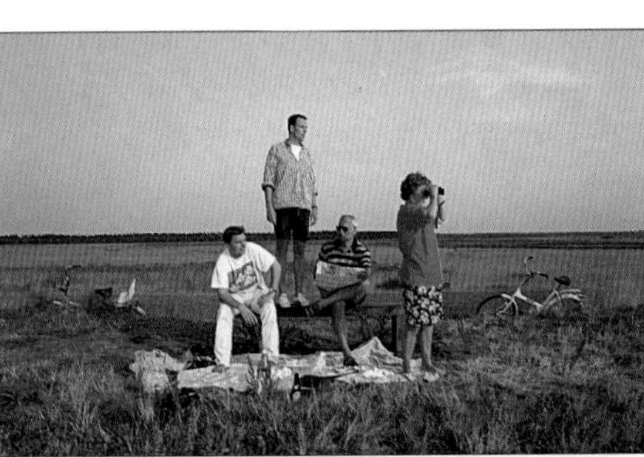

Picnicking
Tables are provided near the Visitors' Center. Picnicking is allowed everywhere except in areas set aside for the animals.

Free White Bicycles
At the Visitors' Center bikes are available for exploring the park.

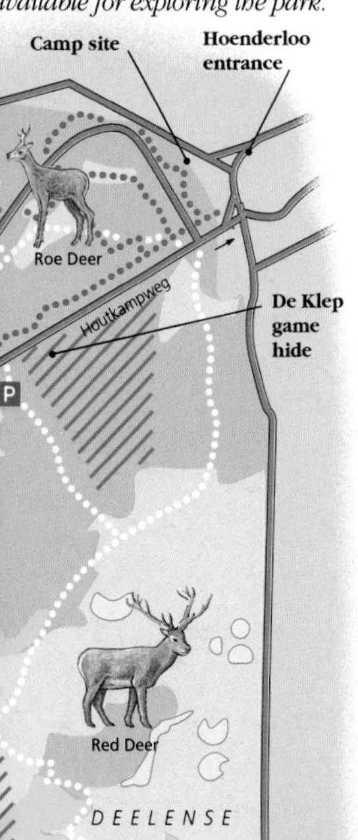

Visitors' Checklist

80 km (50 miles) SE of Amsterdam. Arnhem. ***Entrances*** *at Schaarsbergen, Otterlo, Hoenderloo.*
Nationaal Park Visitors' Center
Houtkampweg, Otterlo.
(0318) 591 627. Apr–Oct: 8am–dusk; Nov–Mar: 9am–dusk.
Museum Kröller-Müller
Houtkampweg 6, Otterlo.
(0318) 591 041. Apr–Oct: 10am–5pm Tue–Sat, 11am–5pm Sun & public hols; Nov–Mar: 10am–5pm Tue–Sat, 1–5pm Sun & public hols.
Park regulations*: Do not camp, or disturb the animals. Vehicles must not leave the road. Do not light fires outside designated areas. Keep dogs on a leash.*

Key

- Main road
- Walk route
- Bike path
- Forest
- Heath
- Sand drifts
- No access

0 kilometers 2
0 miles 1

Game Blinds and Observation Points
Special viewing areas (see map) allow the wildlife, like red deer, moufflon sheep and wild boar, to remain undisturbed.

Star Sights

★ **Museum Kröller-Müller**

★ **Beeldenpark**

Arnhem ㉒

80 km (50 miles) SE of Amsterdam. *133,000. Stationsplein 45. (0264) 420 330. Sat.*

Capital of Gelderland province, Arnhem was all but destroyed between September 17 and 27, 1944, in one of the most famous battles of World War II. The city has since been largely rebuilt, but still retains a number of reminders of the conflict, such as the John Frost Bridge, scene of some of the heaviest fighting. The bridge is named after the commanding officer of the 2nd Parachute Battalion, which fought to hold the bridgehead for four days.

Airborne Museum

Utrechtseweg 232, Oosterbeek.
(0263) 337 710. daily. with assistance.

The museum traces the course of the struggle to take Arnhem, using models, slides and taped commentaries. The collection is in a villa near Oosterbeek, used by the Commander of the 1st British Airborne Division, General Urquhart, as his headquarters during the invasion. The war cemetery nearby is a reminder of all those who died.

John Frost Bridge, Arnhem

Nederlands Openluchtmuseum

Schelmseweg 89. *(0263) 576 123. Apr–Oct: daily.*

Located in a 44-ha (110-acre) wooded park, the Nederlands Openluchtmuseum re-creates the traditional architecture and folklore of the Netherlands from 1800 to 1950. Founded in 1912, about 100 farmhouses, barns, windmills and workshops have since been erected here, many of them furnished in period style. The museum staff dress up in traditional costume and demonstrate the way of life, handicrafts and industry of the old rural communities.

Paleis Het Loo ㉓

STADTHOLDER WILLIAM III (*see p28*) built Het Loo in 1692 as a royal hunting lodge. Generations of the House of Orange used the lodge as a summer palace. Because of its magnificence, it was regarded as the "Versailles of the Netherlands." The main architect was Jacob Roman (1640–1716); the interior decoration and layout of the gardens were the responsibility of Daniel Marot (1661–1752). The building's Classical façade belies the opulence of its lavish interior; after extensive restoration work was completed on both in 1984, the palace was opened as a museum.

Coat of arms (1690) of William and Mary, future king and queen of England.

★ Royal Bedroom of Stadtholder William III *(1713)*
The wall coverings and draperies in this luxurious room are of rich orange damask and blue silk – the colors of the Dutch royal family.

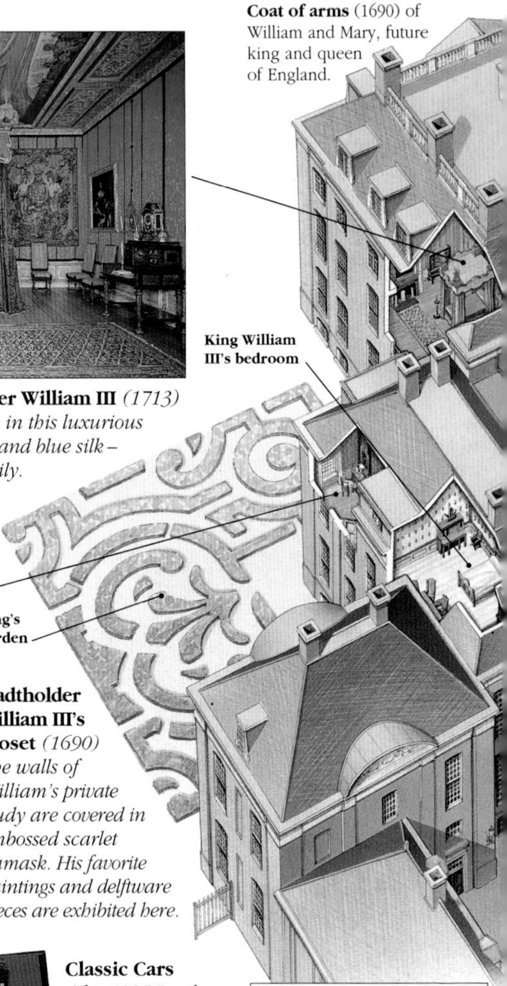

King William III's bedroom

King's Garden

Stadtholder William III's Closet *(1690)*
The walls of William's private study are covered in embossed scarlet damask. His favorite paintings and delftware pieces are exhibited here.

Classic Cars
This 1925 Bentley, nicknamed Minerva, was owned by Prince Hendrik, husband of Queen Wilhelmina. It is one of the royal family's many vintage cars, which are on display in the stable block (1910).

STAR FEATURES

- **★ Old Dining Room**
- **★ Royal Bedroom**
- **★ Formal Gardens**

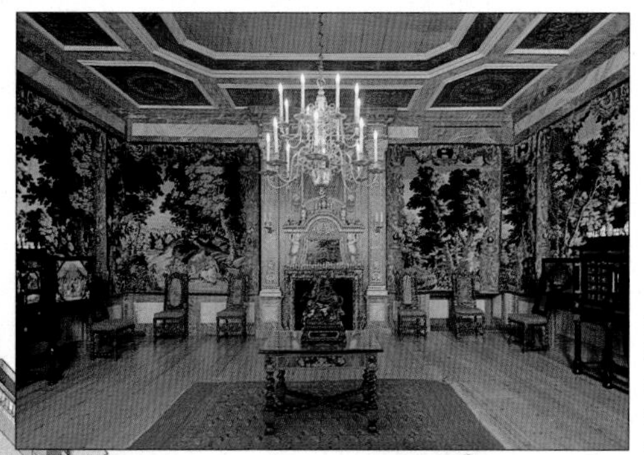

VISITORS' CHECKLIST

85 km (53 miles) SE of Amsterdam. Koninklijk Park 1, Apeldoorn. *(055) 212 244.* *Arnhem.* **Palace** *10am–5pm Tue–Sun (last adm 4:30pm).* **Gardens** *10am–6pm.* *Dec 25.* *gardens only.*

★ Old Dining Room *(1686)*
In 1984, six layers of paint were removed from the marbled walls, now hung with tapestries depicting scenes from Ovid's poems.

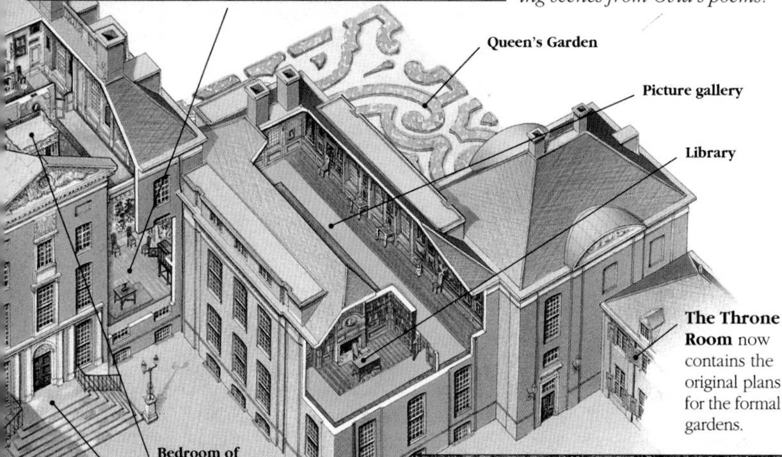

Queen's Garden
Picture gallery
Library
Bedroom of Queen Mary II
Main entrance

The Throne Room now contains the original plans for the formal gardens.

★ Formal Gardens
The gardens combine plants, statuary and fountains in Classical style. The Fountain of the Celestial Sphere stands in the Lower Garden.

Queen's Garden
Paleis Het Loo
Lower Garden
Upper Garden
King's Garden

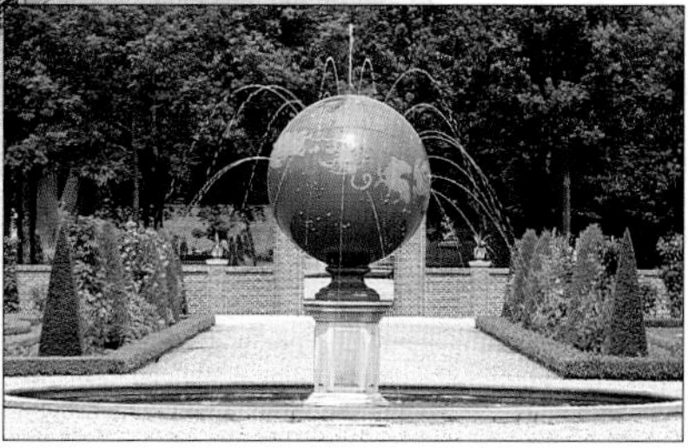

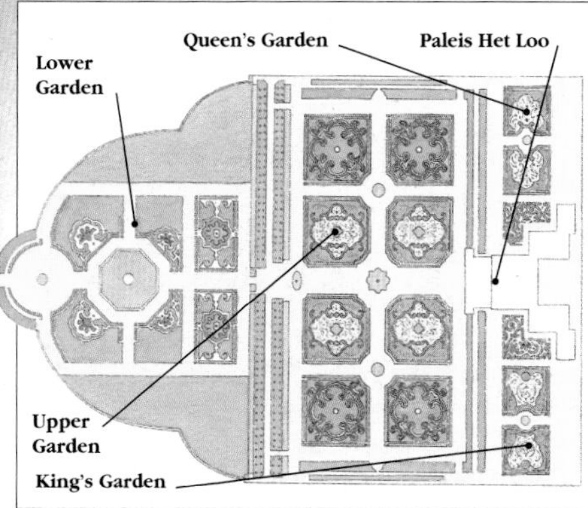

THE FORMAL GARDENS

Old prints, records and plans were used as the guidelines for re-creating Het Loo's formal gardens, which lie in the vast acres behind the palace. Grass was planted over the original walled and knot gardens in the 18th century, and this was cleared in 1975. By 1983, the intricate floral patterns had been re-established, replanting had begun, the Classical fountains were renovated and the water supply fully restored. The garden reflects the late 17th-century belief that art and nature should operate in harmony.

Layout of the formal section of the gardens

TRAVELERS' NEEDS

Where to Stay

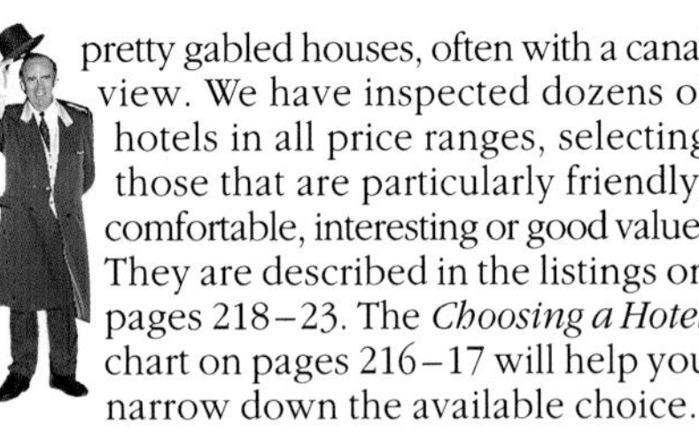

Amsterdam provides top-quality, city-center accommodations to suit everyone's budget. They range from a clutch of luxurious five-star hotels that should impress the most hedonistic traveler to inexpensive hostels for those on a budget. In between there are scores of B&Bs, many occupying pretty gabled houses, often with a canal view. We have inspected dozens of hotels in all price ranges, selecting those that are particularly friendly, comfortable, interesting or good value. They are described in the listings on pages 218–23. The *Choosing a Hotel* chart on pages 216–17 will help you narrow down the available choice.

The Van Ostade Bicycle Hotel in southern Amsterdam ***(see p223)***

Choosing a Hotel

Most of Amsterdam's tourist hotels lie in three areas: the historic center, along the *Grachtengordel* (Canal Ring) and in the Museum Quarter. Since central Amsterdam is compact, wherever you stay, you are within walking distance of most of the city's major attractions. The majority of business-oriented hotels are located in the Nieuw Zuid (New South), which is a little more remote.

Accommodations in Amsterdam's historic center can often be disappointing. There are collections of chain hotels, seedy rooms above cafés and unenticing low-budget hotels around Centraal Station and the Red Light District. Fortunately, there are a few notable exceptions that we recommend *(see pp218–23)*.

You will find the city's most charismatic hotels along the Canal Ring, the majority of which boast beautiful gabled façades and old-fashioned beamed interiors. Despite their charm, you may have to sacrifice some creature comforts, since the rooms can be small, the facilities limited and the stairs treacherously steep.

The quiet 19th-century terraced streets between Leidseplein and Vondelpark house many modest but comfortable establishments that, although not as characterful as the canalside hotels, are conveniently situated close to the main museums and galleries. The VVV *(see p256)* publishes a useful brochure that details the facilities, price and location of virtually all the 300 or so hotels in Amsterdam, with photographs and descriptions. It is on sale at the information desk at Schiphol Airport and VVV offices in the city. It is also available by mail from the Amsterdam VVV and the **NBT** (Netherlands Board of Tourism) in your home country.

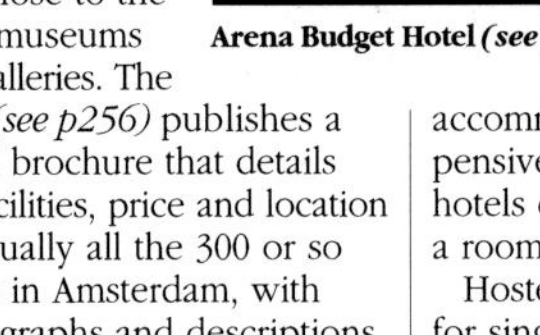

Arena Budget Hotel ***(see p223)***

Room Rates

Room rates usually include tax and a basic breakfast, except at large, expensive hotels where breakfast is almost invariably extra. For those on a tight budget, many B&Bs and small private hotels have rooms without *en suite* facilities at rock-bottom prices. However, canalside accommodations can be expensive and some of these hotels charge a little extra for a room with a canal view.

Hostels are the best option for single travelers, since reductions on the double-room rate at hotels is small, typically around 20 percent. Families and groups of friends, however, can save money by staying in family rooms, common in all types of hotel.

De l'Europe, overlooking Muntplein ***(see p219)***

The breakfast room of the Prinsenhof in Canal Ring South *(see p221)*

Special Offers

Most private hotels drop their rates by a quarter or a third from the beginning of November to the end of March (except over Christmas and the New Year). Some even throw in a complimentary boat trip and free museum admissions. These hotels, which include a couple of dozen choices in all price categories, are featured in the *Winter the Amsterdam Way* brochure. This publication is available by mail from the Amsterdam VVV or the NBT office in your home country.

Amsterdam has a surfeit of chain hotels. Large operators such as **Best Western** and **Holiday Inn** frequently offer special discounts to attract guests, and their weekend rates are substantially cheaper than weekday rates off season.

Booking and Paying

April to May (the tulip season) and July to August are the busiest times of year for tourists. During these periods, book at least a few weeks in advance, especially on weekends when reasonably priced accommodations can dry up completely. For popular hotels along the canals, book well in advance all year.

Since all Amsterdam hoteliers speak English, make reservations directly with the hotel. While most take credit card reservations, some small places will ask for a deposit in the form of a check or money order, usually for the full amount of the first night's stay. The **Netherlands Reservation Center** makes hotel bookings free of charge if you are already in the Netherlands. It will charge a substantial fee should you use the service before you arrive in the country. If you arrive in Amsterdam without accommodation, the KLM desk at Schiphol Airport makes hotel reservations without charge. VVV offices require a small fee for same-day bookings.

Hotel Gradings

The number of stars (from one to five) meted out by the Benelux Hotel Classification system only indicates a hotel's level of facilities. Stars have no bearing on its appeal or location. Many of the city's small hotels are given a low star rating, despite their charm, due to a lack of facilities.

The elegant foyer of the Amstel Inter-Continental *(see p223)*

Using the Listings

The hotels and hostels on pages 218–23 are listed according to area and price category. The symbols summarize the facilities at each of them.

all rooms have bath and/or shower unless otherwise indicated
1 single-rate rooms available
rooms for more than two people available, or an extra bed can be put in a double room
24 24-hour room service
TV television in all rooms
minibar in all rooms
nonsmoking rooms available
air conditioning in all rooms
gym/fitness facilities available in hotel
swimming pool in hotel
business facilities: these include message-taking service, fax service, desk and telephone in each room, and meeting room within hotel
caters to children
wheelchair access
elevator
pets allowed in bedrooms
P hotel parking available
bar
restaurant
credit and charge cards accepted:
AE American Express
DC Diners Club
MC Mastercard/Access
V Visa
JCB Japanese Credit Bureau

Price categories for hotels are based on a standard double room per night, including breakfast, tax and service. Since the majority of hostel accommodation is dormitory style, hostel prices are based on the cost of a single bed in a dormitory.
Ⓕ under *f*125
ⒻⒻ *f*125–250
ⒻⒻⒻ *f*250–400
ⒻⒻⒻⒻ *f*400–600
ⒻⒻⒻⒻⒻ over *f*600

Dining room of the Canal House in the Western Canal Ring *(see p220)*

What to Expect

WHILE SOME stylish B&Bs boast an elegant lounge, only top-of-the-line hotels normally have a restaurant. The vast majority of hotels just offer bed and breakfast, and public areas are limited to a breakfast room and possibly a bar. A Dutch breakfast can include cold meats, cheeses and boiled eggs, but do not expect more than rolls, jam and a hot drink at a no-frills B&B.

It is important to get a detailed description of your room when you book, since many canalside hotels have a number of cramped rooms. In budget B&Bs furnishings can be spartan, but all rooms usually include a TV. If there is a telephone, expect to pay double or triple the normal rate for any call you make.

Wall plaque on the façade of the SAS Royal *(see p218)*

Traveling with Children

WHILE A FEW, small upscale hotels do not welcome children, many big chain hotels offer free accommodation to children under 12 when they share their parents' room. Others offer a half-price rate or even free accommodation for children up to 18, so it is worth phoning around. Babies stay for free almost everywhere. Some places charge for the use of a crib.

The *Choosing a Hotel* chart on pages 216–17 shows which of our recommended hotels have special deals for children.

Gay Hotels

A GAY COUPLE is unlikely to produce a raised eyebrow in most hotels in this tolerant city. Exclusively gay hotels, like the stylish and very popular **New York**, have the advantage of providing a wealth of information on gay hangouts and events. Some hotels, although not exclusively gay, extend a particularly warm welcome to gay guests. Of these, the **Quentin** is now very popular with women, and the **Waterfront** *(see p220)* attracts a mainly male clientele.

English-language publications like *Men to Men* and *Best Guide to Holland* offer comprehensive listings. They can be found in bookshops such as **Intermale**.

Disabled Travelers

THE INFORMATION provided about wheelchair access in our hotel listings relies on the hotels' own assessment of their suitability. The Amsterdam VVV's hotel brochure indicates which four- and five-star hotels have wheelchair access. **SGOA** (Stichting Gehandicapten Overleg Amsterdam) provides comprehensive details on accommodations suitable for people with disabilities. Remember, the stairs in most of the old canalside hotels can be steep, and few have elevators.

Hostels

HOSTELS are very much part of the mainstream tourist culture in Amsterdam. Their convivial cafés are good places for meeting fellow travelers and finding out about popular nightspots. The Amsterdam VVV's hotel brochure lists a broad selection of hostels, and the best four are reviewed in this guide on pages 218–23.

Most of Amsterdam's hostels are independent, except for two run by the **NJHC** (Nederlandse Jeugdherberg Centrale), which offer discounts to members of the International Youth

Hostel Federation (IYHF). Dormitory beds make up the bulk of accommodation in all hostels. Many hostels impose a curfew at night and close for a few hours during the day.

CAMPING

AMSTERDAM VVV's hotel brochure lists five campsites within range of the city center. Most open in spring and close at the end of October, but for the very hardy, some stay open until December. **Vliegenbos** and **Zeeburg** are closest, both about 5 km (3 miles) from the center. Although open to everyone, they are classified as youth sites, as is **Gaasper Camping** so expect late-night parties. Families would do better to head for a quieter site, such as **Amsterdamse Bos**.

Local VVV offices can provide information on campsites elsewhere in the Netherlands, and the NBT in your home country distributes camping brochures covering the whole country. The Netherlands Reservation Center can make camping bookings.

EFFICIENCY APARTMENTS

APARTMENTS for short-term rentals are limited, so canalside efficiencies tend to be expensive. Rental agencies are listed in Amsterdam VVV's hotel brochure; more agencies can be found in the Visitors' Guide section of the Yellow Pages *(Gouden Gids)* *(see p256)*.

Agencies usually insist on a minimum stay of at least one week. Of the hotels recommended in this guide, the Amsterdam Renaissance *(see p219)*, Waterfront *(see p220)* and Acacia *(see p220)* all offer efficiency facilities.

STAYING IN PRIVATE HOMES

A BOOKLET TITLED **Bed & Breakfast Holland** provides a brief description of Dutch homes that take in guests. Around 20 of these are in Amsterdam. Most homes have only two bedrooms and require guests to stay for at least two nights. Some offer evening meals. Prices are charged per person and are competitive with inexpensive B&Bs.

BEYOND AMSTERDAM

THE NBT publishes a thick brochure covering more than 450 hotels throughout the Netherlands. Although this Eyewitness Travel Guide does not cover any hotels outside Amsterdam, the information provided here on booking and paying, hotel ratings, hostels, camping and staying in private homes is applicable.

The bar of Arena Budget Hotel *(see p223)*, a hostel near Oosterpark

DIRECTORY

INFORMATION

NBT (Netherlands Board of Tourism)
225 N. Michigan Ave
Suite 323, Chicago
IL 60601.
Tel *(312) 819-0300.*

GAY HOTELS AND INFORMATION

New York
Herengracht 13, 1015 BA, Amsterdam. **Map** 1 C3.
Tel *624 3066.*
FAX *620 3230.*

Quentin
Leidsekade 89, 1017 PN, Amsterdam. **Map** 4 D1.
Tel *626 2187 or 627 4408.*
FAX *622 0121.*

Intermale
Spuistraat 251, 1012 CR Amsterdam. **Map** 7 B3.
Tel *625 0009.*
FAX *620 3163*

CHAIN HOTELS

(Central reservations toll free in the Netherlands.)

Best Western
Tel *(06) 022 1455.*

Holiday Inn
Tel *(06) 022 1155.*

HOTEL RESERVATIONS

Netherlands Reservation Center
PO Box 404, 2260 AK Leidschendam.
Tel *(70) 320 2500.*
FAX *(70) 320 2611.*

DISABLED TRAVELERS

SGOA (Stichting Gehandicapten Overleg Amsterdam)
Keizersgracht 523, 1017 DP, Amsterdam. **Map** 4 F2.
Tel *638 3838.*

HOSTELS

NJHC (Nederlandse Jeugdherberg Centrale)
Prof. Tulpplein 4, 1018 GX, Amsterdam. **Map** 5 B4.
Tel *551 3155.*

CAMPING

Gaasper Camping
Loosdrechtdreef 7, 1108 AZ, Amsterdam.
Tel *696 7326.*

Amsterdamse Bos
Kleine Noorddijk 1, 1432 CC, Aalsmeer.
Tel *641 6868.*
FAX *640 2378.*

Vliegenbos
Meeuwenlaan 138, 1022 AM, Amsterdam. **Map** 2 F2.
Tel *636 8855.*

Zeeburg
Zuider IJ Dijk 44, 1095 KN, Amsterdam.
Tel *694 4430.*

STAYING IN PRIVATE HOMES

Bed & Breakfast Holland
Theophile de Bockstraat 3, 1058 TV, Amsterdam.
Tel *615 7527.*
FAX *669 1573.*

Amsterdam's Best: Hotels

THE HOTELS RECOMMENDED on these two pages possess an individual charm and character not found in their chain hotel counterparts. All of these recommendations have a typically Dutch atmosphere, ranging from the simple and homey to the ornate, and some have an historical interest. Many of these hotels are impeccably restored 17th-century canal houses offering both canal and garden views, in addition to steep and narrow staircases. So whether you are after a reasonably priced B&B or looking for luxury, there is a huge choice available in Amsterdam.

Canal House
This popular, atmospheric B&B has been beautifully restored by its engaging American owner. (See p220.)

Western Canal Ring

Pulitzer
This surprising, labyrinthine hotel was created by joining together 24 old canal houses and their gardens. (See p221.)

Central Canal Ring

De Filosoof
Perhaps the city's most unusual hotel, "The Philosopher" has rooms named after the world's greatest thinkers, with thematic decor. (See p222.)

Museum Quarter

Ambassade
This classy B&B is an ideal choice for those who want to stay in a charming, gabled canal house without giving up comfort. (See p220.)

Grand Hotel Krasnapolsky
This 130-year-old institution has an excellent choice of restaurants, none more splendid than the Winter Garden shown left. (See p219.)

Grand Amsterdam
The newest of Amsterdam's set of luxury hotels has the air of an opulent country house. (See p218.)

Seven Bridges
On a pretty canal, this refined B&B is filled with antiques and Persian rugs. (See p221.)

Prinsenhof
The dedicated owners of this charmingly decorated, simple canal house B&B provide delightful accommodation at a very reasonable price. (See p221.)

Amstel Inter-Continental
Situated by the side of the Amstel, the city's number one hotel is serene, breathtakingly beautiful and utterly luxurious. (See p223.)

Choosing a Hotel

The hotels and hostels on the following pages have all been inspected and assessed specifically for this guide. This chart shows some of the factors that may affect your choice. For more information on each entry see pages 218–23. They are listed by area and appear alphabetically within their price categories.

		Number of Rooms	Large Rooms	Business Facilities	Under 12s Free in Room	Close to Shops and Restaurants	Quiet Location	Canal Views
Oude Zijde *(see p218)*								
Amstel Botel	ƒƒ	174						■
Doelen Karena	ƒƒƒ	85				■		■
Raeisson SAS Royal	ƒƒƒƒ	243		■		■		
Grand Amsterdam	ƒƒƒƒƒ	166	●	■		■	●	■
Nieuwe Zijde *(see pp218–19)*								
Amsterdam Classic	ƒƒ	33			●	■	●	
Avenue	ƒƒ	50				■		
Rho	ƒƒ	160				■	●	
Singel	ƒƒ	32				■	●	■
Estheréa	ƒƒƒ	73			●	■	●	■
Die Port van Cleve	ƒƒƒ	99			●	■		
De Roode Leeuw	ƒƒƒ	80		■		■		
Sofitel	ƒƒƒ	148		■		■		
Amsterdam Renaissance	ƒƒƒƒ	425		■	●	■		
Golden Tulip Barbizon Palace	ƒƒƒƒ	268		■	●	■		
Grand Hotel Krasnapolsky	ƒƒƒƒ	322	●	■		■		
Holiday Inn Crowne Plaza	ƒƒƒƒ	270		■	●	■		
Swissôtel Amsterdam Ascot	ƒƒƒƒ	109		■	●	■		
Victoria	ƒƒƒƒ	306		■	●	■		
De l'Europe	ƒƒƒƒƒ	100	●	■		■		■
Western Canal Ring *(see p220)*								
Acacia	ƒ	17				■		■
Eben Haëzer	ƒ					■	●	
Van Onna	ƒ	38				■	●	■
Canal House	ƒƒ	26	●			■	●	■
Toren	ƒƒ	43				■	●	■
Central Canal Ring *(see pp220–21)*								
Hans Brinker	ƒ					■		
Agora	ƒƒ	16				■		■
Amsterdam Weichmann	ƒƒ	38				■		■
Waterfront	ƒƒ	9				■		■
Ambassade	ƒƒƒ	52	●			■	●	■
Dikker & Thijs	ƒƒƒ	25		■	●	■		■
American	ƒƒƒƒ	188		■	●	■		■
Pulitzer	ƒƒƒƒ	232	●	■	●	■	●	■
Eastern Canal Ring *(see p221)*								
De Admiraal	ƒƒ	9	●			■		■
Asterisk	ƒƒ	28				■	●	
De Munck	ƒƒ	14				■	●	
Prinsenhof	ƒƒ	10				■		■
Seven Bridges	ƒƒ	11	●			■	●	■
Mercure Arthur Frommer	ƒƒƒ	90	●		●	■	●	
Schiller Karena	ƒƒƒ	95				■		

Price categories for a standard double room per night, including breakfast, tax and service:
Ⓕ under *f* 125
ⒻⒻ *f* 125–250
ⒻⒻⒻ *f* 250–400
ⒻⒻⒻⒻ *f* 400–600
ⒻⒻⒻⒻⒻ over *f* 600

LARGE ROOMS
A significant proportion of standard rooms are larger than average.

NUMBER OF ROOMS
This chart only indicates the number of rooms for hotels, not hostels. The number of beds at each hostel is given in the listings *(see pp218–23)*.

BUSINESS FACILITIES
Includes message-taking service, fax service, desk and telephone in every bedroom, and meeting rooms. Conference facilities are not necessarily available.

	Price	Number of Rooms	Large Rooms	Business Facilities	Under 12s Free in Room	Close to Shops and Restaurants	Quiet Location	Canal Views
MUSEUM QUARTER *(see pp221–2)*								
NJHC Hostel Vondelpark	Ⓕ							
Wynnobel	Ⓕ	11	●			■	●	
Acro	ⒻⒻ	51				■		
Atlas	ⒻⒻ	23		■		■		
De Filosoof	ⒻⒻ	27					●	
Owl	ⒻⒻ	34				■		
Sander	ⒻⒻ	20	●			■		
Jan Luijken	ⒻⒻⒻ	63		■		■		
Amsterdam Marriott	ⒻⒻⒻⒻ	392		■		■		
PLANTAGE *(see pp222–3)*								
Adam and Eva	Ⓕ						●	
Fantasia	Ⓕ	19					●	■
Kitty Muijzers	Ⓕ	10	●					
Bridge	ⒻⒻ	27	●					■
Amstel Inter-Continental	ⒻⒻⒻⒻⒻ	79	●	■			●	■
FARTHER AFIELD *(see p223)*								
Arena Budget Hotel	Ⓕ							
Van Ostade Bicycle Hotel	Ⓕ	15				■	●	
Toro	ⒻⒻ	22	●				●	■
Villa Borgmann	ⒻⒻ	15	●				●	■
Amsterdam Hilton	ⒻⒻⒻⒻ	271		■	●		●	■
Okura	ⒻⒻⒻⒻ	370	●	■	●		●	■

OUDE ZIJDE

Amstel Botel

Oosterdokskade 2–4, 1011 AE. **Map** 8 E1. *626 4247.* *639 1952.* ***Rooms**: 174.* *AE, DC, MC, V, JCB.* ƒƒ

The Amstel Botel, a big, modern boat moored close to Centraal Station, is the only remaining floating hotel in the city. More romantic in concept than reality, the accommodations aboard are neat, but uninspiring and cramped. Although no more spacious, the berths facing the water provide a wonderful view of Amsterdam across the Oosterdok.

Doelen Karena

Nieuwe Doelenstraat 24, 1012 CP. **Map** 7 C4. *622 0722.* *622 1084.* ***Rooms**: 85.* *AE, DC, MC, V, JCB.* ƒƒƒ

A reproduction of Rembrandt's *The Night Watch (see p131)* hangs in this imposing Neo-Classical building, a reminder that the original hung here from 1642 to 1715. Stuccoed walls, marble steps and copper candelabras reveal the hotel's pedigree. Although fading decor betrays the fact that this establishment has seen better days, it is one of the few reasonably priced hotels in central Amsterdam to retain its interior character. Book one of the charming bedrooms overlooking the Amstel (for no extra cost), or spoil yourself in one of the corner suites, which have the best views; some even have their own balcony.

Raeisson SAS Royal

Rusland 17, 1012 CK. **Map** 7 C4. *623 1231.* *520 8200.* *10365.* ***Rooms**: 243.* *AE, DC, MC, V, JCB.* ƒƒƒƒ

Taking up most of the street, the well-run SAS Royal, which opened in 1990, is set around a dramatic state-of-the-art atrium. Despite a predominantly modern appearance, the hotel was developed on the site of several old buildings. These include an 18th-century vicarage, features of which have been preserved and transformed into a lovely candlelit bar. The bedrooms are imaginatively themed in Scandinavian, Oriental, Art Deco or Dutch styles. The hotel also has its own private health center and conference facilities in a building across the road. Both amenities are linked to the hotel by a connecting tunnel.

Grand Amsterdam

Oudezijds Voorburgwal 197, 1012 EX. **Map** 7 C3. *555 3111.* *555 3222.* *13074.* ***Rooms**: 166.* *AE, DC, MC, V, JCB.* ƒƒƒƒƒ

The Grand Amsterdam, opened in 1992, is situated on a peaceful canal just south of the Red Light District. Although it is the city's newest luxury hotel, it occupies one of the most historic locations in the city. The site, first developed as a convent at the beginning of the 15th century, became a royal guest house in the 16th century. The present building, constructed in 1661, was built for the Admiralty and was later used as the city hall. The magnificent premises are set around their own courtyard and a lovely enclosed garden. Highlights inside include luxurious bedrooms in English country-house style, the striking Art Deco Café Roux, serving affordable high-quality French food, and elegant reception rooms.

NIEUWE ZIJDE

Amsterdam Classic

Gravenstraat 14–16, 1012 NM. **Map** 7 B2. *623 3716.* *638 1156.* ***Rooms**: 33.* *AE, DC, MC, V.* ƒƒ

De Drie Fleschjes, an ancient *proeflokaal (see p48)*, leans against the handsome Amsterdam Classic, which was built in 1880 as a distillery. The main attraction of the hotel is its location, overlooking perhaps the most atmospheric cobblestoned square in the city. Inside, the large open-plan lobby-cum-breakfast area and bar is functional and disappointingly modern. The best of the modern-styled bedrooms have been stylishly decorated and contain interesting angular black and brown furniture.

Avenue

Nieuwezijds Voorburgwal 27, 1012 RD. **Map** 7 C1. *623 8307.* *638 3946.* ***Rooms**: 50.* *AE, DC, MC, V, JCB.* ƒƒ

The six-story black-brick Avenue used to be a warehouse belonging to the United East India Company. Although traffic disturbs the front-facing bedrooms of this modest city-center hotel, rooms at the back are quieter. All the rooms are attractive, with beams and wicker furniture. Those on the upper floors at the back have interesting roof-top views. Downstairs, the little breakfast room and bar are functional rather than inviting.

Rho

Nes 5–23, 1012 KC. **Map** 7 B3. *620 7371.* *620 7826.* ***Rooms**: 160.* *AE, MC, V.* ƒƒ

The Rho is tucked away down the Nes *(see p74)*, a narrow backstreet running south from Dam square. It enjoys both peace and quiet and a central location. The hotel's vaulted lobby, with hints of Art Nouveau style, is an original feature of the building, which was constructed in 1908 as a theater. Practical and modern bedrooms do not reflect the character of the period rooms on the ground floor. The choice of facilities offered makes this hotel a good bargain.

Singel

Singel 15, 1012 VC. **Map** 7 B1. *626 3108.* *620 3777.* ***Rooms**: 32.* *AE, DC, MC, V.* ƒƒ

This freshly decorated little hotel occupies three 17th-century canal-side houses. It is located on a pretty northern stretch of the Singel overlooking the Poezenboot (a barge that is home to scores of stray cats). Tasty buffet breakfasts are served in a lime-green room on the ground floor. The bedrooms are small but attractively shaped and brightly decorated with yellow duvets. All the rooms have showers, except the family rooms that come with a bathtub.

Estheréa

Singel 303–309, 1012 WJ. **Map** 7 A3. *624 5146.* *623 9001.* ***Rooms**: 73.* *AE, DC, MC, V, JCB.* ƒƒƒ

The Estheréa occupies four handsome 17th-century redbrick houses on an elegant part of the Singel. It is within easy walking distance of Dam square and Spui. This long-established hotel, decently, though somewhat unexcitingly, furnished in dark wood, is popular with groups. More than half the bedrooms have a canal view, but rooms at the rear tend to be bigger.

Die Port van Cleve

Nieuwezijds Voorburgwal 178–180, 1012 SJ. **Map** 7 B3. *624 4860.* *622 0240.* *13129.* ***Rooms**: 99.* *AE, DC, MC, V, JCB.* ƒƒƒ

The hotel boasts two atmospheric restaurants specializing in Dutch cuisine. Murals of old Amsterdam decorate De Poort restaurant, famous for its steaks, while the more formal De Blauwe Parade restaurant contains a beautiful delft-tile frieze. The hotel stands between two busy streets, near the upscale Magna Plaza shopping center *(see Postkantoor, p78)*, so bedrooms can be noisy. The facilities and furnishings of the standard rooms are dated and spartan. There are some superior rooms, but these cost a little extra.

De Roode Leeuw

Damrak 93–94, 1012 LP. **Map** 7 B2. *555 0666.* FAX *620 4716.* TX *10569.* ***Rooms***: *80.* *AE, DC, MC, V.* ƒƒƒ

The best part of the hotel is at street level, where you can sit all hours of the day on the covered terrace eating pastries, drinking beer and watching the world go by. Behind this a restaurant serves a good buffet breakfast and specializes in traditional Dutch cuisine. The bedrooms are well equipped but plain; ask for one at the back to avoid street noise.

Sofitel

Nieuwezijds Voorburgwal 67, 1012 RE. **Map** 7 B1. *627 5900.* FAX *623 8932.* TX *14494.* ***Rooms***: *148.* *AE, DC, MC, V.* ƒƒƒ

This is a good-quality chain hotel, but somewhat noisy due to its location on a street busy with trolleys and traffic. Like many hotels in the center, its old gabled buildings now contain modern accommodations. However, the standard look is relieved by the beams in the hotel's dozen or so vaulted bedrooms on the top floor. The most striking feature, however, is the bar, where red velvet seating, paneled walls and windows replicate a carriage from the Orient Express.

Amsterdam Renaissance

Kattengat 1, 1012 SZ. **Map** 7 C1. *621 2223.* FAX *627 5245.* TX *17149.* ***Rooms***: *425.* *AE, DC, M, V, JCB.* ƒƒƒƒ

If you want the full range of facilities at a modest room rate, the spacious Amsterdam Renaissance is the best choice. There is a disco, extensive health facilities and a traditional brown café *(see p48)*, along with other restaurants and bars. For those who prefer to cook for themselves, the hotel rents out 43 apartments in old town houses it owns nearby. The hotel also has a business and conference center, which is located across the road in the Lutherse Kerk *(see p78)*.

Golden Tulip Barbizon Palace

Prins Hendrikkade 59–72, 1012 AD. **Map** 8 D1. *556 4564.* FAX *624 3353.* TX *10187 GTPAL.* ***Rooms***: *268.* *AE, DC, MC, V, JCB.* ƒƒƒƒ

A predominantly modern exterior conceals 19 houses dating from the 17th century. Consequently, many of the bedrooms have attractive beamed ceilings. All have first-rate facilities. The chessboard floor and creamy pillars of the lobby, the sprinkling of antiques in the stylish Vermeer restaurant *(see p231)* and the tiny paneled bar lend character to the hotel's public areas. Business and conference facilities are available in St. Olofskapel.

Grand Hotel Krasnapolsky

Dam 9, 1012 JS. **Map** 7 C2. *554 9111.* FAX *622 8607.* TX *12262 KRASNL.* ***Rooms***: *322.* *AE, DC, MC, V, JCB.* ƒƒƒƒ

This landmark hotel began life as a mere coffeehouse in 1866. It has since played host to luminaries as diverse as James Joyce, the Rolling Stones and President Mitterrand. It has the best choice of restaurants of any hotel in Amsterdam, with buffets in the Winter Garden, a Belle Epoque French brasserie and a stylish Japanese restaurant. Afternoon teas are served in the elegant lounge. Its conference and business facilities are good and the bedrooms are comfortable, but due to its location few are peaceful.

Holiday Inn Crowne Plaza

Nieuwezijds Voorburgwal 5, 1012 RC. **Map** 7 C1. *620 0500.* FAX *620 1173.* TX *15183.* ***Rooms***: *270.* *AE, DC, MC, V, JCB.* ƒƒƒƒ

The Crowne Plaza is a cut above the average Holiday Inn, with good business facilities, perky staff and a swimming pool. The hotel's original garden has been covered to make a courtyard café, and a variety of Dutch delicacies can be enjoyed nearby at the Dorrius, a 100-year-old restaurant *(see p231)*. The standard bedrooms are small, but pay a little more and you'll be rewarded with plenty of extra space.

Swissôtel Amsterdam Ascot

Damrak 95–98, 1012 LP. **Map** 7 C2. *626 0066.* FAX *627 0982.* TX *16620.* ***Rooms***: *109.* *AE, DC, MC, V, JCB.* ƒƒƒƒ

This establishment on the corner of Dam Square should appeal to business people who are looking for something more intimate than a vast chain hotel. Breakfast, lunch and dinner are served in an attractive marbled, yet informal, French brasserie. Marble also adorns the bathrooms of the hotel's stylish, modern and well-equipped bedrooms. Rooms facing the square are more expensive, but it is wiser to ask for a quieter room at the rear.

Victoria

Damrak 1–5, 1012 LG. **Map** 7 C1. *623 4255.* FAX *625 2997.* TX *16625.* ***Rooms***: *306.* *AE, DC, MC, V, JCB.* ƒƒƒƒ

Despite the trolleys, trains and canal cruises, which all depart from close to the front doors, the Victoria offers a world removed from the bustle of nearby Centraal Station and the neon of the Damrak. Within the grand Neo-Classical building, leather Chesterfields and oil paintings grace the bar, while pine and potted plants deck out the pleasant restaurant. The fresh, colorful bedrooms have storm windows, and the health center boasts a pool.

De l'Europe

Nieuwe Doelenstraat 2–8, 1012 CP. **Map** 7 C4. *623 4836.* FAX *624 2962.* TX *12081.* ***Rooms***: *100.* *AE, DC, MC, V, JCB.* ƒƒƒƒƒ

The monolithic De l'Europe, dating from 1896, stands opposite the Muntplein, a confluence of waterways and streets carrying every kind of traffic. The location may be noisy, but if you have a weakness for chandeliers, plush drapes, classical music or bedrooms with fleur-de-lis wallpaper, a chaise lounge and a fabulous marble bathroom, this is the place to stay. Added incentives include a serious French restaurant and an amazing swimming pool, which is surrounded by statues and pillars. Many of the rooms have balconies that face directly on to the Amstel, as does the hotel's memorably picturesque waterside terrace.

Western Canal Ring

Acacia

Lindengracht 251, 1016 KH. **Map** 1 B3. *622 1460.* *FAX 638 0748.* ***Rooms**: 17.* *MC, V.* Ⓕ

Inside the wedge-shaped, end-of-terrace Acacia, guests must climb precariously steep stairs to reach simple rooms containing a pine bed and table, a little shower room and not much else. However, the breakfast room is charming, as are the young owners, the van Vliets. They also rent out a houseboat, which sleeps four and has a kitchenette, on an adjacent canal in this peaceful part of the Jordaan.

Eben Haëzer

Bloemstraat 179, 1016 LA. **Map** 1 A4. *Hostel.* *624 4717.* *FAX 627 6137.* ***Beds**: 114.* Ⓕ

This spotlessly clean Christian hostel is not designed for late-night revelers. A midnight curfew operates (1am on weekends) and no drinks are allowed on the premises. There are optional Christian activities.

Van Onna

Bloemgracht 102/104/108, 1015 TN. **Map** 1 A4. *626 5801.* ***Rooms**: 38.* *21.* Ⓕ

Charismatic Loek van Onna's B&B is made up of three canalside houses. He is justifiably proud of the recent modernization of the middle house, which contains an attractive staircase and breakfast room, and neat, modern rooms with *en suite* bathrooms. The untouched old buildings on either side offer much more basic accommodations with shared bathrooms.

Canal House

Keizersgracht 148, 1015 CX. **Map** 7 A1. *622 5182.* *FAX 624 1317.* ***Rooms**: 26.* *AE, DC, MC, V.* ⒻⒻ

Of all the city's small-scale hotels, the Canal House is the most elegant and offers the most antique charm. It occupies two old houses, and all the rooms provide a visual feast. Downstairs, there is an atmospheric bar hung with gilt mirrors and an ornate breakfast room-cum-lounge, in which a grand piano resides under a chandelier and stuccoed ceiling. Antique furnishings also adorn highly individual bedrooms. Those at the front have views of the canal, while back rooms overlook a pretty garden. To preserve the ambience, there's not a TV in sight, and the engaging owner does not welcome children.

Toren

Keizersgracht 164, 1015 CZ. **Map** 7 A1. *622 6033.* *FAX 626 9705.* ***Rooms**: 43.* *AE, DC, MC, V.* ⒻⒻ

The two old houses of the Toren on this ultracivilized stretch of canal are overshadowed by the allure of the nearby Canal House. Bedrooms typically have dated modern furniture, but a few extra guilders buys a canal view and a fair amount of space. Avoid the rooms in the middle of the hotel, which don't even have windows. Downstairs, the breakfast rooms and bar display more character with their small chandeliers and paneled walls. The staff at Toren is helpful and eager to please.

Central Canal Ring

Hans Brinker

Kerkstraat 136–138, 1017 GR. **Map** 7 A5. *Hostel.* *622 0687.* *FAX 638 2060.* ***Beds**: 536.* *AE, DC, MC, V.* Ⓕ

Conveniently close to the nightlife around Leidseplein, this hostel has small dormitories and its own disco. Despite being a bit pricey, it is very popular with backpackers. There is no curfew policy and the lively bar is open until 2am.

Agora

Singel 462, 1017 AW. **Map** 7 B5. *627 2200.* *FAX 627 2202.* ***Rooms**: 16.* *12.* *AE, DC, MC, V.* ⒻⒻ

This modern canalside terraced house has a classic city location overlooking the Singel, near the Bloemenmarkt *(see p123)*. Friendly owners preside over a warren of simple rooms, which boast the odd antique desk or armchair. Those overlooking the canal can sometimes be noisy. The lounge and breakfast area are both nicely decorated.

Amsterdam Wiechmann

Prinsengracht 328–332, 1016 HX. **Map** 1 B5. *626 3321.* *FAX 626 8962.* ***Rooms**: 38.* ⒻⒻ

The charming Mr. Boddy from Oklahoma has been taking in guests at this B&B for about 40 years. His hotel is made up of three canal houses. The corner house, now an attractive blue-tiled breakfast room, was built as a café in 1912. The rest of the hotel seems much older. Persian rugs on polished dark wood floors, beams, antiques and even a suit of armor characterize the elegant reception area and lounge bar. Some antique furniture also graces the unfussy bedrooms, most of which have a canal view.

Waterfront

Singel 458, 1017 AW. **Map** 7 B5. *623 9775.* *FAX 620 7491.* ***Rooms**: 9.* *AE, DC, M, V.* ⒻⒻ

The eye-catching bay windows of this tiny, narrow hotel overlook a busy stretch of the Singel close to the Bloemenmarkt *(see p123)*. Although not exclusively a gay hotel, it is popular with a gay clientele. The enthusiastic owners, the Van Huizens, have capitalized on the hotel's name by installing waterbeds in all except one of the simple but striking modern bedrooms. Sausages and scrambled eggs supplement the traditional Dutch breakfast *(see p212)*. The owners also rent out three studios with kitchenettes on the Amstel.

Ambassade

Herengracht 335–353, 1016 AZ. **Map** 7 A4. *626 2333.* *FAX 624 5321.* *TX 10158.* ***Rooms**: 52.* *AE, DC, MC, V.* ⒻⒻⒻ

This is Amsterdam's most luxurious canalside B&B. Favored by illustrious writers such as Umberto Eco, the hotel is stylish, comfortable and professionally run. It comprises eight beautiful patrician 17th-century houses. The lounges are decorated with chandeliers, rugs on parquet floors and ornate French antiques. The most memorable bedrooms, located at the top of the houses, have beamed, vaulted ceilings and miniature windows. The rooms on lower floors are often spacious and have as many as four windows overlooking Herengracht. The 24-hour room service provides simple meals and drinks.

Dikker & Thijs

Prinsengracht 444, 1017 KE. **Map** 4 E1. *626 7721.* *FAX 625 8986.* ***Rooms**: 25.* *AE, DC, MC, V, JCB.* ⒻⒻⒻ

Located near Leidseplein, the privately owned and recently refurbished Dikker & Thijs offers a change of tempo from the city's traditional canalside residences. Three floors of stylized rooms are predominantly decorated in blacks, pinks and grays, reflecting the hotel's austere, angular Art Deco exterior. Bedrooms looking onto Prinsengracht are the quietest.

American

Leidsekade 97, 1017 PN. **Map** 4 E2. *624 5322.* FAX *625 3236.* TX *12545 CBONL.* ***Rooms**: 188.* *AE, DC, MC, V, JCB.* ⒻⒻⒻⒻ

The spectacular American Hotel dates from the turn of the century and is one of Amsterdam's most distinctive landmarks *(see p110)*. The impressive façade and turreted clock tower bristle with Art Nouveau flourishes. Over the years, bedrooms have lost their authentic period details but, thanks to the installation of storm windows, noise has been reduced. Fortunately, the famous Café Américain *(see p46)*, constantly packed with locals and tourists, has remained largely unchanged, down to library-style desks on which newspapers are read. The hotel's terrace fills a corner of the city's busiest entertainment spot, Leidseplein.

Pulitzer

Prinsengracht 315–331, 1016 GZ. **Map** 1 B5. *523 5235.* FAX *627 6753.* TX *16508.* ***Rooms**: 232.* *AE, DC, MC, V, JCB.* ⒻⒻⒻⒻ

The luxury Pulitzer is probably the city's most imaginative canal house conversion. At least 24 houses along Prinsengracht and Keizersgracht offer bedrooms that cleverly combine 17th- and 18th-century architecture with stylish modern furnishings and art. The complex is set around a lovely courtyard garden, where you can wine and dine in summer. Other creative touches include the hotel's formal French restaurant converted from an old drugstore, a tiled brasserie, an Art Nouveau garden room and a cozy bar. In the summer, champagne cruises leave from the hotel's own landing.

Eastern Canal Ring

De Admiraal

Herengracht 563, 1017 CD. **Map** 7 C5. *626 2150.* FAX *623 4625.* ***Rooms**: 9.* *6.* *AE, DC, MC, V.* ⒻⒻ

This engagingly laid-back B&B stands next to a saucy-looking cabaret off Rembrandtplein and should be avoided by early-to-bedders. Breakfast, served in an amazingly cluttered room full of plants, carriage clocks and paintings, is extra as guests often spend the morning in bed. Many of the atmospheric, beamed bedrooms are massive, particularly the family rooms. No. 12 also has a balcony. There is a five percent surcharge for credit-card payments.

Asterisk

Den Texstraat 14–16, 1017 ZA. **Map** 5 A4. *626 2596.* FAX *638 2790.* ***Rooms**: 28.* *22.* *MC, V.* ⒻⒻ

As the Asterisk is a little way from the center of town, on a residential backstreet near the Heineken Brouwerij *(see p122)*, its rates are good values. Bedrooms within the handsome, four-story, 19th-century house are a decent size and are furnished with good-quality modern units, Impressionist prints and aerial photographs of the city. In the breakfast room, mirrors and stuccowork offer a touch of style. Breakfast is included with cash payment, but extra for credit cards.

De Munck

Achtergracht 3, 1017 WL. **Map** 5 B3. *623 6283.* FAX *620 6647.* ***Rooms**: 14.* *13.* *AE, DC, MC, V, JCB.* ⒻⒻ

The two old gabled buildings of the De Munck rest peacefully on the corner of a leafy little square and cul-de-sac canal. The owner loves 50s and 60s pop music, so pride of place in the lovely basement breakfast room goes to a goldplated Elvis record and a jukebox. Plants, colorful prints and the odd marble fireplace distinguish otherwise sparsely furnished rooms.

Prinsenhof

Prinsengracht 810, 1017 JL. **Map** 5 A3. *623 1772.* FAX *638 3368.* ***Rooms**: 10.* *2.* *AE, MC, V.* ⒻⒻ

The Prinsenhof is one of the best-kept and prettiest of the city's simple canalside B&Bs. With its attractive breakfast room and tastefully decorated bedrooms, the hotel is a good choice if you don't mind sharing a bathroom and can cope with very steep stairs. The first flight of stairs leads straight from the front door, which is operated by a pulley system at reception on the first floor. The many bistros along Utrechtsestraat are just a short walk away. Credit card payments incur a five percent surcharge.

Seven Bridges

Reguliersgracht 31, 1017 LK. **Map** 5 A3. *623 1329.* ***Rooms**: 11.* *6.* *AE, MC, V.* ⒻⒻ

Sitting inconspicuously on arguably Amsterdam's prettiest little canal, the Seven Bridges has evolved over the last 20 years into one of the city's most stylish B&Bs. Although it has no public rooms, steep stairs and a less-than-eager attitude towards children, you may need to book at least a month in advance to stay in one of its beautiful bedrooms. Stripped floorboards, Persian rugs and antique cabinets distinguish both the grand and small rooms. Breakfast is served in your room on fine English china.

Mercure Arthur Frommer

Noorderstraat 46, 1017 TV. **Map** 4 F2. *622 0328.* FAX *620 3208.* TX *14047.* ***Rooms**: 90.* *AE, DC, MC, V.* ⒻⒻⒻ

Mr. Frommer, an American travel guide publisher, established this hotel in the 1960s in a block of two-story, 18th-century houses on a quiet corner of the Canal Ring. Although too sanitized to have real character, the bedrooms are large, with good amenities and shower rooms. The basement bar and breakfast room are gloomy by contrast. Since breakfast costs extra you'd be better off going to a local café.

Schiller Karena

Rembrandtplein 26–36, 1017 CV. **Map** 7 C5. *623 1660.* FAX *624 0098.* ***Rooms**: 95.* *AE, DC, MC, V.* ⒻⒻⒻ

The most distinctive feature of the old-fashioned Schiller is the vast collection of paintings that hangs throughout the hotel's public areas, all the work of the original owner Fritz Schiller. The late 19th-century building has its own café terrace on lively Rembrandtplein. Behind the café lies a big airy dining room with attractive stained-glass sunlights, oak beams and paneling. For peace and quiet, request a bedroom at the back of the hotel, since those at the front are noisy. All the rooms tend to be a little shabby in places.

Museum Quarter

NJHC Hostel Vondelpark

Zanndpad 5, 1054 GA. **Map** 4 D2. *Hostel.* *683 1744.* FAX *616 6591.* ***Beds**: 350.* Ⓕ

Housed in a large chalet on the eastern edge of Vondelpark is one of the two hostels in Amsterdam belonging to the Dutch Youth Hostel Association (NJHC). It offers dormitory accommodations and gives a small discount to members of the Youth Hostel Association.

Wynnobel

Vossiusstraat 9, 1071 AB. **Map** 4 E2. *662 2298.* ***Rooms**: 11.* Ⓕ

The utterly basic Wynnobel, on a quiet street off Vondelpark, is geared towards a bohemian clientele and is a bargain. Steep stairs lead to simple but striking rooms, typically with linoleum, a marble fireplace and old wooden furniture. The rooms are spacious, since none has its own bathroom. A modest breakfast is served in the rooms and each floor shares an old-fashioned bathroom.

Acro

Jan Luijkenstraat 44, 1071 CR. **Map** 4 E3. *662 0526.* FAX *675 0811.* ***Rooms**: 51.* *AE, DC, MC, V.* ⒻⒻ

What the Acro lacks in old-world charm it makes up for in smart modernity, bargain rates and proximity to the upscale shops along PC Hooftstraat *(see p242).* The hotel has a stylish little bar off the foyer and a cafeteria-style breakfast room in the basement. Upstairs, the small bedrooms are bright, well kept and each has an *en suite* shower room. The hotel is popular with tour groups.

Atlas

Van Eeghenstraat, 1071 GK. **Map** 3 C3. *676 6336.* FAX *671 7633.* TX *17081.* ***Rooms**: 23.* *AE, DC, MC, V.* ⒻⒻ

Atlas is one of the city's unheralded architectural delights. This large, detached Art Nouveau house on the southern edge of Vondelpark has floral indulgences on the façade and Gaudiesque embellishments over the windows. The interior is plainer, but all the bedrooms are stylish and have good modern bathrooms. A modest menu of home-made Dutch food is available in the dining room and through room service. The staff is experienced and gives guests a warm welcome.

De Filosoof

Anna van den Vondelstraat 6, 1054 GZ. **Map** 3 C2. *683 3013.* FAX *685 3750.* ***Rooms**: 27.* *23.* *AE, MC, V.* ⒻⒻ

If the stimulants found in Amsterdam's coffee shops *(see p49)* don't deliver the meaning of life to you, search out the modest Hotel de Filosoof on the northern side of Vondelpark. Run by vivacious professional philosopher Ida Jongsma, regular highbrow dinners and meetings are held here and many of the hotel's resident guests are intellectuals. However, this is no stuffy academic retreat. Murals of Plato and Aristotle greet you at the door and most bedrooms have exuberant philosophical or cultural themes. For example, the Plato room is dramatically decorated in black and white with *trompe l'oeil* paintings mounted on pedestals. Classical jazz plays in the velvet-draped breakfast room, which is lined with a library of thought-inducing works, and also in the eye-catching black and white marbled bar.

Owl

Roemer Visscherstraat 1, 1054 EV. **Map** 4 D2. *618 9484.* FAX *618 9441.* ***Rooms**: 34.* *MC, V, JCB.* ⒻⒻ

A stuffed owl in an alcove on the exterior wall provides the name for arguably the best of the many hotels situated on this convenient, quiet street between Leidseplein and Vondelpark. A stylish bar and breakfast room downstairs lead through to a pretty, neat garden. Fresh flowers enliven plain, pine-furnished bedrooms that show signs of wear and tear in places. The cheerful Kos-Brals family have been giving guests a warm welcome here for many years.

Sander

Jacob Obrechtstraat 69, 1071 KJ. **Map** 4 D4. *662 7574.* FAX *679 6067.* TX *18456.* ***Rooms**: 20.* *AE, DC, MC, V.* ⒻⒻ

This small, well-kept hotel stands in a long terrace in the Oud Zuid (Old South), not far from the city's main museums. It has an appealing bar and breakfast room opening onto a pretty little garden to the rear. The bedrooms, although somewhat plain, are comfortable. The more spacious ones even have bays with seating areas.

Jan Luijken

Jan Luijkenstraat 58, 1071 CS. **Map** 4 E3. *573 0730.* FAX *676 3841.* TX *16254 HTJLNL.* ***Rooms**: 63.* *AE, DC, MC, V.* ⒻⒻⒻ

Located in three elegant 19th-century houses, just a stone's throw from the city's main museums and best shops, this well-kept hotel goes out of its way to woo a wide range of guests. Along with excellent business facilities, it offers room service most hours of the day, snacks in the cozy bar and on the garden patio. It also provides free afternoon tea in the stylish peach-colored lounge, and an elaborate buffet breakfast in the basement, which is enlivened with attractive stained-glass windows. The comfortable, well-equipped bedrooms are priced according to size, and the large family rooms come with a sofa bed.

Amsterdam Marriott

Stadhouderskade 19–21, 1054 ES. **Map** 4 D2. *607 5555.* FAX *607 5511.* ***Rooms**: 392.* *AE, DC, MC, V, JCB.* ⒻⒻⒻⒻ

The multistoried Marriott is by no means a showpiece for this American chain, yet it provides all the facilities you would expect from a large cosmopolitan hotel. Business facilities include spacious conference rooms, express check-out and an executive floor. The hotel also contains a number of shops, as well as an attractive grill and seafood restaurant. Front bedrooms face Leidseplein across a busy main road and are noisy. The rooms at the back are quieter and have extensive views over Vondelpark. There are bargain rates for bookings made at least three weeks in advance.

PLANTAGE

Adam en Eva

Sarphatistraat 105, 1018 GA. **Map** 5 B4. *Hostel.* *624 6206,* FAX *638 7200.* ***Beds**: 78.* Ⓕ

Barely a ten-minute walk from Rembrandtplein, this small, easy-going hostel has no nighttime curfew policy. It offers straightforward dormitory accommodations and a sociable bar-cum-restaurant, which stays open until 2am.

Fantasia

Nieuwe Keizersgracht 16, 1018 DR. **Map** 5 B3. *623 8259.* FAX *622 3913.* ***Rooms**: 19.* *MC, V.* Ⓕ

This canalside house, dating from 1773, faces the Amstelhof, a stately retirement home, rather than the usual gabled terraces. Here on the quiet eastern side of the Amstel, the pace of life is slower than on the more fashionable west side. Despite being within easy walking distance of the city center, prices for the old-fashioned, simple bedrooms are very reasonable. The atmosphere is altogether homey, especially in the paneled breakfast room, where the resident cat can often be found snoozing among the clutter of potted plants.

Kitty Muijzers

Plantage Middenlaan 40, 1018 DG. **Map** 6 D2. *622 6819.* ***Rooms**: 10.*

Few traces of the 1990s appear in elderly Kitty Muijzer's somewhat bizarre pension. Located across from the zoo, the hotel is a 15-minute walk or a short trolley ride from the center of Amsterdam. Religious and Classical statues and a profusion of greenery decorate the turn-of-the-century house, which is flooded in a yellowy light from the glass-roofed stairwell. Unequivocally old-fashioned bedrooms, some with decades-old TVs and fridges, are big and comfortably furnished; none has a private bathroom, and basins are often hidden away in cupboards. Children under 12 years old are not welcome.

Bridge

Amstel 107–111, 1018 EM. **Map** 5 B3. *623 7068.* FAX *624 1565.* ***Rooms**: 27.* *AE, DC, MC, V.*

From the Bridge, it is less than a ten-minute stroll along a lovely stretch of the Amstel to the hubbub of Rembrandtplein. Compared to the often cramped canalside hotels in the center of town, the three adjoining brick houses are refreshingly spacious. The roomy bedrooms are furnished in pine with varying degrees of modernity, and the stylish breakfast room is done in rattan style. The hotel leases space downstairs to an Italian restaurant, but recommends that guests eat elsewhere.

Amstel Inter-Continental

Prof. Tulpplein 1, 1018 GX. **Map** 5 B4. *622 6060.* FAX *622 5808.* TX *11004 AMSOTNL.* ***Rooms**: 79.* *AE, DC, MC, V.*

This is undisputably the city's top hotel. Opened in 1867 and painstakingly renovated in 1992 at a cost of about 70 million guilders, its grandeur is overwhelming. The breathtaking hallway is graced with two tiers of pillars and arches and a gilded ceiling. The Amstel's first-class restaurant, La Rive *(see p235)*, the beautiful conservatory sitting room and the elegant swimming pool all open onto a balmy terrace beside the Amstel river. Beautiful fabrics, furniture and paintings enhance stunning bedrooms. Each room also comes with its own superb bathroom, a minibar brimming with cut-glass decanters and, for the industrious, a personal fax machine. Additional treats include a Turkish bath, Rolls Royces and a motor yacht available for use by guests, and limousine service to Schiphol Airport. For a five-star hotel the Amstel is comparatively small, so you often need to book well in advance to secure a room. While the hotel is a 15-minute walk from the city center, this doesn't dissuade guests from staying here, as the cost of a few taxis pales into insignificance beside the final hotel bill.

FARTHER AFIELD

Arena Budget Hotel (Sleep-In)

's-Gravesandestraat 51, 1092 AA. **Map** 6 D4. *Hostel.* *694 7444.* FAX *663 2649.* ***Beds**: 600.*

Located near peaceful Oosterpark, this large hostel also functions as an international center for youth culture and tourism. Although it is a long way from Leidseplein, there is no excuse to be bored here. The hostel has a lively bar, that is open until 2am on weekends, and organizes in-house youth-oriented events, gigs and exhibitions in the summer. There is no curfew policy if you want to explore the nightlife in town.

Van Ostade Bicycle Hotel

Van Ostadestraat 123, 1072 SV. **Map** 4 F5. *679 3452.* FAX *671 5213.* ***Rooms**: 15.* *8.*

A bicycle hangs 6 m (20 ft) up on the wall of this most friendly of B&Bs in the untouristy De Pijp district, south of Sarphatipark. A youthful clientele is attracted by the low prices of the spartan but decent bedrooms, the laid-back atmosphere in the pretty breakfast room and the convenience of being able to rent bikes on the spot. The helpful owners provide city maps and plenty of advice on alternative routes for guests who want to explore the city by bike.

Toro

Koningslaan 64, 1075 AG. **Map** 3 A4. *673 7223.* FAX *675 0031.* ***Rooms**: 22.* *AE, DC, MC, V.*

The Toro is located in a stylish residential district at the southwest corner of Vondelpark. This peaceful spot is a bit far from the city center – a 15-minute stroll through the park or a short trolley ride. Consequently, its rates are real bargains. Tasteful antiques, oil paintings, stained glass, chandeliers and a carved wooden staircase give the mansion the air of a small country house. Some of the Toro's comfortable bedrooms overlook the park's canal and come with a balcony. The same view can also be admired through the French windows of the delightfully airy breakfast room.

Villa Borgmann

Koningslaan 48, 1075 AE. **Map** 3 B4. *673 5252.* FAX *676 2580.* ***Rooms**: 15.* *AE, DC, MC, V, JCB.*

No match for the stylishness of the nearby Toro, this big, airy house built in 1905 nevertheless shares the same enviable peaceful location overlooking the canal on the southern side of Vondelpark. Wicker furniture and floral bedspreads dominate the bedrooms, some of which are very large. The proprietor does not welcome children or backpackers.

Amsterdam Hilton

Apollolaan 138, 1077 BG. **Map** 3 C5. *678 0780.* FAX *662 6688.* TX *11025 HILANL.* ***Rooms**: 271.* *AE, DC, MC, V, JCB.*

This Hilton is a monument to ugly, high-rise architecture, so only the bedrooms on the two executive floors are recommended. Although no one chooses to stay in the Nieuw Zuid (New South) district unless they have business in the area, John Lennon and Yoko Ono staged their notorious "bed in" here in 1969. For a great deal of money, you can stay in what was their suite, now decorated in stark white with quotes, photos and prints of the lovers on the walls. The room also houses a library of Lennon books and CDs and, of course, a guitar.

Okura

Ferdinand Bolstraat 333, 1072 LH. **Map** 4 F5. *678 7111.* FAX *671 2344.* TX *16182.* ***Rooms**: 370.* ***Cots.*** *AE, DC, MC, V, JCB.*

The modern tower block of the plush Okura is a five-minute walk from the RAI Congresgebouw *(see p151)*. The hotel, which is totally geared toward business people, offers excellent conference and banquet facilities. It also has two Japanese restaurants and a French restaurant with panoramic views of the city. A shopping arcade and beautiful suites round out the perks. To lure guests to stay on, most room rates are halved on weekends.

Restaurants, Cafés and Bars

Although the Netherlands does not enjoy the gastronomic reputation of France or Italy, the chances of finding good food at a reasonable price in Amsterdam are high. Many cafés and bars serve tempting snacks, and some, known as *eetcafés*, provide a full three-course menu *(see pp236–7)*. In addition to the city's selection of Dutch restaurants, where portions are invariably generous, there are also hundreds of other places to try, offering a range of culinary delights from around the world. The following pages will help you locate the best quality food and most exciting cuisine in all price categories. *Choosing a Restaurant* on pages 228–9 gives summaries of the key features of restaurants included in this guide. A detailed review on each of the selected restaurants is provided on pages 230–35.

The brightly decorated dining area of the Gauguin *(see p233)*

Where to Eat

Amsterdam is a small city, and most of the restaurants listed in this guide are fairly central and easy to find. The highest concentrations of restaurants are to be found along Van Baerlestraat in the Museum Quarter, in the Red Light District and along Spuistraat in the Nieuwe Zijde, on Reguliersdwarsstraat in the Eastern Canal Ring and in the Jordaan. Bargain meals can be enjoyed in any of the city's *eetcafés*.

What to Eat

In the past, Dutch home cooking and snacks were traditionally offered in *eetcafés*, and Indonesian-based cuisine was the main cheap alternative. French food was served in the more expensive restaurants. Today, there is a much greater choice of international cuisine available and many of the city's restaurants combine French cooking techniques with seasonal Dutch ingredients.

Since much of Indonesia was once a Dutch colony, Amsterdam is one of the best places in Europe to sample its diverse flavors. Much of the cooking may lean too heavily toward the Chinese style for purists, but it is possible to sample genuine Indonesian recipes. Japanese and Thai food is also popular and affordable. Italian cooking is another favorite and the standard is improving. Indian, Mexican and African food can also be found, but the quality is variable.

On the whole, vegetarians are well catered to here. The chart on pages 228–9 shows which restaurants have a good selection of vegetarian dishes.

What to Drink

Beer is the drink of preference in most Dutch cafés and bars, and all have a wide selection of local and imported brews *(see p48–9)*. Wine is widely available and nearly all restaurants in Amsterdam offer a good choice, with emphasis on French wines. Most Spanish and Italian restaurants also have an interesting range of their own local wines. A special symbol is awarded to

Amsterdam's famous floating Chinese restaurant, the Sea Palace *(see p230)*

those restaurants listed in this guide that offer an exceptionally good choice of wines.

Restaurants specializing in traditional cuisine tend to have the best selection of *jenevers* (Dutch gin) *(see p48–9)*.

How Much to Pay

Dutch people like to know exactly how much they are going to pay for a meal, so almost all restaurants display a menu in the window. This gives the prices, which include tax (BTW) and service. Prices vary greatly in the city and a meal at a luxurious restaurant can cost more than *f* 185 per person. However, if you are on a budget, Amsterdam has a wide choice of places serving meals at under *f* 50 per person. The cost of drinks is extra and the markup levied by a restaurant, especially on cheap wine, can be high.

Enjoying attentive service – a feature of eating out in Amsterdam

Opening Times

Since the Dutch don't view lunch as a the main meal of the day, few restaurants are open during the day. However, many designer bars and brown cafés *(see pp236–7)* serve lunch from around noon to 2pm. In most restaurants, dinner is served from 6pm onward, and last orders are often taken as early as 10pm. Nowadays, however, some kitchens are deciding to stay open longer. Some restaurants, particularly those in the central areas, now take orders until 11pm, and a few remain open considerably later. Traditionally, many do not open at all on Mondays,

Guests sitting along the Prinsengracht outside Kort *(see p234)*

although this is also changing. For details of café and bar opening times, see *Light Meals and Snacks* on pages 236–7.

Making a Reservation

When visiting one of the city's more celebrated restaurants, it is always wise to book in advance. The listings on pages 228–9 indicate where booking is advisable.

Popular brown cafés and designer bars can also become crowded in the evening, but few of them take reservations.

Reading the Menu

The menus at many tourist restaurants are written in Dutch, French and English. However, as most waiters and waitresses in the city speak good English, and often another European language, it is rarely a problem ordering a meal anywhere in Amsterdam. For more details on what to order, see pages 226–7.

Etiquette

Most restaurants in Amsterdam are relaxed, so casual or semiformal dress is suitable almost everywhere. Although there is nothing to stop you from dressing up, no one insists on a tie. For details of eating out with children, see page 253.

Smoking

Generally, there are no areas set aside for nonsmokers in Amsterdam's restaurants, brown cafés or designer bars.

Wheelchair Access

Visitors with disabilities can get into the majority of ground-floor restaurants in the city. However, toilets can be difficult to get to as access to them is often via steep stairs.

Tipping

A service charge of 15 percent is automatically included in checks at restaurants, cafés and bars. Most Amsterdammers round up a small check to the largest whole guilder and larger ones to the nearest *f* 5. The tip is left as change rather than included on a credit-card slip.

Using the Listings

Key to symbols in the listings on pp228–9.

- fixed-price menu
- V vegetarian dishes
- wheelchair access
- outdoor eating
- good wine list
- live music
- ★ highly recommended
- credit cards accepted:
- *AE* American Express
- *DC* Diners Club
- *MC* Master Card/Access
- *V* Visa
- *JCB* Japanese Credit Bureau

Price categories for a three-course meal for one, including cover charge, tax and service, but without wine or other drinks:

ⓕ up to *f* 50
ⓕⓕ *f* 50–*f* 60
ⓕⓕⓕ *f* 60–*f* 75
ⓕⓕⓕⓕ over *f* 75

What to Eat in Amsterdam

Patates frites (French fries) and mayonnaise

Traditional Dutch food is hearty and wholesome, prepared with simple ingredients. Bread, cold meat and cheese are often eaten for breakfast and lunch. Snacks such as French fries are sold from street stalls *(see p236)*, and there are many bakeries selling tempting cakes. Ethnic dishes are also popular, and the city enjoys some of the best Indonesian cuisine in Europe.

Typical Dutch Breakfast
Breakfast usually consists of bread and butter with a slice of ham or cheese.

Bitterballen en Frikadellen
Deep-fried meatballs and spicy, sausage-shaped rissoles are served with mustard.

Uitsmijter
This filling snack consists of a slice of bread with cheese or ham, topped with a fried egg.

Crispbread with Hagelslag
Strands of chocolate (hagelslag) *are sprinkled on bread.*

Fresh Raw Herring
Raw herring is marinated and eaten as an entrée or snack with onion or gherkins.

Coffee and Speculaas
Spicy cookies called speculaas *are ideal with coffee, usually served strong and black.*

Bread and Cheeses
The most popular cheeses are Edam and Gouda, sometimes flavored with herbs or seeds. Cheese is often eaten with rye, whole wheat or white bread.

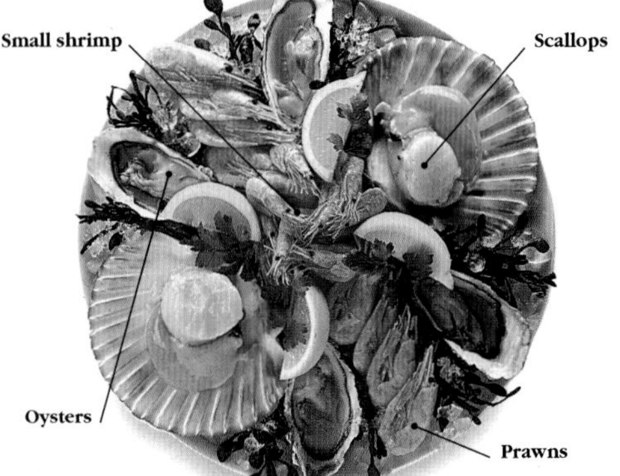

Fruits de Mer
Fresh seafood such as oysters, prawns, shrimp and scallops are served on a bed of ice and seaweed.

Plaice with Vegetables
Grilled fish is often eaten as a main dish, served with butter, boiled potatoes and carrots.

Stamppot
This is a typical Dutch stew of puréed potatoes, vegetables and smoked sausage.

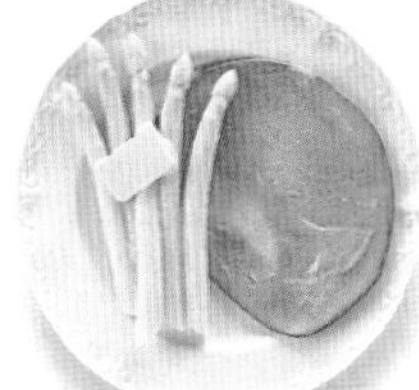

White Asparagus and Ham
Thick slices of boiled Dutch ham are served with white asparagus and melted butter.

Erwtensoep
A wholesome, thick pea soup, it is served with boiled, smoked sausage and bacon.

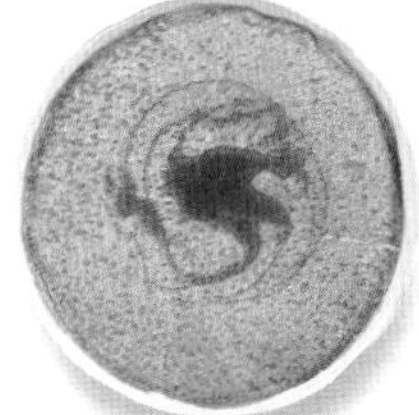

Large Pancake with Stroop
Pannekoeken, *or pancakes, are a popular dessert, covered with a thick syrup or* stroop.

Limburgse Vlaai
Served hot or cold, Limburg pie is made with bread dough and filled with fruit.

Strawberries and Yogurt
Yogurt is delicious as a light dessert, sprinkled with sugar and served with fresh fruit.

INDONESIAN CUISINE

Indonesian food, introduced from the former Dutch colony, is usually eaten in the form of a *rijsttafel* (rice table). It consists of a large, shared bowl of noodles or rice, with up to 25 smaller dishes of meat, fish and vegetables, with various sauces.

Bami goreng (fried noodles, chicken, shrimp, garlic, chili and vegetables)

Babi asam pedas (spicy pork)

Udang bakar (grilled tiger shrimp)

Satay daging (marinated beef)

Ayam panike (chicken in aromatic sauce)

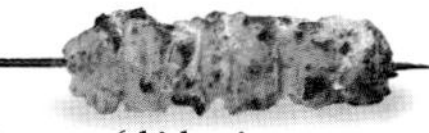

Satay ayam (chicken in peanut sauce)

Gado gado (vegetable salad with peanut sauce)

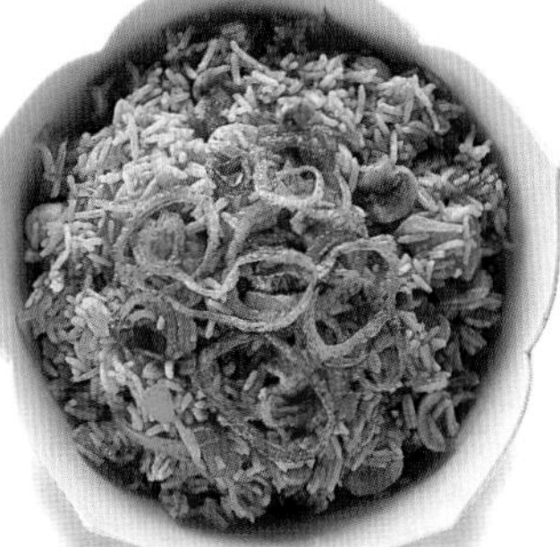

Nasi goreng (fried rice with beef or pork, mushrooms, soy sauce and shrimp paste)

Choosing a Restaurant

The restaurants in this guide have been selected for their good value or exceptional food. This chart highlights some of the factors which may influence your choice. Entries are alphabetical within price category. For more details on the restaurants, see pages 230–35. Information on cafés and bars is on pages 236–7.

Restaurant	Price	Ethnic	Late Opening	Fixed-Price Menu	Vegetarian Dishes	Outdoor Tables	Special Wine List	Attractive Setting
Oude Zijde *(see p230)*								
Oriental City *(Chinese)*	Ⓕ	●	■	●	■			
A Road to Manila *(Philippine)* ★	Ⓕ	●	■	●	■			
Hemelse Modder *(European)*	ⒻⒻ				■	●		
Sea Palace *(Chinese)*	ⒻⒻ	●	■	●	■			●
Tom Yam *(Thai)*	ⒻⒻ	●		●	■			
Café Roux *(French/modern British)* ★	ⒻⒻⒻ		■		■	●	■	
Nieuwe Zijde *(see pp230–31)*								
Beaume *(Mediterranean/European)* ★	Ⓕ		■	●	■	●		
Centra *(Spanish)*	Ⓕ		■					
Kantjil & de Tijger *(Indonesian)* ★	Ⓕ	●	■	●	■	●		
Krua Thai *(Thai)* ★	Ⓕ	●	■	●	■	●		
Luden *(French/Dutch)*	Ⓕ		■	●	■	●		
Treasure *(Chinese)* ★	Ⓕ	●	■	●	■			
De Compagnon *(French)*	ⒻⒻ		■	●	■			
Dorrius *(Dutch)*	ⒻⒻ		■	●	■		■	●
De Kooning van Siam *(Thai)*	ⒻⒻ	●	■	●	■			
Lucius *(Fish)* ★	ⒻⒻ		■	●		●	■	●
De Silveren Spiegel *(French)* ★	ⒻⒻⒻ			●	■	●	■	●
Vasso *(Italian)* ★	ⒻⒻⒻ		■	●	■	●	■	●
D'Vijff Vliegen *(Dutch)*	ⒻⒻⒻ			●	■	●	■	●
Vermeer *(French/modern Dutch)* ★	ⒻⒻⒻⒻ		■	●	■		■	
Western Canal Ring *(see pp231–2)*								
Burger's Patio *(Italian)*	Ⓕ		■		■	●		
Speciaal *(Indonesian)* ★	Ⓕ	●	■	●	■			
Claes Claesz *(Dutch)*	ⒻⒻ		■	●				
Prego *(Italian)*	ⒻⒻ		■	●	■		■	
Taddy Zemmel *(French/Dutch)* ★	ⒻⒻ		■	●	■	●	■	
D'Theeboom *(French)* ★	ⒻⒻ		■	●	■	●	■	
Bordewijk *(French)* ★	ⒻⒻⒻ		■	●	■		■	●
Chez Georges *(Belgian)* ★	ⒻⒻⒻ		■	●	■		■	
Toscanini *(Italian)*	ⒻⒻⒻ		■		■		■	
Christophe *(French)* ★	ⒻⒻⒻⒻ		■	●	■	●	■	
Central Canal Ring *(see pp232–4)*								
Café Cox *(European)*	Ⓕ		■		■			
De Expressionist *(French)*	Ⓕ		■	●	■			
Lulu *(French)* ★	Ⓕ		■	●	■			
Mayur *(Indian)*	Ⓕ	●	■	●	■			
Swaagat *(Indian)* ★	Ⓕ	●	■	●	■	●		
Tout Court *(French)*	ⒻⒻ		■	●	■			
Zomer's *(French/Dutch)* ★	ⒻⒻ		■		■			
Dynasty *(Asian)* ★	ⒻⒻⒻ	●	■	●	■	●	■	●
Gauguin *(Asian/European)*	ⒻⒻⒻ		■	●	■	●		●
Sichuan Food *(Chinese)*	ⒻⒻⒻ	●	■	●	■			
Het Tuynhuys *(French/Dutch)* ★	ⒻⒻⒻ		■	●	■	●	■	●
Hosokawa *(Japanese)*	ⒻⒻⒻⒻ	●	■	●	■			●
't Swarte Schaep *(French/Dutch)*	ⒻⒻⒻⒻ		■	●	■		■	●

Price categories are for a three-course meal for one, excluding wine, plus all unavoidable extra charges such as cover, service and tax:

Ⓕ up to *f* 50
ⒻⒻ *f* 50–60
ⒻⒻⒻ *f* 60–75
ⒻⒻⒻⒻ over *f* 75

★ Means highly recommended.

Fixed-Price Menu
Restaurant offering a menu of two to three courses for a set price including coffee but excluding wine and other drinks.

Vegetarian Dishes
Restaurant that has a particularly good selection of vegetarian dishes.

Late Opening
Last orders accepted at or after 10:30pm.

Attractive Setting
Restaurant with a good view or pleasant setting such as an attractive canalside.

	Price	Ethnic	Late Opening	Fixed-Price Menu	Vegetarian Dishes	Outdoor Tables	Special Wine List	Attractive Setting
Eastern Canal Ring *(see p234)*								
An *(Japanese)* ★	Ⓕ	●		●	■			
Indrapura *(Indonesian)* ★	ⒻⒻ	●	■	●	■	●		●
Kort *(French)* ★	ⒻⒻ			●	■	●		●
Tempo Doeloe *(Indonesian)* ★	ⒻⒻ	●	■	●	■			
Le Zinc... et les Dames *(French)*	ⒻⒻ		■	●	■		■	●
Van Vlaanderen *(French/Belgium)* ★	ⒻⒻⒻ		■	●	■		■	
Museum Quarter *(see pp234–5)*								
Overakker *(French/Dutch)*	Ⓕ		■	●	■			
Brasserie Bark *(Fish)*	ⒻⒻ		■		■	●		
Bartholdy *(Mediterranean)*	ⒻⒻ		■	●	■			
Zabar's *(Mediterranean)*	ⒻⒻ		■		■			
Le Garage *(French)* ★	ⒻⒻⒻ		■	●			■	●
Raden Mas *(Indonesian)* ★	ⒻⒻⒻ	●	■	●	■		■	
Beddington's *(French/British)* ★	ⒻⒻⒻⒻ		■	●	■		■	●
De Trechter *(French)*	ⒻⒻⒻⒻ		■	●	■		■	
Plantage *(see p235)*								
La Rive *(French)* ★	ⒻⒻⒻⒻ		■	●	■	●	■	●
Farther Afield *(see p235)*								
Beau Bourg *(French/European)*	ⒻⒻ		■	●	■			
Kaiko *(Japanese)* ★	ⒻⒻ	●	■	●				
Mangerie de Kersentuin *(French/Dutch)*	ⒻⒻ		■	●	■		■	

OUDE ZIJDE

Oriental City

Oudezijds Voorburgwal 177–179. **Map** 7 C3. *626 8352.* V AE, DC, MC, V. *11:30am–11pm daily.* Ⓕ

Very popular with Chinese locals, this large, bustling Chinese restaurant has an enormous menu that offers plenty of choice. One of the best times to go is on Sundays at lunch time when whole families congregate for *dim sum* accompanied by Chinese tea. The same owner also runs Golden Chopsticks, a new, brightly lit "canteen" restaurant next door. Try the roast duck, *won ton* soup and one of the *bami* (noodle dishes).

A Road to Manila

Geldersekade 23. **Map** 8 D2. *638 4338.* V ★ AE, DC, MC, V. *5–11pm daily.* Ⓕ

This Philippine restaurant, located on the edge of the Red Light District, is one of Amsterdam's best-kept secrets. The lively personality of the chef/owner Toni Moralsi is reflected in the interior decor and hospitality. Its interesting mixture of Asian and Spanish dishes demonstrate how Philippine cuisine can be one of the most varied in the world. Start with the tapas and move on to *adobong manok* (chicken marinated in coconut vinegar, bay leaf, black pepper and fresh garlic), or *asadong kambing* (marinated goat in mushroom and Spanish pepper sauce).

Hemelse Modder

Oude Waal 9. **Map** 8 E3. *624 3203.* V *6–10pm Tue–Sun.* ⒻⒻ

Located on an attractive, quiet canalside, this restaurant serves a mixed meat and vegetarian menu. It was set up by squatters who originally cooked on weekends as a hobby. They have now been operating professionally for seven years. The menu is largely inspired by French and Italian cuisine and includes a selection of daily meat and fish specialties. Indonesian-style recipes have recently been added to the vegetarian menu.

Sea Palace

Oosterdokskade 8. **Map** 8 E1. *626 4777.* V AE, DC, MC, V. *noon–11pm daily.* ⒻⒻ

If you cannot make it to the floating emporiums of Hong Kong, then this is the next best thing. Moored in the Oosterdok near Centraal Station, this floating Chinese restaurant provides a wonderful view of Amsterdam. It has traditionally been seen as a fun place to go to with friends rather than a treat for Asian gourmets, but recently the food has improved. The enormous menu includes Cantonese staples like *won ton* soup along with more unusual dishes such as Peking soup with Szechuan shrimp. There is also a well-thought-out wine selection.

Tom Yam

Staalstraat 22. **Map** 7 C4. *622 9533.* V AE, DC, MC, V. *6–10pm daily.* ⒻⒻ

Previously, chef/owner Jos Boomgaardt was a well-known Dutch chef cooking French food. After his travels in Asia, he turned his attentions to the Thai kitchen. His small restaurant now offers the aromas and spices that are symbolized in the name Tom Yam, based on the dish *Tom Yam Kung* (a spicy soup of shrimp with lemon grass, chilies, mint, coriander, garlic and lime leaves). His well-balanced repertoire of ethnic cuisine will appeal to both experts and beginners alike and is accompanied by an imaginative wine list.

Café Roux/ Grand Amsterdam

Oudezijds Voorburgwal 197. **Map** 7 C3. *555 3560.* V ★ AE, DC, MC, V. *noon–3pm, 6–11pm daily.* ⒻⒻⒻ

This restaurant offers a unique opportunity to experience dishes made famous by Albert Roux at a very reasonable price. It continues to win over the Dutch public with a wonderful mixture of French and modern British cuisine. A typical selection of dishes could include *les deux boudins aux deux pommes* (black and white sausage with potato and apple), *coquilles St Jacques à la Parisian* (scallops) and *tarte tatin* for dessert. It is wise to book in advance as locals and guests staying at the Grand Amsterdam *(see p218)* have all discovered this to be one of the best restaurants in town.

NIEUWE ZIJDE

Beaume

Spuistraat 266. **Map** 7 A3. *422 0423.* V ★ *(only above f 50) AE, DC, MC, V.* *noon–midnight daily.* Ⓕ

This restaurant is well known for its combinations of flavors and ingredients based on Mediterranean cooking. As this place also manages to keep prices low, it is always busy. The menu changes frequently, but in order to see the kitchen at its best, go for the "catch of the day," fresh from the fish market, or one of the dishes of the day. Simple items such as wild spinach salad with duck *confit* are excellent. It is wise to book in advance to be sure of getting a table.

Centra

Lange Niezel 29. **Map** 8 D2. *622 3050.* *1–11pm daily.* Ⓕ

Some restaurants have the knack of surviving changes of fashion and public taste. This Spanish restaurant, located right in the heart of the Red Light District, is one of them. Its spartan interior reflects a no-nonsense approach towards the repertoire of classic dishes, such as *tortilla* and *paella*, washed down with a good selection of Spanish wines. Due to its location, the restaurant attracts a lively mix of visitors and locals.

Kantjil & de Tijger

Spuistraat 291–293. **Map** 7 A3. *620 0994.* V ★ AE, DC, MC, V. *5–11pm daily.* Ⓕ

The combination of Amsterdam School architecture and a modern interior disguises the fact that this is one of the very few restaurants in Amsterdam to provide authentic Indonesian food. The menu features well-known Indonesian dishes such as *nasi goreng* (fried rice dish), along with lesser-known regional dishes. First timers should order a *rijsttafel (see p227)*, which offers a complete range of dishes. Service can be a little slow, but the food is well worth the wait.

Krua Thai

Spuistraat 90a. **Map** 7 B1. *620 0623.* V ★ MC, V. *5–10:30pm daily.* Ⓕ

Thai hospitality and enthusiasm add greatly to the enjoyment of this small, casual restaurant's range of aromatic specialties. By far the easiest way to order is from one of Krua Thai's set menus. However, for a truly memorable meal, it is worth asking your waiter to help you select an interesting combination of soups, salads, curries and other main dishes from the extensive à la carte menu.

Luden

Spuistraat 306. **Map** 7 A4. *622 8979.* V AE, DC, MC, V. *noon–3pm Mon–Fri, 6–11pm daily.* Ⓕ

Luden is a simple but stylish restaurant. The mix of French/Dutch regional and seasonal cuisine in the restaurant is excellently priced and the service is friendly. Luden's policy of allowing diners to make up their own menu from the selection of dishes for a set price has been very influential in changing Dutch eating habits in the last few years, and it now has a string of imitators. However, this restaurant is still one of the best, so make sure to book in advance.

Treasure

Nieuwezijds Voorburgwal 115. **Map** 7 B2. *626 0915.* ★ *AE, DC, MC, V. noon–3pm, 5–10:30pm daily.* Ⓕ

Most Chinese food in Amsterdam is a strange concoction of Indonesian-style cuisine and dishes cooked with tomatoes and fruit. Treasure is one of the few places where you can eat genuine specialties from Canton, Beijing, Shanghai and Szechuan provinces, prepared with great attention to detail and served in an attractive setting. An added attraction is the new *dim sum* bar, which offers a wide selection of enticing steamed or fried Cantonese snacks.

De Compagnon

Guldehandsteeg 17 (near Warmoesstraat). **Map** 8 D1. *620 4225.* *AE, MC, V. 6–11pm Wed–Mon.* ⒻⒻ

It is well worth tracking down this tiny restaurant located in a small alley near Centraal Station. Inside, a clutter of tables are squeezed onto two levels. Culinary photographs on the wall of the bar put you in the mood for the selection of French dishes from the menu, which is recited to you by the friendly and helpful staff. It is advisable to book early since De Compagnon is a great favorite with people in the know.

Dorrius

Nieuwezijds Voorburgwal 5. **Map** 7 C1. *420 2224.* *AE, DC, MC, V, JCB. noon–11pm daily.* ⒻⒻ

Dorrius first opened as a restaurant at the end of the 19th century, but had been closed for many years before a new restaurant revived the name. When the owners were applying to use the name of their famous predecessor, its original 1890s interior was discovered in storage and they used these furnishings and decor in the new premises. The restaurant, which is now one of the few places in Amsterdam that serves genuine Dutch food, consequently maintains a genuinely period ambience. You can try typical dishes such as *erwtensoep*, a thick pea soup *(see p227)*, *paling* (eel) and *stokvis* (salted cod). The choice of desserts includes buttermilk ice cream and cinnamon *parfait* with black currant sauce. Large portions add to the authenticity.

De Kooning van Siam

Oudezijds Voorburgwal 42. **Map** 8 D2. *623 7293.* *AE, DC, MC, V. 6–10:30pm daily.* ⒻⒻ

At this relaxed Thai restaurant, authentic food is presented in an interior that recalls old Siam as well as 17th-century Amsterdam. Red, green and yellow curries, chicken soup with coconut milk and fresh Thai basil are just some of the flavors to be found on an extensive menu that makes few concessions to European tastes. A wonderful array of dishes awaits you.

Lucius

Spuistraat 247. **Map** 7 B3. *624 1831.* ★ *AE, DC, MC, V. 5pm–midnight Mon–Sat.* ⒻⒻ

Amsterdam is short of specialty seafood restaurants, considering the fantastic range of fresh produce available. Lucius offers a wide selection on its menu, such as Dutch flatfish, salmon, mussels and oysters. The daily specials may include more exotic fish such as swordfish or gold bream and there is always a meat dish, just in case. Chablis is one of the many well-known wines available to accompany your meal.

De Silveren Spiegel

Kattengat 4. **Map** 7 C1. *624 6589.* ★ *AE, DC, MC, V. 6–10pm Mon–Sat.* ⒻⒻⒻ

There has been a restaurant of one form or another on this site for 200 years. The building itself dates from 1614 and the dining room, which has been restored to its original 17th-century style, retains an intimate atmosphere. The staff is enthusiastic and there is a good seasonal selection of Dutch produce. Their shrimps, scallops and lamb are all highly recommended, and you can choose from one of the best wine lists in Amsterdam.

Vasso

Rozenboomsteeg 12–14. **Map** 7 B4. *626 0158.* ★ *AE, MC, V. 6–10:30pm daily.* ⒻⒻⒻ

Plain, simple ingredients are the hallmark of the best Italian cooking, and this rustic restaurant, with its color-washed walls and wooden floor, provides the perfect setting in which to sample them. There are daily specials and a regional set menu as well as a concise seasonal menu. Dishes like crab risotto, wild duck, and aniseed ice cream with chocolate will certainly tempt anyone wanting more than pasta or pizza. There is an extensive wine list that changes regularly. It is essential to book early.

D'Vijff Vliegen

Spuistraat 294–302. **Map** 7 A3. *554 6015 or 624 8369.* *AE, DC, MC, V. 5:30–10:30pm daily (10pm winter).* ⒻⒻⒻ

"The Five Flies" is a 350-year-old Dutch restaurant which uses only fresh, local produce to create a mixture of traditional Dutch dishes as well as less heavy modern cuisine. In the authentic period dining rooms, brass nameplates on the chairs display the names of famous guests and reveal that Elvis Presley once ate here. The restaurant also offers 50 different Dutch gins.

Vermeer/Golden Tulip Barbizon Palace

Prins Hendrikkade 59–72. **Map** 8 D1. *556 4885.* ★ *AE, DC, MC, V. noon–3pm Mon–Fri, 6–10:30pm Mon–Sat.* ⒻⒻⒻⒻ

Vermeer is one of the best restaurants in which to taste modern Dutch/French cuisine. The two-course lunch menu offers a good introduction to chef Ron Schouwenburg's delightful cuisine, which incorporates a wide range of culinary influences. Specialties include fresh goat-cheese soufflé with roasted garlic, Dutch snails, and salmon with braised peppers. The efficient service and luxurious surroundings enhance the culinary delights of this excellent restaurant. The extensive wine list also contains some real gems.

Western Canal Ring

Burger's Patio

2e Tuindwarsstraat 12 (near Westerstraat). **Map** 1 B3. *623 6854.* *AE, DC, MC, V. 6–11pm daily.* Ⓕ

An excellent example of a café-cum-restaurant that stands up to more expensive competition. Quality ingredients are used to produce a range of Italian dishes such as *carpaccio* (slices of raw beef) and *saltimbocca* (veal with Parma ham), with *tiramisu* for dessert. French fries with mayonnaise provide a local touch. The 1950s-style interior with kitsch lights sets the scene for a relaxed dinner with very friendly service. If you have to wait for a table, the owner will even come and get you from the pub across the street.

For key to symbols *see p225*

Speciaal

Nieuwe Leliestraat 142. **Map** 1 B4. *624 9706.* ★ *AE, MC, V. 5:30–11pm daily.* Ⓕ

With a well-established reputation built up over a number of years, many people consider this to be the best Indonesian restaurant in the area. Traditional dishes are served in a crowded and casual atmosphere. Most people will try the *rijsttafel (see p227)*, which may include *satay*, *ayam* (chicken), *ikan* (fish), *telor* (egg) and *rendang* (beef), as well as various condiments such as shredded coconut, sweet-and-sour vegetables and *krupuk* (shrimp crackers). It is advisable to book in advance.

Claes Claesz

Egelantiersstraat 24–26. **Map** 1 B4. *625 5306.* *AE, MC, V. 6–11pm Thu–Sun.* ⒻⒻ

Claes Claesz occupies the premises of a former poorhouse, which was built in 1616. Some amusing touches now characterize this small Dutch restaurant, such as ice buckets made from tiny garden pails, plates sporting the Dutch children's alphabet and toast racks on the table. Portions are generous, and dishes served include farmer's paté, poached salmon and pancakes filled with vanilla ice cream. The special *jenevers (see p48)* on offer here can be addictive. These and the local Jordaan character will put you in the mood for a highly enjoyable evening.

Prego

Herenstraat 25. **Map** 7 A1. *638 0148.* *AE, MC, V. 6–10:30pm Mon–Sat.* ⒻⒻ

A very popular restaurant with regular customers, who appreciate the homestyle cooking of Prego's female Sardinian chef. The menu, which is displayed on a blackboard, changes frequently and includes a wide selection of market-fresh meat and fish dishes. The staff is very helpful and knowledgeable, not least about the excellent wine list. This is not exclusively Italian but includes a range of wines to complement the food. It is advisable to book in advance.

Taddy Zemmel

Prinsengracht 126. **Map** 1 B4. *620 6525.* ★ *AE, MC, V. 6–10:30pm Tue–Sun.* ⒻⒻ

From the theatrically designed interior, with distressed walls and hops used as floral decoration, to kosher bonbons and cakes from Michelin-star chef Constant Fonk (based in his own restaurant in Hoorn), this is very definitely a restaurant with a difference. Main courses are all well made, and the desserts are really worth waiting for. The food is complemented by an interesting wine list which contains many French country wines at affordable prices. The friendly service and ambience are also great attractions and in summer the large terrace is always full.

D'Theeboom

Singel 210. **Map** 7 A3. *623 8420.* ★ *AE, DC, MC, V. 6–10:30pm Tue–Sun.* ⒻⒻ

French chef Georges Thubert is a professional. His ability to provide excellent cuisine and wine in an imaginatively decorated restaurant at a reasonable price is almost too good to be true. A typical meal could include mussel salad with seaweed, lamb in a herb crust, followed by cinnamon ice cream with warm cherries. The wine list has something for everyone, and includes an especially good choice of Rhône wines. Theeboom's pleasant canalside setting provides another good reason to dine here.

Bordewijk

Noordermarkt 7. **Map** 1 C3. *624 3899.* ★ *AE, MC, V. 6:30–10:30pm Tue–Sun.* ⒻⒻⒻ

Bordewijk, with its striking 1950s-cum-1980s interior, is one of the best restaurants in Amsterdam. Well-informed staff can help visitors select the ideal combination of food and wine. If you choose, for example, red mullet with wild spinach, *bouillabaisse* sauce and razor shell filled with pesto and garlic, then a *Moulins de Citran* (Bordeaux rosé) is available as the perfect complement. It attracts many regular guests, so it is advisable to book early.

Chez Georges

Herenstraat 3. **Map** 7 A1. *626 3332.* ★ *AE, DC, MC, V. 6–11pm. Sun & Wed.* ⒻⒻⒻ

Despite its modest façade, this small, homey restaurant is one of the busiest in Amsterdam. Belgian chef Georges François serves star-quality dishes ranging from duck-liver salad to a three-color chocolate mousse with a caramel *coulis*. The delights of the kitchen are accompanied by an impressive wine list and Georges' family are all involved in providing friendly and helpful service. Such is the demand for a table on weekends, that reservations often need to be made two weeks in advance.

Toscanini

Lindengracht 75. **Map** 1 C3. *623 2813.* *6–10:30pm daily.* ⒻⒻⒻ

The general impression of space in this busy Italian restaurant is unusual for Amsterdam. You can watch your meal being prepared with plenty of Italian temperament in Toscanini's open kitchen, which adds to the enjoyment. The menu offers plenty of choice, including a good cross section of typical Italian dishes. Although service can be slow, even a little off at times, this is a popular restaurant with a good reputation for the quality of its food. You will need to book in advance.

Christophe

Leliegracht 46. **Map** 7 A2. *625 0807.* ★ *AE, DC, MC, V. 7–11pm Mon–Sat.* ⒻⒻⒻⒻ

Jean-Christophe Royer from Toulouse is one of Amsterdam's star chefs. He concentrates his talents on producing high-quality dishes from south of the "sun-belt," an imaginary line that runs between Bordeaux and Avignon. You can choose wines from Madiran, Jurançon and Limoux, among others, to accompany dishes such as galette of eggplant with fresh anchovies, veal knuckle and cooked figs with thyme ice cream.

Central Canal Ring

Café Cox

Marnixstraat 429. **Map** 4 D1. *620 7222.* *AE, DC, MC, V. 12:30–2:30pm, 5:30–11:30pm daily.* Ⓕ

Although Cox also functions as a café on the ground floor, it is worth visiting the restaurant upstairs for its range of European dishes. Located near Leidseplein, it makes an ideal place to visit on a trip to the theater or movies. Go late if you are looking for a young crowd and a busy ambience.

De Expressionist

Runstraat 17d. **Map** 4 E1. *627 0618.* *AE, DC, MC, V. 6–10:30pm Sun–Thu, 6–11pm Fri & Sat.* Ⓕ

This modern, casual restaurant has no pretensions. Its crowded interior has an open kitchen that delivers dishes such as mushroom pasta with duck liver, sole with shrimp sauce and lamb with mango. There is also a fixed-price menu and the service is good but relaxed.

Lulu

Runstraat 8. **Map** 4 E1.
624 5090. ★ *AE, DC, MC, V.* *6–11pm daily.* ƒ

The tongue-in-cheek interior of this friendly bistro is balanced by tasty French regional dishes like *confit* of duck, *salade paysanne* and prune-and-armagnac ice cream. Chef/owner Erwin Debye takes his love of France to even greater lengths with background music by the likes of Edith Piaf and Charles Aznavour. Be sure to book in advance.

Mayur

Korte Leidsedwarsstraat 203.
Map 4 E2. *623 2142.* *AE, DC, MC, V.* *12:30–2:30pm Sat & Sun, 5–11pm daily.* ƒ

This spacious restaurant, located near Leidseplein, offers some of the best Indian food in Amsterdam. It specializes in a range of Tandoori dishes, which are authentically spiced. As the Dutch have not yet acquired a taste for Indian food, many of the clientele are tourists. Don't let this put you off; Mayur's soberly comfortable interior and convivial service make all visitors feel at home.

Swaagat

Lange Leidsedwarsstraat 74. **Map** 4 E2.
638 4702. ★ *AE, DC, MC, V.* *Apr–Sep 12:30–3pm, 5–11pm daily.* ƒ

Swaagat is one of the new breed of Indian restaurants. The large photographs of Indian elephants, dancers and the Taj Mahal that hang in the pleasant modern interior put you in the mood for its good-value dishes. There are no beef or pork dishes on the menu, making it popular with Indian clients, but the enthusiastic owner will happily talk you through the available choices. Dishes are prepared with top-quality ingredients and are presented in Tandoori style or as curries such as *roghan josh*, which is a house specialty. Try one of the set menus if you are having difficulty choosing.

Tout Court

Runstraat 13. **Map** 4 E1.
625 8637. *AE, DC, MC, V.* *noon–11:30pm Mon–Fri; 1–11:30pm Sat & Sun.* ƒƒ

Chef/owner John Fagel comes from one of the most famous culinary families in the Netherlands, with numerous brothers involved in many of the top restaurants throughout the country. The kitchen is open late, giving plenty of time to try a delicious assortment of French regional dishes with carefully selected wines to match. If you happen to know any Amsterdam celebrities then you may recognize some of the people around you. It is advisable to book well in advance since this is a very popular restaurant.

Zomer's

Prinsengracht 411. **Map** 4 E1.
638 3398. ★ *AE, DC, MC, V.* *5:30–10:30pm Tue–Sun.* ƒƒ

Zomer's is a wise choice if you want to enjoy good, reasonably priced food in pleasant surroundings with service to match. Local items like Dutch shrimps, classic *entrecôte* dishes, mushrooms in red wine plus a variety of more exotic dishes are all included on this restaurant's comprehensive menu. Portions are large and well balanced. The accompanying wines are affordably priced too, making an evening at Zomer's a great value for the money.

Dynasty

Reguliersdwarsstraat 30. **Map** 7 B5.
626 8400 or 627 9924. ★ *AE, DC, MC, V.* *6–11pm.* *Tue.* ƒƒƒ

This restaurant offers upscale, refined Southeast Asian cuisine in a colorful and well-designed interior. A variety of individual menus and carefully composed set menus give diners the opportunity of enjoying dishes from a cross section of Asian countries, such as Thailand, Vietnam and China. There is also a first-class wine list that contains a range of wines that have been carefully selected to complement the herbs and spices in the food. In the summer, an attractive open-air terrace behind the dining room provides a wonderful setting for a romantic evening meal.

Gauguin

Leidsekade 110. **Map** 4 D1.
622 1526. *AE, DC, MC, V.* *6–10:30pm Wed–Sun.* ƒƒƒ

A riot of South Sea colors hits you as you enter one of the more spectacular interiors in Amsterdam. The restaurant's slogan "Where East meets West" is imaginatively reflected by the cultural mix of ingredients in dishes such as salmon and samosa, Thai chicken with lemon and chili or *crème brûlée* with exotic fruits. Australian clients may find this familiar, but the experience is new for most people. A suitably varied wine list provides ample opportunity to experiment. The waterside location adds to the restaurant's overall atmosphere.

Sichuan Food

Reguliersdwarsstraat 35. **Map** 7 B5.
626 9327. *AE, DC, MC, V.* *5–11pm daily.* ƒƒƒ

It is unusual to come across a Chinese restaurant with one Michelin star, so it is always worth investigating them when you do. Despite its name, nearly half the dishes come from other provinces and consist of fairly typical standards like Peking duck and Cantonese *dim sum.* If you are feeling more experimental, the selection of Szechuan dishes, which rely heavily on chilies and Chinese peppers, should catch your eye. Friendly and informative service will help you make your selection of less-familiar dishes and makes a visit to this intimate restaurant worthwhile.

Het Tuynhuys

Reguliersdwarsstraat 28. **Map** 7 B5.
627 6603. ★ *AE, DC, MC, V.* *noon–2pm Mon–Fri; 6–10:30pm daily.* ƒƒƒ

In Amsterdam's Golden Age *(see pp24–7)*, this former coach house was owned by a wealthy Dutch merchant. The building has since been beautifully renovated as a restaurant in a mixture of Dutch and Portuguese styles, and the attractive interior is always worth a look. Tiles and metal furniture have been used to retain an old-fashioned garden atmosphere and the courtyard offers a perfect setting for a relaxing meal during the warm summer months. The service is friendly at Tuynhuys and the food is an attractive blend of French and Dutch country dishes, which are prepared with a range of good fresh produce.

Hosokawa

Max Euweplein 22 (near Leidseplein). **Map** 4 E2. *638 8086.* *AE, DC, MC, V.* *noon–2:30pm Mon–Fri; 6–11pm daily.* ƒƒƒƒ

This Japanese restaurant is renowned for its *teppan* dishes. The social aspect of sitting around the *teppan* (an iron grill plate) as the chef cooks your meal in front of you at your table is a large part of the enjoyment, and is very popular with the Dutch. You can also try other Japanese delicacies like *sashimi* (raw fish), *yakitori* (skewer of grilled chicken) or *tempura* (deep-fried seafood or vegetables). The *teppan* style of Japanese cooking demands years of experience, so it is worth going to a well-established restaurant like Hosokawa to find a chef with the required expertize. Naturally, this standard of service comes at a price.

't Swarte Schaep

Korte Leidsedwarsstraat 24. **Map** 4 F2. *622 3021.* V *AE, DC, MC, V, JCB.* *noon–11pm daily.* ⒻⒻⒻⒻ

Housed in a building that dates from 1687, this restaurant offers a high standard of cooking and a cozy Dutch ambience. There is also a surprisingly large selction of wines and other drinks – an apéritif made from champagne and lychee liqueur will certainly wake up your taste buds. The constantly changing menu could include a *parfait* of goose liver wrapped in truffles, snail ravioli in balsamico, lobster timbale in veal sauce and a dessert made from figs. Service can be slow, but is always attentive.

Eastern Canal Ring

An

Weteringschans 199. **Map** 5 A4. *627 0607.* V ★ *No drink license.* *6–10pm Wed–Sun.* Ⓕ

Homestyle meals are unusual in Japanese restaurants, but at An you have the chance to sample the dishes that are enjoyed daily by most Japanese. Typical examples include *yakiniku* (grilled meat), *tonkatsu* (marinated pork fried in breadcrumbs) and *tempura* (deep-fried seafood or vegetables), all of which are served with rice, *miso* soup and pickles. This restaurant ia a real bargain.

Indrapura

Rembrandtplein 42. **Map** 7 C5. *623 7329.* V ★ *AE, DC, MC, V.* *5–11pm daily.* ⒻⒻ

The thousands of islands that make up Indonesia produce an enormous variety of gastronomic styles. In Indrapura's modern colonial interior, you can enjoy the traditions of Java (sweet in taste, no pork), Sumatra (spicy with an Indian influence) and smaller islands whose cuisines owe more to Thai cooking. The restaurant also has a range of wines to go with even the hottest dishes on the menu. Leave room for the delicious fermented black-rice dessert, which is a must.

Kort

Amstelveld 12. **Map** 5 A3. *626 1199.* V ★ *AE, DC, MC, V.* *Sep–Apr: noon–2:30pm, 6–10pm daily (11pm Fri–Sat).* *Tue (Sep–Jun).* ⒻⒻ

Kort is housed in a 17th-century church on a cobblestone square overlooking houseboats, canals and gabled houses. It is an ideal setting in which to enjoy adventurous French/Dutch cuisine. Dishes such as guinea fowl in citric sauce can be challenging when it comes to choosing the wine. Kort's varied wine list, however, manages to complement some of the fuller flavors on the menu and contains a good selection of half bottles. This restaurant is an ideal venue for anyone seeking an authentic Amsterdam experience slightly off the usual tourist route.

Tempo Doeloe

Utrechtsestraat 75. **Map** 5 A3. *625 6718.* V ★ *AE, DC, MC, V.* *6–11pm daily.* ⒻⒻ

If you are looking for real Indonesian food, then ring the doorbell of this restaurant to gain access to the domain of chef Don Ao. Hot dishes are very well indicated on the menu and, since the cooking is authentic, hot really means hot! If this does not appeal to you, there are many options that show off the more delicate side of Indonesian cuisine. Friendly, hospitable staff is always on hand to help you order dishes to suit your palate.

Le Zinc… et les Dames

Prinsengracht 999. **Map** 5 A3. *622 9044.* V *MC.* *5:30–11pm Tue–Sat.* ⒻⒻ

The rustic interior of this recently renovated canalside warehouse provides a perfect setting for the homestyle French regional cooking provided by the popular first-floor restaurant. The menu is concise and offers a daily three-course selection. Dishes on offer range from *saucisson de Lyon* to fried cod, followed by *tarte tatin.* There is also a well-chosen and reasonably priced selection of ten wines, which are sold by the glass, carafe or bottle. These wines are also available in the ground-floor bar, which makes an ideal setting in which to enjoy a predinner drink. It is advisable to book in advance.

Van Vlaanderen

Weteringschans 175. **Map** 5 A4. *622 8292.* V ★ *AE, MC, V.* *6:30–10:30pm Mon–Sat.* ⒻⒻⒻ

One of the newest restaurants in Amsterdam but set to become one of the most interesting. A light, modern interior is the setting where Belgian chef Marc Philippart reveals his repertoire of classic French dishes such as *salade gourmande.* The daily specials and the seasonal menus may also feature modern combinations like red mullet with blood sausage, duck liver and wild spinach in a *bouillabaisse.* Attention to the quality of the ingredients and the distinctive full flavors make this a memorable place. The wine list offers an interesting selection, from the house wine right through to the more expensive bottles. Well-informed staff adds to the pleasure of dining here.

Museum Quarter

Overakker

Overtoom 160–162. **Map** 4 D2. *683 3552.* *AE, DC, MC, V.* *6–11pm Tue–Sun.* Ⓕ

An attractive international/French menu, good-quality table settings and a fresh-looking, modern interior with Japanese touches could give the impression that prices in this restaurant are bound to be high. However, you will be pleasantly surprised by the reasonable cost of eating here. The set menu may include a *confit* of guinea fowl with Indonesian and Chinese spices, followed by *bitterkoekjes* and advocaat ice cream with a caramel sauce. The restaurant's location near Leidseplein makes this an ideal choice for visitors planning a trip to the theater.

Brasserie Bark

Van Baerlestraat 120. **Map** 4 D4. *675 0210.* V *AE, DC, MC, V.* *noon–3pm Mon–Fri, 5:30pm–12:30am daily.* ⒻⒻ

Surprisingly, despite the availability of fish in Amsterdam, this is one of the very few specialty fish restaurants in the city. It is usefully located close to the Concertgebouw in one of the city's main restaurant areas, so the surrounding competition helps to keep standards up and prices down. Dutch and French oysters, lobster, grilled salmon and lobster bisque (always a good test of the kitchen) are among the selection of classic dishes always available here. The appetizers also features a vegetarian as well as some meat options for variety. Another good reason to pay a visit to Bark's is that it stays open unusually late.

Bartholdy

Van Baerlestraat 35–37. **Map** 4 D4. *662 2655.* V *AE, DC, MC, V.* *5:30–11pm daily.* ⒻⒻ

The concert menu at Bartholdy should interest music and food lovers alike. It allows you to eat the first two courses of your meal, then dash across to the Concertgebouw *(see p128)* for the performance, before returning for the final two courses. The cuisine is French based, but many of the dishes also incorporate some Mediterranean and North African ingredients. This pleasant restaurant proves that it is possible to serve interesting meals at a reasonable price, and offer friendly service as well. It is worth visiting even if you don't have any concert tickets booked.

Zabar's

Van Baerlestraat 49. **Map** 4 D4.
679 8888. V *MC.* *11am–11pm Mon–Fri, 5:30–11pm Sat.* ƒƒ

Zabar's was one of the first places in the Netherlands to offer the combinations of food found in Californian and Australian restaurants. Its highly adventurous Mediterranean-based menu makes use of a wide range of ingredients to produce dishes such as zucchini soup, pasta, grilled tuna and sweetbreads with lamb. In addition to a mold-breaking culinary freedom, Zabar's continuing popularity is guaranteed by its highly inventive wine selection, which perfectly complements the food.

Le Garage

Ruysdaelstraat 54–56. **Map** 4 E4.
679 7176. ★ *AE, DC, MC, V.* *noon–2pm Mon–Fri, 6–11pm daily.* ƒƒƒ

Unique in Amsterdam, this busy, bustling brasserie is lined with red-plush benches and closely packed tables. Regulars are attracted by the in-crowd who frequent Le Garage, and use the large wall mirrors for people-watching. Chef/owner Joop Braakheken is well known for his cooking program on Dutch television. His enthusiasm for food is reflected in the lively French regional menu. There is also a late supper and a dieters' menu. The extensive wine selection is well balanced with some really good deals, and all desserts come with suggestions for a suitable dessert wine or liquor. Book early and enjoy yourself.

Raden Mas

Stadhouderskade 6. **Map** 4 D2.
685 4041. V ★ *AE, DC, MC, V.* *5–11pm daily.* ƒƒƒ

Raden Mas provides a complete evening out for diners who like being spoiled. After a warm welcome at the door, you are shown into the restaurant's luxurious Oriental interior where you are treated to live piano music and attentive service. The extensive menu offers a broad selection of Indonesian dishes, ranging from a choice of *rijsttafel* *(see p227)* to a whole lobster served in a light Indonesian sauce. The wine list is also impressive. If you are in the mood for a gastronomic feast, plenty is offered to tempt you to splurge. However, if you choose carefully, it is still possible to eat for a reasonable price here.

Beddington's

Roelof Hartstraat 6–8. **Map** 4 E5.
676 5201. V ★ *AE, DC, MC, V.* *noon–2pm Tue–Fri, 6–10:30pm Mon–Sat.* ƒƒƒƒ

Flavors and taste are central to Chef Jean Beddington's cooking, as exhibited in her signature dish, monkfish Tandoori with cumin sauce. Influences from many cuisines are blended to achieve the required flavors, and top-quality ingredients are used to guarantee the taste. While the inclusion of Stilton and port on the menu may betray Jean's English roots, her cross-cultural outlook makes it difficult to pigeon-hole her cooking. Her creative philosophy is also reflected in Beddington's striking, designer interior. It is advisable to book in advance.

De Trechter

Hobbemakade 63. **Map** 4 E4.
671 1263. V *AE, DC, MC, V.* *6–10:30pm Tue–Sat.* ƒƒƒƒ

Jan de Wit is a single-minded chef with roots set deeply in classic French cooking. He uses only the best raw ingredients to create exquisite Michelin-star dishes. These include expensive items such as Sevruga caviar, *foie gras* and lobster, as well as more humble produce such as cod. Specialties include chicory soup with Roquefort and walnuts, and sweetbreads with chanterelles in a sauce of mushroom-and-veal stock. The wines are generally expensive, but include a reasonably priced selection from the southwest of France.

PLANTAGE

La Rive

Prof. Tulpplein 1. **Map** 5 B4.
622 6060. V ★ *AE, DC, MC, V.* *noon–2pm Mon–Fri, 6:30–10:30pm daily.* ƒƒƒƒ

The grandeur of the Amstel Hotel *(see p223)* is reflected in its elegant riverside dining room, presided over by chef Robert Kranenborg. This is one of the best restaurants in Amsterdam. The menu reflects Kranenborg's long experience in top establishments in France and Belgium. Dishes like skate fried in sesame oil with carrots, artichoke hearts with poultry breast in a sherry dressing or caramelized apple croquettes with a ginger sorbet confirm his careful selection of ingredients. A less expensive two-course lunch menu provides a useful preview to the interesting flavors on offer, but for the full works, treat yourself to a meal in the glorious wine room, or on the terrace during the summer.

FARTHER AFIELD

Beau Bourg

Emmalaan 25. **Map** 3 B4.
664 0155. V *AE, DC, MC, V.* *noon–3pm Mon–Fri, 6–11pm daily.* ƒƒ

This brasserie-cum-restaurant is elegantly decorated in a mixture of contemporary styles. Dishes include platters of oysters to whet the appetite, *gazpacho* and *coq au vin*. Friendly service helps to make this an enjoyable place for a reasonably priced lunch or dinner. It is ideally located for visitors to the Vondelpark and is a short trolley ride from the museums.

Kaiko

Jekerstraat 114.
662 5641. ★ *AE, DC, MC, V.* *6–10:30pm Mon–Wed, Fri & Sat.* ƒƒ

It is worth going a little out of the center of Amsterdam in order to find the best *sushi* in town. A simple set menu offers eight pieces of *sushi*, a rolled *sushi*, *miso* soup, salad and dessert. More extensive menus allow you to explore the full range of Japanese cuisine including *sashimi* (raw fish) and *tempura* (deep-fried shrimp or vegetables in batter). If possible, get a seat at the counter of this small restaurant in order to see the skillful way chef/owner Kobayashi prepares the food.

Mangerie de Kersentuin

Dijsselhofplantsoen 7. **Map** 4 D5.
664 2121. V *AE, DC, MC, V.* *6–11pm Mon–Sat.* ƒƒ

While some restaurants regard a down-to-earth approach as an excuse for lowering standards, the Mangerie de Kersentuin uses this formula to produce delicious food in relaxed surroundings at an excellent price. Far from being ordinary, the cooking is imaginative and brings out the full flavors of the top-quality ingredients that are used in the creation of a broad selection of dishes. Genuinely friendly service adds to the pleasure of dining at this unpretentious restaurant.

For key to symbols *see p225*

Light Meals and Snacks

In addition to the normal assortment of burger joints, pizzerias and the like, most Dutch cafés and bars serve food ranging from simple bar snacks to a three-course meal. Those that offer lunch-time snacks and an evening meal are generally known as *eetcafés*. While the choice of dishes tends to be limited, the quality is generally high and prices are often very reasonable. Some *eetcafés* have started serving more adventurous dishes and generally offer a good vegetarian selection. However, café and bar kitchens close early and it is difficult to get a meal after 9pm. For more information on cafés and bars, including a selection of the top ten in Amsterdam, see pages 46–7.

Bars and Street Stands

Almost all bars serve a range of snacks. The standard selection of nibbles includes olives, chunks of Dutch cheese served with mustard and *borrelnoten* (nuts with a savory coating). More substantial tapas-like snacks include *bitterballen* (deep-fried meatballs), *vlammetjes* (deep-fried batter envelopes similar to meat and vegetable spring rolls) and *osseworst* (a spicy mince-beef sausage).

Given the maritime tradition of the Netherlands, it is worth trying the fish dishes available in bars and from stands on the street, such as herring served with onion or gherkins. Pizza, sandwiches and hamburgers are also commonly available from stands. However, the most popular snack from street stands is french fries or *patat frites*, which are served with mayonnaise in a plastic tray or a paper cone *(see p226)*.

Pancake Houses

Pancakes *(pannekoeken)* are popular, inexpensive light meals in Amsterdam. The French-style *crêpe* is believed to have been adopted in the Netherlands during the Napoleonic occupation *(see pp28–9)* as a way of using up leftovers.

These days there is nothing penny-pinching about the wide range of sweet and savory toppings available at most pancake houses in Amsterdam. It is not uncommon to find up to 70 varieties offered and you can usually combine any of these to create the pancake of your choice. The best places include **Bredero**, **De Carrousel**, **Meerzicht**, **The Pancake Bakery** and **Het Pannekoekhuis**. Portions may seem small, but they are deceptively filling. Pancakes and waffles served with syrup are also available as the staple snack at smoking coffeeshops *(see p49)*.

Brown Cafés and Bars

The term *eetcafés* is most commonly applied to traditional brown cafés *(see also p48)*. These often offer much better value and a more relaxed atmosphere than many small restaurants. Outstanding brown cafés include **De Prins**, **Het Molenpad**, **Carel's**, **De Reiger** and **Frascati**, which have extensive and appealing menus. Not suprisingly, they often get crowded and it can be hard to find a free table.

The majority of basic *eetcafés* just offer filling homemade fare, such as soup, sandwiches, salads, omelets and fries. The only unfamiliar dishes you are likely to come across are *uitsmijter* (a large open sandwich with roast beef or ham, topped with fried eggs) and *erwtensoep* (a thick pea soup with pork). Of the cheaper, more down-to-earth varieties of *eetcafés*, **De Doffer** and **Aas van Bokalen** both serve filling food that is an excellent value. Aas van Bokalen is widely considered to provide one of the best deals in the city and De Doffer has the attraction of a billiard room. Both places attract a young, lively crowd and are popular with students.

However, an increasing number of Amsterdam's cafés and bars are becoming more ambitious in the food they offer. **Café Cox**, located in De Stadsschouwburg *(see p111)*, is a perfect example of this more adventurous approach. At smart *eetcafés*, the menu is rarely limited to a single style or national cuisine. A notable exception to this rule is **Van Puffelen**, which offers more formal French-style dishes. Meals are served in the back extension of this intimate brown café, which has an impressive 19th-century interior.

Designer Bars

An extensive range of food is offered in some of the more upscale designer bars *(see p49)*. This type of bar is invariably more expensive than other types of cafés and bars in the city and in most cases the quality of the fare does not justify such inflated prices. **Café Schiller**, housed in a beautiful Art Deco building on Rembrandtplein, is an honorable exception. Amid portraits of 1930s cabaret stars painted by Frits Schiller, you can enjoy a reasonable selection of snacks and meals in an evocative period bar. Both **Het Land van Walem** and **De Balie** also serve tasty food in a stylish setting. **Morlang**, next door to Het Land van Walem, is less chic, but the food is a better value, and the trendy **Café Esprit** is popular with Kalverstraat shoppers.

Specialist Cafés

If you feel like trying something different, sample the delicious Belgian home cooking at the Flemish cultural center **De Brakke Grond**, where meals are served in both the café and the restaurant. **De Zotte** also serves down-to-earth Flemish food and stocks a huge variety of Belgian beers. While the quality is not as exceptional, the portions are large enough to soak up the strongest of beers.

Probably the best value meal in town is served at **Terzyde**. One enormous home-cooked dish, which could be anything from chili con carne to pasta, is served every night at this modern "neighborhood" café.

Directory

Pancake Houses

Bredero
Oudezijds Voorburgwal. 244. **Map** 7 C3.
622 9461.

De Carrousel
HM van Randwijckplantsoen 1 (near Weteringschans).
Map 4 F3.
627 5880.

Meerzicht
Koenenkade 56.
Amstedamse Bos.
679 2744.

The Pancake Bakery
Prinsengracht 191.
Map 1 B4.
625 1333.

Het Pannekoekhuis
Prinsengracht 358.
Map 1 B4.
620 8448.

Brown Cafés and Bars

Aas van Bokalen
Keizersgracht 335.
Map 1 B5.
623 0917.

Carel's Café
Voetboogstraat 6.
Map 7 B4.
622 2080.

Café Cox
Marnixstraat 427.
Map 4 D1.
620 7222.

De Doffer
Runstraat 12.
Map 4 E1.
622 6686.

't Doktertje
Rozenboomsteeg 4.
Map 7 B4.
626 4427.

Frascati
Nes 59.
Map 7 B4.
624 1324.

Het Molenpad
Prinsengracht 653.
Map 4 E1.
625 9680.

De Pieper
Prinsengracht 424.
Map 4 E1.
626 4775.

De Prins
Prinsengracht 124.
Map 1 B4.
624 9382.

De Reiger
Nieuwe Leliestraat 34.
Map 1 B4.
624 7426.

De Tuin
2e Tuindwarsstraat 13 (near Westerstraat).
Map 1 B3.
624 4559.

Van Puffelen
Prinsengracht 377.
Map 1 B4.
624 6270.

Proeflokalen and Modern Tasting Bars

De Drie Fleschjes
Gravenstraat 18.
Map 7 B2.
624 8443.

Gollem
Raamsteeg 4.
Map 7 A4.
626 6645.

Henri Prouvin
Gravenstraat 20.
Map 7 B2.
623 9333.

In De Wildeman
Kolksteeg 3.
Map 7 C1.
638 2348.

L&B Limited
Korte Leidsedwarsstraat 82.
Map 4 E2.
625 2387.

Grand Cafés and Designer Bars

De Balie
Kleine Gartmanplantsoen 10.
Map 4 E2.
624 3821.

Café Américain
American Hotel, Leidseplein 28–30.
Map 4 E2.
624 5322.

Café Esprit
Spui 10.
Map 7 B4.
622 1967.

De Jaren
Nieuwe Doelenstraat 20.
Map 7 C4.
625 5771.

De Kroon
Rembrandtplein 17.
Map 7 C5.
625 2011.

Het Land van Walem
Keizersgracht 449.
Map 7 A5.
625 3544.

Café Luxembourg
Spuistraat 22.
Map 7 B4.
620 6264.

Morlang
Keizersgracht 451.
Map 7 A5.
625 2681.

Café Schiller
Rembrandtplein 26.
Map 7 C5.
624 9846.

Vertigo
Nederlands Filmmuseum, Vondelpark 3
Map 4 D2.
612 3021.

Smoking Coffeeshops

The Bulldog
Leidseplein 13–17.
Map 4 E2.
627 1908.

La Chocolata
Spuistraat 51.
Map 7 B1.
622 6241.

The Grasshopper
Oudebrugsteeg 16.
Map 7 C1.
626 1529.

Global Chillage
Kerkstraat 51.
Map 4 E1.
639 1154.

Rookies
Korte Leidsedwarsstraat 145–147.
Map 4 E2.
639 0978.

Rusland
Rusland 16.
Map 7 C4.
627 9468.

Siberia
Brouwersgracht 11.
Map 1 C3.
623 5909.

De Tweede Kamer
Heisteeg 6.
Map 7 A4.
627 5709.

Coffeeshops and Salons de Thé

Arnold Cornelis
Van Baerlestraat 93.
Map 4 D4.
662 1228.

Back Stage
Utrechtsedwarsstraat 67.
Map 5 A3.
622 3638.

Berkhoff
Leidsestraat 46.
Map 4 E1.
624 0233.

Café Françoise
Kerkstraat 176.
Map 4 F2.
624 0145.

Metz & Co
Keizersgracht 455.
Map 4 F1.
624 8810.

PC
PC Hooftstraat 83.
Map 4 D3.
671 7455.

Pompadour
Huidenstraat 12.
Map 7 A4.
623 9554 .

Specialty Cafés

De Brakke Grond
Nes 43.
Map 7 C3.
626 0044.

Terzyde
Kerkstraat 59.
Map 4 E1.
626 2301.

De Zotte
Raamstraat 29.
Map 4 E1.
626 8694.

Shops and Markets

AMSTERDAM has a huge range of shops and markets, so if you are present-hunting, you will find no shortage of ideas. Most of the large clothing and department stores are to be found in the Nieuwe Zijde, especially along Kalverstraat *(see p72)*, but there are many other shopping areas to discover. The narrow streets that cross the Canal Ring, such as Herenstraat and Hartenstraat, contain a diverse array of specialist shops selling everything from ethnic fabrics and beads to unusual games and handmade dolls. The best luxury fashion is to be found on the classy PC Hooftstraat and Van Baerlestraat. However, if you are looking for a bargain, take time to explore the street markets and numerous secondhand shops. Here you can pick up recent fashion items and worn leather jackets cheaply.

Atrium of the Magna Plaza in the former Postkantoor

Opening Hours

STORES ARE usually open from 9am or 10am to 6pm Tuesday to Saturday and from 1pm to 6pm on Monday *(see p256)*. In the city center, shops stay open until 9pm on Thursdays. However, legislation does allow storekeepers in the city center to remain open between 7am and 10pm seven days a week if they so wish. Retailers are most likely to take advantage of this law in the run up to Sinterklaas *(see p53)* and during the Christmas period.

How to Pay

CASH IS the most popular method of payment, so if you intend to use a credit card, do ask if they are accepted before buying. Although cards are becoming more widely accepted, department stores often require purchases to be paid for at a special register, and smaller stores may only accept them for nonsale items and goods costing more than *f*100. Eurocheques are accepted in most stores and, if you have a bank account in the Netherlands, direct debits are becoming popular. If you run out of guilders, some tourist stores take foreign currency, but offer a poor rate of exchange.

Tax Exemption

MOST DUTCH GOODS are subject to value added tax (BTW) of either 17.5 percent for clothes and other goods, or 6 percent for books. Non-EU residents are entitled to a refund, subject to certain conditions. Stores that stock the relevant forms will have a sign saying "Tax free for tourists." On leaving the country, this form must be stamped by customs who will then send it back to the store. The store will eventually refund you the tax paid. Unless your purchase is an expensive one, you may find that it is not worth the effort involved.

Stoeltie Diamonds *(see p242)*

Sales

SALES TAKE PLACE mainly in January and July but smaller shops and boutiques may offer discount items at any time. *Uitverkoop* describes anything from a going-out-of-business sale to a clearance sale, while *korting* merely indicates that discounts are being offered.

Near the end of a sale, further discounts, which will be calculated at the cash register, are often subtracted from the marked-down price. Beware of clothes racks marked, for example, *VA 40* or *Vanaf 40* since this sign means "From 40" – the items cost *f* 40 or more, rather than exactly *f* 40.

Department Stores and Malls

PERHAPS AMSTERDAM'S best-known department store is **De Bijenkorf** on Dam square, often described as the Dutch Harrods. It has a huge perfumery, and stocks a wide range of men's and women's clothing, plus toys, soft furnishings and household goods. At Christmas it devotes a whole floor to decorations. Both **Maison de Bonneterie** and **Metz & Co** are more exclusive. Among the less expensive stores, **Hema** is very popular for household goods, children's clothes and underwear. Also popular for basic items is **Vroom & Dreesman**, which is working hard to update its range of clothing.

The only shopping mall in central Amsterdam is Magna Plaza, which is housed in the old Postkantoor building *(see p78)*. The impressive, vaulted interior of this former main post office now contains a huge assortment of upscale boutiques and shops.

Markets

AMSTERDAMMERS' love of street trading is most graphically illustrated on April 30 during Queen's Day *(see p50)*, when Amsterdam turns into the biggest flea market in the world, as local people crowd the city to sell off all their unwanted junk. Such is the crush of eager bargain hunters that the entire city center is closed to traffic during the festivities.

Since Amsterdam still resembles a collection of small villages, every district has its own local market. The best-known of these, because of its size, is the Albert Cuypmarkt *(see p122)* in the Pijp district, which sells a wide assortment of food, both Dutch and ethnic. This market is also good for cheap clothes and reasonably priced flowers.

Apart from the local markets, Amsterdam has a wide range of specialty markets. Visitors to the city and residents alike are drawn to the excellent array of seasonal flowers for sale at the Bloemenmarkt *(see p123)*. Another market popular with tourists is Waterlooplein flea market *(see p63)*. Despite the crowds, vigilant collectors can still seek out the odd bargain among the bric-a-brac; there is also a selection of new and second-hand clothes for sale.

Browsers will be fascinated by the hundreds of stalls at the Looier Kunst Antiekcentrum *(see p113)*, which sell anything from antique dolls to egg cups. Every Wednesday and Saturday on the Nieuwezijds Voorburgwal there is a specialist market for stamp and coin collectors. Gourmets should head for the Noordermarkt *(see p92)*, which holds an organic food market on Saturdays. The best prices, however, are to be found about 25 km (16 miles) northwest of Amsterdam. The **Zwarte Markt** (Black Market) in Beverwijk, open on Saturdays, is perhaps Europe's largest indoor flea market. Next door, the **Oosterse Markt** (Eastern Market), open weekends, has a cross-section of Oriental merchandise, including rugs, carpets, pottery, crafts and food.

MEXX, a fashionable boutique on PC Hooftstraat *(see p126)*

Smoked fish on display at the Albert Cuypmarkt

Specialty Shops

Dotted throughout Amsterdam are dozens of small specialty shops. One of the more unusual is **Condomerie Het Gulden Vlies**, located in a former squat, which sells condoms from all over the world. Equally unusual is **Christmas World**, which sells festive adornments all year round, and **Party House**, which has a vast collection of paper decorations. **Hot Shop** and **Capsicum Natuurstoffen** have a huge selection of exotic silks and linens, while **Copenhagen 1001 Kralen** has more than 1,000 different types of beads. It is also worth making time to explore **Stilett** for hand-painted T-shirts, **Vliegertuig** for kites, **Koffie Keizer** for tea and coffee, or treat yourself to an array of wonderful-smelling herbs at **Hooy & Co**.

Books, Newspapers and Magazines

Since books are subject to value added tax in the Netherlands, you may find them slightly more expensive than at home. English-language books are generally available, particularly at **The American Book Center** and **WH Smith**. Holiday reading can be picked up very cheaply at second-hand book-stores, such as **De Slegte**. Collectors of comics should not miss a visit to **Lambiek**.

Amsterdam does not have its own English-language newspaper, but most city-center newsstands stock foreign papers. *Het Financieel Dagblad* has a daily business update in English and publishes a weekly English-language edition. Both *Time Out Amsterdam* and *What's On* are useful listings magazines *(see p256)*.

A selection of seasonal flowers, including sunflowers, roses and lilies

What to Buy in Amsterdam

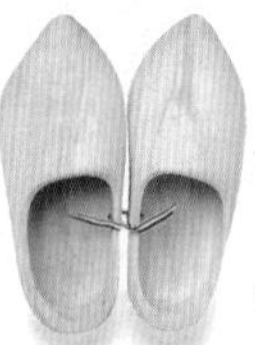

Traditional wooden clogs

AMSTERDAM HAS hundreds of tourist shops selling souvenirs, but those looking for something different will find a better selection of genuine Dutch items in one of the city's specialty stores or even at an ordinary supermarket. Authentic delftware is only found at a handful of licensed dealers, but there are still many jewelers selling anything from uncut stones to secondhand diamond rings. Dutch cheese, chocolate and locally produced beers and *jenevers* offer a flavor of the city, while a bunch of flowers is always appreciated.

Ceramics
Finely detailed model canal houses can be be bought singly or by the row.

Droste chocolate pastilles

Sweet and salty varieties of drop licorice

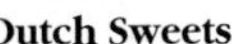

Dutch Sweets
Handmade Belgian chocolates and Droste pastilles are both delicious, but salty licorice is an acquired taste.

Handmade Belgian chocolates

Flowers
Bulbs and cut flowers are colorful reminders of the city and, due to greenhouse production, many blooms are available all year round.

Tulip bulbs

A bunch of fresh tulips

Gouda Cheese
There are many types of Gouda of different maturity (see p242). *Any store will be happy to let you try a slice before making a purchase.*

Two popular brands of beer

Beer in Amsterdam
A huge variety of imported, bottled beers, as well as many local brews, are sold in Amsterdam (see p242).

Sturdy stone flagons of *jonge* and *oude jenever (see pp48–9)* – also available in flavored varieties

Dutch windmill prints

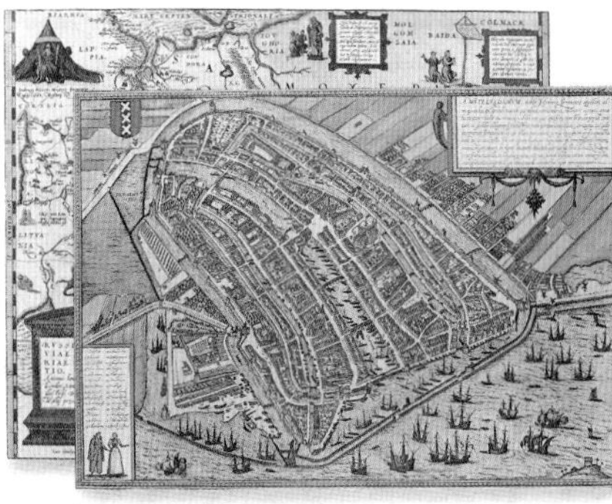
Reproductions of old maps of Amsterdam and Russia

Old Maps and Prints

Historically famous for cartography, Amsterdam has a good selection of new and old maps, and many second-hand bookshops stock etchings.

Diamond brooch

Chain-link, diamond-encrusted bracelet

Diamonds

Diamond cutting was first established in Amsterdam during the 16th century. The city is still one of the major diamond centers.

Different colored brilliant-cut diamonds

ROYAL DELFT

In response to the demand for Chinese design, more than 30 factories sprang up in Delft in the 17th century, producing distinctive blue-and-white porcelain *(see p195)*. Today, only De Porceleyne Fles still makes real delftware. Items from this factory are sold with a certificate of authenticity.

Pynaker tobacco jar influenced by Japanese Imari ware

Plate painted in traditional delft blue

Polychrome jug painted in colors used on 17th-century majolica

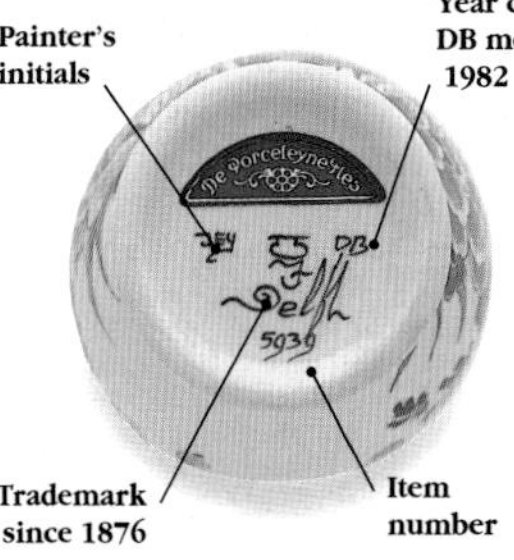

Genuine De Porceleyne Fles marks

Delft-blue vase

17th-century plate made for rich family

Decorative 17th-century fireplace tile

Antique Delft

Old delftware is highly sought after and expensive, but delft fireplace tiles can be picked up less expensively.

Where to Shop in Amsterdam

THE NETHERLANDS IS JUSTLY famous for its flowers, beer and cheese. A wide choice of these indigenous products is available in Amsterdam, which has also long been regarded as the world center for diamonds. Owing to the large numbers of overseas settlers living in Amsterdam and the cosmopolitan outlook of its residents, it is easy to find a selection of foreign goods in the city. These range from Indonesian beads to French designer wear.

Fashion and Clothes

VAN BAERLESTRAAT and PC Hooftstraat contain numerous designer boutiques such as **MEXX**, offering top names like Katharine Hamnet and the leading French and Italian designer labels. The stylish set from the Canal Ring haunt **Hobbit** and **Pauw** for timeless clothes and accessories.

Boutiques in the Nieuwe Zijde offer less pricey items. The French designer **Agnès B** has her own shop along Rokin selling classic designer wear, and **Puck en Hans**, also on Rokin, caters to the wackier end of high fashion. Along Kalverstraat, **Mac & Maggie** stock cheaper, up-to-the-minute clothes for teenagers, while **Sissy Boy** specializes in more refined classic suits and eye-catching designs.

Fanatics of secondhand clothes will find well-priced and stylish selections at stores such as **Zipper**. For the widest choice of fashionable boots and shoes, **Dr. Adams** is almost a Dutch institution.

Antiques and Furnishings

WHILE YOU CAN pick up the odd bargain on Waterlooplein *(see p63)* and at the Noordermarkt *(see p92)*, the best place for antiques is around Spiegelgracht. A wide selection of antiques shops in the area sells everything from 17th-century tiles to icons. The **Amsterdam Antiques Gallery** in particular has a good reputation for the range of its stock. It is also interesting to visit an auction house. Both **Sotheby's** and **Christie's** have branches in Amsterdam. Looier Kunst en Antiekcentrum *(see p113)*, has a potpourri of odds and ends, while **De Haas** and **Object Art Deco** have good collections of 20th-century furniture and accessories. If you like to barter, **Tut Tut** buys and sells antique toys.

Flowers and Bulbs

NO DUTCH PERSON would dream of visiting a friend without a bunch of flowers, so Amsterdam is crowded with flower shops. Worth visiting are **Riviera**, for a vast assortment of colorful domestic blooms and **Gerda's Bloemenwinkel** for its stock of tropical flowers.

Cut flowers are cheapest at Albert Cuypmarkt *(see p122)*, but Bloemenmarkt *(see p123)* has a better selection, as well as hundreds of bulbs and tubers. It also sells potted plants, but due to customs regulations, these usually can't be exported.

Diamonds

AMSTERDAM has a long tradition of cutting and polishing diamonds *(see p30)*. It is still possible to purchase loose stones and diamonds in a new setting at one of the city's many diamond-cutting centers such as **Stoeltie Diamonds** or Coster Diamonds *(see p128)*. The city is also well stocked with jewelers, several specializing in diamonds. The best secondhand jewelry can be found in the fascinating antiques shops around Spiegelgracht.

Cheese

AS THE DUTCH are fussy about their cheese, you can buy a good selection from supermarkets such as **Albert Heijn**, street markets and at specialty stores. Instead of buying the red-wax-covered Edam, try one of the many varieties of Gouda. Mature Gouda *(overjarige kaas)* has a rich, salty taste and crumbly texture, while young Gouda *(meikaas)* is fresh and curdy. This cheese is also sold with cumin *(leidsekaas)* or cloves *(nagelkaas) (see p226)*.

Chocolates

VERKADE AND DROSTE are the best-known makes of chocolate in the Netherlands. For a treat, visit **Pompadour**, for its delicious handmade chocolates, or a branch of the upscale Belgian chocolate specialist, **Leonidas**.

Beers and Spirits

THE DUTCH ARE knowledgeable beer drinkers. Along with brand-name lagers like Heineken, Grolsch and Amstel, a huge range of bottled beers are offered. Local specialties include Zatte, a rare, bottle-fermented beer and Wieckse Witte, a white beer. Specialty shops like **De Bierkoning** offer the widest choice and best advice.

The Dutch spirit *jenever*, the "father" of gin, is often sold in stone bottles and flavored with herbs or fruit *(see p48)*.

Pottery and Glassware

BLUE-AND-WHITE POTTERY is stocked by most tourist stores, but only items with a certificate are real delftware. **Rinascimento** and **Focke & Meltzer** sell the real thing from De Porceleyne Fles, one of the original delft potteries.

The Jordaan is the best place to hunt for modern pottery, while **Glasgalerie Kuhler** has a stunning range of modern glass, and **Het Klei Kollektief** offers an ever-changing choice of bright ceramics.

Posters and Prints

THE BEST PLACES to find good reproductions of paintings are in museum stores. **Art Unlimited** offers an excellent selection of the less famous Dutch scenes. A fascinating range of old etchings can be found at **Old Prints** and among the stalls at the Oudemanshuispoort *(see p61)*.

Directory

Department Stores

De Bijenkorf
Damrak 1.
Map 7 B2.
621 8080.

Hema
Reguliersbreestraat 22.
Map 7 C5.
624 6506.
Nieuwendijk 174.
Map 7 B2.
623 4176.

Maison de Bonneterie
Rokin 140–142.
Map 7 B4.
626 2162.

Metz & Co
Keizersgracht 455.
Map 7 A5.
624 8810.

Vroom & Dreesman
Kalverstraat 201.
Map 7 B5.
622 0171.

Markets Outside the City

Oosterse Markt and Zwarte Markt
Industriegbied aan de Buitenlanden, Beverwijk Oost (near Haarlem).
(025) 126 2626.

Specialty Shops

Capsicum Natuurstoffen
Oude Hoogstraat 1.
Map 7 C3.
623 1016.

Christmas World
Nieuwezijds Voorburgwal 137–9. **Map** 7 B3.
622 7047.

Condomerie Het Gulden Vlies
Warmoesstraat 141.
Map 7 C2. *627 4174.*

Copenhagen 1001 Kralen
Rozengracht 54.
Map 1 B4.
624 3681.

Hooy & Co
Kloveniersburgwal 12.
Map 8 D3.
624 3041.

Hot Shop
Nieuwe Hoogstraat 24.
Map 7 C3.
625 5850.

Koffie Keizer
Prinsengracht 180.
Map 1 B4.
624 0823.

Party House
Rozengracht 93b.
Map 1 B4.
624 7851.

Stilett
Damstraat 14.
Map 7 B3.
625 2854.

Vliegertuig
Gasthuismolensteeg 8.
Map 7 A3.
623 3450.

Books, Newspapers and Magazines

The American Book Center
Kalverstraat 185.
Map 7 B5.
625 5537.

Lambiek
Kerkstraat 78.
Map 7 A5.
626 7543.

De Slegte
Kalverstraat 48–52.
Map 7 B3.
622 5933.

WH Smith
Kalverstraat 152.
Map 7 B4.
638 3821.

Fashion and Clothes

Agnès B
Rokin 126.
Map 7 B4.
627 1465.

Dr. Adams
Oude Doelenstraat 5.
Map 7 C3.
622 3734.

Hobbit
Van Baerlestraat 44.
Map 4 D3.
664 0779.

Mac & Maggie
Kalverstraat 6 & 172.
Maps 7 B3 & 7 B5.
628 1039.

MEXX
PC Hooftstraat 118.
Map 4 D3.
675 0171.

Pauw
Leidsestraat 16. **Map** 7 A5.
626 5698.

Puck en Hans
Rokin 66. **Map** 7 B4.
625 5889.

Sissy Boy
Kalverstraat 210.
Map 7 B4.
626 0088.

Zipper
Huidenstraat 7.
Map 7 A4.
623 7302.

Antiques and Furnishings

Amsterdam Antiques Gallery
Nieuwe Spiegelstraat 34.
Map 4 F2.
625 3371.

Christie's
Cornelis Schuytstraat 57.
Map 3 C4.
575 5255.

De Haas
Kerkstraat 155.
Map 4 F2.
626 5952.

Object Art Deco
Leliegracht 4. **Map** 7 A2.
627 1622.

Sotheby's
Rokin 102. **Map** 7 B4.
627 5656.

Tut Tut
Elandsgracht 109, Looier Markt. **Map** 1 A5.
627 7960.

Flowers and Bulbs

Gerda's Bloemenwinkel
Runstraat 16. **Map** 4 E1.
624 2912.

Riviera
Herenstraat 2–6.
Map 7 A1.
622 7675.

Diamonds

Stoeltie Diamonds
Wagenstraat 13–17.
Map 8 D5.
623 7601.

Cheese

Albert Heijn
Waterlooplein 129–31.
Map 8 E4. *624 1249.*
Many other branches.

Chocolates

Leonidas
Damstraat 11. **Map** 7 B3.
625 3497.

Pompadour
Huidenstraat 12.
Map 7 A4.
623 9554.

Beers and Spirits

De Bierkoning
Paleisstraat 125.
Map 7 B3.
625 2336.

Pottery and Glassware

Focke & Meltzer
PC Hooftstraat 65–7.
Map 4 E3.
664 2311.

Galleria d'Arte Rinascimento
Prinsengracht 170.
Map 1 B4.
622 7509.

Glasgalerie Kuhler
Prinsengracht 134.
Map 1 B4.
638 0230.

Het Klei Kollektief
Hartenstraat 19.
Map 7 A3.
622 5727.

Posters and Prints

Art Unlimited
Keizersgracht 510.
Map 7 A5.
624 8419.

Old Prints
Spiegelgracht 27.
Map 4 F2.
628 8852.

Entertainment in Amsterdam

Amsterdam offers a diverse array of world-class entertainment. A variety of performances are staged in hundreds of places throughout the city, ranging from the century-old Concertgebouw *(see p128)* to the 17th-century IJsbreker café on the Amstel *(see p248)*. The Dutch passion for American jazz draws international greats like BB King, Pharaoh Sanders and Nina Simone to annual events such as the Blues Festival and Drum Rhythm Festival *(see p50)*. The city's most popular events take place in the summer and include the Holland Festival *(see p51)* and the World Roots Festival *(see p51)*. There is a huge choice of multilingual plays and movies throughout the year. There is also plenty of free entertainment from the multitude of street performers and live bands in late-night bars and cafés.

Entertainment Information

The most useful source of entertainment information is *Uitkrant*, a free listings magazine *(see p256)*. It is printed monthly and is available from bookstores, cafés and tourist offices. Although written in Dutch, it is easy to follow and offers the most comprehensive daily listings of what's going on.

Amsterdam's tourist office, the **VVV** *(see also p256)*, also publishes an English-language listings magazine every two weeks called *What's On in Amsterdam*. It can be picked up for a nominal fee at VVV offices and some newsstands, or free issues can be found in selected hotels and restaurants. Daily newspapers such as *De Volkskrant, Het Parool, NRC Handelsblad* and *De Telegraaf* publish their own listings on Thursdays, although they are mainly excerpts from *Uitkrant*.

Late-night bar in the Red Light District

Another popular English-language guide is *Time Out Amsterdam*, which is published monthly and gives a more critical view of music, art and film. Along the same lines and focusing on a more youthful audience is the free Dutch magazine *Agenda*, found in most bars and cafés.

Booking Tickets

Amsterdam's major classical music, opera and dance performances, such as those by the Dutch National Ballet, are likely to be sold out weeks ahead of time. It is advisable to book tickets in advance to get the day, time and seats of your choice. For most other events, it is possible to buy tickets on the same day.

The main reservations office for entertainment and all cultural activities is the **AUB** (Amsterdam Uitburo), which is located next to the Stadsschouwburg *(see p111)* in Leidseplein. You can make reservations, pick up tickets in advance (a booking fee is charged) and obtain information in person or over the telephone. You can also make bookings at the venue itself, or through the VVV offices or the **Dutch Tourist Information Office**, which offers a booking service for theaters. Tickets to major rock concerts can be obtained at the VVV, AUB, **Nieuwe Muziek Handel** and at some of the large record shops in the city center. Although some of the most

The Stopera complex, home to the Dutch national opera and ballet companies

The Neo-Classical-style pediment of the Concertgebouw *(see p128)*

popular club dates need to be booked in advance, entrance to nightclubs like the Paradiso and De Melkweg *(see pp110–11)* can usually be bought at the door. Going to the movies is popular with Amsterdammers, so it is advisable to get tickets in the afternoon for evening performances during a movie's opening week. Most multi-screen theaters provide a Dutch-speaking automated booking service. All booking offices are usually open from Monday to Saturday, between 9am and 6pm, or later. Credit cards are generally not accepted and it is important to collect reserved tickets at least an hour before the show starts, or the tickets may be resold.

Theater sign on Nes *(see p74)*

Discount Tickets

Entry to some performances can be obtained at bargain prices for holders of the Cultureel Jongeren Passport (CJP). Valid for one year, it is available to anyone under the age of 26 for *f* 20. Some hotels include discounts to certain cultural events as part of their package deals, so check details with your travel agent. Theaters usually offer a 30 percent discount from Monday to Thursday. Several venues, such as the Concertgebouw *(see p128)* and the Westerkerk *(see p90)*, have free lunch-time concerts throughout the year.

Facilities for the Disabled

Nearly all Amsterdam's major theaters, movie and concert halls have unrestricted wheelchair access and assistance is always available. A number of the city's smaller venues, however, are housed in old buildings not designed with the disabled in mind. Places like the IJsbreker *(see p248)* will make special arrangements if they are notified beforehand. Movie theaters also provide facilities for the visually and hearing-impaired. Always telephone the box office a couple of days before your visit and specify what you need.

Open-Air Entertainment

As Amsterdammers are avid supporters of theater and classical and contemporary music, there are plenty of open-air events going on in the summer. In the heart of the city, the Vondelpark open-air theater *(see p128)* stages a wide variety of free concerts and theater performances. The restored turn-of-the-century Nederlands Filmmuseum *(see p129)* is housed in a pavilion in the park. During the summer, free screenings and documentaries are shown, as well as silent movies that are sometimes accompanied by live music.

The Prinsengracht classical music concert *(see p51)* is performed in August on a group of canal barges. On the outskirts of the city, the scenic Amsterdamse Bos *(see p155)* is the setting for productions of Shakespeare, Chekhov and other classical dramatists, staged in the open-air theater. In the south, Amstelpark *(see p154)* is the spot for De Parade each July *(see p51)*. Amsterdammers also enjoy rowing on the Amstel, where rowing clubs operate from a boathouse near Amstelpark.

Useful Addresses

AUB
Leidseplein 26. **Map** 4 E2.
☎ *621 1211.*

Dutch Tourist Information Office
Damrak 35. **Map** 7 C2.
☎ *638 2800.*

Nieuwe Muziek Handel
Leidsestraat 50. **Map** 7 A5.
☎ *623 7321.*

VVV
Stationsplein 10. **Map** 8 D1.
☎ *06 3403 4066.*
Leidseplein 106. **Map** 4 E2.
☎ *06 3403 4066.*

Customers enjoying café life in the popular Thorbeckeplein

Theater, Dance and Film

THEATER AND DANCE are important aspects of cultural life in Amsterdam, and performances take place throughout the year at dozens of sites all over the city. Experimental theater can be found in one of the oldest streets in the city, along the Nes *(see p74)*. Theaters on the Nes, such as De Brakke Grond, are also popular spots for radical theater productions. The city's main locations for dance include the Felix Meritis, Meervaart, Muziektheater, Stadsschouwburg and the Dutch Dance Laboratory, for experimental productions. The Dutch love movies and, though Amsterdam has only a few large movie-theater complexes, there is a surprising number of places that show a variety of movies, from first-run, mainstream and art, to foreign-language, revival and gay.

THEATER AND CABARET

AMSTERDAM HAS more than 50 theaters and boasts a number of English-speaking companies. **De Stalhouderij**, a converted stable in the Jordaan, is home to the Stalhouderij company. This is a collective of Dutch, English, American and Australian actors and directors. Performances are held in an intimate setting, and usually attract audiences of around 35 people. The Toneelgroep Amsterdam is the resident theater company at **Stadsschouwburg** *(see p111)*, and the **Theater Bellevue** and the **Felix Meritis** *(see p113)* are both important spots for touring companies.

Experimental theater can be found at a range of locations throughout Amsterdam, including the **Westergasfabriek** and the former public bathhouse, **De Bochel** (Hunchback), which is home to a resident theater cooperative of the same name. De Trust is a small theater company that was founded in 1988 and specializes in translating Austrian and German plays, while the Orkater musical theater company often holds performances at Stadsschouwburg and the Theater Bellevue.

The annual Holland Festival *(see p51)* offers a prestigious series of opera, theater and dance performances. It features international talent such as Peter Brook, Peter Zadek and John Jesurum. The International Theater School Festival presents innovative performances at **De Brakke Grond**, **Frascati** and other places on the Nes *(see p74)* at the end of June. The **Soeterijn Theatre** has a full program of lively productions from developing countries.

Downriver from the Muziektheater, near the smart Amstel Inter-Continental *(see p223)*, the **Koninklijk Theater Carré** plays host to long-running musicals such as *Les Misérables* and *Cyrano*. This is often the setting for elegant premieres attended by members of the Dutch royal family. Closer to the Muziektheater and also facing the Amstel is the charming 17th-century **De Kleine Komedie**. It can seat an audience of up to 500 and offers a perfect setting for cabaret. It also features stand-up comedy and occasionally has English-language theater productions. Although De Kleine Komedie is closed throughout the summer, such is its reputation in Europe, that bookings must be made at least three months in advance.

Summer outdoor theater can be seen at the **Vondelpark** open-air theater *(see p128)* and at the Amsterdamse Bos *(see p155)*, a woodland park on the edge of town. Here, a pathway lined with Classical Greek statuary leads to a 1,800-seat amphitheater, the venue for performances of Shakespeare and Chekhov. In the south of Amsterdam, the Amstelpark *(see p154)* is the venue for De Parade, a tent city erected each summer (late July/early August) where international dance, theater and circus acts perform. Merry-making often carries on into the early morning hours.

DANCE

THE NETHERLANDS possesses two world-class ballet companies, the Dutch National Ballet and the Nederlands Dans Theater (NDT). The Dutch National Ballet is housed in the 1,600-seat **Muziektheater** *(see p63)*, which provides magnificent views along the Amstel river, and is renowned for its classical and modern repertoire.

The NDT regularly performs in theaters throughout the city. Ballets from the Czech artistic director, Jiri Kylian, form the majority of the programming. In addition to the core company, the NDT also has two other companies, NDT2 and NDT3. NDT2 is a younger company made up of dancers aged 18–21 who perform the work of established choreographers such as Hans van Manen. It also performs the works of younger choreographers such as Lionel Hoche and Paul Lightfoot. NDT3 is composed of former members of the original Nederlands Dans Theater. These highly experienced dancers, who are all over the age of 40, perform shows of unparalleled technical expertise and control.

Dance is often performed at Stadsschouwburg and at the Felix Meritis, Amsterdam's 18th-century concert hall and one of its earliest performance venues. Westergasfabriek, the former gasworks, also holds dance performances.

Amsterdam is a laboratory for experimental dance, and many innovative performances can be seen throughout the city. They are not confined to any one place though, so it is best to check the entertainment listings, such as *Uitkrant* and *Time Out Amsterdam (see p256)*, for full details. Experimental dance can be enjoyed regularly at top venues like the Stadsschouwburg and the **Meervaart**. Companies to look out for include Introdans, who combine jazz with flamenco alongside other varieties of ethnic dance, and Opus One, who mix jazz, classical ballet and tap. Needless to say, the Nederlands Dans Theater's repertoire also includes experimental dance routines.

The Holland Festival in June *(see p51)* is used as the principal platform for premieres of shows by top choreographers from both the Nederlands Dans Theater and the Dutch National Ballet. The International Theater School Festival, also in June, focuses increasingly on dance, with performances taking place in the historic street of Nes *(see p74)*, which is one of the very oldest parts of the city.

Film

Amsterdammers love going to the movies, and there are more than 45 theaters in the city. All movies are screened in the original language with subtitles. Movie lovers should not miss the plush Art Deco Tuschinski Theater *(see p123)*. Constructed between 1918 and 1921, this theater features a luxurious foyer, stained-glass windows, tables, sofas and lamps. First-run movies often open at the Tuschinski, and this is often the place to catch public appearances by Dutch and international movie stars.

It is easy to find out which movies are showing where, as each theater has a listing at its entrance, and details are also posted in bars and cafés.

Programs change on a Thursday, and most new movie listings, carried in the daily newspapers, are printed on that day. *De Filmkrant* is a highly regarded, free monthly movie magazine that carries complete listings, which are written in Dutch but are very easy to understand. The ticket prices vary from *f* 12–18, depending on whether it is a matinee or an evening screening, although some longer movies can command a slightly higher admission price.

Some of the larger movie complexes offer afternoon matinees during the week and these usually begin at 2pm. On the weekend the schedule varies. Many of the mainstream theaters, such as the **City** and the **Alhambra**, often schedule several special showings of children's movies on the weekend. Seldom, if ever, home to a first-run or European premiere, movies at the Alhambra theater tend to run until every last person in Amsterdam has seen them.

Evening shows usually begin at either 6:30pm or 7pm, and there is a second showing at 9pm or 9:30pm, although a few theaters have an 8pm screening. Be prepared for the intermission, which is known as the *pauze*. This is a 15-minute obligatory break that is usually scheduled to coincide exactly with the most exciting scene of the movie.

If you suddenly get the urge to see a movie and don't particularly mind what it is, check out Leidseplein *(see p110)*, one of the biggest gathering areas in Amsterdam where movie theaters, cafés, restaurants and bars abound.

First-run and mainstream theaters that are found within a two-minute walking distance of Leidseplein include the **Calypso** and the **Bellevue Cinerama**, which are two separate and fairly glittery complexes that are right next to each other and share the same box office. There is also the high-profile, seven-screen, 2,094-seat **City** complex.

Revival and art-house theaters near Leidseplein include the **Alfa**, a former dance hall that is tucked behind the ABN Bank that overlooks Leidseplein (walk down the alley between the bank and De Bailie *(see p49)*, a popular theater bar). There is also the Cinecenter, on a side street just off the main square across from De Melkweg *(see p110)*; and for a real treat, **Bioscope de Uitkijk**, which is a short walk along Leidsestraat to Prinsengracht. This small 158-seat theater specializes in movie classics and, best of all, refuses ever to indulge in the dreaded *pauze*. Dating from 1913, De Uitkijk is Amsterdam's oldest theater.

Directory

Theater and Cabaret

De Bochel
Andreas Bonnstraat 28.
Map 5 C4.
☎ *668 5102.*

De Brakke Grond
Vlaams Cultureel Centrum, Nes 45.
Map 7 C3.
☎ *626 6866.*

De Kleine Komedie
Amstel 56–58.
Map 5 B3.
☎ *626 5917.*

Felix Meritis
Keizersgracht 324.
Map 1 B5.
☎ *623 1311.*

Frascati
Nes 59.
Map 7 B4.
☎ *626 6866.*

Koninklijk Theater Carré
Amstel 115–125.
Map 5 B3.
☎ *622 5225.*

Soeterijn Theatre
Linnaeusstraat 2.
Map 6 E3.
☎ *568 8500.*

Stadsschouwburg
Leidseplein 26.
Map 4 E2.
☎ *624 2311.*

De Stalhouderij
1e Bloemdwarsstraat 4.
Map 1 B4.
☎ *626 2282.*

Theater Bellevue
Leidsekade 90. **Map** 4 D1.
☎ *624 7248.*

Westergasfabriek
Haarlemmerweg 10.
Map 1 A1. ☎ *621 1211.*

Vondelpark
Map 4 D3.

Dance

Meervaart
Osdorpplein 205.
☎ *610 7498.*

Muziektheater
Waterlooplein 22.
Map 8 D5. ☎ *625 5455.*

See also under
Felix Meritis
Stadsschouwburg
Westergasfabriek

Film

Alfa
Hirschgebouw, Leidseplein. **Map** 4 E2.
☎ *627 8806.*

Alhambra
Weteringschans 134.
Map 4 E2.
☎ *623 3192.*

Bioscope de Uitkijk
Prinsengracht 452.
Map 4 E2.
☎ *623 7460.*

Calypso/Bellevue Cinerama
Marnixstraat 400.
Map 4 D1.
☎ *623 4876.*

City
Leidseplein. **Map** 4 E2.
☎ *623 4579.*

Classical Music and Opera

AMSTERDAM IS A CITY with a long and rich tradition in classical music and opera. The principal orchestral halls house some of the world's finest musical events. The city has also acquired a reputation as a center for early music and organ recitals, with performances in traditional settings such as the English Reformed Church or the Oude Kerk. In summer, concerts can be enjoyed as you relax in one of the city's beautiful parks.

ORCHESTRAL, CHAMBER AND CHORAL MUSIC

AMSTERDAM'S music centerpiece is the **Concertgebouw** *(see p168)*, famous for its acoustics and home to the celebrated Royal Concertgebouw Orchestra. International orchestras and soloists come here regularly, and each summer it hosts Robeco Groep concerts, which are famous for showcasing young talent. Early music is also performed here, often by the world-famous Amsterdam Baroque Orchestra and the Orchestra of the Eighteenth Century.

The **Beurs van Berlage** *(see p78)* was originally the city's stock and commodities exchange and is now the residence of the Netherlands Philharmonic Orchestra. Many of the country's fine orchestras and chamber choirs perform here. The **RAI** is principally a convention center, but it is often the setting for classical music and opera events. The **Tropenmuseum** *(see pp152–3)* often features traditional music from developing countries. Modern classical music, opera and choirs can also be heard at De Melkweg *(see pp110–11)* and the Paradiso *(see p251)*.

Although **Cristofori's** main business is buying, restoring and selling grand pianos, it also organizes orchestral, chamber and choral concerts. Many performers are internationally renowned artists who can often be called upon to talk about their work before or after a performance.

The **IJsbreker**, which overlooks the Amstel, was once a stopping-point for 17th-century icebreakers. Today, it is the most popular place for innovative modern music.

MUSIC IN CHURCHES

CHURCHES in Amsterdam offer concerts throughout the year. The city prides itself on its 42 historic church organs, and those in the **Oude Kerk** *(see pp68–9)* and the **Nieuwe Kerk** *(see pp76 – 7)* are particularly magnificent.

Carillon concerts are often held in the Oude Kerk and, at lunchtime, on Tuesdays in the **Westerkerk** *(see p90)*. The 17th-century **English Reformed Church** holds concerts that range from Baroque to modern. In the summer, free lunch-time concerts are given by new ensembles and young musicians – monthly programs are available from the church. The **Thomaskerk**, built only a few decades ago to serve the south of the city, holds a free lunch-time concert every other Tuesday.

OPERA

BUILT IN 1988, the **Muziektheater** houses the Stadhuis (town hall) and the Dutch National Opera. Its nickname, the Stopera, is a combination of both names *(see p63)*. It is one of Europe's most up-to-date theaters and features an internationally famous repertoire, as well as lesser-known and some experimental works. Opera can also be seen at the Stadsschouwburg *(see p111)* on Leidseplein. More experimental opera is performed at the **Westergasfabriek** and sometimes at nightclubs such as the Paradiso and De Melkweg *(see p251)*. Also, check the Holland Festival listings for world premieres *(see p51)*.

OPEN-AIR CONCERTS

THE PRINSENGRACHT concert *(see p51)* takes place in late August. Musicians perform on barges on the canal in front of the Pulitzer Hotel *(see p221)*. Concerts also take place in the Vondelpark open-air theater and the Amsterdamse Bos *(see p155)*, and at various other parks throughout the city.

DIRECTORY

ORCHESTRAL, CHAMBER AND CHORAL MUSIC

Beurs van Berlage
Damrak 243.
Map 7 C2.
627 0466.

Concertgebouw
Concertgebouwplein 2–6.
Map 4 D4.
671 8345.

Cristofori
Prinsengracht 579.
(near Molenpad)
Map 4 E1.
626 8485.

IJsbreker
Weesperzijde 23.
Map 5 C4.
668 1805.

RAI
Europaplein.
549 1212.

Tropenmuseum
Linnaeusstraat 2.
Map 6 E3.
568 8215.

MUSIC IN CHURCHES

English Reformed Church
Begijnhof 48.
Map 7 B4.
624 9665.

Nieuwe Kerk
Dam.
Map 7 B2.
628 8168.

Oude Kerk
Oudekerksplein 23.
Map 7 C2.
624 9183 or 625 8284.

Thomaskerk
Prinses Irenestraat 36.
676 7587.

Westerkerk
Prinsengracht 281.
Map 1 B4. *624 7766.*

OPERA

Muziektheater
Waterlooplein 22.
Map 8 D5.
625 5455.

Westergasfabriek
Haarlemmerweg 10.
Map 1 A1. *581 0425.*

Pop, Rock and Nightclubs

AMSTERDAM is bursting with live music. From the omnipresent street entertainers to a whole variety of music forums and nightclubs, as well as countless music cafés, it is hard to avoid the city's rock, pop and club scene. Concerts and clubs tend to be inexpensive and relaxed, with few places having a strict door policy or dress code. Local bands and musicians are encouraged, and many places receive subsidies from the local council, so tickets, with the exception of the big-name concerts, rarely cost more than *f* 15. Some of the best bands can be enjoyed for the price of a drink. Fierce competition means that concerts and clubs come and go faster than the city's trams. For the latest information and gig guides, consult the free *Pop Uitlijst,* available from the AUB ticket service and VVV tourist offices *(see p245)*; both sell advance tickets for major concerts. The free magazine *Uitkrant* and English-language *What's On* and *Time Out Amsterdam* all carry concert listings *(see p244).*

Pop and Rock

MANY BIG NAMES tend to bypass Amsterdam and head for Rotterdam's Ahoy and Utrecht's Vredenburg stadiums instead. However, mainstream pop concerts are occasionally held at the RAI *(see p151).* Middle-of-the-road artists tend to play in large theaters, such as the Theater Carré *(see p145),* **Nieuwe de la Mar** and the Theater Bellevue *(see p247).* The Marcanti Plaza and Escape nightclubs *(see p251)* host dance and soul acts.

For most Amsterdammers, rock and pop are synonymous with two places – the **Paradiso** and **De Melkweg**. The Paradiso, housed in a converted church just off Leidseplein, is more prestigious. De Melkweg is housed in a former dairy, hence the name the "Milky Way" *(see pp110–11).*

Both the Paradiso and De Melkweg offer an extremely varied program: rock, pop, dance, rap and world music. The standards range from chart-toppers and cult heroes to local hopefuls trying their luck at one of the regular talent nights. Big-name bands that come to play in Amsterdam invariably turn up at one of these two places.

Of the commercial venues, one of the most sophisticated is **Naar Boven**, offering pop, rock, blues and jazz music to a cocktail-sipping audience in designer surroundings. Not far away, **Parker's** features a similarly wide variety of music to Naar Boven but the spot itself is slightly less luxurious. The brown café **De Korte Golf** opts for guitar rock and attracts a mainly student crowd, while followers of rock 'n' roll should visit the **Cruise-Inn**. The recently refurbished **Arena** is part of the Sleep-In budget hotel *(see p223),* where locals and backpackers cram in for a diet of grunge, metal and punk rock. British, American and eastern European bands also perform regularly. Several other budget hotels, such as the **Hotel Kabul** and **The Last Waterhole**, found in the Red Light District *(see p60),* also feature live rock.

Blues music alternates with rock at the loud and crowded **De Kroeg**. Smoky, sweaty and beer-soaked, this place may not seem particularly inviting, but the atmosphere is convivial. Combine this with a visit to the **Korsakoff**, where anything goes – from heavy metal to hiphop. Primarily a dance club, Korsakoff also hosts bands on Friday and Saturday nights.

One experience unique to Amsterdam is "squat-rock." Some of the city's abandoned building (squats) frequently host gigs on weekends. The emphasis is on alternative music – punk, rap and experimental. The events are irregular and publicized by posters and flyers. The best spots are **PH31** and **Vrankrijk**.

From May to September, free concerts are held every Sunday afternoon in the Vondelpark open-air theater *(see pp128–9),* often featuring some of the country's top pop acts.

Jazz

THERE MAY WELL BE more jazz clubs in Amsterdam than anywhere else in the world. The relaxing rhythms of jazz music are perfectly suited to the mood of the brown cafés and bars *(see pp46–9).*

The city's jazz flagship is the **Bimhuis**, a place that takes its music seriously. Commonly known as the "Bim," it could be described as pretentious, but it is the best place for contemporary jazz, and it has an international reputation.

The many jazz cafés dotted around the city are very popular. Most of them are small brown cafés where local bands perform. Late opening and free entry boost their appeal, although drinks cost a little above average. Most cafés hold weekly jam sessions, when anyone can take the stage.

Around Leidseplein are the **Alto Jazz Café**, the **Bourbon Street** and the **Bamboo Bar**. Alto is best on Wednesday evenings when Hans Dulfer, the so-called "father" of the Amsterdam jazz scene, is in residence. His daughter Candy is a regular attraction at the **De Heeren van Aemstel**. **De Engelbewaarder** has popular jam sessions on Sunday afternoons and **'t Heerenhuys** is also worth checking out. In the old port, the **Joseph Lam Jazz Club** offers Dixieland jazz. Parker's, Naar Boven and the Vondelpark open-air theater *(see pp128–9)* are also popular jazz clubs. Grand cafés such as **Café Zilver** and **Café du Lac** have jazz on Saturday evenings and Sunday afternoons.

The Dutch passion for jazz turns to frenzy in the summer, with a festival in almost every town. In July, the North Sea Jazz Festival *(see p51),* held in Den Haag, attracts some of the world's biggest names in jazz. The May Drum Rhythm Festival *(see p50)* explores the influences of rock, dance and world music on jazz.

World Music and Folk

In the Netherlands the world-music scene has been heavily influenced by its many immigrant communities. The West Indian, Indonesian, Maghreb, West African, Surinamese and Turkish traditions are thriving, and are actively encouraged by the city's authorities. A varied program of ethnic, classical and popular concerts is offered at the Soeterijn theater *(see p246)*. Groups from around the world appear there on a regular basis, with a strong emphasis on Asian music.

The **Akhnaton** is a multicultural youth center. Its main strengths are Caribbean, African and Arabic music. In addition, there are regular performances by reggae, rap, and salsa artists. These styles also show up on the dance nights.

De Melkweg, and to a lesser extent the Paradiso and Arena, also schedule world music – De Melkweg hosts a colorful World Roots Festival *(see p51)* in June. Live salsa is a nightly attraction at the **Caneçao Rio** bar, and on weekends in the foyer of the **Iboya** theater.

The indigenous folk music of the Netherlands is an acquired taste. It sounds like a combination of traditional German folk music, French *chanson* and old sea shanties. Large cafés around Rembrandtplein, including the **Rembrandt** and **Hof van Holland**, provide folk music for tourist consumption. For a more authentic experience, head for the Jordaan. In bars like **De Twee Zwaantjes** and **Café Nol** regulars sometimes burst into joyous song.

Anglo-Saxon and Celtic-style folk plus blues appear at **De String**. Some Irish pubs like **Mulligan's** and **The Blarney Stone** also have Celtic music.

Nightclubs

Amsterdam is known for its trendsetting nightclub scene. There is little pretension here, and the mood is relaxed and carefree.

Most clubs open at 11pm but don't really get going before 1am. They usually close at 4am during the week, and 5am on Friday and Saturday nights. Entrance prices are relatively low and drinks are reasonably priced. Few clubs enforce a strict dress code, but they do reserve the right to refuse admission. It is an established custom to tip the doormen approximately *f* 5 on the way out. Amsterdam was one of the very first cities to embrace house music during the late 1980s. It still dominates most clubs, but there is now more variety offered. DJs and music vary from one night to the next, so check listings for details.

The only exclusive club is the **Roxy**. This is a converted theater, where the beautiful people of Amsterdam gather to rub shoulders with whichever stars are in town. Lines do develop on weekends and there is a members-only policy, though it often applies only during busy times.

The nearby **Richter**, with its earthquake-inspired decor, attracts the Roxy's spillover and plays similar music, but is easier to get into. Another lively competitor is **Seymour Likely 2**. Organized by a group of artists, it is well worth paying a visit for the quirky decor alone – chains and padded walls, novelty art and barrack-style bunk beds as seats.

The classiest place of all for dancing is the **Lido**, the disco downstairs from the Holland Casino. This is evening dress territory, but the atmosphere is electric on weekends. A less upscale version is **Hollywood**.

Far more friendly and less pretentious is **Mazzo**. Though small and intimate, it attracts a young and trendy crowd that prefers to enjoy the latest progressive house sounds from the top DJs without having to dress up for the occasion.

Amsterdam's students have established their own club, **Dansen Bij Jansen**. The two sweaty dance floors in this rambling club are packed on weekends. You will need a student card to get in, but provided you look the part there should be no problem.

The leading nonhouse club in town is the **Soul Kitchen**, with its varied and enjoyable menu of soul, funk and jazz-dance. For a varied choice of music, the **Odeon** plays house music on the ground floor, '60s–'80s classic disco upstairs and jazz-dance in the basement. The city's two biggest dance halls are **Escape** and the **Marcanti Plaza**, which attract a young from out-of-town crowd each weekend. The nightclubs and discos around Leidseplein, such as **Cash** and **Bunnies**, are more like extended bars with small dance floors, catering to tourists and attracting a wide age range. Mainstream and chart music tend to be played.

Gay Clubs

Clubbing is at the heart of Amsterdam's gay scene. The best-known venue is **iT**, a large and glitzy disco off Rembrandtplein. The techno sounds and camp floor shows attract a trendy, mainly gay male crowd. Thursdays and Sundays are officially "mixed" nights. This kind of crossover is not unusual, and most gay clubs will rarely turn away women or straight men.

April's Exit, in Reguliersdwarsstraat, is a smaller, less-camp version of iT. Up the road, the designer café **Havana** has a small, friendly dance floor upstairs, which is open until 1am, and until 2am on weekends. There is no admission charge and it is a good location for meeting people.

Less popular, but still lively, the **Homolulu** offers a mixture of house, pop and hi-NRG sounds. On weekends, the gay community center, **COC Amsterdam**, organizes a popular mixed disco. **De Trut** is housed in the basement of a famous former squat and packs in young gays and lesbians on Sunday nights. The decor is seedy, but the dance floor is big and the drinks are cheap.

For lesbians, there are fewer options – details of events can be obtained from the **Gay and Lesbian Switchboard**. One regular fixture is the Mona Lisa party, held on a monthly basis at **Vrouwenhuis** (women's house). The music ranges from blues and soul in the early evening and then moves on to house. The decor is imaginative and the atmosphere friendly.

Directory

Pop and Rock

Arena
's-Gravesandestraat 51. **Map** 6 D4. *694 7444.*

Cruise-Inn
Zeeburgerdijk 272. **Map** 6 F2. *692 7188.*

Hotel Kabul
Warmoesstraat 38–42. **Map** 8 D2. *623 7158.*

Korsakoff
Lijnbaansgracht 161. **Map** 4 D1. *625 7854.*

De Korte Golf
Reguliersdwarsstraat 41. **Map** 7 B5. *626 5435.*

De Kroeg
Lijnbaansgracht 163. **Map** 4 D1. *420 0232.*

The Last Waterhole
Oudezijds Armsteeg 12. **Map** 8 D2. *624 4814.*

De Melkweg
Lijnbaansgracht 234. **Map** 4 E2. *624 1777.*

Naar Boven
Reguliersdwarsstraat 12. **Map** 7 B5. *623 3981.*

Nieuwe de la Mar
Leidsekade 90. **Map** 4 D1. *623 3462.*

Paradiso
Weteringschans 6–8. **Map** 4 E2. *623 7348.*

Parker's
Voetboogstraat 5a. **Map** 7 B4. *420 1711.*

PH31
Prins Hendriklaan 31. **Map** 3 B4. *673 6850.*

Vrankrijk
Spui 216. **Map** 7 B4.

Jazz

Alto Jazz Café
Korte Leidsedwarsstraat 115. **Map** 4 E2. *626 3249.*

Bamboo Bar
Lange Leidsedwarsstraat 66. **Map** 4 E2. *624 3993.*

Bimhuis
Oudeschans 73. **Map** 8 E3. *623 1361.*

Bourbon Street
Leidsekruisstraat 6–8. **Map** 4 E2. *623 3440.*

Café du Lac
Haarlemmerstraat 118. **Map** 1 C3. *624 4265.*

Café Zilver
Rembrandtplein 19. **Map** 7 C5. *623 8101.*

De Engelbewaarder
Kloveniersburgwal 59. **Map** 8 D3. *625 3772.*

't Heerenhuys
Herengracht 114. **Map** 7 A1. *622 7685.*

De Heeren van Aemstel
Thorbeckeplein 5. **Map** 7 C5. *620 2173.*

Joseph Lam Jazz Club
Van Diemenstraat 8 (near Houtmankade). **Map** 1 B1. *622 8086.*

World Music and Folk

Akhnaton
Nieuwezijds Kolk 25. **Map** 7 C1. *624 3396.*

The Blarney Stone
Nieuwendijk 29. **Map** 7 C1. *623 3830.*

Café Nol
Westerstraat 109. **Map** 1 B3. *624 5380.*

Caneçao Rio
Lange Leidsedwarsstraat 68. **Map** 4 E2. *626 1500.*

Hof van Holland
Rembrandtplein 5. **Map** 7 C5. *623 4650.*

Iboya
Korte Leidsedwarsstraat 29. **Map** 4 E2. *623 7859.*

Mulligan's
Amstel 100. **Map** 7 C5. *622 1330.*

Rembrandt
Rembrandtplein 3. **Map** 7 C5. *623 0688.*

De String
Nes 98. **Map** 7 B3. *625 9015.*

De Twee Zwaantjes
Prinsengracht 114. **Map** 1 C3. *625 2729.*

Nightclubs

Bunnies
Korte Leidsedwarsstraat 29. **Map** 4 E2. *622 6622.*

Cash
Leidseplein 12. **Map** 4 E2. *627 6544.*

Dansen Bij Jansen
Handboogstraat 11. **Map** 7 B4. *620 1779.*

Escape
Rembrandtplein 11. **Map** 7 C5. *622 3542.*

Hollywood
Singel 447. **Map** 7 B5. *623 3984.*

Lido
Max Euweplein 62 (near Leidsekruisstraat). **Map** 4 E2. *620 1006.*

Marcanti Plaza
Jan van Galenstraat 6–8. **Map** 1 C1. *682 3456.*

Mazzo
Rozengracht 114. **Map** 1 A5. *626 7500.*

Odeon
Singel 460. **Map** 7 C5. *624 9711.*

Richter
Reguliersdwarsstraat 36. **Map** 7 B5. *626 1573.*

Roxy
Singel 465. **Map** 7 C5. *620 0354.*

Seymour Likely 2
Nieuwezijds Voorburgwal 161. **Map** 7 B2. *420 5062.*

Soul Kitchen
Amstelstraat 32. **Map** 8 D5. *620 2333.*

Gay Clubs

COC Amsterdam
Rozenstraat 14. **Map** 1 B5. *623 4079.*

April's Exit
Reguliersdwarsstraat 42. **Map** 7 B5. *625 8788.*

Gay and Lesbian Switchboard
623 6565.

Havana
Reguliersdwarsstraat 17. **Map** 7 B5. *620 6788.*

Homolulu
Kerkstraat 23. **Map** 7 A5. *624 6387.*

iT
Amstelstraat 24. **Map** 8 D5. *625 0111.*

De Trut
Bilderdijkstraat 165. **Map** 3 C1. *612 3524.*

Vrouwenhuis
Nieuwe Herengracht 95. **Map** 8 E5. *625 2066.*

CHILDREN'S AMSTERDAM

As a lively, cultural city, Amsterdam can be a fascinating place to visit with children. Its network of canals is fun to explore and many of the squares are alive with street musicians and performers. The city's many parks offer a wide range of outdoor activities and the streets are lined with tempting stores, restaurants, cafés and food stalls. Even in summer, there is no guarantee of good weather, but you can always find something to do on wet days. Some theaters and museums are geared for children and there is nearly always an English-language film showing that is suitable for children.

PRACTICAL ADVICE

If you are visiting Amsterdam with a very young child, a baby sling or pouch is essential. While the city center is small enough to be covered on foot, maneuvering a heavy stroller around the cobbled streets can be tough. Negotiating one of Amsterdam's notoriously steep flights of stairs or getting on a crowded trolley or canal boat with a stroller is virtually impossible, and they are actually banned in some of the museums.

For sightseeing, it is worth taking a boat trip. Details on the options available are on pages 276–7. Most of the operators offer discounts to children under 12 and allow toddlers to travel free. Trolleys are another efficient way to get around *(see p272)*, although they tend to be crowded at peak periods. Like all other forms of public transportation in the city, children under four ride free and under-12s travel at half price.

Children are welcome at the majority of hotels in Amsterdam *(see p212)*. Some of the bigger ones even provide babysitting facilities. If your hotel does not offer this, **Babysit Centrale Kriterion** provides reliable child care. The service is 24-hour, but bookings must be made between 5:30pm and 7pm.

BABYSITTING SERVICE

Babysit Centrale Kriterion
Roetersstraat 170.
☎ *624 5848.*

THEATERS AND MUSEUMS

Many theaters, such as the **Kindertheater Elleboog** and **De Krakeling**, hold children's shows on Wednesdays, and the Vondelpark *(see p128)* stages weekly open-air shows in summer.

Seasonal attractions include the traditional Christmas circus at the Koninklijk Theater Carré *(see p145)*. The VVV's monthly publication, *Uitkrant*, contains a complete listing, which is easy to understand, despite being written in Dutch *(see p256)*.

Rangda witch from Bali at the Kindermuseum

A number of Amsterdam's museums have sections which are geared for children. The Technology Museum NINT *(see p150)* is one of the best for older children, with its wide range of hands-on exhibits and buttons to press. The Nationaal Luchtvaartmuseum Aviodome *(see p155)* is a big favorite with anyone who is interested in airplanes and space travel. Adventurous 6- to 12-year-olds will like the exhibitions at Tropenmuseum's Kindermuseum *(see pp152–3)*, which brings to life the cultures and traditions of the developing world. Would-be pirates love climbing aboard the *Amsterdam*, a full size replica of an 18th-century East Indiaman moored outside the Nederlands Scheepvaart Museum *(see pp146–7)*. The waxworks at Madame Tussauds Scenerama *(see p74)* are also worth a visit, although small children may be upset by a few of the more gruesome exhibits. Most of Amsterdam's museums offer substantial discounts to children and toddlers under four normally get in free.

CHILDREN'S THEATERS

Kindertheater Elleboog
Passeerdersgracht 32. **Map** 4 E1.
☎ *626 9370.*

De Krakeling
Nieuwe Passeerderstraat 1. **Map** 4 D1.
☎ *624 5123.*

ZOOS AND CITY FARMS

Since Artis zoo incorporates both indoor and outdoor animal pens, along with a Planetarium and the Geologisch Museum, it is a great place to

Crocodiles basking in the Reptile House of Artis zoo *(see pp142–3)*

The full-size replica of the *Amsterdam*, outside the Scheepvaart Museum

visit whatever the weather conditions *(see pp154–5)*. Cheaper, but less extensive, animal viewing options in and around the city include the animal enclosure in the Amsterdamse Bos *(see p155)*, donkeys and llamas in the Vondelpark *(see p128)* and free-roaming Highland cattle in the Amstelpark *(see p154)*.

Sports and Recreation

Amsterdam's parks provide a whole range of activities that children will enjoy. The Vondelpark *(see p128)* has well-maintained playgrounds, free puppet shows and face-painting sessions at the Milk Bar in summer. The Amstelpark and Amsterdamse Bos have a range of activities covered on pages 154 and 155, respectively. The Electrische Museumtramlijn *(see p155)* runs regular round trips to and from the Amsterdamse Bos in vintage trolleys. You can also camp in designated campsites in this park *(see p213)*.

There are a number of indoor swimming pools on the outskirts of Amsterdam, the best of which is **Miranda Bad**, a tropical paradise with water slides, a beach and a wave machine. Indoor pools tend to close during the summer holidays and are replaced by the outdoor pools, like the municipal pool in Twiske, a rural park north of the IJ. The seaside, which is only 20 minutes away by train, has miles of clean, sandy coastline.

Perhaps the most fun can be had simply exploring Amsterdam's network of canals by renting canal bikes *(see p277)*. Should you arrive during a hard winter, when the canals are frozen, then your children will never forget the thrill of skating around the city.

Swimming Pools

Miranda Bad
De Mirandalaan 9.
☎ *644 6637.*

Eating Out

Children may not be welcome in some of the more expensive restaurants, but most places are tolerant. Many cafés and restaurants offer a children's menu such as chicken, French fries and *appelmoes* (applesauce). Don't miss tea time at the **Kinderkoek Kafe** on Wednesday afternoons, when the food is cooked and served by children. Adults are not admitted unless accompanied by a child. Amsterdam also has a good choice of pancake houses *(see p236)*, with a huge selection of toppings. Other treats include delicious *poffertjes*, tiny puffed-up pancakes loaded with butter and confectioner's sugar.

If hunger strikes when you are on the move, few children do not like French fries with mayonnaise, available at many street stalls all over town *(see p236)*.

Children's Cafés

Kinderkoek Kafe
Oudezijds Achterburgwal 193.
Map 2 D5. ☎ *625 3257.*

Shopping

Alongside an assortment of large toy stores selling anything from computer games to the latest Barbie accessories, there are also a few small stores that sell traditional wooden and handcrafted toys. Look for the exquisite dollhouse furniture at **De Kleine Nicolaas**.

Good children's clothes can be found at most department stores, but for something out of the ordinary go to **Oilily**, an exclusive children's shop that opened in 1993.

Shops for Children

De Kleine Nicolaas
Bilderdijkstraat 61. **Map** 3 C1.
☎ *616 2694.*

Oilily
PC Hooftstraat 131-133. **Map** 4 D3.
☎ *672 3361.*

Children resting weary legs outside Kort café and restaurant *(see p225)*

Survival Guide

Practical Information

Amsterdam is a cosmopolitan city and visitors should find its citizens, who are often multilingual, helpful and friendly. The official networks for helping tourists, whether with information about sights or medical attention, are efficient and straightforward. Telephones, parking meters and cash machines may seem familiar to European visitors, but other tourists will need to follow instructions closely. One of the particular pleasures of visiting the city is to enjoy the relatively car-free environment. Trolleys, water transportation, bicycles and pedestrians are all given a much higher priority in the center than motor vehicles. Indeed, the ideal ways to explore are on foot *(see pp270–71)*, or by bicycle *(see pp274–5)*.

Exploring the city on foot

The VVV office on Stationsplein, opposite Centraal Station

Tourist Information

Very few cities are as well-equipped to help visitors as Amsterdam, and in general the Netherlands has a comprehensive network of tourist information centers. The state-run organization is known as *Vereniging Voor Vreemdelingenverkeer* – literally, the "Association for Alien Traffic" – this is universally abbreviated to **VVV**, and pronounced "fay-fay-fay."

The familiar logo of the VVV

Beware of the tourist offices and accommodations agencies in the city that are not related to the VVV: the accommodations they offer can be expensive, of poor quality and sometimes found in unpleasant locations.

The VVV

There are three VVV offices in Amsterdam, and almost 450 throughout the Netherlands. The multilingual staff can provide useful information on sights, entertainment, events, transportation, walks and tours. They will also change money and book hotels, excursions, plays, shows and concerts (all for a small fee). Most VVV leaflets and maps are also available from newsstands and museums around the city. If you are seeking information before you travel, the **NBT** (Netherlands Board of Tourism) produces its own brochures, maps and useful leaflets.

Arena

This center caters especially to the independent traveler on a tight budget, and welcomes people of all ages. It comprises not only a Budget Hotel with about 600 beds *(see p223)*, but a pop concert and exhibition hall, café, restaurant and a youth information center. Arena's concert hall is the third largest in Amsterdam.

Entertainment

Posters and listings in the city's bars and cafés are an immediate guide to entertainment in Amsterdam *(see p244)*. The VVV produces an English-language magazine entitled *What's On*. This contains some useful information, but it can't match the English-language *Time Out Amsterdam*, available from most newsstands. The free monthly *Uitkrant* has comprehensive listings, and, though in Dutch, is accessible to non-Dutch speakers.

Of the other free, English-language monthly listings, *Arena* is perhaps the best. It is youthful, good for live music and has an invaluable section with services and numbers.

AUB Uitburo *(see p244)* gives information on and sells advance tickets for the city's theaters and concerts, for a tiny fee. Libraries and theaters supply entertainment handouts and display film listings.

Some of the most comprehensive Amsterdam listings, in English and Dutch

Museum Card and entrance tickets

Museum Card

The very successful Museum Card *(Museumjaarkaart)* appears expensive, but it does provide admission to more than 400 museums throughout the Netherlands. This includes all the major ones in Amsterdam, although it does not cover their special exhibitions. Valid for a year, and with separate cards for adults and under 18s, you will recoup the cost of your card after about ten visits. The card can be bought from VVV and NBT offices and all the participating museums.

Disabled Visitors

For such a forward-looking city, Amsterdam sometimes disregards the needs of people with disabilities, although there is information available *(see p213)*. While museums, galleries, movie theaters, theaters and now churches often have wheelchair access and adapted rest rooms, getting around from place to place can be a problem. Cobblestone streets make life very difficult for wheelchair users, and public toilets with easy access are virtually nonexistent.

P

KN-06-VG

Sign for disabled parking

Opening Times

Opening times for retailers in Amsterdam do vary enormously, but each store has its own hours of business posted on the door *(see p238)*. Stores right in the center of town may be open between the hours of 7am and 10pm all week, including Sundays *(see p238)*. Opening hours that are of most interest to visitors are 11am until 5pm from Monday to Saturday. In the center, Thursday is *koopavond* or shopping night, when the stores close around 9pm. Banks normally open from 9am to 4 or 5pm, though many in the city center stay open till 7pm on Thursday. The GWK *(see p260)* now runs a 24-hour service. Many of the state-run museums are closed on Monday, and open from 10am to 5pm, Tuesday to Saturday and from 1 to 5pm on Sunday. The museums also adopt these Sunday hours for all national holidays *(see p53)*, apart from New Year's Day, when they are always closed.

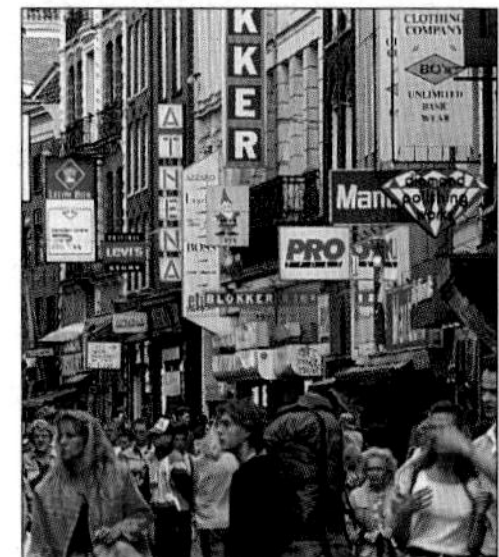

Shoppers on Kalverstraat

Language and Etiquette

People whose mother tongue is English will not have a language problem in Amsterdam. Nearly all Dutch people speak some English, but it's appreciated if you can handle a few niceties, such as saying *Dag* (Good day) before asking a Dutch person whether they speak English. This guide has a phrase book on pages 311–12. The Dutch are quite liberal in many ways, but they retain a few conventions. Expect your hand to be shaken a lot, and if you are out with a crowd, introduce yourself or people may think you are standoffish. When eating out, the Dutch tend to pay for their own share of the bill.

Directory

Tourist Information

Arena
's-Gravesandestraat 51.
Map 6 D4.
☎ *694 7444.*

Centraal Station VVV
Stationsplein 10.
Map 8 D1.
☎ *06 340 34066.*

Leidseplein VVV
Leidseplein 1.
Map 4 E2.
☎ *06 340 34066.*

Stadionplein VVV
Van Tuyll Van Serooskerkenweg 125.
☎ *06 340 34066.*

NBT Offices Worldwide

Australia
6th Floor,
5 Elizabeth Street,
Sydney, NSW 2000.
☎ *2 387 6644.*
FAX *2 223 6665.*

Canada
Suite 710, 25 Adelaide Street East, Toronto, Ontario M5C 1Y2.
☎ *(416) 363-1577.*
FAX *(416) 363-1470.*

UK
PO Box 523,
London SW1E 6NT.
☎ *0891 200 277.*
FAX *0171 828 7941.*

US
East: 21st Floor,
355 Lexington Avenue,
New York, NY 10017.
☎ *(312) 819-0300.*
FAX *(312) 819-1740.*

Central: Suite 326,
225 N. Michigan Avenue,
Chicago, IL 60601.
☎ *(312) 819-0300.*
FAX *(312) 819-1740.*

West: Suite 305,
90 New Montgomery Street,
San Francisco,
CA 94105.
☎ *(312) 819-0300.*
FAX *(312) 819-1740.*

Personal Security and Health

Policeman on wheels

After a recent clean-up by the authorities, Amsterdam is now one of the safest cities in Europe. It does have a reputation for crime, most of which is drug-related, but tourists should not be affected by this provided they act sensibly. It is a good idea, however, to take out travel insurance which should cover any loss of money or personal items. For those who do find themselves in trouble, the city has efficient emergency services and facilities ranging from an **HIV Positive Line** to a **Legal Advice Center**.

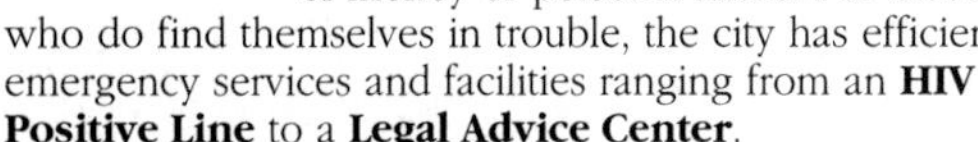

Damrak leading to Centraal Station: a place to be wary of pickpockets

Members of the armed Dutch police force

Personal Property

While Amsterdam is safer than most American and European cities, theft is still a cause for concern. Pickpockets work crowded tourist areas and on the trolleys, especially in summer, so take precautions: don't put wallets and money in back pockets, leave handbags exposed or flash cash around.

Bicycle and car theft, particularly of foreign vehicles, is also a problem. Muggings are fairly rare, but it is best to avoid parks and poorly lit places at night. Women would also be wise not to frequent bars and cafés late at night. Finally, don't take photographs of prostitutes in the Red Light District, since it is considered rude.

If you are the victim of theft or assault, report it to the nearest police station. You are required to report any personal injury. In serious cases or emergencies, call the **Emergency Services**.

Medical Treatment and Insurance

All travelers should consider purchasing travel insurance. Non-EU nationals are obliged to carry medical insurance, taken out before they arrive.

Discuss your medical coverage with your insurer before leaving the US. If you know that you will need to obtain prescriptions while you are abroad, find out in advance exactly how to do this. Your local consulate may be able to help. It is probably also a good idea to take out private insurance, which should cover sending you home in an emergency.

Minor problems can be dealt with by a drugstore *(drogist)* that stocks nonprescription drugs. For a prescription, go to a pharmacy *(apotheek)*, open from 8:30am to 5:30pm Monday to Friday. Details of pharmacies open outside normal hours are posted in all

Fire engine

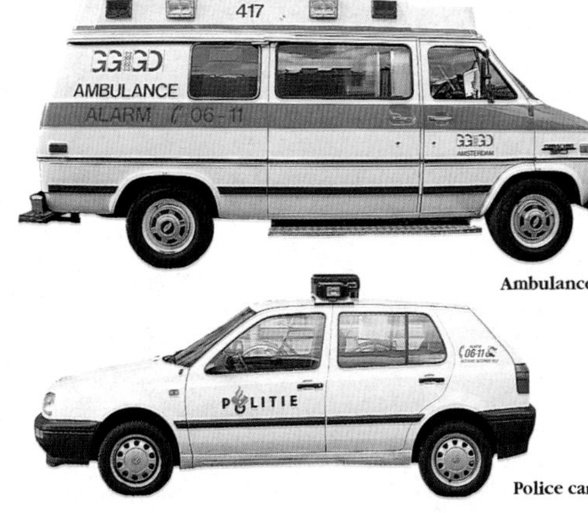

Ambulance

Police car

pharmacy windows and in the afternoon newspaper *Het Parool.* The **Central Medical Service** *(Centraal Doktersdienst)* will direct you to the nearest pharmacy open outside normal hours, and can also refer you to an on-duty GP or supply the name of a dentist.

Minor accidents are treated in hospital outpatient clinics, open 24 hours a day, and the VVV *(see p256)* can advise on these. In an emergency, make your way to a hospital with an emergency room, or call an ambulance.

MOSQUITOES

ATTRACTED by the canals, mosquitoes can be a real irritant. Residents and regular summer visitors deal with them in various ways. Burning coils, ultraviolet tubes, mosquito nets, repellent sprays and antihistamine creams and tablets are available from large pharmacies or supermarkets.

A selection of mosquito repellents

DRUGS

THOUGH SOFT DRUGS have not been legalized in the Netherlands, the police tend to ignore the possession of small amounts of marijuana. They also tolerate the sale of small amounts in designated "smoking" coffeeshops *(see p49)*. Hard drugs are a completely different matter. The Zeedijk area has been cleaned up but is still best avoided late at night, and anyone caught with hard drugs will certainly be prosecuted. Never attempt to take drugs out of the country; penalties are stiff.

Hash Museum sign *(see p61)*

LOST PROPERTY

TO HELP with insurance claims, you must report lost or stolen property as soon as possible, preferably to a police station in the vicinity of the loss. They hold recovered items for a day or so before sending them to the main police lost-and-found office. If you lose your passport, you must tell your consulate *(see p265)*. For items lost on public transportation, try **Centraal Station** or the GVB head office *(see p273)*.

DIRECTORY

PHARMACIES

Dam
Damstraat 2.
Map 7 C3.
624 4331.

Jordaan
Westerstraat 180.
Map 1 B3.
624 9252.

Koek Schaeffer & van Tijen
Vijzelgracht 19.
Map 4 F3.
623 5949.

Proton
Utrechtsestraat 86.
Map 5 A3.
624 4333.

Het Witte Kruis
Rozengracht 57.
Map 1 A5.
623 1051.

HOSPITALS

Academisch Medisch Centrum
Meibergdreef 9.
566 9111 or 566 3333.

Lucas Ziekenhuis
Jan Tooropstraat 164.
510 8911.

Onze Lieve Vrouwe Gasthuis (with emergency room)
1e Oosterparkstraat 279.
Map 6 D4. *599 9111.*

VU Academisch Ziekenhuis
De Boelelaan 1117.
444 4444.
24-hour first aid:
444 3636.

EMERGENCY SERVICES

Ambulance, fire & police
06 11.

HOTLINES

AIDS Helpline
06 022 2220.
2–10pm Mon–Fri.

Central Medical Service
06 3503 2042.

Crisis Helpline
675 7575.
9am–3am Mon–Thu, 24 hours a day Fri–Sun.

HIV Positive Line
616 6242.
1–4pm Mon, Wed & Fri; 8pm–1:30pm Tue & Thu.

Legal Advice Center
Bureau voor Rechtshulp, Spuistraat 10. **Map** 7 B1.
626 4477 (call during office hours for appointment).

SEXUAL ABUSE

De Eerste Lijn
612 7576.
10:30am–11:30pm Mon–Fri, 3:30–11:30pm Sat & Sun. (for those who have experienced violence)

TOSG
612 7576.
10:30am–11:30pm. (if you are threatened, attacked or raped)

Blijf-van-m'n-lijf-huis
(Don't Touch My Body House) *638 7636.*
24 hours a day.

POLICE

Headquarters
Elandsgracht 117.
Map 1 B5.
559 9111.

Main Police stations
Lijnbaansgracht 219.
Map 4 E2.
559 2310.

Warmoesstraat 44.
Map 7 C2.
559 2210.

LOST-AND-FOUNDS

Centraal Station
NS Lost Property Information, Stationsplein 15.
Map 8 D1.
557 8544.
7am–11pm daily.
(After 10 days, items found on trains are forwarded to NS Afdeling Gevonden Voorwerpen, Daalsedijk 4, 3500 HA Utrecht.)

Police
Stephensonstraat 18.
559 3005.
noon–3:30pm.

Banking and Local Currency

Amsterdammers are strangely partial to cash transactions and, surprisingly, credit cards are not as universally acceptable in the Netherlands as in other countries. The larger hotels, stores and most restaurants will, however, accept the major credit cards. Many will also take traveler's checks, with appropriate identification, and Eurocheques with a Eurocard. The latter is now the second-most-favored form of payment after cash.

Amsterdam has an excellent exchange network, and transactions are virtually hassle-free for visitors, particularly English speakers. There is no limit to the amount of currency you can bring into the country.

ABN-AMRO automatic cash machine

GWK exchange counter at Schiphol Airport

Checks

Traveler's checks are still a good way to carry the bulk of your money. They are useful for paying hotel bills, but if you use them in a restaurant, for example, the management is not required to pay you the change (ie, exchange money on your behalf).

If you have a European bank account, Eurocheques with a guarantee card are an easy alternative. These can be exchanged for cash in most Dutch banks.

Changing Money

You can change currency in banks *(see p257)*, **American Express** offices and post offices. These all charge a small commission when exchanging currency. The independent exchange bureaus charge an exorbitant commission and give a poor exchange rate, but the official ones, **GWK** *(grenswisselkantoorbureaux)*, are fair.

If you arrive by ferry, don't change money on the boat, where you can pay for things in dollars. Wait until you can visit the GWK just after getting off. This stays open for day and night arrivals. Avoid changing your money in hotels, since their charges tend to be very high.

Rabobank

High street bank logo

Credit Cards

The main credit cards can be used to obtain money, provided you require at least *f*300. The exchange rate is slightly better than for currency. Cards can be used in automatic cash machines at most banks and post offices. Access, Mastercard, Eurocard, American Express, Banknet, Diner's Club and Visa are the most commonly accepted, but Europass can also be used. Post office

Directory

Banks and Cash Machines

ABN-AMRO
Koningsplein/Singel 429–435.
Map 7 B4. *624 3097.*

ING Bank
Damrak 80.
Map 7 C1. *550 3100.*

Postbank
Singel 250–256.
Map 7 A3. *556 3311.*

American Express

Damrak 66. **Map** 7 C1.
520 7777.

GWK

Centraal Station.
Map 8 D1. *627 2731.*
24 hours daily.

Schiphol Airport Station.
601 0507. *24 hours daily.*

Amstel Station.
693 4545. *8am–8pm Sat–Wed, 8am–9pm Thu–Fri.*

Lost or Stolen Cards and Checks

American Express
642 4488.

Diner's Club
06 0334.

Eurocard/Mastercard
010 2070 789.

Visa
06 022 4176.

American Express Traveler's Checks
06 022 0100.

cash machines accept only Eurocard and Mastercard. Few Dutch banks will advance you cash against credit cards.

CURRENCY

THE DUTCH currency is the guilder *(gulden)*, formerly called the florin. It is usually abbreviated before the amount as *f* or *fl*, or occasionally *Hfl*, *Dfl* or *NLG*. The guilder breaks down into 100 cents, written as c after the number. It is worth noting that the Dutch don't like giving out change, so try to provide the exact money or a sum close to the value of your purchase.

Single cents are still used for some prices, but since the Dutch no longer have 1c or 2c coins, the amount will be rounded up or down to the nearest five cents. It is difficult to get *f* 250 and *f* 1000 bills changed, so don't use them in stores and cafés. Embossed symbols on Dutch bills enable blind and partially sighted people to identify their value.

Bank Notes
The lowest denomination of Dutch bill is f 10 and the highest f 1000. There are two f 100 bills in circulation: the one shown here and an older design in brown depicting a bird. Dutch bills are colorful, decorated with figures or themes relating to Dutch history and culture.

f 1000 bill

f 250 bill

f 100 bill

f 50 bill

f 25 bill

f 10 bill

f 2.50

f 1

f 5

25 cents

Coins
Dutch coins, shown here actual size, are worth 5c (stuiver), *10c* (dubbeltje), *25c* (kwartje), *f 1, f 2.50* (rijksdaalder) *and, in circulation since 1992, f 5. The 5c is copper-colored, the 10c, 25c, f 1 and f 2.50 are silver-colored and the new f 5 is gold-colored. The 25c coin is useful for local telephone calls* (see p262).

10 cents

5 cents

Using Amsterdam's Telephones

BEFORE 1989, telephone and postal services in the Netherlands were part of the same state-run company, PTT. They are now run independently of each other, though telephone booths and post offices still carry the characteristic PTT logo. Services continue to be among the best in Europe, but both telephones and mail are in the process of radical change. The phones in particular sometimes suffer from "improvements" involving extensive number changes and overloading, while the postal service is also undergoing changes, such as increased rates, resulting from privatization.

Telephone kiosks located inside the PTT Telecom Telecenter

Sign for telephone center

Telephone Centers

THERE ARE SEVERAL privately owned telephone centers in Amsterdam. The best known is **Telecenter**, run by PTT. From here you can make local, national and international calls and pay for them afterward with cash, credit cards, traveler's checks or Eurocheques. Telecenter offers fax, telex and photocopying facilities, and sells stamps and phone cards.

The times for international discount-rate calls vary. For Australia and New Zealand, they are midnight–7am and 3–8pm, plus weekends; for Canada and the US, 7pm–10am plus weekends; for the United Kingdom and Ireland, 8pm– 8am plus weekends.

Telecenter
Raadhuisstraat 48.
Map 7 A2. *484 3654.*
8am–2am daily.

Using a Card Phone

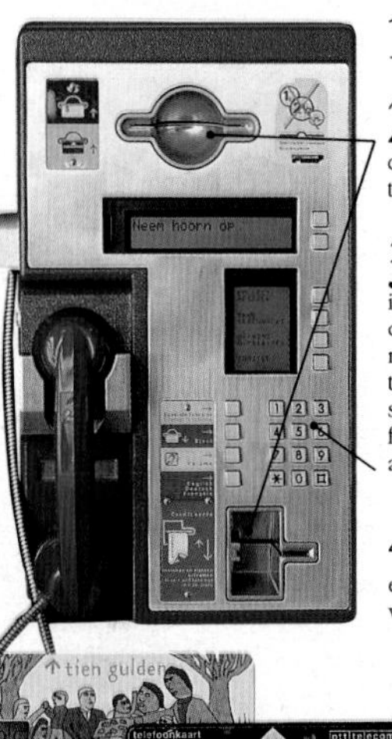

1 Lift the receiver.

2 Insert phone card or credit card. Wait for dial tone – a low hum.

3 Dial the number. The ringing tone in the Netherlands comprises long medium-pitch tones. The busy signal is slightly faster. Instructions are also in English.

4 Replace the receiver at the end of the call and withdraw card.

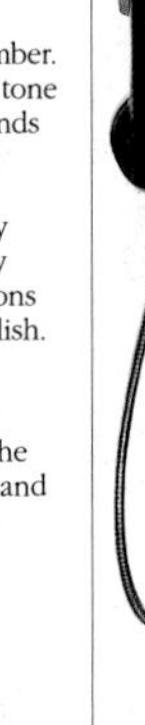

Colorful selection of pictorial phone cards

Using a Coin-Operated Phone

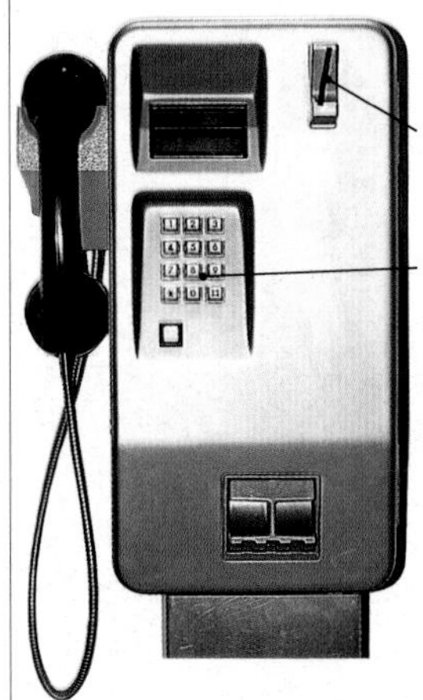

1 Lift the receiver.

2 Insert the coins and wait for dial tone – a low hum.

3 Dial the number. Remember that the ringing tone in the Netherlands comprises long medium-pitch tones. The busy signal is slightly faster. Instructions are also in English.

4 Replace the receiver at the end of the call and collect any unused coins.

25c *f* 1 *f* 2.50

Using the Telephone

Public telephones in Amsterdam can be found on the street, at railroad stations, in post offices and at telephone centers. The city's green-trimmed, booth pay phones take 25c, *f*1 and *f*2.50 coins; a digital display tells you how much credit remains after a call, but only wholly unused coins are returned. Two 25c coins will be more than enough for a local call. Most of the new booths contain card phones, which take credit cards and phone cards. The latter can be bought at telephone centers, post offices and railroad stations. A card giving 20 local calls costs *f*5, and *f*10 and *f*25 cards are also available. Instructions for coin- and card-operated telephones are in English and Dutch. Cafés and bars often have pay phones that the public may use, but these may start at 50c a call. Most hotels have IDD (International Direct Dialing) units, but telephone costs on your bill are likely to be inflated.

PTT telephone booth at station

Reaching the Right Number

- Internal information, dial 06 8008.
- International information, dial 06 0418.
- Local and international operator, dial 06 0410.
- To phone US, dial 001 followed by number.
- To phone UK, dial 0044 followed by the number, omitting the 0 from the area code.
- To phone Australia, dial 0061 followed by number.
- To phone New Zealand, dial 0064 followed by number.
- To phone Irish Republic, dial 00353 followed by number.

Postal Services

Amsterdam's numerous post offices all bear the PTT logo. Apart from offering the usual postal services – stamps, telegrams, *poste restante* (mail-holding service) – they will also change currency and traveler's checks, and have telephone, telex and fax services. The main post office also has photocopying facilities and sells stationery and stamps.

A selection of decorative Dutch postage stamps

Sending a Letter

When you want to mail letters going abroad or outside Amsterdam, use the *overige* slot in any of the mail collection boxes to be found throughout the city.

Letters up to 20 g (.7 oz) can be sent anywhere in Europe – not just within the EU – for the same rate, while destinations farther afield cost slightly more. Postal charges have in fact been increasing at intervals since privatization. There are often long lines for stamps *(postzegels)* at post offices and it is more often simpler and quicker to purchase them at the same time as purchasing your postcards at tobacconists or souvenir shops.

Most post offices are open weekdays 9am–5pm, but may open later and close earlier.

Poste Restante

Mail can be sent to Amsterdam *poste restante.* When you collect your mail, be sure to take along some form of photo identification, such as a passport or driver's license.

Directory

Main Post Office
Hoofdpostkantoor PTT, Singel 250–256.
Map 7 A2.
☎ *556 3311.*
◯ *9am–6pm Mon–Fri, 9am–1pm Sat.*
Poste restante ◯ *8am–7pm Mon–Fri, 9am–noon Sat.*

Main Sorting Office
Oosterdokskade 3.
Map 8 F1. ☎ *523 8111.*
◯ *9am–9pm Mon–Fri, 9am–noon Sat.*

Postal Information
☎ *06 0417.*
◯ *9am–6pm Mon–Fri, 10am–1pm Sat.*

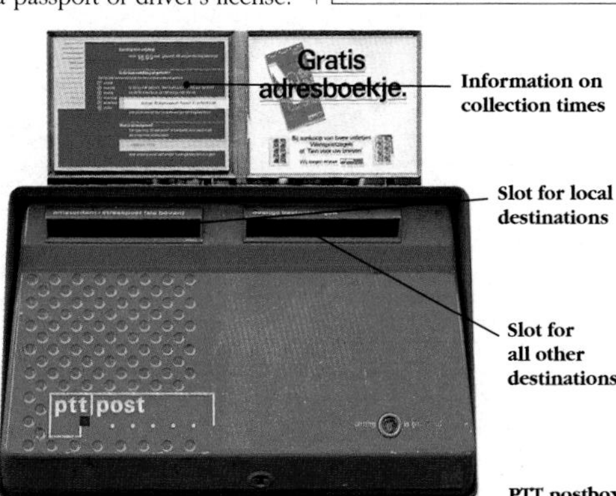

PTT postbox

Additional Information

Prepacked tulip bulbs in Bloemenmarkt

Visas and Customs

For a stay lasting up to three months, Australian, EU, New Zealand and US nationals need only a valid passport. EU nationals over 17 years of age are entitled to import limitless goods for personal use, except for tobacco and alcohol on which duty has already been paid. The limits are: 800 cigarettes; 400 small cigars; 200 cigars; 1 kg of tobacco; 10 liters of spirits; 20 liters of fortified wine; 90 liters of wine; 110 liters of beer.

Diamond brilliants

Bulbs can be brought into the UK, but the US requires an inspection certificate. Non-EU members buying diamonds can reclaim VAT on returning home. Phone the free **Customs Information** line for details.

Cats and dogs may be brought in, providing they have a certificate of inoculation against rabies.

Duty-Free Goods

Citizens of non-EU countries, and EU nationals who buy goods in duty-free outlets, must abide by the following restrictions: 200 cigarettes or 50 cigars or 250 g of tobacco; 1 liter of spirits or 2 liters of fortified wine or 2 liters of nonsparkling wine; 50 g of perfume; 500 g of coffee; 100 g of tea; other goods or gifts to the value of ƒ125.

Toilets

Amsterdam is short on public facilities, and visitors, especially women, often have to resort to using the facilities situated in hotels, museums and cafés. This is acceptable practice, although a few cafés and bars will charge 25c–50c whether you are a customer or not. Large stores also expect 30c or more, while station toilets have attendants who will insist on a tip. Parents will also have to pay 30c for baby-changing facilities in large stores. The only café with toilets for disabled people is 't Nieuwe Café, located in Dam square.

Sign for public facilities

Browsing among the bottles in the duty-free shop at Schiphol Airport

Conversion Table

Imperial to Metric
1 inch = 2.54 centimeters
1 foot = 30 centimeters
1 mile = 1.6 kilometers
1 ounce = 28 grams
1 pound = 454 grams
1 US pint = 0.47 liters
1 US gallon = 3.8 liters

Metric to Imperial
1 centimeter = 0.4 inch
1 meter = 3 feet 3 inches
1 kilometer = 0.6 miles
1 gram = 0.04 ounces
1 kilogram = 2.2 pounds
1 liter = 2.1 US pints

Time

Like all its neighboring countries, the Netherlands is on Central European Time, 1 hour ahead of Greenwich Mean Time in winter and 2 hours ahead in the summer. Sydney is 9 hours ahead in winter (8 in summer), Johannesburg 2 (1 in summer); New York is 6 hours behind in winter (7 in summer), Los Angeles 9 (10 in summer).

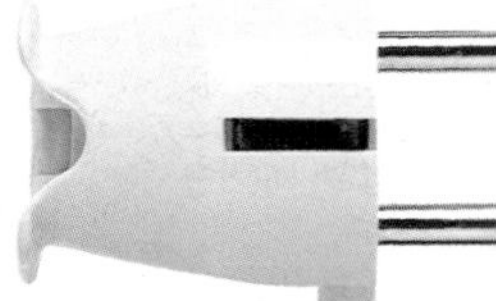

Standard continental plug

Electricity

The voltage in the Netherlands is 220, 50-cycle AC, and compatible with British equipment, but since the Dutch use two-pin continental plugs you will need an adapter.

American visitors need to convert their equipment or buy a transformer. Dutch wall sockets require a larger plug than those used in the US.

Television

The five main channels of Dutch TV serve standard European fare, but most hotels and homes have cable TV, with 20 or so channels available, including French, German, Belgian and Italian stations. Other cable channels offered include BBC1 and BBC2; NBC Superchannel, offering largely American programming and international news; CNN; and the Euroversion of MTV, with pop and rock videos 24 hours a day. All British and American shows are subtitled on the Dutch and Belgian channels, but are dubbed on the French, Italian and German channels.

Radio

In the Netherlands, news is broadcast on Dutch Radio 1 (747kHz), pop music on Radio 3 (96.8MHz) and classical music on Radio 4 (98.9MHz). It is also possible to pick up BBC Radio 4 on 198kHzAM and the World Service on 648kHzAM. Stations of all kinds are often opening in the city, aimed especially at youth.

Newspapers

Most foreign newspapers reach the city center by lunch time on publication day. The widest variety is sold at **Athenaeum Nieuwscentrum** and **WH Smith**, and includes the *Wall Street Journal*, *International Herald Tribune*, the *Guardian* and other North American and European newspapers.

A selection of newspapers available

Embassies and Consulates

Most embassies are located in the Dutch administrative capital of Den Haag *(see pp186–7)*, which is a 45-minute train ride from Centraal Station. Some countries, however, also have special consular facilities situated in Amsterdam. These include the UK, USA, France, Germany and Italy.

For a comprehensive list of offices in the city, consult the main Amsterdam telephone directory under *Consulaat*.

Directory

Embassies and Consulates

Australia
Carnegielaan 14,
2517 KH Den Haag.
(070) 310 8200.
9am–12:30pm, 1:15–5:15pm Mon–Thu.

Canada
Sophialaan 7,
2514 JP Den Haag.
(070) 361 4111.
9am–1pm, 2:30–4pm Mon–Fri.

Ireland
Dr Kuyperstraat 9,
2514 BA Den Haag.
(070) 363 0993.
10am–12:30pm, 2:30–5pm Mon–Fri.

New Zealand
Mauritskade 25,
2514 HD Den Haag.
(070) 346 9324.
9am–12:30pm, 1:30–5:30pm Mon–Thu.
Visa enquiries: 9am–12:30pm Mon–Fri.

South Africa
Wassenaarseweg 40,
2596 CJ Den Haag.
(070) 392 4501.
9am–noon, 2–4pm Mon–Fri.

UK Consulate
Koningslaan 44.
Map 3 B4.
General enquiries:
676 4343.
Visa enquiries:
675 8121.
9am–noon, 2–3:30pm Mon–Fri (visa collections only).

UK Embassy
Lange Voorhout 10,
2514 ED Den Haag.
(070) 364 5800.

US Consulate
Museumplein 19.
Map 4 E3.
664 5661 or 679 0321.
8:30–noon Mon–Fri. (visa applications only).

US Embassy
Lange Voorhout 102,
2514 EJ Den Haag.
(070) 310 9209.

Religious Services

Anglican
Episcopal Christ Church
Groenburgwal 42.
Map 5 A2.
624 8877.
Services in English: 10:30am & 7:30pm Sun.

Dutch Reformed Church
Oude Kerk *(see pp68–9)*
Oudekerksplein 1.
Map 7 C2.
625 8284 or 624 9183.
Mar–Oct: 11am–5pm daily, Nov–Feb: 1–5pm Fri–Sun.
Service: 11am Sun.
Westerkerk *(see p90)*
Prinsengracht 281.
Map 1 B4.
624 7766.
10am–4pm Mon–Sat.
Service: 10:30am Sun.

English Reformed Church
Begijnhof 48 *(see p75)*
Map 1 C5.
624 9665.
Jun–Sep: 2–4pm Mon–Fri. Service in English: 10:30am Sun. Service in Dutch: 7pm Sun.

Jewish
Orthodox Community Amsterdam
PO Box 7967, Van der Boechorstraat 1008.
646 0046.
9am–5pm Mon–Fri.
Jewish and Liberal Community Amsterdam
Jacob Soetendorpstraat 8.
642 3562.
9am–5pm Mon–Thur, 9am–3pm Fri.
Services: 8pm Fri, 10am Sat.

Muslim
THAIBA Islamic Cultural Center
Kraaiennest 125.
698 2526.
Prayers: daily.

Quaker
Religious Genootsch der Vrienden
Vossiusstraat 20.
Map 4 D3. *679 4238.*
Meeting: 10:30am Sun.

Roman Catholic
St. John & St. Ursula
Begijnhof 30. **Map** 1 C5.
622 1918.
10am–6pm Mon–Sat.
Services: 9am & 5pm Mon–Fri, 9am Sat, 10am Sun. Service in English: 12:15pm Sun. Service in French: 11:15pm Sun.

Customs Information

06 0143 (free phone).

Newsstands

Athenaeum Nieuwscentrum
Spui 14–16. **Map** 7 B4.
623 3933.

WH Smith
Kalverstraat 152.
Map 7 B3. *638 3821.*

GETTING TO AMSTERDAM

One of Europe's most popular tourist destinations, Amsterdam is easily accessible by plane, bus, car, ferry and train. Since the autumn of 1994, travelers from the UK have also been able to reach Amsterdam via the Channel Tunnel. Each method has its own benefits and disadvantages, and the choice will largely depend on whether time, money or comfort is the priority. Whichever you choose, it's always worth making a few inquiries to find the best deal to suit your requirements. Not only is there a wide selection of "packages" and special-interest holidays available, but prices can fluctuate widely throughout the year, and new ventures are emerging all the time.

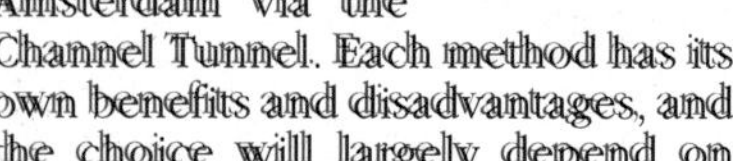

KLM's hotel bus into the city center

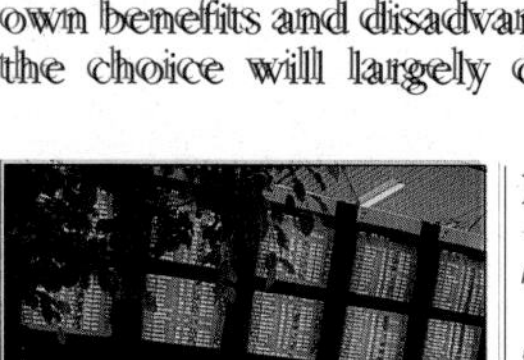
Flight information from the departures board at Schiphol

By Air

There is an immense choice of flights to Amsterdam from the UK and the Republic of Ireland, with seven carriers operating direct flights. These include the national airlines **Aer Lingus**, **British Airways** and **KLM**. Inexpensive trips are advertised in the travel sections of national newspapers and in listings magazines, and are also available through discount agencies. Smaller operators are usually, but not always, less expensive than the national airlines. Flights are very quick – under an hour from London, for example.

There are dozens of inclusive package deals. Organized through a reliable agency, these can be far cheaper than booking a ferry or flight and separate accommodations.

Using Amsterdam Airport Schiphol

All the airport signs at Schiphol are color-coded: yellow ones indicate the transfer desks and gates, green ones the amenities such as coffee bars, restaurants, stores, children's play area and well-equipped baby rooms. For business people and those in transit, there is an amazing range of facilities from business center and conference rooms to sauna and golf and fitness centers.

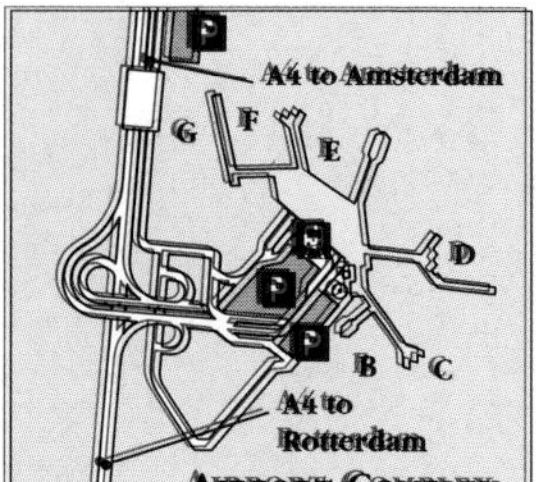

Airport Complex

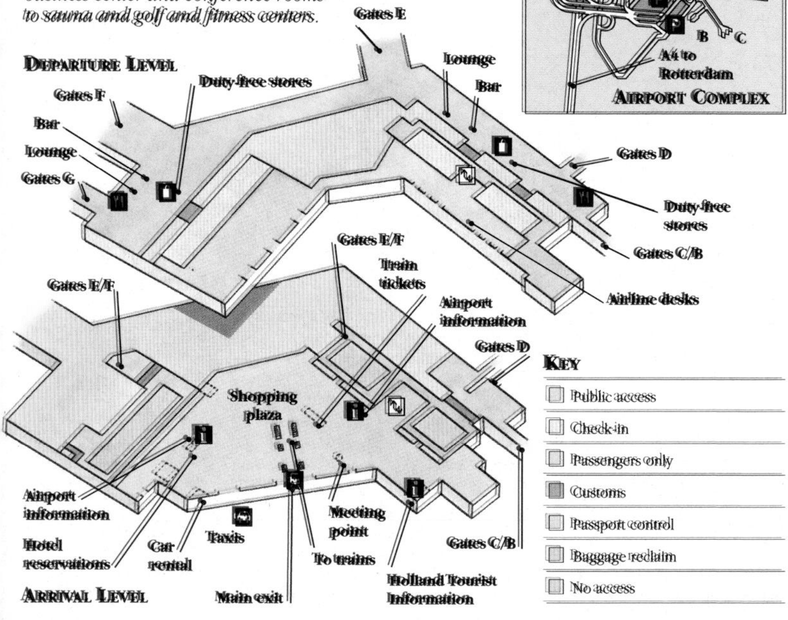

A4 to Amsterdam
G
F
E
D
B
C
A4 to Rotterdam

Departure Level

Gates E
Lounge
Bar
Duty-free stores
Gates F
Bar
Lounge
Gates G
Gates D
Duty-free stores
Gates C/B
Airline desks

Arrival Level

Gates E/F
Gates E/F
Train tickets
Airport information
Gates D
Shopping plaza
Airport information
Hotel reservations
Car rental
Taxis
Main exit
To trains
Meeting point
Holland Tourist Information
Gates C/B

Key

Public access
Check-in
Passengers only
Customs
Passport control
Baggage reclaim
No access

Planes on runway at Amsterdam Airport Schiphol

LONG-DISTANCE FLIGHTS

AMSTERDAM is a popular stopover for overseas visitors to Europe. You can fly from many US cities to Schiphol, and operators running nonstop services on scheduled flights include the Dutch company **Martinair**, **Delta**, **TWA**, **United Airlines** and **Northwest Airlines/KLM**. These last two also offer free or reduced-price connecting flights. Other operators fly via the major European capital cities, such as Paris and Rome, but London is probably the cheapest trans-Atlantic destination, with uniquely varied connections. Fare prices vary according to season, with APEX the best year-round option. The leader in the field of charter flights from the US is Martinair which offers mid-range prices on nonstop flights from a number of cities.

Better still are the fares of the "seat consolidators," who buy unsold seats from the major carriers and sell them at a huge reduction. For bargain flights, check out the free weeklies and travel sections of newspapers. Several companies offer excellent-value package tours. KLM has the widest range of options, but as always, it's well worth shopping around. The best route for visitors from Australia and New Zealand is also a London stopover, since scheduled flights direct to Amsterdam are expensive. **STA Travel**, which has offices in Australia, New Zealand and the US, is a source of expert advice for independent travelers.

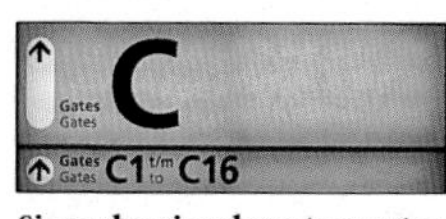

Signs showing departure gates

Travel poster from the 1950s advertising KLM's European flights

ARRIVING AT SCHIPHOL

AMSTERDAM AIRPORT Schiphol has maintained its single terminal status and remains one of the world's most modern, efficient, clean and user-friendly airports. In the welcoming arrivals hall, you will find a tourist information desk, a post office, exchange office and baggage facilities.

There are three main ways of getting into the center of Amsterdam, 18 km (11 miles) to the northeast. Despite its name, the KLM Hotel Bus Service is open to anyone: you don't have to come by KLM, or be staying at one of the six hotels in the city center where it stops. These buses leave from outside the main exit every 30 minutes between 6:30am and 3pm, with a final departure at 5pm.

Taxis are plentiful at the stand outside the arrivals hall, but the rule that cabbies are required to wear ties and jackets hardly justifies the high taxi fares. The best method of all for getting to Amsterdam center is by train.

Transfer desk at Schiphol

FROM SCHIPHOL BY RAIL

FOR THE SCHIPHOL AIRPORT rail service, just walk into the shopping plaza, buy a ticket to Amsterdam's Centraal Station and catch the next train. Free luggage carts can be taken right onto the platform.

Trains run every 15 minutes between 6am and midnight, after which they run hourly. The journey takes about 20 minutes, and the fare is cheaper than the bus. There are also rail connections from Schiphol to the majority of stations in the Netherlands.

Railroad platform at Schiphol Plaza – destination Amsterdam

Beware of pickpockets at Amsterdam's Centraal Station

By Ferry

The Dutch railways, Nederlands Spoorwegen, in conjunction with **Stena Sealink** and **British Rail**, operate a twice-daily boat-train service from London to Amsterdam via Harwich and the Hook of Holland. The total journey time is about 11 hours. **P&O**'s rival twice-daily service from Felixstowe to Zeebrugge has no linked rail ticket. British Rail operates an integrated service from London via Dover and Ostend, taking a total of 13 hours, and a faster version by Jetfoil, which lasts nine hours. **North Sea Ferries** sail daily from Hull to Rotterdam; the crossing takes 14 hours. The other cross-Channel routes viable for Amsterdam are run by **Sally Lines**, from Ramsgate in England to Ostend in Belgium and Dunkirk in France.

The logo of Dutch Railways

By Train

Students and those under 26 can benefit from discount rail travel both to and within the Netherlands. The Inter-Rail pass, which is valid in 26 countries, and the Freedom pass both allow 3, 5 or 10 days' unlimited travel in the Netherlands. For details on these offers call British Rail's **European Information Line**. You don't even have to be a young person or a student to qualify for some of the deals offered.

All trains arrive at Centraal Station, including those from Schiphol Airport. The station has two decent cafés, public toilets, police on patrol, a lost-and-found office, baggage lockers, bike rental and all the amenities of a big terminal.

However, it's very crowded and a magnet for pickpockets, drug pushers and con artists. Head for Stationsplein by the main entrance, following signs to the VVV *(see p256)*. Avoid the rear entrance, a prostitute hangout. On Stationsplein, beware of smooth-talking hotel touts. The trolley stops are only a few yards from the entrance, and the bus stops are across the square to the left. All trolley and bus routes start here *(see pp272–3)*. The VVV office is the white pavilion building found on your left, and the GVB municipal transportation authority office is located to its right.

By Bus

Long-distance bus travel can be a cheap, although sometimes tiresome, option for those visiting Amsterdam. The choice lies between **Eurolines**, crossing by ferry (Dover–Calais or Ramsgate–Ostend), and **Hoverspeed City Sprint** (Dover–Calais) traveling by hovercraft. Both companies run at least two daily services in summer from London to Centraal Station in Amsterdam, and at least one service a day in winter.

With all the various transportation permutations available to UK–Amsterdam travelers, it's worth finding the one that best suits your needs of time, money or comfort.

Comfortable travel by bus

By Car

In Europe only the Irish, the British and northern Scandinavians have to cross the sea to get to Amsterdam. An ever-expanding highway system makes it easy to reach the Netherlands from most of western, central and southern

Cars parked on Noorder Dijk, between the North Sea and IJsselmeer

Taking the car and bicycles

Europe. A valid driver's license is sufficient for driving in the Netherlands, although many car-rental firms and the automotive club **ANWB** (Royal Dutch Touring Club) favor an international one. To take your own car into the Netherlands you will need proof of registration, valid insurance documents, a road safety certificate from the country of origin and an international identification disk. Drivers from Australia, New Zealand, Ireland and the United Kingdom must remember that the Dutch drive on the righthand side.

Major roads (marked N) are well-maintained, but Dutch highways (labeled A) have narrow lanes, traffic lights and sometimes no hard shoulder. European routes are labeled E.

There are three levels of speed limits: 120 km/h (75 mph) on highways, 80 km/h (50 mph) outside cities and 50 km/h (30 mph) in urban areas. From the A10 ring road, the S-routes (marked by blue signs) take you to the center of Amsterdam.

The ANWB provides a breakdown service for members of other car clubs, like AAA. A nonmember can pay for the ANWB's services, or become a temporary ANWB member.

Driving in Amsterdam

Be careful of cyclists and trolleys when driving in the city. Trolleys take precedence and cyclists need ample space. Take care when turning, and allow cyclists priority. Much of the city center is one-way, and when driving in the canal area, remember that the water should be to your left. Main roads with priority are marked by a white diamond with a yellow center; otherwise priority is to the right.

The blue signs guiding you to city centers

Directory

Airlines in Britain and Ireland

Aer Lingus
London
0181 899 4747.
Dublin
1844 4747.

Air UK
01345 666777.

British Airways
From within London
0181 897 4000.
From outside London
0345 222 111.

British Midland
0345 554 554.

KLM
London
0181 750 9000.
Dublin
1284 3823.

Airlines in US

British Airways
(800) 247-9297.

Delta
(800) 241-4141.

KLM
(800) 374-7747.

Martinair (charter)
(800) 627-8462.

Northwest Airlines
(800) 225-2525.

TWA
(800) 221-2000.

United Airlines
(800) 538-2929.

Sta Travel

Australia
2 218 9866.
New Zealand
9 309 9723.
UK
0171 937 9921.
US
(617) 266-6014.

Schiphol Airport

Information Service
06 350 34050.

Airline Offices

Aer Lingus
Heiligeweg 14. **Map** 7 B4.
623 8620.

Air UK
Walaardt Sacrestraat 250, Schiphol Airport.
601 0633.

British Airways
Neptunusstraat 33, Hoofddorp.
02503 50066.

British Midland
World Trade Centre Strawinskylaan 721.
662 2211.

Delta
De Boelelaan 7–8.
661 0051.

KLM
G Metsusstraat 2–6.
Map 4 E4.
649 3633.

Northwest Airlines
Weteringschans 85c.
Map 4 E2.
627 7141.

TWA
Singel 540.
Map 7 B5.
627 4646.

United Airlines
World Trade Centre Strawinskylaan 831.
662 3236.

Ferry Operators

North Sea Ferries
01482 377 177.

P&O European Ferries
0181 575 8555.

Sally Lines
London
0181 858 1127.
Kent
01843 595 522.

Stena Sealink
Kent
01233 647 047.
Essex
01255 243 333.

British Rail Information

British Rail
European information line
0171 834 2345.

British Bus Information

Eurolines UK Ltd
01582 404 511.

Hoverspeed City Sprint
01304 240 101.

Breakdown

ANWB
24-hour emergency service
070 314 1414.

GETTING AROUND AMSTERDAM

THE BEST WAY to see Amsterdam is on foot. Almost everything of interest is within comfortable walking distance. The city's layout is quite simple, with its concentric canals *(grachten)* and interlocking roads, but it can seem confusing at first. The *Street Finder (see pp278–91)* will help you negotiate the maze of narrow streets. The simplest way to orient yourself is to remember that, starting from the Singel, the main canals are arranged in the alphabetical sequence of Herengracht, Keizersgracht, Prinsengracht and Singelgracht. Houses are numbered starting at Centraal Station and finishing, with the high numbers, at the Amstel. Amsterdam is not a city to drive around and there are limited and expensive facilities for motorists.

Street sign indicating district

Pedestrian crossing, Dam square

WALKING

BEFORE EMBARKING on a walk around the city, make sure that you are wearing sensible shoes – the brick-cobbled streets can be tiring as well as hazardous. Another problem is dog mess, so look down before looking up to admire canalside architecture.

Some people may not be used to trolleys and bicycles, remember to look both ways when crossing trolley routes (trolleys can be almost silent), and keep off the cycle paths.

Many pedestrian crossings are regulated by lights. Those without lights only indicate what is thought to be a suitable place to cross the road, and cars are not required to stop for you.

WALKING TOURS

THE CANAL WALK on pages 94–105 takes in some of the city's grandest canals. The Guided Walk along the Historic Waterfront *(see pp160–61)* explores Amsterdam's trading history. For a tour of the tranquil Jordaan and the Western Islands, see pages 158–9.

Walks organized by **Yellow Bike Tour** pass many of the important buildings and monuments around the Canal Ring and in the Jordaan. Details are available from the VVV *(see pp256–7)* and hotels. Two contrasting walks by **Camilles Pleasure Tours** take you through the famous Red Light District *(see p60)*. A daytime walk concentrates on some of the city's oldest buildings; the nighttime walk visits the lesser-known streets. Again, details are available from VVV and hotels. **Amsterdam Travel & Tours** covers the Red Light District, while guides from **Mee in Mokum** take you around historic Amsterdam. **Archivisie** covers the heart of the city, including examples of Amsterdam School architecture *(see p97)* and medieval areas.

The penalty for illegal parking

CARS IN AMSTERDAM

ALTHOUGH THE CITY is not suited to car traffic and the VVV advises visitors not to tour Amsterdam by car, provisions are made for those who visit the city as part of a broader car trip. Remember, however, that parking is difficult, booting prevalent and theft rife, so it is wise to follow some simple rules.

If you're staying in a hotel, book one with secure parking facilities and leave your car while you are in and around Amsterdam. If you are coming from outside, park on the outskirts of the city

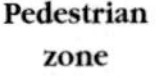
Pedestrian zone

Pedestrian crossing

Right only

Bridge open – turn off engines

End of right of way

Give way

in a "P&R" (park and ride) and take public transportation into the center. If you decide to drive into town, use a parking lot rather than a meter or roadside space. Finally, if you do park in a public place, remove your car radio and any other other valuables.

Space for parking in the city is at a premium, especially on the streets, and meters on the main canal banks are rarely free during the day. Most meters are limited to two hours. Don't park if the meter is out of order – you could get fined or booted. If you use a lot, first put money in the ticket machine, which can be far from the parking place. Be sure to display the ticket inside your windshield.

Illegally parked cars get booted or towed away and you will be also fined. If you are booted, report it to the nearest **Dienst Parkeerbeheer**, or call **Klem-hulp**.

There are now many 24-hour covered parking lots, such as **De Kroon and Zn Parking** and **Byzantium**, and 23,000 official parking places. Uncovered lots are free from midnight to early morning. All city lots are marked by a white P on a square blue background. A three-day parking pass is available for *f* 50 from all Parkeerbeheer offices and some hotels.

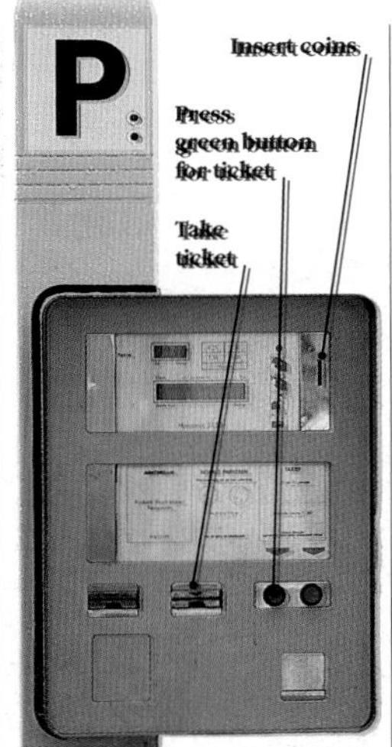

A pay-and-display ticket machine

Car Rental

To rent a car, you must be 21 or over and possess a license and passport. Some companies also insist on a minimum of one year's driving experience. Most of the major agencies have offices in the city, and at Schiphol Airport, but local Dutch firms are significantly cheaper. All outlets require a substantial deposit.

Taxis

The best ways to find a cab are to pick one up at a taxi stand, or call one from **Taxicentrale**, which runs a 24-hour service. You will find that the response is fast, except on Friday and Saturday nights. Rates are generally high, so only give a small tip, unless your driver has been particularly helpful.

Taxi drivers waiting patiently for a fare

Directory

Walking Tours

Amsterdam Travel & Tours
☎ 627 6236.

Archivisie
☎ 625 8908.

Camilles Pleasure Tours
☎ 694 9597.

Mee in Mokum
☎ 625 1390.

Yellow Bike Tour
☎ 620 6940.

Parking Lots

De Kroon and Zn Parking
Muziektheater, Waterlooplein.
Map 8 D5. ☎ 638 0919.

Byzantium
Tesselschadestraat 1.
Map 4 D2. ☎ 616 6416.

Europarking
Marnixstraat 250.
Map 4 D1. ☎ 623 6694.

Museumplein (uncovered).
Map 4 D5. ☎ 671 6418.

Prinsengracht 542.
Map 4 E2.
☎ 625 9852.

Parking Amsterdam Centraal
Prins Hendrikkade 20.
Map 2 D3. ☎ 638 5330.

Parking Advice

Dienst Parkeerbeheer
Bakkerstraat 13.
Map 7 C5.
☎ 639 2469.

Cruquiuskade 25.
Map 6 F2. ☎ 555 9833 *(for towed vehicles).*

Korte Leidsedwarsstraat 2.
Map 4 E2. ☎ 523 3120.

Prins Hendrikkade 108.
Map 8 E2. ☎ 555 4849.

Booting

Klem-hulp
☎ 620 3750.

Car Rental

Adam's Rent-a-Car
Nassaukade 344.
Map 4 D1. ☎ 685 0111.

Avis
Nassaukade 380.
Map 4 D1. ☎ 683 6061.

Budget
Overtoom 121.
Map 3 C2.
☎ 612 6066.

Diks
Gen. Vetterstraat 51–55.
☎ 617 8505.

Hertz
Overtoom 333.
Map 3 A3. ☎ 612 2441.

Kuperus
Middenweg 175.
Map 6 F5.
☎ 693 8790.

Taxis

Taxicentrale
☎ 677 7777.

Taxi Stands

Centraal Station
☎ 570 4200.

Dam square
☎ 570 4201.

Elandsgracht
☎ 570 4209.

Leidseplein
☎ 570 4203.

Muziektheater
☎ 570 4212.

Nieuwmarkt
☎ 570 4205.

Rembrandtplein
☎ 570 4206.

Spui
☎ 570 4213.

Tropenmuseum
☎ 570 4504.

Public Transportation

AMSTERDAM'S INTEGRATED public transportation system, with Centraal Station the focal point, is efficient and inexpensive. The **OVR** gives detailed information on all forms of public transportation within the city and the rest of the Netherlands, but does not make reservations. Tickets for travel around Amsterdam can be bought from machines and on trolleys and buses, but the cheapest way to travel is to buy a *strippenkaart*, available from the **GVB**, VVV and Arena *(see p257)*, and at newsstands.

Trolley terminus at Centraal Station

Watch out for trolleys

TROLLEYS

AMSTERDAM'S 17 TROLLEY lines, whose routes are shown on a free transit map, obtainable from the GVB, are the most common form of transportation in the city. Trolleys start operating at 6am on weekdays and slightly later on weekends. They end before midnight, when night buses take over. Yellow boards at the trolley and bus stops give the name of the stop, the route numbers it serves and the stops along those routes. Maps and diagrams in the shelters are helpful, but if you are not sure, ask the driver, conductor or fellow passengers. You can get on or off by any of the three doors, but on trolleys with a conductor, use the rear door only when boarding. If you need to buy a ticket, you can board at the front and pay the driver, but this can be difficult at rush hour. If you have children or luggage, keep one foot on the bottom step when you board, to hold the door open. Trolleys are awkward for the elderly and people with strollers, and impossible for those with a mobility problem.

Stops are usually announced, but if you're not sure where to get off, ask for guidance. Press a button inside the trolley to open the doors, and take care when getting off as many stops are in the middle of the road.

BUSES

LIKE THE TROLLEYS, the majority of Amsterdam's buses start out at Centraal Station, but they branch out from the city center and largely complement the trolley network. The

No. 35 bus serving the north of the city from Centraal Station

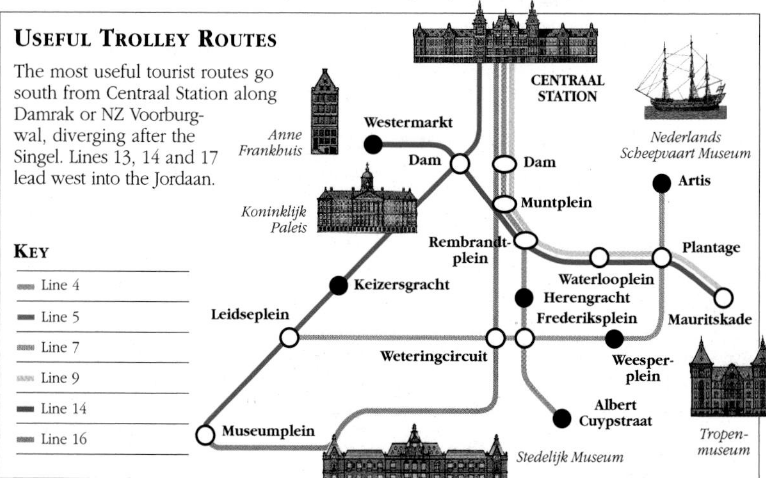

USING THE STRIPPENKAART

Time indicator

Insert *strippenkaart* here

Strippenkaart stamping machine

1 Starting from the top, fold top strip back and stamp the second one for one person traveling in central Amsterdam for up to one hour. The stamp indicates time and date of travel and zone in which you have boarded.

2 For a second person traveling in the center, stamp here as well, to validate two more strips.

3 For a subsequent trip that crosses into two zones, such as a visit from Dam square to the Olympic Quarter *(see p154)*, validate the next three strips by stamping the *strippenkaart* here.

eastbound routes, on the other hand, serve the Scheepvaart Museum *(see 146–7)*, which is not served by a trolley.

Buses have the same system as the trolleys, but you must board by the front door. While the majority of tourists are unlikely to use buses during the day, the night buses that cover for the trolleys after midnight are useful.

Night-bus stops feature a black square with a special number on it, running from 71 to 77. Unfortunately the buses stop between 2am and 4am, so the only options after a night out are walking or taking a taxi.

METRO

AMSTERDAM'S underground system comprises only three lines, all terminating at Centraal Station. Mainly used by commuters, it is of little use to tourists as it only covers four stations in the center, all on the eastern side – Amsterdam CS, Nieuwmarkt, Waterlooplein and Weesperplein. The Metro runs for half an hour longer than trolleys on weekdays, and the ticketing system is the same. Take care at night when stations are popular with drug dealers.

METRO SNELTRAM

Sign for Metro station

Checking a train timetable

TRAINS

THE DUTCH national railroad company, Nederlandse Spoorwegen, runs a busy network, which is considered one of the best in the world. It is reliable, clean and reasonably priced. The OVR (Openbaar Vervoer Reisinformatie) office gives a mass of information on rail trips for tourists, plus details of special fares, such as family rovers, which allow you to stop off en route to your destination. It does not, however, sell tickets, which are sold at the ticket office. Information and bookings for rail travel abroad is available from the **Nederlandse Spoorwegen Internationale** office, which is located near the OVR on Stationsplein.

TROLLEY AND BUS TICKETS

THE STRIPPENKAART (ticket strip), available in multiples of 15 units, allows you to travel all over the Netherlands. Each unit, or strip, covers one zone, even when changing trolley, bus or Metro. Counting from the top, leave blank the number of strips required for your trip by folding them back and stamping the next one in the machine. Most sights are in the central zone, so for most trips you will need to validate only two strips per person traveling. Any number of people can travel on a single *strippenkaart*, providing it still has enough unused strips left.

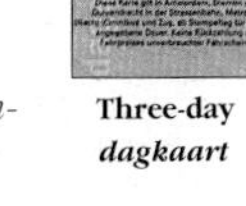

Three-day *dagkaart*

Tickets for one hour's unlimited travel can be purchased on board, but cost proportionally more. The *dagkaart* (day ticket), extendable for up to 9 days, and a season ticket are both on sale from the GBV.

DIRECTORY

GVB (Gemeente Vervoer Bedrijf)
Stationsplein 14. **Map** 2 E3.
06 9292. 7am–9pm Mon–Fri, 8am–9pm Sat.

GVB Head Office
Prins Hendrikkade 108–114.
8:30am–4:30pm Mon–Fri.

Nederlandse Spoorwegen Internationale
Stationsplein 15.
Map 2 E3. *620 2266.*
6:30am–10:15 daily
(for international rail travel information and reservations).

OVR (Openbaar Vervoer Reisinformatie)
Stationsplein 13a.
Map 2 E3.
06 9292.
6:30am–midnight Mon–Fri, 7am–midnight Sat & Sun
(for information on all public transport in the Netherlands).

Getting Around by Bicycle

THE BICYCLE is the ideal form of transportation in Amsterdam. More than half a million people cycle to school or work, and use a bicycle to shop or go out in the evening. The city's traffic system is biased in favor of bicycles, with an excellent network of integrated bike lanes *(fietspaden)*, dedicated traffic lights and road signs, and special routes linking different parts of the city. More and more tourists are adopting this way of exploring Amsterdam and its environs. You can bring your own bicycle, rent one for just a day or join a bike tour.

Bicycle safety helmet

Promoting the pleasures of biking

Bike tour crossing Nieuwe Herengracht

Rules of the Road

AMSTERDAM'S TRAFFIC can appear to be chaotic at first, so above all always remember to ride on the right. Be aware that motorists, trolley drivers and other cyclists will not necessarily recognize you as an inexperienced tourist.

Motorists and other cyclists have priority when entering your road from the right, unless otherwise stated. Trolleys have priority, if only because they are bigger and can't be steered, so don't argue with them. Always keep a wary ear open for their distinctive rattle and stay clear. If you are not sure who has right of way – or anything else err on the side of caution. You will need to be patient with pedestrians who are clearly tourists and unfamiliar with the local rules of the road. Dutch cyclists are naturally anarchic and often ride through red lights, but don't try to follow their example. Many novices dismount at busy junctions and cross on foot, to be on the safe side.

Trolley tracks should be used only by trolleys, buses, taxis and emergency services. If you have to move inside the tracks to pass a stationary vehicle, do so at an angle, otherwise your front wheel may get stuck. Also watch out for people emerging from parked cars, and foreign buses whose drivers may be unsympathetic to cyclists. You may cycle two abreast, but only if you do not block traffic. Don't carry passengers on your bike, or ride on sidewalks or pavements – even though the Amsterdammers do.

You are legally required to have reflector bands on both wheels and a large reflector at the back, as well as lights. Don't try to copy the Amsterdammers, who tend not to use lights at night. And, although the locals don't bother, it is a wise precaution to wear a helmet.

For a flat tire or mechanical problem, head for one of the many bicycle stores *(fietsenmaker)* found around the city.

Crossing trolley tracks at a safe angle

Buying a Bicycle

BE CAREFUL when buying a bicycle. A cheap one for sale on the street will almost certainly have been stolen, and an expensive one from a specialty store will probably end up being stolen. On the other hand, it's worth buying a secondhand bargain if you are staying for a few weeks and plan to do a fair amount of cycling. There are quite a number of reputable secondhand dealers in Amsterdam, and you'll find that some rental companies also sell bicycles.

Traffic lights for bicycles

Bicycles allowed

No entry except to bicycles and mopeds

Renting a Bicycle

Bike rental stores abound in Amsterdam. All require a deposit, but some will accept your passport instead of cash. Rental costs start at around *f*10 a day with deposits varying from *f*50 to *f*200. Tandems are available, but do cost more.

The brakes on most Dutch bikes are worked by back-pedaling. This can take some practice, so if you think you'll find it difficult, insist on a cycle with handlebar brakes.

A selection of bicycles for rent

Bicycle Security

Bicycle theft is rife, so it's essential to lock your bike even when parking for just a few minutes. Fasten both front wheel and frame to a post or railings with a metal U-shaped lock. Rental shops are happy to advise on security matters, and will normally provide a lock in the rental price.

A metal U-lock

Transporting a bike long-distance

Taking Your Own Bicycle

Taking a bicycle on the ferry to the Netherlands is free. When you book your ferry ticket, inform the clerk of your plans. If you're traveling to one of the British ferry ports by train, you will need to book the bicycle on British Rail. On your arrival in the Netherlands, if you want the bike to go with you by train, buy a ticket for it. To take your bicycle by air, you must make a cargo booking with the airline at least a week in advance. It will have to be included in your 20-kg (44-lb) luggage allowance, and you must pay any excess. Remove the wheels and fold down the handlebars for transportation.

Bicycle Tours

Guided bicycle tours are increasingly popular as a way of discovering the city and its environs at a sedate pace. The price of the tours usually includes bicycle rental. **Yellow Bike** organizes tours in Amsterdam, and you can book tours at their office or at one of the VVV offices *(see p256)* from April to October.

If you want to go it alone, the VVV also provides maps with routes, bike lanes and refreshment stops. Arena Budget Hotel *(see p223)* produces an excellent folder with suggestions and maps for bike trips around and outside the city. City tours usually take about 3 hours, country trips are longer at around 7 hours.

MacBike's multilingual biking guide for energetic visitors

Directory

Bicycle Rental

Bulldog
Oudezijds Voorburgwal 126.
Map 7 C3.
624 8248.

Damstraat Rent-a-Bike
Pieter Jacobsdwarsstraat 11.
Map 7 C3.
625 5029.

Holland Rent-a-Bike
Damrak 247.
Map 7 C2.
622 3207.

Koenders Take-a-Bike
Centraal Station, Stationsplein 6.
Map 8 D1.
624 8391.
Utrechtsedwarsstraat 105.
Map 5 A3.
623 4657.

MacBike
Marnixstraat 220.
Map 4 D1.
626 6964.
Nieuwe Uilenburgerstraat 116.
Map 8 E4.
620 0985.

Rent-a-Bike
Stationsplein 33.
Map 8 D1.
625 3845.

Sint Nicolaas Rent-a-Bike
Sint Nicolaasstraat 16.
Map 7 B2.
623 9715.

Stalling Amstel
Amstelstation, Julianaplein.
692 3584.

Take-a-Bike Zijwind
Ferdinand Bolstraat 168.
Map 4 F5. 673 7026.

Tarde Rent-a-Bike
Keizersgracht 248.
Map 1 B5. 620 5417.

Yellow Bike
Nieuwezijds Kolk 29.
Map 7 C1.
620 6940.

Bicycle Tours

Cycle Tours
Keizersgracht 181.
Map 1 B4. 627 4098.

Yellow Bike
See under Bicycle Rental.

Secondhand Bicycles

Groenewoud
2e H De Grootstraat 12.
Map 1 A4. 684 4270.

John Fiets Inn
Nieuwe Keizersgracht 64.
Map 8 F5. 623 0666.

MacBike
See under Bicycle Rental.

Getting Around by Canal

AMSTERDAM HAS EVOLVED around its network of canals, earning it the name "Venice of the North." Though the canals were built for moving goods rather than people, today they provide a marvelous means of viewing the city's splendid sights, as well as its everyday life. Canal boats offer a huge variety of tours to satisfy the most diverse requirements, and are usually featured in tourist brochures. Boat trips are particularly well-suited to those without the time to explore on foot or by trolley, or to the elderly and families with children, who are not able to walk long distances.

A brightly decorated row boat

Embarkation point for P Kooij

Canal Tours

THERE ARE MANY operators in Amsterdam offering canal tours with foreign-language commentaries. Boats depart from a number of embarkation points, mainly from opposite Centraal Station along Prins Hendrikkade, the Damrak and along the Rokin. Many *rondvaartboten* (tour boats) have glass tops, some of which can be opened in good weather. It is not always necessary to book seats for tours, but it is wise to do so for lunch time, evening and dinner cruises, especially during the peak tourist season.

Night cruises can feature wine-and-cheese parties, a stop at a pub or a romantic candlelit dinner. **Lovers** cruises are among the most reasonable while **P Kooij** are perhaps the most upscale. In addition to the city-center tours, **Artis Express** operates a special service from Centraal Station to Artis *(see pp142–3)*, the Scheepvaart Museum *(see pp146–7)* and Tropenmuseum *(see pp152–3)*. On hot days, it is a good idea to go for P Kooij, since it has more open-topped boats than its rival companies.

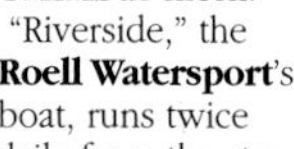

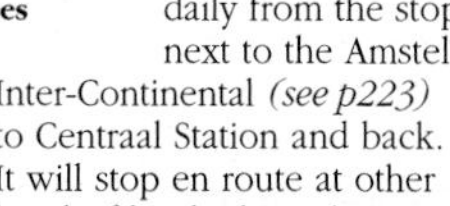

Brochures and ticket for canal cruises

Canalbus

THE CANALBUS SERVICE runs every 25 minutes on a set route from the Singelgracht via the Rijksmuseum *(see pp130–133)* to Centraal Station and back. It stops at Leidseplein, Leidsestraat/Keizersgracht and at Westerkerk for Anne Frankhuis *(see pp90–91)*. The trip takes about an hour, and you can get on or off at any of the stops along the route. It is claimed that the canalbus is the first boat in Europe to run on gas.

Unlike canal tours, canalbuses have no commentary. A day ticket can be purchased, and the canalbus is also available on Fridays and Saturdays for candlelit wine-and-cheese cruises, starting from the Rijksmuseum. It is generally advisable to book these beforehand at a **Canalbus** kiosk.

"Riverside," the **Roell Watersport**'s boat, runs twice daily from the stop next to the Amstel Inter-Continental *(see p223)* to Centraal Station and back. It will stop en route at other hotels if booked in advance.

Canal tour on the Oude Schans, showing the Montelbaanstoren in the background

The Museum Boat on Singelgracht

Museum Boat

A RECENT INNOVATION, the **Museum Boat** takes in, and stops near, all the major city sights. Tours start every 30 minutes daily, between 10am and 3:30pm, from opposite Centraal Station. You can buy an ordinary ticket, which gives unlimited use for one day, or otherwise a combination ticket, which gives entrance to three museums at discount rates. Both can be bought at VVV offices *(see p256)*, at the Centraal Station lock or any landing points. Details of landing areas are on the transportation map on the inside back cover of this guide.

Polished interior of a water taxi

Water Taxis

WATER TAXIS are more convenient than canal boats for sightseeing and parties, and are in fact rarely used as taxis. They are also expensive – more than *f*120 an hour for an 8-seater and three times that for a 35-seater. Some boats are old-fashioned, with wooden interiors. Food, drinks and guides can also be booked in advance. If you want to use one of these boats as a taxi, hail one as it goes past, or order one from the **Water Taxi Centrale**. Fares are not cheap – around *f*2 a minute.

Canal taxi logo

Sightseeing by canal bike

Canal Bikes

THE KEEP-FIT WAY to see the city is by canal bike. These are really two- or four-seat pedal boats. Propelling them requires considerable energy, but children love them and when you've had enough, you can stop for a drink.

You can pick up or leave a pedal boat at any of the canal-bike moorings in the city center: Prinsengracht at the Westerkerk, Keizersgracht near Leidsestraat, Leidseplein between the Marriott and American hotels, and along the Singelgracht just outside the Rijksmuseum. These four locations operate from 9:30am to 7pm every day, and until 10:30pm during July and August.

Between November and March only the mooring at Singelgracht is open. Ponchos are provided in wet weather and included in the price, along with a route-planning map of Amsterdam.

Directory

Canal Trips

Amstel
Nicolaas Witsenkade 1a, opposite Heineken Brouwerij.
Map 4 F2.
☎ *626 5636.*

Artis Express
Prins Hendrikkade 25, opposite Centraal Station.
Map 8 D1.
☎ *622 2181.*

Best of Holland
Prins Hendrikkade 25, opposite Centraal Station.
Map 8 D1.
☎ *623 1539.*

Canalbus
Weteringschans 24
Map 4 E2.
☎ *623 9886.*

Holland International
Prins Hendrikkade 33a, opposite Centraal Station.
Map 8 D1.
☎ *622 7788.*

Lindenbergh
Damrak 26. **Map** 8 D1.
☎ *622 2766.*

Lovers
Prins Hendrikkade 25, opposite Centraal Station.
Map 8 D1.
☎ *622 2181.*

Meijer
Jetty 5, Damrak.
Map 8 D1.
☎ *623 4208.*

Museum Boat
Stationsplein 8.
Map 8 D1.
☎ *622 2181.*

P Kooij
Opposite Rokin 125.
Map 7 B4.
☎ *623 3810.*

Roell Watersport
Mauritskade 1, opposite Amstel Inter-Continental. *(Mon-Sat).*
Map 5 B4.
☎ *692 9124.*

Water Taxi Centrale
Stationplein 8.
Map 8 D1.
☎ *622 2181.*

Street Finder

The page grid superimposed on the *Area by Area* map below shows which parts of Amsterdam are covered in this *Street Finder*. The map references given for all sights, hotels, restaurants, shopping and entertainment spots described in this guide refer to the maps in this section. A complete index of the street names and places of interest marked on the maps follows on pages 288–91. The key, set out below, indicates the scales of the maps and shows what other features are marked on them, including transportation terminals, emergency services and information centers. All the major sights are clearly marked so they are easy to locate.

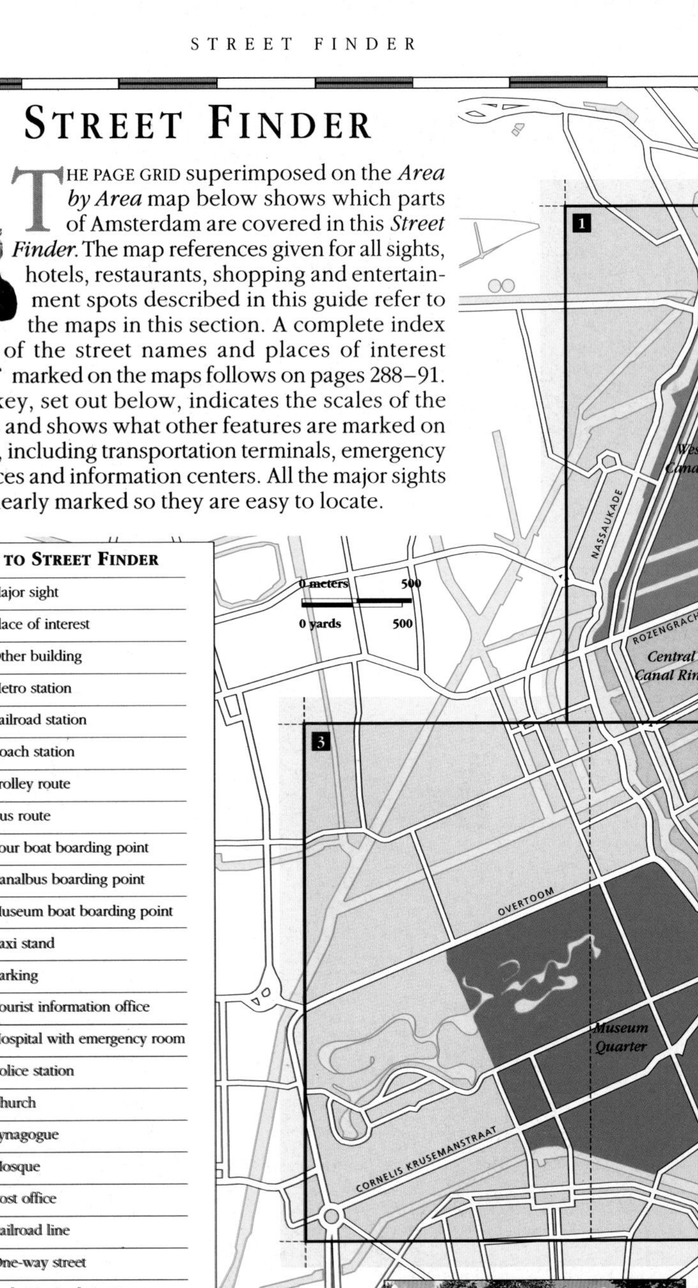

Key to Street Finder

- Major sight
- Place of interest
- Other building
- Metro station
- Railroad station
- Coach station
- Trolley route
- Bus route
- Tour boat boarding point
- Canalbus boarding point
- Museum boat boarding point
- Taxi stand
- Parking
- Tourist information office
- Hospital with emergency room
- Police station
- Church
- Synagogue
- Mosque
- Post office
- Railroad line
- One-way street
- Pedestrianized street

Scale of Maps 1–6

0 meters 250
0 yards 250
1:12,000

Scale of Maps 7–8

0 meters 100
0 yards 100
1:7,000

Fresh fruit for sale in the Noordermarkt ***(see p92)***

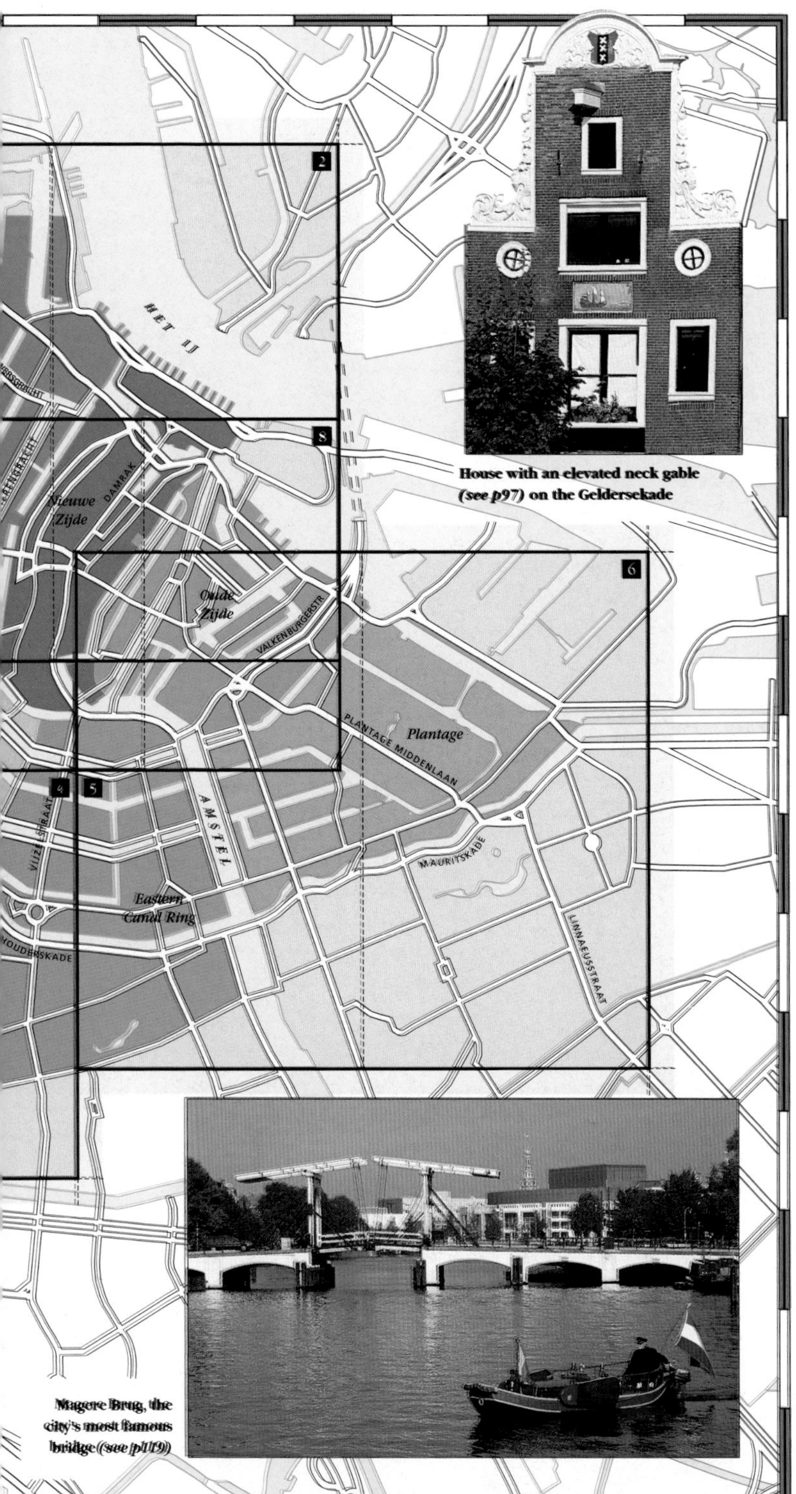

House with an elevated neck gable *(see p97)* on the Geldersekade

Magere Brug, the city's most famous bridge *(see p119)*

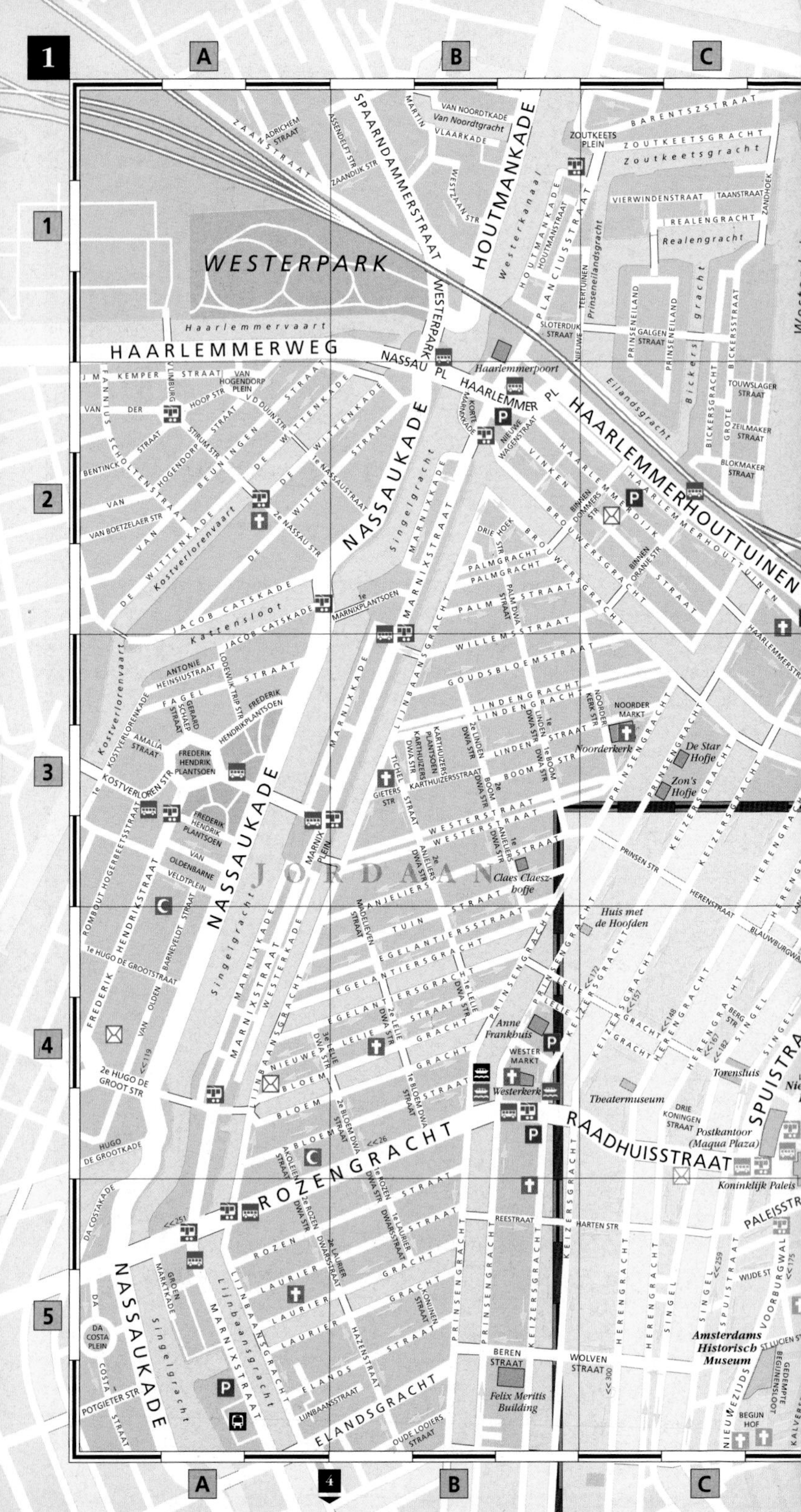

1
A
B
C
WESTERPARK
Haarlemmervaart
HAARLEMMERWEG
NASSAUKADE
HOUTMANKADE
SPAARNDAMMERSTRAAT
WESTERPARK
NASSAU PL
HAARLEMMER PL
HAARLEMMERHOUTTUINEN
Haarlemmerpoort
Westerkanaal
Zoutkeetsgracht
Realengracht
Prinseneilandsgracht
Bickersgracht
Eilandsgracht
Kostverlorenvaart
Kattensloot
Singelgracht
JORDAAN
Noorderkerk
De Star Hofje
Zon's Hofje
Claes Claesz-hofje
Huis met de Hoofden
Anne Frankhuis
Westerkerk
Theatermuseum
Torensluis
Postkantoor (Magna Plaza)
Koninklijk Paleis
RAADHUISSTRAAT
ROZENGRACHT
SPUISTRAAT
Amsterdams Historisch Museum
Felix Meritis Building
ELANDSGRACHT
Lijnbaansgracht
PRINSENGRACHT
KEIZERSGRACHT
HERENGRACHT
SINGEL
NOORDER MARKT
WESTER MARKT
BEGIJNHOF
4

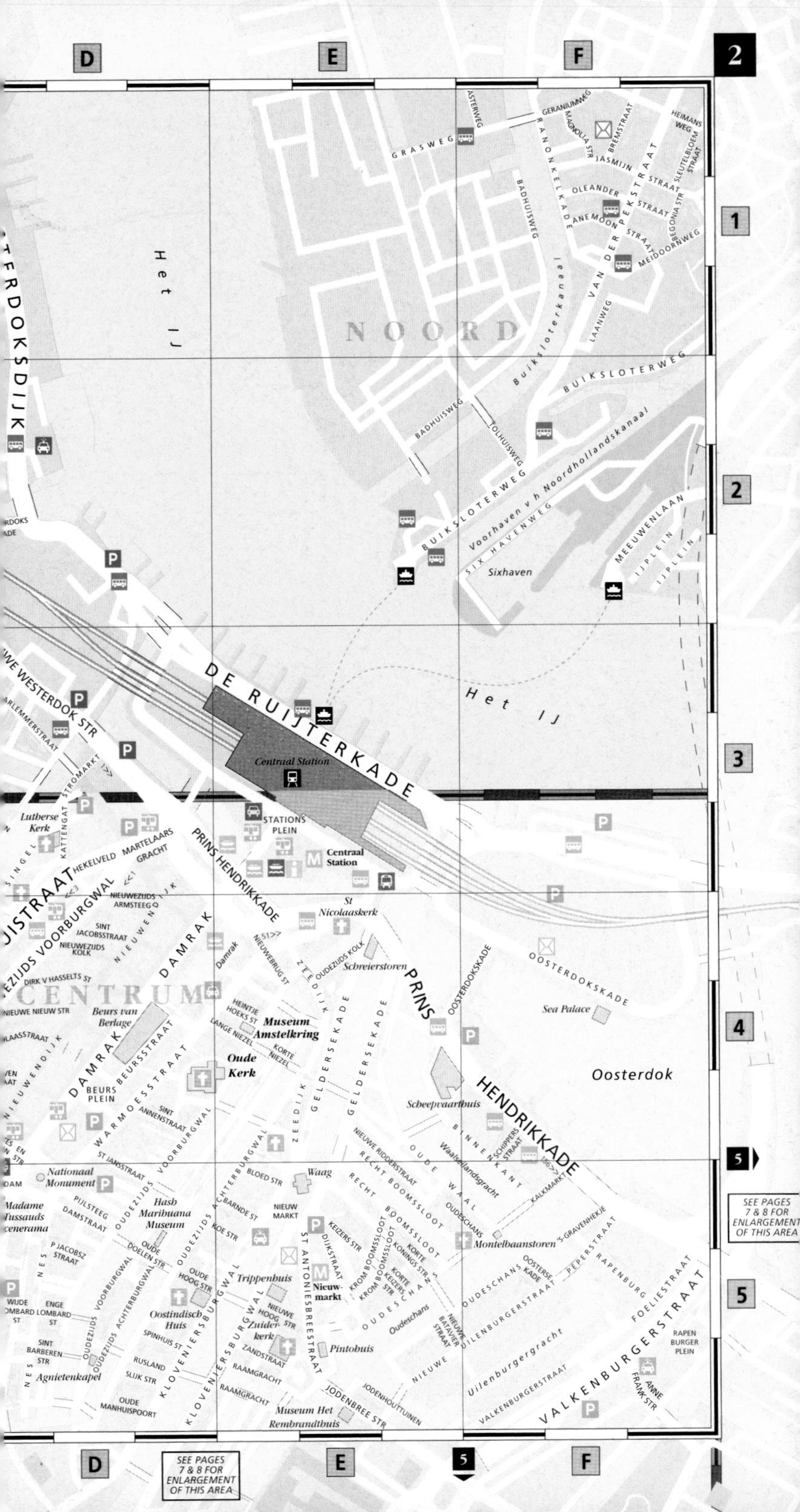

2
D
E
F
1
2
3
4
5
Het IJ
NOORD
Sixhaven
DE RUIJTERKADE
Centraal Station
STATIONS PLEIN
PRINS HENDRIKKADE
St Nicolaaskerk
Schreierstoren
Museum Amstelkring
Oude Kerk
Beurs van Berlage
CENTRUM
DAMRAK
Scheepvaartbuis
Oosterdok
Sea Palace
Waag
Nieuw-markt
Trippenbuis
Zuiderkerk
Oostindisch Huis
Pintobuis
Montelbaanstoren
Nationaal Monument
Madame Tussauds Scenerama
Hash Marihuana Museum
Agnietenkapel
Museum Het Rembrandtbuis
Lutherse Kerk
VALKENBURGERSTRAAT
BUIKSLOTERWEG
Voorhaven v h Noordhollandskanaal
SEE PAGES 7 & 8 FOR ENLARGEMENT OF THIS AREA
SEE PAGES 7 & 8 FOR ENLARGEMENT OF THIS AREA

3
A
B
C
1
2
3
4
5
OUD WEST
OVERTOOM
VONDELPARK
OUD ZUID
Hollandse Manège
VAN KINSBERGEN STR
CABOTSTRAAT
MARCO POLO STRAAT
ADMIRALENGRACHT
WITTE DE WITHSTRAAT
VAN SPEIJKSTRAAT
CHASSÉSTRAAT
SCHIMMELSTRAAT
BELLAMY PLEIN
KWAKERSSTRAAT
BILDERDIJKSTRAAT
Bilderdijk KADE
DA COSTA
JAN HANZENSTRAAT
BELLAMY STRAAT
WENSLAUER STRAAT
HASEBROEKSTRAAT
TEN KATE STRAAT
KINKERSTRAAT
TOLLENSSTRAAT
JACOB VAN LENNEPSTRAAT
Jacob van Lennepkanaal
BAARSJESWEG
Kostverlorenvaart
2e KOSTVERLORENKADE
VAN BRAKEL STRAAT
DAVISSTRAAT
COLUMBUSPLEIN
POSTJESWEG
Postjeswetering
POSTJESKADE
STUYVESANTSTRAAT
CRYNSSEN STRAAT
V RENSSELAER STR
NEPVEU STR
BONAIRE STR
BORGER STRAAT
LOOTSSTRAAT
PIETER LANGENDIJKSTRAAT
STARINGSTRAAT
NICOLAAS BEETS STRAAT
BORGER SCHOOLMEESTER STRAAT
ANNA SPENGLERSTRAAT
W GASTHUISPLEIN
2e CONSTANTIJN HUYGENS
ARIE BIEMOND STR
JELTJE DE BOSCHKEMPERPAD
HELMERS PLANTSOEN
1e HELMERSSTRAAT
BREDERODE STRAAT
STARING PLEIN
GERARD BRANDTSTRAAT
ANNA VAN DEN VONDELSTRAAT
VONDELSTRAAT
WILHELMINA KANAAL
RHIJNVIS FEITH STRAAT
J J CREMERPLEIN
Kostverlorenkade
3e KOSTVERLORENKADE
KATTENLAAN
SCHOOL STR
RUTJIGENHOF
SAXENBURGER STR
REYER ANSLO STR
VONDELKERK STR
FREDERIKS STR
ZOCHERSTRAAT
VAN EEGHENSTRAAT
WILLEMSPARK
CORNELIS SCHUYTSTRAAT
VAN BREESTRAAT
J VERHULST
KONINGSLAAN
EMMA LAAN
EMMA PLEIN
ORANJE NASSAULAAN
PRINS HENDRIKLAAN
KONINGINNEWEG
VALERIUS STRAAT
EMMASTRAAT
DUFAY STRAAT
J VERHULST STR
LASSUS STRAAT
DE LAIRESSESTRAAT
J J VIOTTASTR
SAXEN WEIMAR
WALDECK PYRMONTLAAN
SOPHIALAAN
AMSTELVEENSE WEG
HENDRIK JACOBSZ STRAAT
OKEGHEM STRAAT
VALERIUSPLEIN
JAN VAN GOYENKADE
Amstelkanaal
ALBERT HAHNPLANTSOEN
WILLEM WITSEN STR
BREITNERSTRAAT
CORNELIS KRUSEMAN STR
LOMAN
VAART STR
DES PRES STR
LASTMANKADE
Noorder
APOLLOLAAN
HAVEN STRAAT
BERTELMAN PL
BERTELMANSTRAAT
PIETER
KOCHSTRAAT
OLYMPIAKADE
OLYMPIAWEG
OLYMPIA STRAAT
OLYMPIAPLEIN
SPEER STR
THESEUS STR
HERCULES STR
SPORTPARK OLYMPIA PLEIN
TITIAANSTRAAT
LEONARDO STRAAT
RAPHAELSTRAAT
MICHELANGELO STR
VERONESE STRAAT
MINERVALAAN
RUBENSSTRAAT
GERRIT VAN DER
<<219
<<128
<<165
<<17
<<91
210>>

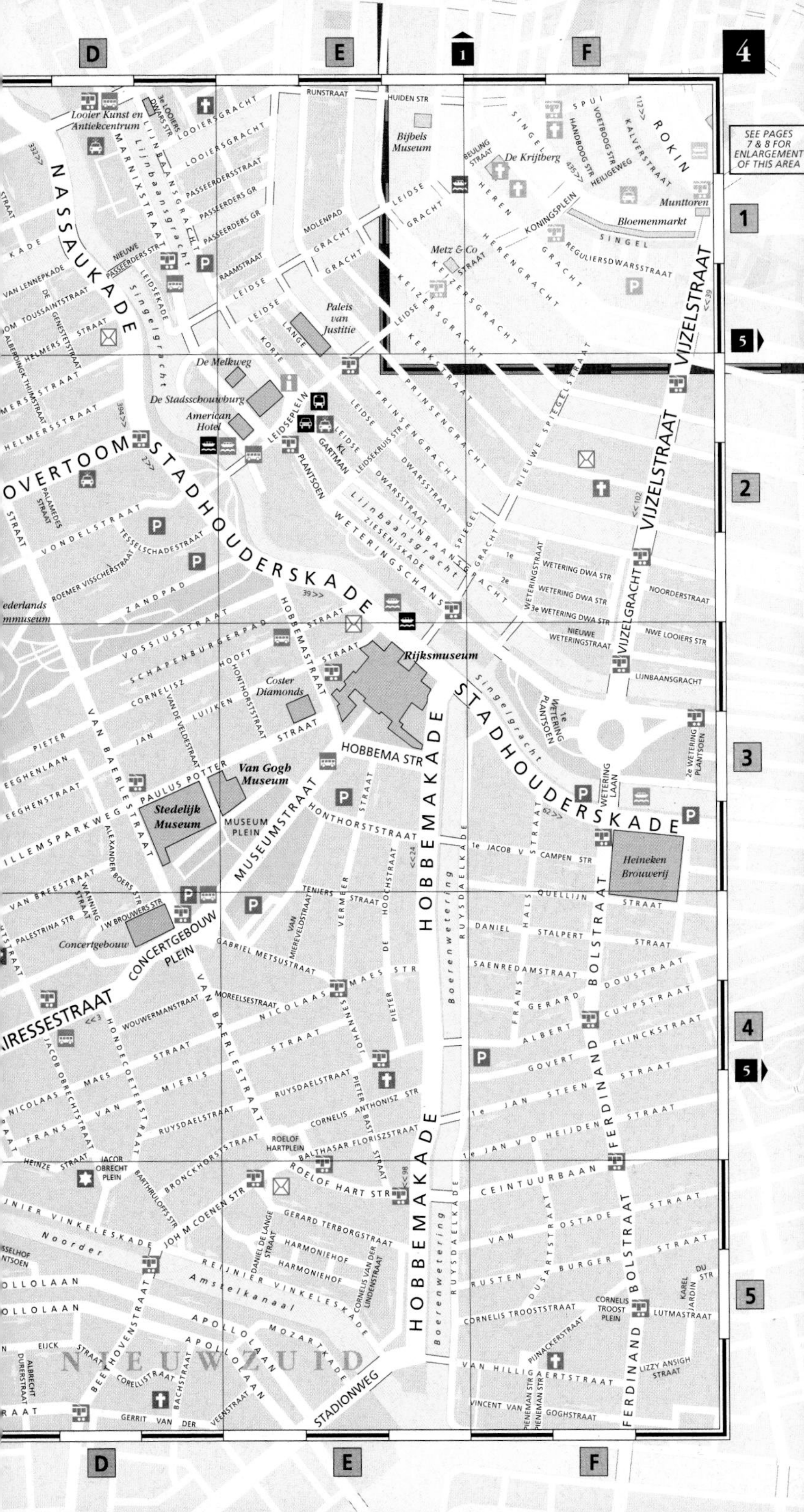

D
E
1
F
4
SEE PAGES 7 & 8 FOR ENLARGEMENT OF THIS AREA
Looier Kunst en Antiekcentrum
LOOIERSGRACHT
PASSEERDERSSTRAAT
PASSEERDERS GR
NIEUWE PASSEERDERS STR
NASSAUKADE
MARNIXSTRAAT
Lijnbaansgracht
Singelgracht
LEIDSEKADE
RAAMSTRAAT
RUNSTRAAT
HUIDEN STR
Bijbels Museum
BEULING STRAAT
De Krijtberg
SPUI
VOETBOOG STR
HANDBOOG STR
HEILIGEWEG
KALVERSTRAAT
ROKIN
Munttoren
KONINGSPLEIN
Bloemenmarkt
SINGEL
REGULIERSDWARSSTRAAT
LEIDSE GRACHT
MOLENPAD
HERENGRACHT
Metz & Co
KEIZERSGRACHT
LEIDSE KERKSTRAAT
PRINSENGRACHT
VIJZELSTRAAT
Paleis van Justitie
LANGE LEIDSE DWARSSTRAAT
KORTE LEIDSE DWARSSTRAAT
De Melkweg
De Stadsschouwburg
American Hotel
LEIDSEPLEIN
KL GARTMAN PLANTSOEN
LEIDSEKRUIS STR
NIEUWE SPIEGELSTRAAT
SPIEGEL GRACHT
WETERINGSCHANS
ZIESENISKADE
OVERTOOM
STADHOUDERSKADE
VAN LENNEPKADE
TOUSSAINTSTRAAT
DE GENESTETSTRAAT
HELMERS STRAAT
ALBERDINGK THIJMSTRAAT
HELMERSSTRAAT
PALAMEDES STRAAT
VONDELSTRAAT
TESSELSCHADESTRAAT
ROEMER VISSCHERSTRAAT
ZANDPAD
Nederlands Filmmuseum
1e WETERINGSTRAAT
WETERING DWA STR
2e WETERING DWA STR
3e WETERING DWA STR
NIEUWE WETERINGSTRAAT
VIJZELGRACHT
NOORDERSTRAAT
NWE LOOIERS STR
LIJNBAANSGRACHT
VOSSIUSSTRAAT
SCHAPENBURGERPAD
HOBBEMASTRAAT
HOOFT
HONTHORSTSTRAAT
Coster Diamonds
Rijksmuseum
CORNELISZ
LUIJKEN STRAAT
JAN
VAN DE VELDESTRAAT
PIETER
HOBBEMA STR
HOBBEMAKADE
Singelgracht
1e WETERING PLANTSOEN
2e WETERING PLANTSOEN
WETERING LAAN
Heineken Brouwerij
VAN BAERLESTRAAT
PAULUS POTTER
Van Gogh Museum
Stedelijk Museum
MUSEUM PLEIN
MUSEUMSTRAAT
HONTHORSTSTRAAT
EEGHENLAAN
EEGHENSTRAAT
WILLEMSPARKWEG
ALEXANDER BOERS STR
VAN BREESTRAAT
WANNING STRAAT
J W BROUWERS STR
PALESTRINA STR
Concertgebouw
CONCERTGEBOUW PLEIN
TENIERS STRAAT
VAN MIEREVELDSTRAAT
VERMEER
DE HOOCHSTRAAT
1e JACOB V CAMPEN STR
QUELLIJN STRAAT
DANIEL STALPERT STRAAT
RUYSDAELKADE
Boerenwetering
FRANS HALS STRAAT
SAENREDAMSTRAAT
DOUSTRAAT
GERARD
ALBERT CUYPSTRAAT
FLINCKSTRAAT
GOVERT STRAAT
JAN STEEN STRAAT
1e JAN V D HEIJDEN STRAAT
FERDINAND BOLSTRAAT
GABRIEL METSUSTRAAT
MAES STR
NICOLAAS
PIETER
MOREELSESTRAAT
WOUWERMANSTRAAT
JOHANNES VERHULSTSTRAAT
RUYSDAELSTRAAT
PIETER BAST STRAAT
ANTHONISZ STR
CORNELIS
BALTHASAR FLORISZSTRAAT
ROELOF HARTPLEIN
ROELOF HART STR
HONDECOETERSTRAAT
JACOB OBRECHTSTRAAT
MAES
MIERIS
NICOLAAS
VAN
FRANS
HEINZE STRAAT
JACOB OBRECHT PLEIN
BARTHRULOFFS STR
BRONCKHORSTSTRAAT
JOH M COENEN STR
GERARD TERBORGSTRAAT
DANIEL DE LANGE STRAAT
HARMONIEHOF
CORNELIS VAN DER LINDENSTRAAT
CEINTUURBAAN
VAN OSTADE STRAAT
DUSARTSTRAAT
BURGER STRAAT
RUSTEN
KAREL DU JARDIN STR
CORNELIS TROOST PLEIN
CORNELIS TROOSTSTRAAT
LUTMASTRAAT
PIJNACKERSTRAAT
VAN HILLIGAERTSTRAAT
LIZZY ANSIGH STRAAT
PIENEMAN STR
VINCENT VAN GOGHSTRAAT
REIJNIER VINKELESKADE
Noorder Amstelkanaal
APOLLOLAAN
MOZARTKADE
BEETHOVENSTRAAT
CORELLISTRAAT
BACHSTRAAT
VEENSTRAAT
GERRIT VAN DER
STADIONWEG
EIJCK STRAAT
ALBRECHT DURERSTRAAT
NIEUW ZUID
2
3
5

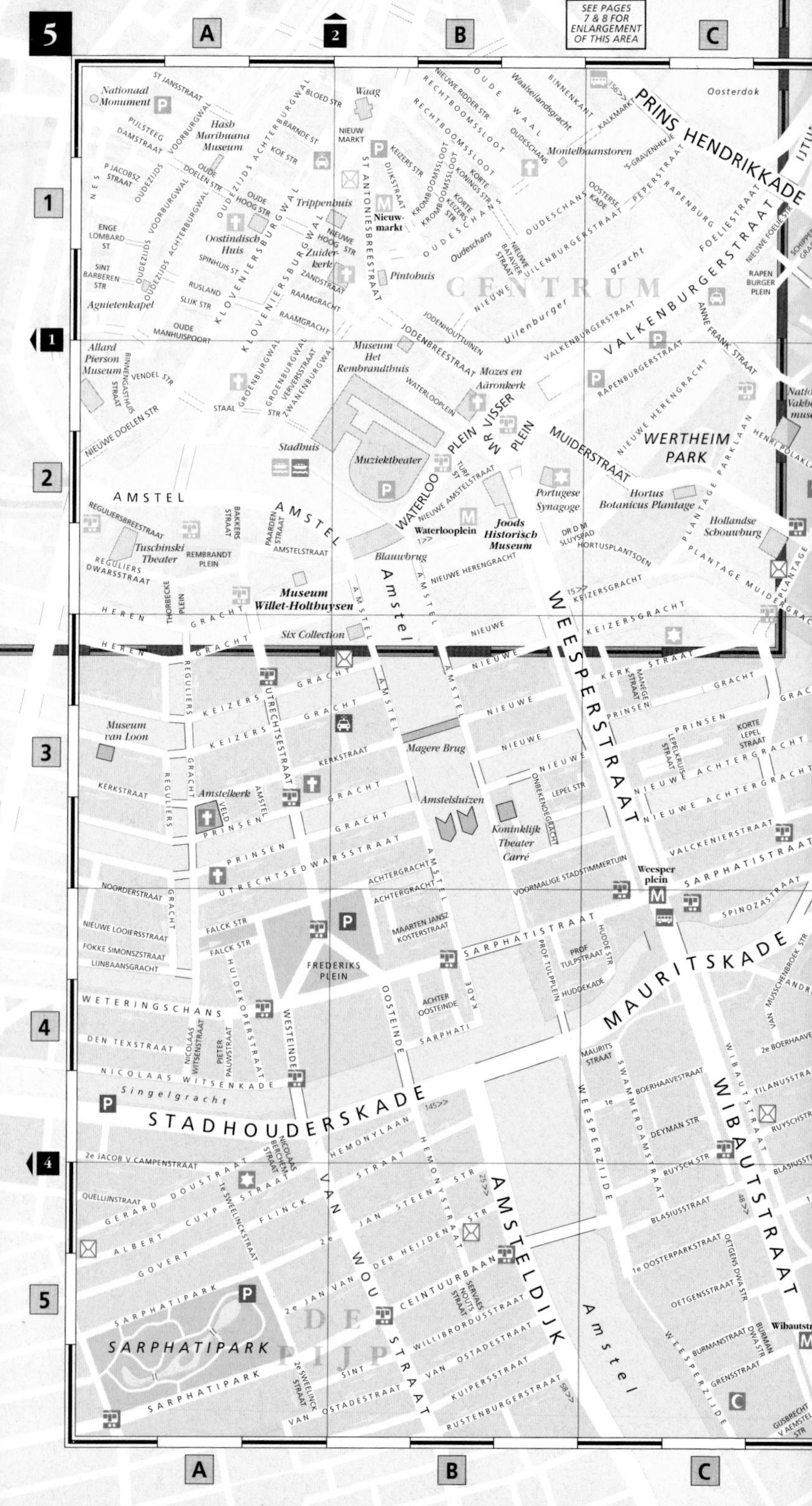

5
A
B
C
SEE PAGES 7 & 8 FOR ENLARGEMENT OF THIS AREA
Nationaal Monument
Hash Marihuana Museum
Waag
Trippenhuis
Nieuwmarkt
Oostindisch Huis
Zuiderkerk
Pintohuis
Montelbaanstoren
Agnietenkapel
CENTRUM
PRINS HENDRIKKADE
Oosterdok
Allard Pierson Museum
Museum Het Rembrandthuis
Mozes en Aäronkerk
Stadhuis
Muziektheater
WERTHEIM PARK
Portugese Synagoge
Hortus Botanicus Plantage
Hollandse Schouwburg
AMSTEL
Tuschinski Theater
Waterlooplein
Joods Historisch Museum
Blauwbrug
Museum Willet-Holtbuysen
Six Collection
Amstel
WEESPERSTRAAT
Museum van Loon
Magere Brug
Amstelkerk
Amstelsluizen
Koninklijk Theater Carré
Weesper plein
FREDERIKS PLEIN
MAURITSKADE
STADHOUDERSKADE
Singelgracht
WIBAUTSTRAAT
AMSTELDIJK
DE PIJP
SARPHATIPARK
Wibautstr
1
2
3
4
5

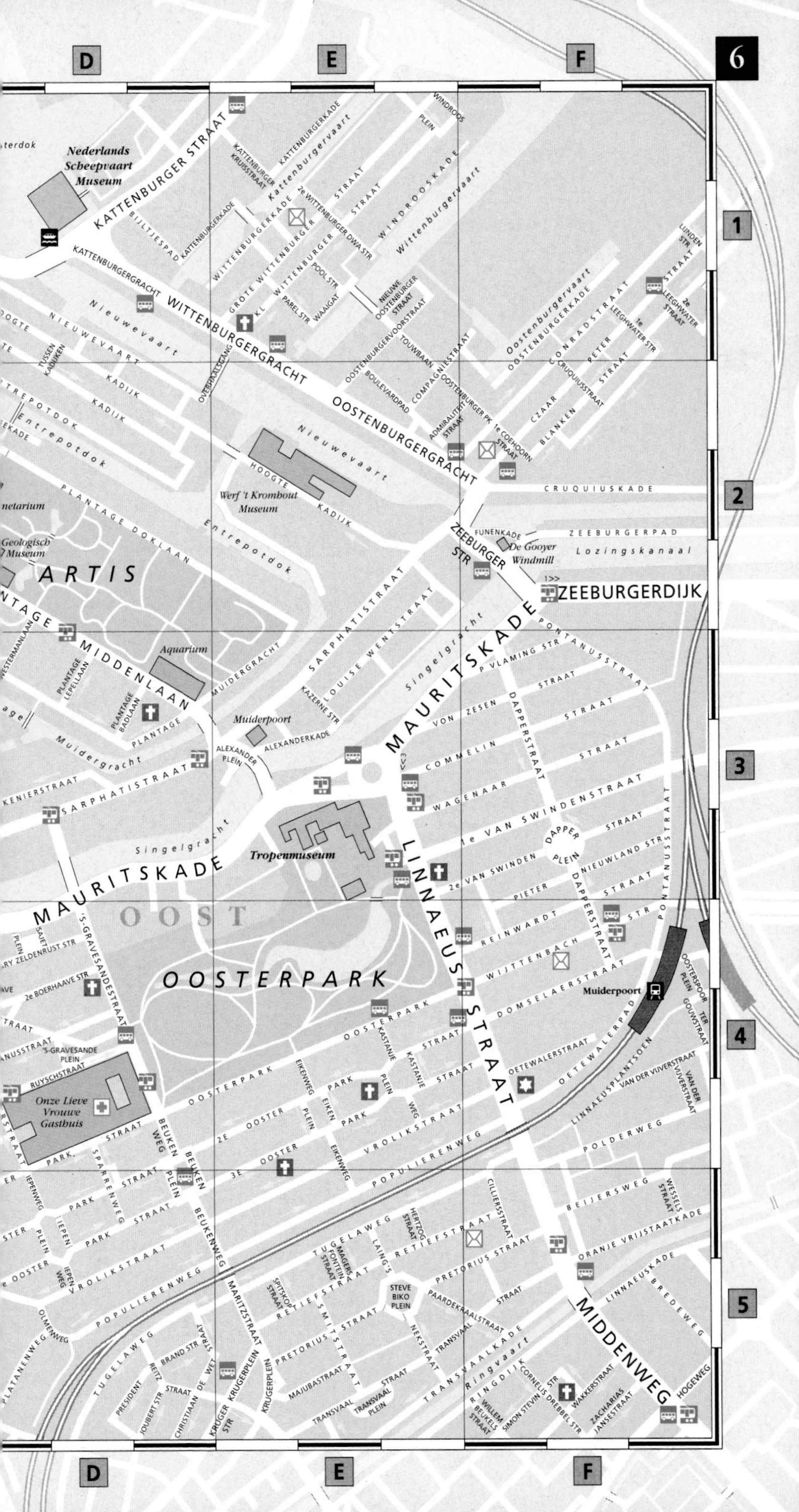
D
E
F
1
2
3
4
5
Nederlands Scheepvaart Museum
KATTENBURGER STRAAT
KATTENBURGERGRACHT
WITTENBURGERGRACHT
OOSTENBURGERGRACHT
Nieuwevaart
Kadijk
Entrepotdok
Werf 't Krombout Museum
ARTIS
Geologisch Museum
PLANTAGE MIDDENLAAN
PLANTAGE DOKLAAN
Aquarium
Muiderpoort
ALEXANDERPLEIN
SARPHATISTRAAT
MAURITSKADE
Singelgracht
Tropenmuseum
LINNAEUSSTRAAT
OOST
OOSTERPARK
Onze Lieve Vrouwe Gasthuis
CRUQUIUSKADE
ZEEBURGERPAD
Lozingskanaal
De Gooyer Windmill
ZEEBURGERDIJK
DAPPERSTRAAT
DAPPERPLEIN
Muiderpoort
MIDDENWEG
POPULIERENWEG
VROLIKSTRAAT
LINNAEUSKADE
STEVE BIKO PLEIN
Ringvaart
TRANSVAALKADE
KRUGERPLEIN
MARITZSTRAAT
HOGEWEG
D
E
F

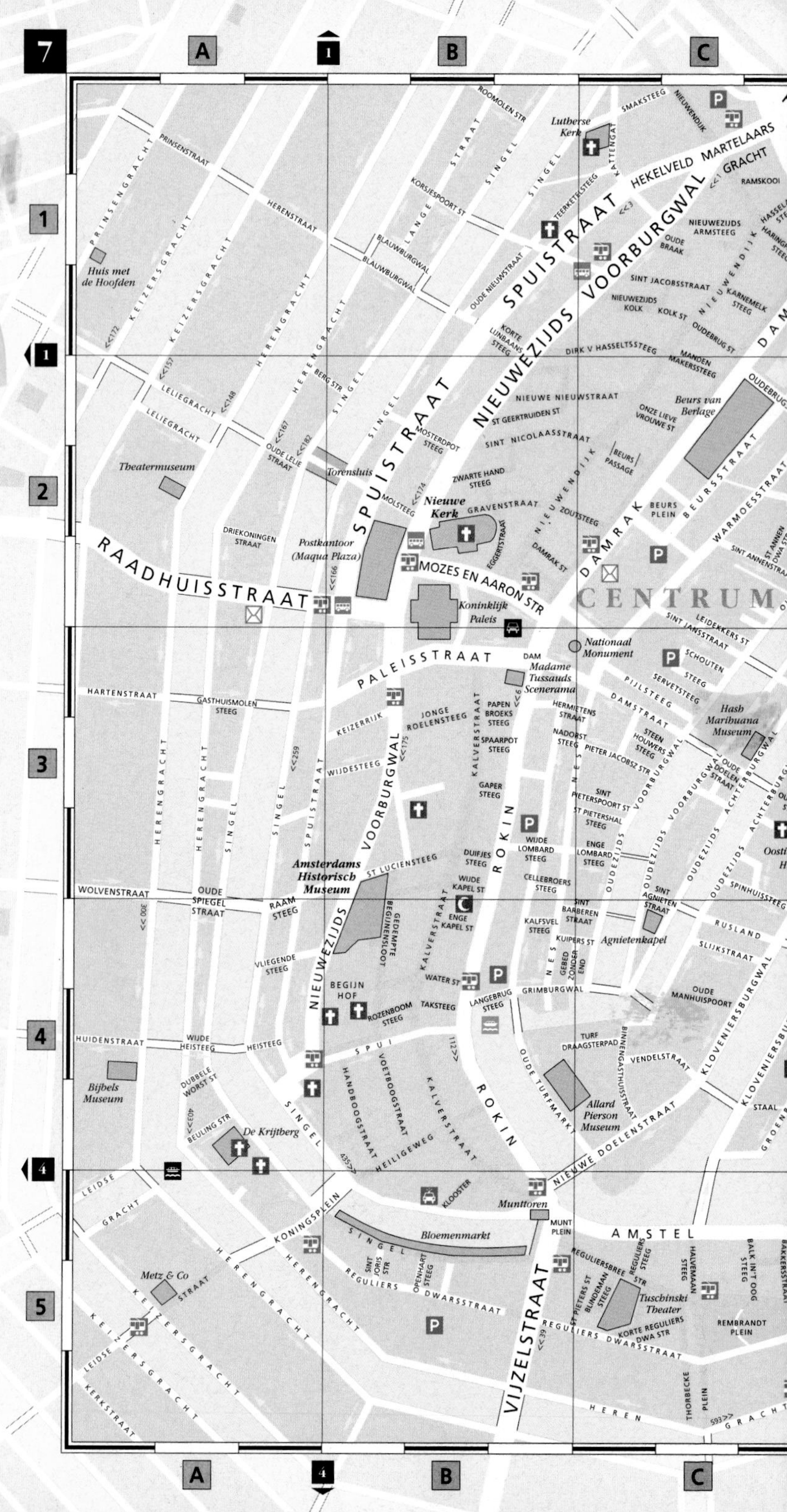
A
B
C
1
2
3
4
5
PRINSENSTRAAT
PRINSENGRACHT
HERENSTRAAT
Huis met de Hoofden
KEIZERSGRACHT
HERENGRACHT
SINGEL
ROOMOLEN STR
LANGE STRAAT
KORSJESPOORT ST
BLAUWBURGWAL
OUDE NIEUWSTRAAT
Lutherse Kerk
KATTENGAT
TEERKETELSTEEG
SMAKSTEEG
NIEUWENDIJK
HEKELVELD
MARTELAARS GRACHT
RAMSKOOI
SPUISTRAAT
NIEUWEZIJDS VOORBURGWAL
NIEUWEZIJDS ARMSTEEG
OUDE BRAAK
SINT JACOBSSTRAAT
NIEUWEZIJDS KOLK
KOLK ST
KARNEMELK STEEG
OUDEBRUG ST
KORTE LIJNBAANS STEEG
DIRK V HASSELTSSTEEG
MANDEN MAKERSSTEEG
DAMRAK
LELIEGRACHT
BERG STR
OUDE LELIE STRAAT
NIEUWE NIEUWSTRAAT
ST GEERTRUIDEN ST
MOSTERDPOT STEEG
SINT NICOLAASSTRAAT
ONZE LIEVE VROUWE ST
Beurs van Berlage
OUDEBRUG
BEURS PASSAGE
BEURSSTRAAT
Theatermuseum
Torensluis
ZWARTE HAND STEEG
MOLSTEEG
Nieuwe Kerk
GRAVENSTRAAT
ZOUTSTEEG
BEURS PLEIN
WARMOESSTRAAT
ST ANNEN DWA ST
SINT ANNENSTRAAT
DRIEKONINGEN STRAAT
Postkantoor (Maqua Plaza)
EGGERTSTRAAT
DAMRAK ST
RAADHUISSTRAAT
MOZES EN AARON STR
Koninklijk Paleis
CENTRUM
SINT JANSSTRAAT
LEIDEKKERS ST
Nationaal Monument
DAM
PALEISSTRAAT
Madame Tussauds Scenerama
SCHOUTEN STEEG
SERVETSTEEG
PIJLSTEEG
DAMSTRAAT
HARTENSTRAAT
GASTHUISMOLEN STEEG
KEIZERRIJK
JONGE ROELENSTEEG
KALVERSTRAAT
PAPEN BROEKS STEEG
HERMIETENS STRAAT
NADORST STEEG
STEEN HOUWERS STEEG
Hash Marihuana Museum
PIETER JACOBSZ STR
OUDE DOELEN STRAAT
ACHTERBURGWAL
WIJDESTEEG
SPAARPOT STEEG
GAPER STEEG
SINT PIETERSPOORT ST
ST PIETERSHAL STEEG
NES
ROKIN
WIJDE LOMBARD STEEG
ENGE LOMBARD STEEG
OUDEZIJDS VOORBURGWAL
Amsterdams Historisch Museum
ST LUCIENSTEEG
DUIFJES STEEG
WIJDE KAPEL ST
CELLEBROERS STEEG
SPINHUISSTEEG
WOLVENSTRAAT
OUDE SPIEGEL STRAAT
RAAM STEEG
GEDEMPTE BEGIJNENSLOOT
ENGE KAPEL ST
SINT BARBEREN STRAAT
SINT AGNIETEN STRAAT
RUSLAND
KALFSVEL STEEG
KUIPERS ST
Agnietenkapel
SLIJKSTRAAT
VLIEGENDE STEEG
GEBED ZONDER END
WATER ST
BEGIJN HOF
ROZENBOOM STEEG
TAKSTEEG
LANGEBRUG STEEG
GRIMBURGWAL
OUDE MANHUISPOORT
KLOVENIERSBURGWAL
HUIDENSTRAAT
WIJDE HEISTEEG
HEISTEEG
SPUI
VOETBOOGSTRAAT
TURF DRAAGSTERPAD
BINNENGASTHUISSTRAAT
VENDELSTRAAT
Bijbels Museum
DUBBELE WORST ST
HANDBOOGSTRAAT
OUDE TURFMARKT
Allard Pierson Museum
STAAL
BEULING STR
De Krijtberg
HEILIGEWEG
NIEUWE DOELENSTRAAT
LEIDSE GRACHT
KONINGSPLEIN
KLOOSTER
Munttoren
MUNT PLEIN
AMSTEL
Bloemenmarkt
SINT JORIS STR
OPENHART STEEG
REGULIERSBREE STR
REGULIERS STEEG
HALVEMAAN STEEG
BALK IN'T OOG STEEG
BAKKERSSTRAAT
Metz & Co
REGULIERS DWARSSTRAAT
VIJZELSTRAAT
ST PIETERS ST
BLINDEMAN STEEG
Tuschinski Theater
KORTE REGULIERS DWA STR
REMBRANDT PLEIN
LEIDSE STRAAT
KERKSTRAAT
THORBECKE PLEIN
HERENGRACHT
GROENB

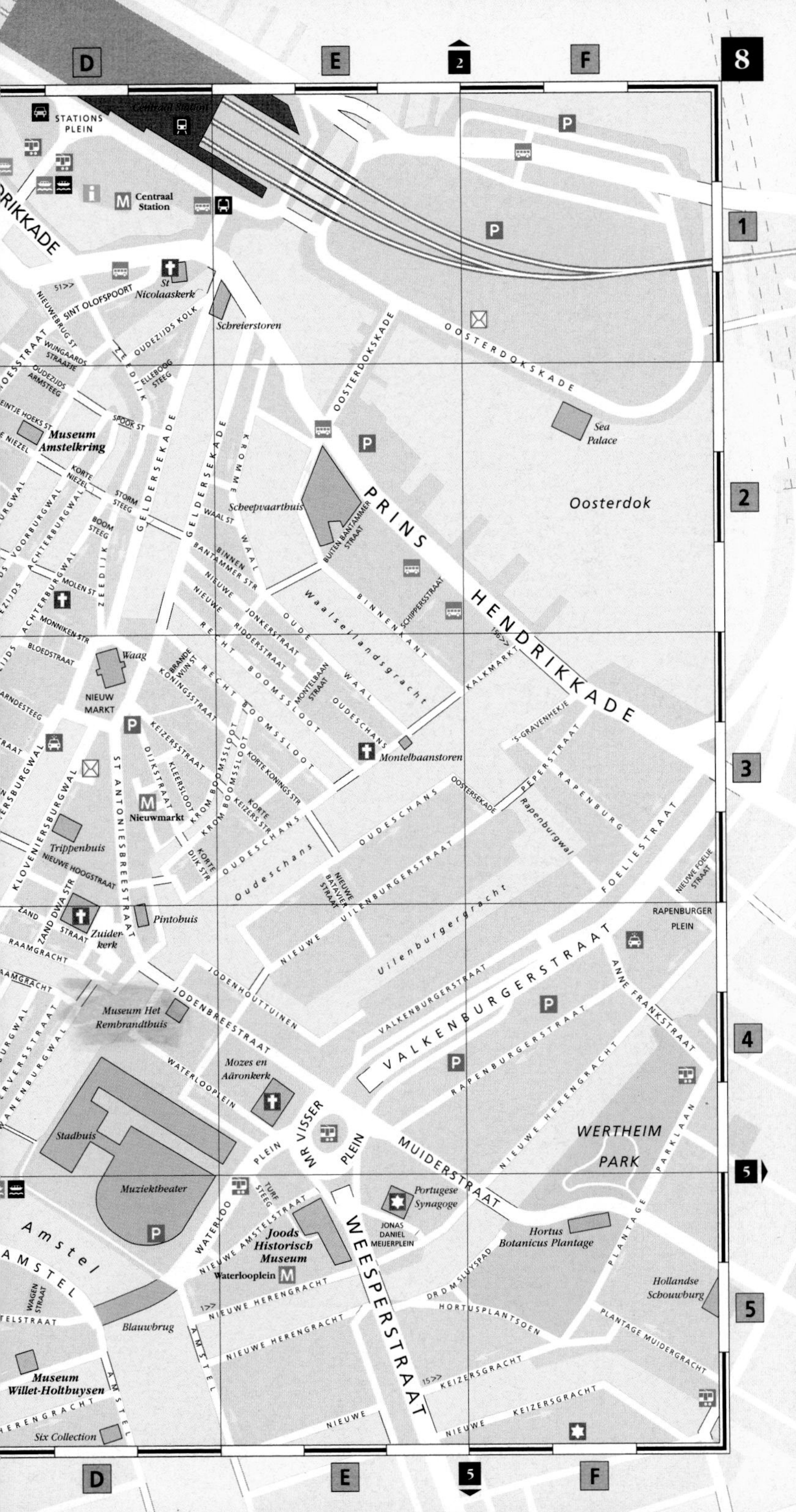

D
E
2
F
8
Centraal Station
STATIONS PLEIN
Centraal Station
St Nicolaaskerk
Schreierstoren
SINT OLOFSPOORT
OUDEZIJDS KOLK
ZEEDIJK
OOSTERDOKSKADE
Museum Amstelkring
Sea Palace
Oosterdok
Scheepvaarthuis
PRINS HENDRIKKADE
GELDERSEKADE
KROMME WAAL
BINNENKANT
Waalseilandsgracht
OUDE WAAL
Waag
NIEUW MARKT
Montelbaanstoren
OUDESCHANS
Oudeschans
KALKMARKT
RAPENBURG
Rapenburgwal
FOELIESTRAAT
RAPENBURGER PLEIN
Nieuwmarkt
Trippenhuis
ST ANTONIESBREESTRAAT
KLOVENIERSBURGWAL
NIEUWE HOOGSTRAAT
Pintohuis
Zuiderkerk
Uilenburgergracht
NIEUWE UILENBURGERSTRAAT
VALKENBURGERSTRAAT
JODENBREESTRAAT
JODENHOUTTUINEN
Museum Het Rembrandthuis
Mozes en Aäronkerk
WATERLOOPLEIN
ANNE FRANKSTRAAT
RAPENBURGERSTRAAT
NIEUWE HERENGRACHT
WERTHEIM PARK
PARKLAAN
Stadhuis
Muziektheater
MR VISSER PLEIN
MUIDERSTRAAT
Portugese Synagoge
JONAS DANIEL MEIJERPLEIN
Hortus Botanicus Plantage
PLANTAGE
Joods Historisch Museum
Waterlooplein
WEESPERSTRAAT
Amstel
AMSTEL
Blauwbrug
DR D M SLUYSPAD
HORTUSPLANTSOEN
PLANTAGE MUIDERGRACHT
Hollandse Schouwburg
Museum Willet-Holthuysen
Six Collection
KEIZERSGRACHT
NIEUWE KEIZERSGRACHT
1
2
3
4
5
5

Street Finder Index

IJ is treated as y in Dutch

General Index

Page numbers in **bold** type refer to main entries

A

B

C

D

I

L

M

P

Q

R

S

Z

Acknowledgments

DORLING KINDERSLEY would like to thank the following people whose help and assistance contributed to the preparation of this book.

MAIN CONTRIBUTORS

Robin Pascoe has lived in Amsterdam for the past 15 years. She is a freelance journalist and writes for various Dutch newspapers. She also works for the Dutch national news agency ANP, the international development news agency IPS, and the BBC.

Christopher Catling has been visiting the Netherlands for over ten years, since writing his first guide for business travelers in 1984. He has since written a further four guides to Amsterdam and the Netherlands. Besides this guide, he has contributed to four *Eyewitness Travel Guides:* Florence and Tuscany, Venice and the Veneto, Great Britain and Italy.

ADDITIONAL PHOTOGRAPHY

Steve Gorton, Clive Streeter

ADDITIONAL ILLUSTRATIONS

Arcana (Graham Bell), Richard Bonson, Stephen Conlin, Roy Flooks, Mick Gillah, Kevin Goold, Stephen Gyapay, Chris Orr, Ian Henderson, Philip Winton, John Woodcock

EDITORIAL ASSISTANCE

Susan Churchill, Debbie Scholes, Seán O'Connell, Caroline Radula-Scott

DESIGN ASSISTANCE

Martin Cropper, Anthea Forlee, Annette Jacobs

INDEX

Hilary Bird

SPECIAL ASSISTANCE

Greet Tuinman, Charlotte van Beurden, Poppy

PHOTOGRAPHY PERMISSIONS

Dorling Kindersley would like to thank the following for their kind permission to photograph at their establishments:

Airborne Museum, Arnhem; Allard Pierson Museum; Amstelkring Museum; Amsterdams Historisch Museum/Willet-Holthuysen Museum; Artis Zoo; Aviodrome; Beurs van Berlage; Boerhaave Museum, Leiden; Carré Theater; Concertgebouw; Coster Diamonds; Domkerk, Utrecht; Electrische Museumtramlijn; Europoort, Rotterdam; Filmmuseum; Frankendael; Anne Frankhuis; Grote Kerk, Alkmaar; Grote Kerk, Edam; Hash Marihuana Museum; Heineken Museum; Hollandse Schouwburg; Hortus Botanicus, Leiden; Joods Historisch Museum; Justitie Hall; Koninklijk Paleis; Krijtberg; Kröller-Müller Museum and National Park, Otterlo; Nederlands Scheepvaart Museum; Madurodam, Den Haag; Maritime Museum, Rotterdam; Monnickendam; Nieuwe Kerk; Nieuwe Kerk and Oude Kerk, Delft; Oude Kerk; Paleis Het Loo, Apeldoorn; Peace Palace, Den Haag; Portugese Synagoge; Prince William V Gallery, Den Haag; Prinsenhof, Leiden; Prison Gate Museum, Den Haag; RAI International Exhibition Centre; Rijksmuseum; Rijksmuseum, Utrecht; Rijksmuseum van Oudheden, Leiden; Rijksmuseum van Speelklok Tot Pierement, Utrecht; St. Bavo, Haarlem; St. Nicolaaskerk; SAS Hotel; Scheveningen Sea Life Centre; Sint Janskerk, Gouda; Stadhuis-Muziektheater; Stedelijk Museum; Stedelijk Molenmuseum, Leiden; Technologie Museum; Teylers Museum, Haarlem; Theater Museum; Tropenmuseum; Vakbonds Museum; Van Gogh Museum; Van Loon Museum; Verzetsmuseum; Werf 't Kromhout Museum; Westerkerk; Westfries Museum, Hoorn; Zuiderzee Museum.

PICTURE CREDITS

t = top; tl = top left; tc = top center; tr = top right; trc = top right center; cla = center left above; ca = center above; cra = center right above; cl = center left; c = center; cr = center right; clb = center left below; cb = center below; crb = center right below; bl = bottom left; b = bottom; bc = bottom center; br = bottom right; (d) = detail.

Every effort has been made to trace the copyright holders, and we apologize in advance for any unintentional omissions. We would be pleased to insert the appropriate acknowledgments in any subsequent edition of this publication.

Works of art have been reproduced with the permission of the following copyright holders: © ABC/MONDRIAAN ESTATE/HOLTZMAN TRUST, LICENSED BY ILP 1995: 136br; © ADAGP, PARIS AND DACS, LONDON 1995: 136cl, 200t; © DACS, LONDON 1995: 38bl, 136bl, 201tl; © JASPER JOHNS/DACS LONDON/VAGA NEW YORK: 137cb.

The Publishers are grateful to the following museums, photographers and picture libraries for permission to reproduce their photographs:

AKG, LONDON: 20clb, 22cl, 23c, 24cl, 26br, 27t, 101tr, 130tc, 185tr, 209c; Niklaus Strauss 137br; AMSTELKRING MUSEUM: 84bl, 85cr, 85br; AMSTERDAMS HISTORISCH MUSEUM: 16, 21bc, 22–3c, 23tc, 23crb, 23bl, 24–5c, 25clb, 28cl, 29t, 29cb, 30cl, 31cr, 38cl, 81t, 81tr, 81cr, 81br, 82tl, 82b, 83t,

83b, 90b, 94, 120cl, 120c, 120bl, 121cr; ANP PHOTO: 35tc, 35crb, 35bl.

B&U INTERNATIONAL PICTURE SERVICE: 35tl, 35tr, 51cr, 53b, 101bl, 105br, 180cl, 203t; BOYMANS-VAN BEUNINGEN MUSEUM, ROTTERDAM: 200cl, 200b, 201tc, 201cr, 201br; © ADAGP Paris and DACS London 1995 *La Méditerranée* Aristide Maillol 1905 200t; © DACS London 1995 *Mother and Child* Constant 1951 201tl; BRIDGEMAN ART LIBRARY: Christie's London *The Groote Market Haarlem with the Church of St. Bavo* Gerrit Berckheyde c.1668 176t; Giraudon/Musée Crozatier Le Puy-en-Velay France *King Louis XIV* 27br; Kremlin Museums Moscow 28bl; Private Collection *The Oude Zijds Voorburgwal in Amsterdam* Cornelius Springer 44cl; Private Collection *Self-Portrait Kazimir Malevich* 137cr; Stapleton Collection Delft tile 19th century 192tl.

CAMERA PRESS: Karsh of Ottawa 137tr; JEAN-LOUP CHARMET: Musée de l'Armée 28br; COLORSPORT: 34cla.

JAN DERWIG: 99tr, 151b, 224b, 266cl, 267cr; DRENTS MUSEUM, ASSEN: 18bl.

MARY EVANS PICTURE LIBRARY: 9c, 19cra, 19bc, 21bl, 23br, 24bl, 25br, 27bl, 29br, 30cb, 30bc, 31bl, 33crb 55c, 163c; Louis Raemaehois 32bc; Jean Veber 31br.

FOTO NATURA: Fred Hazelhoff 205cb.

GAUGUIN RESTAURANT: 224cl; GEMEENTEARCHIEF, AMSTERDAM: 19tl, 21ca, 21cb, 22tl, 22bc, 29cr, 45b, 99tl, 99cl, 100clb, 101br, 102bl, 103tr, 103cr, 104tr, 105tr, 105cr; GEMEENTEARCHIEF, KAMPEN: 21tl.

FRANS HALS MUSEUM, HAARLEM: 25tl, 28–9c, 178t, 178bl, 178br, 179tl, 179tr, 179bl, 179br; VANESSA HAMILTON: 97tl, 101cr, 104cl; ROBERT HARDING PICTURE LIBRARY: 58tr; Peter Scholey 116t; Adam Woolfitt 11br; HULTON-DEUTSCH COLLECTION: 38t.

ICONOGRAFISCH BUREAU: 103tl; THE IMAGE BANK: Bernard van Berg 52cr; Fotoworld 50b; INTERNATIONAL FLOWER BULB CENTER: 24bc, 180bc, 181tl, 181cla, 181cl, 181clb, 181bl; INTERNATIONAL INSTITUTE OF SOCIAL HISTORY: 32tl.

JEWISH HISTORICAL MUSEUM: 64cl.

KRÖLLER-MÜLLER MUSEUM: 204tl; MAURITSHUIS, DEN HAAG: 188t, 188c, 188bl, 189t, 189cr, 189br, 189bl, 193tl; MGM CINEMAS BV: 33cr; MUNICIPAL MUSEUM DE LAKENHAL, LEIDEN: 184b; MUSEUM HUIS LAMBERT VAN MEERTEN, COLLECTION RBK: 195t.

NATIONAL FIETSMUSEUM VELORAMA, NIJMEGEN: 31tl, 274tr; NETHERLANDS ARCHITECTURE INSTITUTE ARCHIVE: 98cl; Isaac Gosschalk 105cl; De Klerk 33t, 97cra.

PICTURE BOX: Lee Auteur 156; © PHOTO RMN, PARIS: 8–9; PRENTENKABINET DER RIJKSUNIVERSITEIT, LEIDEN: 30br.

RANGE PICTURES: 26tr; MUSEUM HET REMBRANDTHUIS: 59b; RETROGRAPH ARCHIVE LTD: 267bl; Martin Breese 30tl; RIJKSMUSEUM-FOUNDATION, AMSTERDAM: 24tl, 26tl, 28cla, 38c, 40b, 130cl, 130b, 131t, 131c, 131br, 132t, 132b, 133t, 133b; RIJKSMUSEUM PALEIS HET LOO, APELDOORN: E Boeijinga 206tr, 206cl, 207tl; AAW Meine Jansen 206bl; R Mulder 206clb; ROYAL PALACE, AMSTERDAM: Erik Hemsmerg 25tr, 37cr, 70, 74t.

SCHEEPVART MUSEUM: 17b, 26cr, 27c,146tl; SCIENCE PHOTO LIBRARY/Earth Satellite Corporation: 10cl; HARRY SMITH HORTICULTURAL COLLECTION: 34b; SPAARNESTAD FOTOARCHIEF: 33c, 97tr, 99cb; STEDELIJK MUSEUM, ALKMAAR: 32c; STEDELIJK MUSEUM, AMSTERDAM: 136tr, 137tl, 137tc; © ABC/Mondriaan Estate/Holtzmann Trust, licenced by ILP 1995 *Composition in Red, Black, Blue, Yellow and Grey* Piet Mondriaan 1920 136br; © ADAGP Paris and DACS London 1995 *Portrait of Artist with Seven Fingers* Marc Chagall 1912–13 136cl; © DACS London 1995 *Red Blue Chair* Gerrit Rietveld 1918 136bl; © DACS London 1995 *Steltman Chair* Gerrit Rietveld 1963 38bl; © Jasper Johns/DACS London/VAGA New York 1995 *Untitled* Jasper Johns 1965 137cb; STEDELIJK MUSEUM DE LAKENHAL, LEIDEN: 104br; TONY STONE IMAGES: 173cl, 268bl; Kim Blaxland 181tr; David Hanson 208–9; John Lamb 2–3; Manfred Mehlig 162–3; Rohan 100t.

HANS TULLENERS: 99cr, 100cr, 102c.

UNIVERSITEITSBIBLIOTHEEK VAN AMSTERDAM: 96tr; VINCENT VAN GOGH (FOUNDATION), VAN GOGH MUSEUM, AMSTERDAM: 38br, 134t, 134c, 134bl, 134br, 135t, 135cr, 135crb.

WESTERN AUSTRALIAN MARITIME MUSEUM: 26ca; WORLD PICTURES: 95cr.

ZEFA: CPA 52b; Steenmans 53c; Streichan 45t.

Front Endpaper: All special photography except ROYAL PALACE AMSTERDAM Erik Hemsmerg trc.

Jacket: All special photography except TELEGRAPH COLOUR LIBRARY/Masterfile front t.

Phrase Book

In Emergency

Help!	**Help!**	Help
Stop!	**Stop!**	Stop
Call a doctor	**Haal een dokter**	Haal uhn **dok**-tur
Call an ambulance	**Bel een ambulance**	Bell uhn ahm-bew-**luhns**-uh
Call the police	**Roep de politie**	Roop duh poe-**leet**-see
Call the fire department	**Roep de brandweer**	Roop duh **brahnt**-vheer
Where is the nearest telephone?	**Waar is de dichtstbijzijnde telefoon?**	Vhaar iss duh **dikhst**-baiy-zaiyn-duh tay-luh-**foan**
Where is the nearest hospital?	**Waar is het dichtstbijzijnde ziekenhuis?**	Vhaar iss het **dikhst**-baiy-zaiyn-duh **zee**-kuh-houws

Communication Essentials

Yes	**Ja**	Yaa
No	**Nee**	Nay
Please	**Alstublieft**	Ahls-tew-**bleeft**
Thank you	**Dank u**	Dahnk-ew
Excuse me	**Pardon**	Pahr-**don**
Hello	**Hallo**	Hallo
Goodbye	**Dag**	Dahgh
Good night	**Slaap lekker**	Slaap **lek**-kah
Morning	**Morgen**	**Mor**-ghuh
Afternoon	**Middag**	**Mid**-dahgh
Evening	**Avond**	**Ah**-vohnd
Yesterday	**Gisteren**	**Ghis**-tern
Today	**Vandaag**	Vahn-**daagh**
Tomorrow	**Morgen**	**Mor**-ghuh
Here	**Hier**	Heer
There	**Daar**	Daar
What?	**Wat?**	Vhat
When?	**Wanneer?**	Vhan-**eer**
Why?	**Waarom?**	Vhaar-**om**
Where?	**Waar?**	Vhaar
How?	**Hoe?**	Hoo

Useful Phrases

How are you?	**Hoe gaat het ermee?**	Hoo ghaat het er-**may**
Very well, thank you.	**Heel goed, dank u**	Hayl ghoot, dahnk ew
How do you do?	**Hoe maakt u het?**	Hoo maakt ew het
See you soon.	**Tot ziens**	Tot zeens
That's fine	**Prima**	**Pree**-mah
Where is/are?	**Waar is/zijn?**	Vhaar iss/zayn...
How far is it to...?	**Hoe ver is het naar...?**	Hoo vehr iss het naar...
How do I get to ...?	**Hoe kom ik naar...?**	Hoo kom ik naar...
Do you speak English?	**Spreekt u engels?**	Spraykt ew **eng**-uhls
I don't understand.	**Ik snap het niet**	Ik snahp het neet
Could you speak slowly?	**Kunt u langzamer praten?**	Kuhnt ew **lahng**-zahmer praa-tuh
I'm sorry	**Sorry**	Sorry

Useful Words

big	**groot**	ghroaht
small	**klein**	klaiyn
hot	**warm**	vharm
cold	**koud**	khowt
good	**goed**	ghoot
bad	**slecht**	slekht
enough	**genoeg**	ghuh-**noohkh**
well	**goed**	ghoot
open	**open**	open
closed	**gesloten**	ghuh-**slow**-tuh
left	**links**	links
right	**rechts**	rekhts
straight ahead	**rechtdoor**	rehkht dohr
near	**dichtbij**	dikht baiy
far	**ver weg**	vehr vhekh
up	**omhoog**	om-**hoakh**
down	**naar beneden**	naar buh-**nay**-duh
early	**vroeg**	vroohkh
late	**laat**	laat
entrance	**ingang**	**in**-ghahng
exit	**uitgang**	**ouht**-ghang
toilet	**wc**	vhay say
occupied	**bezet**	buh-**zett**
free (unoccupied)	**vrij**	vraiy
free (no charge)	**gratis**	**ghraah**-tiss

Making a Telephone Call

I'd like to place a long-distance call.	**Ik wil graag interlokaal telefoneren**	Ik vhil ghraakh **inter**-loh-kaahl tay-luh-foe-**neh**-ruh
I'd like to make a collect call.	**Ik wil 'collect call' bellen**	Ik vhil 'collect call' **bel**-luh
I'll try again later.	**Ik probeer het later nog wel eens**	Ik pro-**beer** het laater nokh vhel ayns
Can I leave a message?	**Kunt u een boodschap doorgeven?**	Kuhnt ew uhn **boat**-skhahp **dohr**-ghay-vuh
Could you speak up a little please?	**Wilt u wat harder praten?**	Vhilt ew vhat **hahr**-der **praah**-tuh
Local call	**Lokaal gesprek**	Low-**kaahl** ghuh-**sprek**

Shopping

How much does this cost?	**Hoeveel kost dit?**	Hoo-**vayl** kost dit
I would like	**Ik wil graag**	Ik vhil ghraakh
Do you have...?	**Heeft u...?**	Hayft ew...
I'm just looking.	**Ik kijk alleen even**	Ik kaiyk alleyn **ay**-vuh
Do you take credit cards?	**Neemt u credit cards aan?**	Naymt ew credit cards aan
Do you take traveler's checks?	**Neemt u reischeques aan?**	Naymt ew **raiys**-sheks aan
What time do you open?	**Hoe laat gaat u open?**	Hoo laat ghaat ew opuh
What time do you close?	**Hoe laat gaat u dicht?**	Hoo laat ghaat ew dikht
This one.	**Deze**	**Day**-zuh
That one.	**Die**	Dee
expensive	**duur**	dewr
cheap	**goedkoop**	ghoot-**koap**
size	**maat**	maat
white	**wit**	vhit
black	**zwart**	zvhahrt
red	**rood**	roat
yellow	**geel**	ghayl
green	**groen**	ghroon
blue	**blauw**	blah-ew

Types of Shops

antique shop	**antiekwinkel**	ahn-**teek**-vhin-kul
bakery	**bakker**	**bah**-ker
bank	**bank**	bahnk
bookstore	**boekwinkel**	**book**-vhin-kul
butcher	**slager**	slaakh-er
cake shop	**banketbakkerij**	bahnk-**et**-bahk-er-aiy
cheese shop	**kaaswinkel**	**kaas**-vhin-kul
delicatessen	**delicatessen**	daylee-kah-**tes**-suh
department store	**warenhuis**	**vhaar**-uh-houws
drugstore	**apotheek**	ah-poe-**taiyk**
fish seller	**viswinkel**	**viss**-vhin-kul
greengrocer	**groenteboer**	**ghroon**-tuh-boor
hairdresser	**kapper**	**kah**-per
market	**markt**	mahrkt
newsstand	**krantenwinkel**	**krahn**-tuh-vhin-kul
post office	**postkantoor**	**pohst**-kahn-tor
shoe shop	**schoenenwinkel**	**sghoo**-nuh-vhin-kul
supermarket	**supermarkt**	**sew**-per-mahrkt
tobacconist	**sigarenwinkel**	see-**ghaa**-ruh-vhin-kul
travel agent	**reisburo**	**raiys**-bew-roa

Sightseeing

art gallery	**gallerie**	ghaller-ee
bus station	**busstation**	**buhs**-stah-shown
bus ticket	**strippenkaart**	**strip**-puh-kaahrt
cathedral	**kathedraal**	kah-tuh-**draal**
church	**kerk**	kehrk
closed on public holidays	**op feestdagen gesloten**	op **fayst**-daa-ghuh ghuh-**slow**-tuh
day return	**dagretour**	**dahgh**-ruh-tour
garden	**tuin**	touwn
library	**bibliotheek**	bee-bee-yo-**tayk**
museum	**museum**	mew-**zay**-uhm
railroad station	**station**	stah-**shown**
round trip	**retourtje**	ruh-**tour**-tyuh
one-way ticket	**enkeltje**	**eng**-kuhl-tyuh
tourist information	**VVV**	fay fay fay
town hall	**stadhuis**	staht-**houws**
train	**trein**	traiyn

Staying in a Hotel

Do you have a vacant room?	**Zijn er nog kamers vrij?**	Zaiyn er nokh **kaa-mers** vray
double room with double bed	**een twees persoonskamer met een twee persoonsbed**	uhn **tvhay**-per **soans**-kaa-mer met uhn **tvhay**-per- **soans** beht
twin room	**een kamer met een lits-jumeaux**	uhn **kaa-mer** met uhn lee-zjoo-**moh**
single room	**eenpersoons-kamer**	**ayn**-per-**soans-kaa-mer**
room with a bath,	**kamer met bad**	**kaa-mer** met baht
shower	**douche**	doosh
porter	**kruier**	**krouw**-yuh
I have a reservation.	**Ik heb gereserveerd**	Ik hehp ghuh-ray-sehr-**veert**

Eating Out

Do you have a table?	**Is er een tafel vrij?**	Iss ehr uhn **tah**-fuhl vraiy
I want to reserve a table.	**Ik wil een tafel reserveren**	Ik vhil uhn **tah**-fuhl ray-sehr-**veer**-uh
The check, please.	**Mag ik afrekenen**	Mukh ik **ahf**-ray-kuh-nuh
I am a vegetarian.	**Ik ben vegetariër**	Ik ben fay-ghuh-**taahr**-ee-er
waitress/waiter	**serveerster/ober**	Sehr-**veer**-ster/**oh**-ber
menu	**de kaart**	duh kaahrt
cover charge	**het couvert**	het koo-**vehr**
wine list	**de wijnkaart**	duh **vhaiyn**-kaart
glass	**het glas**	het ghlahss
bottle	**de fles**	duh fless
knife	**het mes**	het mess
fork	**de vork**	duh fork
spoon	**de lepel**	duh **lay**-pul
breakfast	**het ontbijt**	het ont-**baiyt**
lunch	**de lunch**	duh lernsh
dinner	**het diner**	het dee-**nay**
main course	**het hoofdgerecht**	het **hoaft**-ghuh-rekht
appetizer, first course	**het voorgerecht**	het **vohr**-ghuh-rekht
dessert	**het nagerecht**	het **naa**-ghuh-rekht
dish of the day	**het dagmenu**	het **dahgh**-munh-ew
bar	**het cafe**	het kaa-**fay**
café	**het eetcafe**	het **ayt**-kaa-**fay**
rare	**rare**	'rare'
medium	**medium**	'medium'
well-done	**doorbakken**	dohr-**bah**-kuh

Menu Decoder

aardappels	**aard**-uppuhls	potatoes
azijn	aah-**zaiyn**	vinegar
biefstuk	**beef**-stuhk	steak
bier, pils	beer, pilss	beer
boter	boater	butter
brood/broodje	broat/**broat**-yuh	bread/roll
cake, taart, gebak	'cake', taahrt, ghuh-**bahk**	cake, pastry
carbonade	kahr-bow-**naa**-duh	pork chop
chocola	show-coa-**laa**	chocolate
citroen	see-**troon**	lemon
cocktail	cocktail	cocktail
droog	droakh	dry
eend	aynt	duck
ei	aiy	egg
garnalen	ghahr-**naah**-luh	shrimp
gebakken	ghuh-**bah**-ken	fried
gegrild	ghuh-**ghrillt**	grilled
gekookt	ghuh-**koakt**	boiled
gepocheerd	ghuh-posh-**eert**	poached
gerookt	ghuh-**roakt**	smoked
geroosterd brood	ghuh-**roas**-tert broat	toast
groenten	**ghroon**-tuh	vegetables
ham	hahm	ham
haring	**haa**-ring	herring
hutspot	huht-spot	hot pot
ijs	aiyss	ice, ice cream
jenever	yuh-**nay**-vhur	gin
kaas	kaas	cheese
kabeljauw	kah-buhl-**youw**	cod
kip	kip	chicken
knoflook	**knoff**-loak	garlic
koffie	coffee	coffee
kool, rode of witte	coal, **roe**-duh off **vhit**-uh	cabbage, red or white
kreeft	krayft	lobster
kroket	crow-**ket**	ragout in bread-crumbs, deep-fried
lamsvlees	**lahms**-flayss	lamb
lekkerbekje	**lek**-kah-bek-yuh	fried fillet of haddock
mineraalwater	meener-**aahl**-vhaater	mineral water
mosterd	**moss**-tehrt	mustard
niet scherp	neet skehrp	mild
olie	**oh**-lee	oil
paling	**paa**-ling	eel
pannekoek	**pah**-nuh-kook	pancake
patat frites	pah-**taht** freet	French fries
peper	**pay**-per	pepper
poffertjes	**poffer**-tyuhs	tiny buckwheat pancakes
rijst	raiyst	rice
rijsttafel	**raiys**-tah-ful	Indonesian meal
rode wijn	**roe**-duh vhaiyn	red wine
rookworst	**roak**-vhorst	smoked sausage
rundvlees	**ruhnt**-flayss	beef
saus	souwss	sauce
schaaldieren	**skaahl**-deeh-ruh	shellfish
scherp	skehrp	hot (spicy)
schol	sghol	plaice
soep	soup	soup
stamppot	**stahm**-pot	sausage stew
suiker	**souw**-ker	sugar
thee	tay	tea
tosti	**toss**-tee	cheese on toast
uien	**ouw**-yuh	onions
uitsmijter	**ouht**-smaiy-ter	fried egg on bread with ham
varkensvlees	**vahr**-kuhns-flayss	pork
vers fruit	fehrss frouwt	fresh fruit
verse jus	**vehr**-suh zjhew	fresh orange juice
vis	fiss	fish/seafood
vlees	flayss	meat
water	**vhaa**-ter	water
witte wijn	**vhih**-tuh vhaiyn	white wine
worst	vhorst	sausage
zout	zouwt	salt

Numbers

1	**een**	ayn
2	**twee**	tvhay
3	**drie**	dree
4	**vier**	feer
5	**vijf**	faiyf
6	**zes**	zess
7	**zeven**	**zay**-vuh
8	**acht**	ahkht
9	**negen**	**nay**-guh
10	**tien**	teen
11	**elf**	elf
12	**twaalf**	tvhaalf
13	**dertien**	**dehr**-teen
14	**veertien**	**feer**-teen
15	**vijftien**	**faiyf**-teen
16	**zestien**	**zess**-teen
17	**zeventien**	**zayvuh**-teen
18	**achtien**	**ahkh**-teen
19	**negentien**	**nay-ghuh**-teen
20	**twintig**	**tvhin**-tukh
21	**eenentwintig**	**aynuh**-tvhin-tukh
30	**dertig**	**dehr**-tukh
40	**veertig**	**feer**-tukh
50	**vijftig**	**faiyf**-tukh
60	**zestig**	**zess**-tukh
70	**zeventig**	**zay**-vuh-tukh
80	**tachtig**	**tahkh**-tukh
90	**negentig**	**nayguh**-tukh
100	**honderd**	**hohn**-durt
1000	**duizend**	**douw**-zuhnt
1,000,000	**miljoen**	mill-**yoon**

Time

one minute	**een minuut**	uhn meen-**ewt**
one hour	**een uur**	uhn ewr
half an hour	**een half uur**	uhn hahlf ewr
half past one	**half twee**	hahlf tvhay
a day	**een dag**	uhn dahgh
a week	**een week**	uhn vhayk
a month	**een maand**	uhn maant
a year	**een jaar**	uhn jaar
Monday	**maandag**	**maan**-dahgh
Tuesday	**dinsdag**	**dins**-dahgh
Wednesday	**woensdag**	**vhoons**-dahgh
Thursday	**donderdag**	**donder**-dahgh
Friday	**vrijdag**	**vraiy**-dahgh
Saturday	**zaterdag**	**zaater**-dahgh
Sunday	**zondag**	**zon**-dahgh

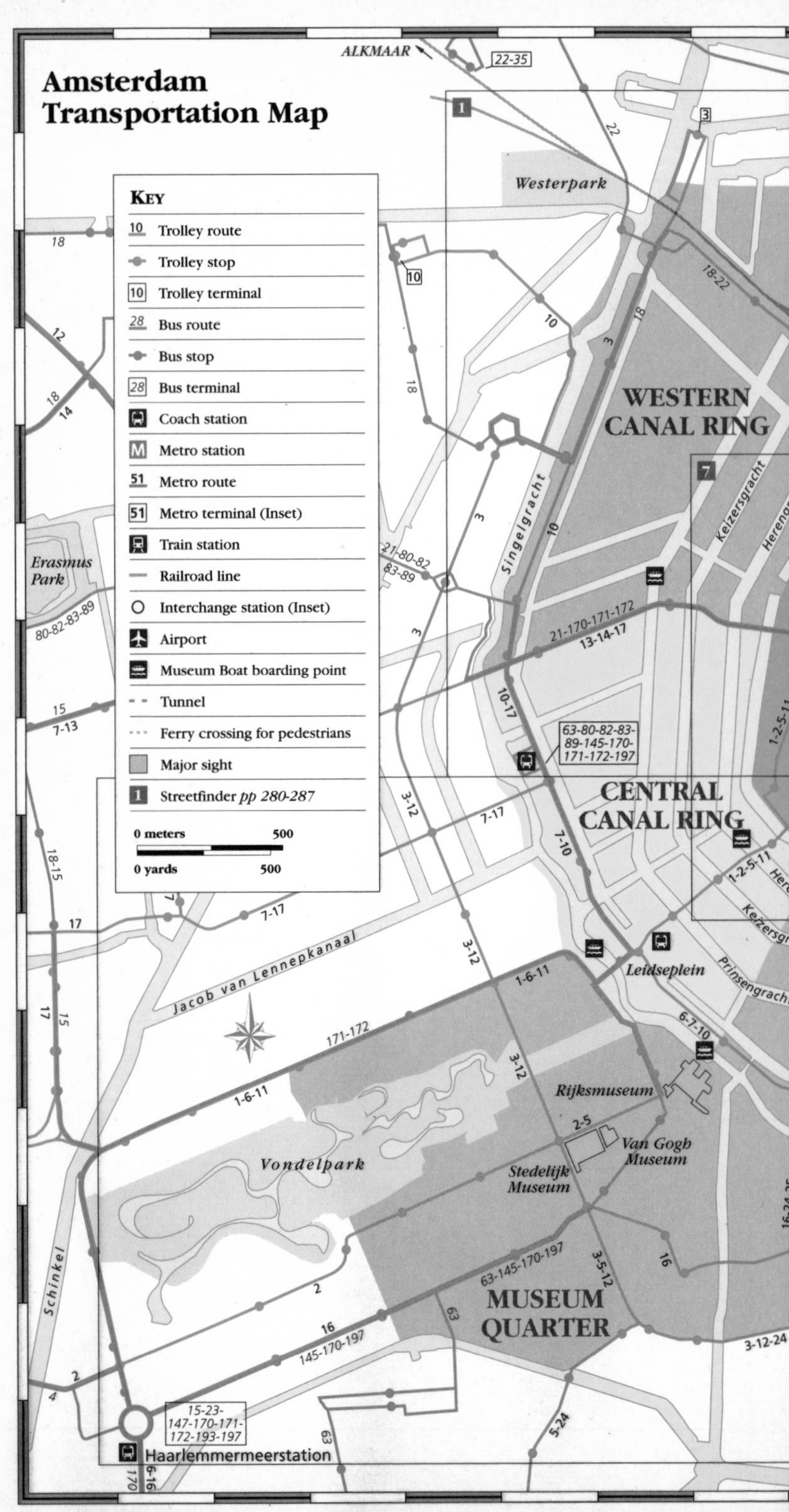

Amsterdam Transportation Map
KEY
Trolley route
Trolley stop
Trolley terminal
Bus route
Bus stop
Bus terminal
Coach station
Metro station
Metro route
Metro terminal (Inset)
Train station
Railroad line
Interchange station (Inset)
Airport
Museum Boat boarding point
Tunnel
Ferry crossing for pedestrians
Major sight
Streetfinder pp 280-287
0 meters 500
0 yards 500
ALKMAAR
22-35
Westerpark
WESTERN CANAL RING
Keizersgracht
Herengracht
Singelgracht
Erasmus Park
80-82-83-89
21-80-82
83-89
21-170-171-172
13-14-17
10-17
63-80-82-83-89-145-170-171-172-197
CENTRAL CANAL RING
7-17
3-12
7-10
1-2-5-11
Prinsengracht
Leidseplein
Jacob van Lennepkanaal
18-15
171-172
1-6-11
6-7-10
Rijksmuseum
2-5
Van Gogh Museum
Stedelijk Museum
Vondelpark
63-145-170-197
3-5-12
16-24-25
MUSEUM QUARTER
3-12-24
145-170-197
Schinkel
15-23-147-170-171-172-193-197
5-24
Haarlemmermeerstation